MAKE ART
MAKE MONEY

MAKE ART MAKE MONEY

Lessons from Jim Henson on Fueling Your Creative Career

ELIZABETH HYDE STEVENS

LAKE UNION PUBLISHING

PRAISE FOR *MAKE ART MAKE MONEY*

"Stevens captures Jim Henson's legacy beautifully. . . . Full of practical insights, Make Art Make Money is above all a reminder—a manifesto, were the word not so tragically worn by now—that you don't need to survive on lettuce soup in order for your art to be authentic." —Maria Popova, *Brain Pickings*

"There are plenty of books out there about how to make money from your art. This is a book about how to make money SERVE your art." —Jeremy Meyers, *Deeper Context*

"Author Elizabeth Hyde Stevens has been interested in the tension between commercial success and artistic integrity in Henson's life for a while. She's taught a course at Boston University called "Muppets, Mickey, and Money," and now has a new e-book that attempts to distill Henson's career into useful principles for creative people." —Kevin Hartnett, *Boston Globe*

"In 2011, Elizabeth Hyde Stevens wrote an in-depth examination of the Muppets as an entertainment property in the years after Jim Henson's death in 1990. It was a fascinating essay on how characters so intricately linked to their creator's performance function as artistic properties owned by a corporation following an artist's death. Now Stevens is back with a book about Henson himself, and how he juggled the art and commerce sides of his work." —Kevin McFarland, *AV Club*

"Stevens has done a remarkable job at deconstructing the life and work of Henson in a way that thoroughly explains what made him a successful artist. Just like a meal spent with Henson would be life-changing, this book opens up the reader to ways of acting and thinking, as modeled by Henson that will surely aid in the growth of one's artistic goals." —C.T., *Nerd Lunch*

"Lovers of Muppets, lovers of art, and all those who aspire to make a creative living will take pleasure in Stevens's wise and entertaining book." —C.J. Hauser, author of *The From-Aways*

Originally published as a Kindle Serial, September 2013

Printed in the United States of America.

Published by Lake Union Publishing, Seattle

www.apub.com

ISBN-10: 1477817387
ISBN-13: 9781477817384

Library of Congress Control Number: 2013919512

Cover Designed by Inkd Inc

CONTENTS

For my mother, Joanne, and for Jim Henson

THE ARTIST'S PROBLEM

ART VS. MONEY

In 1968, Jim Henson performed a skit on *The Ed Sullivan Show* called "Business, Business," which he cowrote with Jerry Juhl. In it, there are two kinds of creatures, and they are locked in conflict.

On one side, the creatures make sounds like a cash register and a slot machine. They recite a poem written in business-ese: "Corporate profits, exculpates, mutual fund, interest rates."

On the other side, the creatures have naïve voices and lightbulb heads. They ask, "Love? Beauty? Joy?"

Ca-ching! The battle is on.

"Brotherhood, hope, peace!" says one side.

"Option, market, possibility, eight-point-one over counter utility," says the other.

It's a war of ideologies.

"Friendship!"

"Income!"

"Beauty!"

"Money!"

Business opens fire. The idealists fire back. Business explodes! Then disappears. Silence.

Cautiously, the idealists look around. They have won. "Peace?" says one. "Success!" says the other. Their lightbulbs go off.

"Victory? Opportunity! Comfort . . . security . . ." The lightbulbs flash faster. "Benefits, growth, wealth, diversity, dividends, profit, capital, economy, business, business, BUSINESS, BUSINESS!"

Ed Sullivan's adult audience laughs at Henson's goofy puppets. One man in a suit turns to his wife and raises an eyebrow.[1]

"Business, Business" implies that business and idealism are diametrically opposed. The idealist is attacked not just by the establishment, but also from within, where greed starts to change one's motives.

For the most part, money *is* the enemy of art. Artists know this from experience; you are rarely compensated well for following your muse. You could make a lot more if you left art behind to work in sales, management, or finance. This is no accident. Put simply, great art wants quality, whereas good business wants *profit*. Quality requires many man-hours to produce, and as any accountant will tell you, this cuts significantly into your profit. Great artists fight *for* such expenditures, whereas successful businessmen fight *against* them. The exceptions, those entrepreneurial visionaries who do fight for quality—a Walt Disney or a Steve Jobs—fight an uphill battle. To the CFOs, the man-hours that quality *requires* are simply gratuitous overhead to be cut in the name of cheaper, faster profits.

This problem was perhaps most eloquently stated in a 1979 book by former Harvard professor Lewis Hyde. *The Gift* is elucidating yet mysterious. Above the bar code, it labels itself "Literary Criticism" and "Sociology." Yet, to quote Margaret Atwood's endorsement on the back cover, it is "the best book I know of for talented but unacknowledged creators." For artists, Hyde's book approaches a form of self-help.

The Gift shows us *why* artists don't make money: because art is, anthropologically speaking, a gift. Trouble arises in societies when a person tries to convert a gift into a commodity. "When gifts are sold," Hyde writes, "they change their nature as much as water changes when it freezes, and no rationalist telling . . . can replace the feeling that is lost."[2] This would be the case if, say, *Sesame Street* were taken over by a for-profit company, with advertisements, opportunistic spin-offs, and direct-to-video releases. No longer a gift to the children of the world, *Sesame Street* would become a commodity produced by a corporation that views children as consumers. Gifts, on the other hand, are given in sacrifice with no hope of return, except for perhaps a karmic faith in shared humanity. When we lose the *feeling* of the gift—the gratitude, awe, and communality of it—the gift is reduced to a shell of what it was. It doesn't work like it should—on our emotions. It is just a trinket with no intrinsic power.

Using tribal peoples as examples, Hyde explains that art has a special set of rules by which it circulates, whereas commodities of the market have another, very different set of rules. For art to truly affect us, it needs to be, in a sense, "given." For a commodity to be successful, it needs to be bought and sold. The market economy is zero-sum, where selling an item is to lose it, and paying money is to become poorer. The gift economy, on the other hand, grows with each transaction, with gratitude and societal bonds being an "increase" for both the giver and recipient. It is a cumulative wealth, because in a sense, we feel "richer" the more we give others, and they too feel "rich" in spirit. Using Hyde's elegant theory, we can easily define what is and isn't art. Art is a gift, and anything that is not a gift *in some sense* is not art.

Let us leave Hyde for a moment to see if this jibes with the world we know. If we examine the hardest-working, most-talented, most-enduring, and most-genius artists, they tend to be in the stage of their career when they are just about to make it big. "His early albums are still the best," we say, or put another way, "She hasn't done anything interesting since she got that three-book deal." Before artists become successful, they give it their all as an act of social faith with no set schedule for repayment. They are "making a name for themselves" or "hoping to strike it big" and trust that society will give them a career in return. This is the gift. But once an artist enters the market economy, profits start to demand giving less and charging more.

It is not the artist's fault, but rather the result of an unhappy union: an artisan working in a gift economy but trying to survive in a market economy. For example, the woman who gave me the best massage of my life was doing it to practice for a job interview. It was free. But in order to make a profit—to actually *survive* as an artist—one can't afford to be generous all the time. A year into working professionally, that masseuse needed hand surgery and stopped offering deep-tissue techniques. You can give a masterpiece massage once a week, but to actually make enough to live, she wound up overworking her muscles and joints to the point that it damaged her. Giving it her all wasn't financially feasible. It wasn't that she *wanted* to sacrifice the quality of her art, but in order to pay her rent, to survive as an artist, she had to give less. Profit demands this. It's Economics 101.

In essence, capitalism does not reward art that is a gift. In spite of this economic reality, as a society we value the art of the genius, and we naturally reject the sham-art of the entrepreneur, that is, commodity-art. It is true that all too often the larger society does become duped by saccharine holiday jingles, corporate art sculptures, clip-art GIFs on sales flyers, and Hyde's example, the formulaic romance novel written by focus-group surveys. Yet, on these objects, our cultural critics usually reach a unanimous judgment. They are designed to *take*, not to give. These objects are not art because they lack generosity, and given enough time, history inevitably proves it.

We intuitively reject art when the cost to make it is less than the cost to buy it. How many times have you scoffed at the ridiculous price some art collector paid for a Warhol, a Pollock, a Rothko? That's not art, you say. I could make one of those in my sleep. It's just a status-seeker's luxury, pure market speculation, you say. It's no longer art, and if it is, it isn't *great* art—it's not something you have to take your grandchildren to see so that they may one day show their grandchildren.

But as much as we know and value art—as a society—we expect our best artists to starve. Herman Melville died penniless and depressed, as did Van Gogh. The National Endowment for the Arts works on this principle—that there is art out there that is *too good* to make any money. The endowment model does seem to fit nicely with Hyde's art-as-gift philosophy, but it also bespeaks a sad fatalism—that artists *can't* make money.

Yet art and money *do* occasionally dance. Hyde acknowledges this with caution. "There are three primary ways," he tells us, "in which modern artists have resolved the problem of their livelihood: they have taken second jobs, they have found patrons to support them, or they have managed to place the work itself on the market and pay the rent with fees and royalties."[3] At various points in Jim Henson's career—as we will see—the artist used each of these methods, but more than any, he used the market. The art of the Muppets is inarguably "commercial," though it is also much more.

Of the three routes, Hyde says, the first two (quite often teaching and grants) are the easier ways for an artist to *protect* his art from money—to "mark the boundary between his art and the market." When we exchange our art for money directly, without a clear boundary, the art can easily become contaminated by market demands. Hyde writes:

> It is not hard to distinguish between writing poems and working the night shift in a hospital, and easier still for the poet to know he is no Guggenheim. But the artist who sells his own creations must develop a more subjective feel for the two economies [gift and market] and his own rituals for both keeping them apart and bringing them together. He must, on the one hand, be able to disengage from the work and think of it as a commodity. He must be able to reckon its value in terms of current fashions, know what the market will bear, demand fair value, and part with the work when someone pays the price. And he must, on the other hand, be able to forget all that and turn to serve his gifts on their own terms. If he cannot do the former, he cannot hope to sell his art, and if he cannot do the latter, he may have no art to sell, or only a commercial art, work that has been created in response to the demands of the market, not in response to the demands of the gift.[4]

Hyde's book is an amazing exploration of the problem, but as he writes in the afterword, it is not "a very practical book."[5] The afterword touches briefly on auspicious avenues for artists—universities and foundations. However, these institutions are currently glutted, saturated with artists. And their power over artists is so high that they themselves contaminate art as much as the market—demanding arcane fashions appreciated by a handful of academics. I have seen rooms full of poets lamenting the politics of tenure and grant writing, and the effects it has on their work, and I have thought, where has all our *hope* gone? Jim Henson's work was poetry, and yet his eyes always danced with hope and laughter, because he knew how to work the market for the purposes of art. In this book, I propose the path less traveled, the dimly lit third avenue, Jim Henson's Muppety "shoot-the-moon" route. In a word—entrepreneurship, a very *uncommon* entrepreneurship.

If you are turned off by the greed and avarice of the business world, know that part of the problem is that you—*artists*—aren't there yet in great enough numbers. There is a New Testament story in which Jesus expels the money-chargers from the temple. It has lingered in my mind as a strong literary image because it resonates with my own hope for a better world. It is powerfully dramatized in the 1971 musical *Jesus Christ Superstar*, where Jesus sings, "My temple should be a house of prayer, but you have made it a den of thieves!"

While in the Bible Jesus emerges victorious, in Lloyd Webber's musical he just slinks off—a dejected martyr. This version is more true to our American mythos; we accept the victory of money over art and welcome the artist's destruction in righteous, sulky pessimism. This is the struggle in which artists of our era are stuck knee-deep. Artists are the members of society who trust that gifts are worth giving for their own sake and not for what you can get back. But avoiding money merely assures that the only ones in the temple will be the thieves. One does not rid the temple of the money-chargers by singing alone; one expels them by occupying the space they currently hold and keeping it. It is time for the faithful to reenter the market.

HENSON'S SOLUTION

MAKE ART MAKE MONEY

In "Business, Business," Jim Henson's idealists fight back and beat the business-heads, but when they do, they turn into capitalists. Its irony may seem fatalistic. Yet it's not that Henson was pessimistic or perverse; it's just that he saw things from a different perspective. It may seem sad to young idealists, but this seemingly contradictory evolution is actually the *solution* to the artist's problem.

"Business, Business" was a comment on the times. In 1968—the year of this sketch—a generation was coming of age that outnumbered its parents. It was *tuning in*—to free love, drugs, rock music, and youth collectives. The children of 1968 were rejecting the old order and trying to live more authentic lives. The lightbulb idealists in "Business, Business" were flower children, baby boomers, hippies.

But Henson was not. In 1968, he was thirty-one—placed *just* in between the boomers and their parents. In generation theory, Henson was a member of the Silent Generation, Americans born in the hardship of the Depression and raised in war, and yet paradoxically this time produced many of the creative visionaries who would inspire the boomers to mass hippiedom. The popular musicians of the sixties—the Beatles and the Stones—were ten years older than the boomers. They weren't the flower children of the sixties; they were more like the babysitters, the gurus. In America, Grace Slick and John Fogerty were both born *before* the 1946 baby boom. It is to these Silent Generation pied pipers that we should rightly attribute much of the sixties' cultural change, more so than the generation who followed their song.

Only six short months after 1967's Summer of Love in San Francisco, Jim Henson made "Business, Business." It clearly reflects the events of its time, but from the perspective of someone living halfway between both worlds. Not a boomer at all, he lived in New York City with his wife and a few kids and made a good living. Having made hundreds of television ads, Henson was already a capitalist when he made "Business, Business." And we could even conclude that the skit describes his own conversion from idealism to capitalism. In 1968, he had an agent who got him TV appearances on *Ed Sullivan* and freelance commercial gigs hawking products as unhippielike as IBM computers and Getty oil.

Yet Jim Henson's business wasn't oil—it was art. While today, most artists are too timid to admit it, Henson freely referred to himself as an "artist," and his agent went even further, calling him "artsy-craftsy."[6] Henson may have worked in show business, but he'd also traveled in Europe as a young man, sketching pictures of its architecture. He owned a business, but his business rested on the ideas the idealists were shouting—brotherhood, joy, and love. He wore a beard. Biographers would say it was to cover acne scars, but in the context of the late sixties, it aligns Henson with a category of people that is unmistakable. Though a capitalist, he was also a staunch artist.

Growing up in the 1940s, Henson was a self-described Mississippi Tom Sawyer who played in the swamp, often went shoeless,[7] and loved to sketch. He joined a puppetry club at his high school in Hyattsville, Maryland, and in 1954, at the age of eighteen, made his first puppet for a television audition. Henson had fallen in love with TV when his family bought their first set only four years earlier.[8] His show *Sam and Friends* aired on Washington's WRC-TV from 1956 to 1961, when he also made humorous, tongue-in-cheek commercials. At the age of twenty-seven, Henson moved his family to New York City, where in the 1960s he did many variety appearances on *Ed Sullivan* and *The Jimmy Dean Show* and made experimental films, pilots, and projects like *Time Piece* and *The Cube*.

In 1969, at the age of thirty-three, Henson collaborated with Children's Television Workshop (CTW) to make *Sesame Street*, the first nonprofit children's show on television, which made him a worldwide star. In the early 1970s, he used this success to make *The Muppet Musicians of Bremen*, *The Frog Prince*, and other TV specials as well as recurring characters for the first year of *Saturday Night Live*. After Henson spent years pitching, British entertainment mogul Lew Grade funded Henson's *Muppet Show* series, which ran from 1976 to 1981 all around the world. After an HBO movie called *Emmet Otter's Jug-Band Christmas,* Henson made his first Hollywood film, the 1979 hit *The Muppet Movie*. In the 1980s, Henson became a mogul himself, making two more Muppet movies; the elaborate fantasy films *The Dark Crystal* and *Labyrinth*; classic TV specials like *The Christmas Toy*, *The Tale of the Bunny Picnic*, and *A Muppet Family Christmas*; and lush TV series like the Toronto-based *Fraggle Rock* and *The Storyteller*. Henson's spin-off series *Muppet Babies* ran for eight years, encouraging creativity to a new generation on Saturday mornings.

The artist was creating the Disney World attraction *Muppet*Vision 3D* when he died suddenly in 1990 from a rare infection. When you think of leaving an artistic legacy of lasting good, I don't think you can aim much higher than Henson's—the work he created is beloved by so many, twenty-three years after his death, in more than a hundred different countries.

So let us return now to "Business, Business." If art and money are at odds, which side was Jim Henson *really* on? If you watch the skit, the clue is in the characters' voices. Of the Slinky-necked business-heads and idealist-heads, Henson was really both and neither, because in "Business, Business," he parodies *both*. Locked in conflict, they sound like blowhards and twerps, respectively, but they were both facets of his life. As an employer to two other men, Henson was the boss man—the suit, cash register, and slot machine—who wrote the checks. But he also got together with his friends to sing, laugh, and play with puppets in the kind of collectivism that hippies celebrated.

In the same month that Henson performed "Business, Business" on Ed Sullivan, he was working on a documentary called *Youth '68* that aired as part of the *NBC Experiment in Television* series. In it, Henson interviews both street hippies out in LA and weary grandparents in Omaha with smoking pipes. Musicians slurred poetic about revolution and old folks complained, "They don't have respect for their parents like they used to."[9] It took someone like Henson—living forever in between them—to give us the full picture. There is a saying that goes like this: "Beware of artists. They mix with all classes of society and are therefore the most dangerous." In order for Henson's art to have the universal power it did, this mixing had to include "the establishment"—what we could call "the business class."

But today—especially with Generation X and Millennials—serious artists often refuse contact with business. Large numbers of liberal-arts graduates bristle when presented with the corporate world, rejecting its values to protect their ideals. Devoted artists move home to a parent's basement to complete their masterpieces, while the more pragmatic artists live in cloistered "Neverland" artist collectives, grant-funded arts colonies, and university faculty lounges. *Youth '68* still feels contemporary, because we never *solved* this conflict. The clothing choices of suits and hipsters still mean what they did in 1968. In 99 percent of cases, you can tell if a man on the street works in finance or acrylic—not because these are mutually exclusive professions, but because we wear our battle colors to show we have chosen a side. It is as if the 1960s opened up a rift in American culture that was never healed. It's 2013—more than forty years on—and if you squint your eyes, the flamboyant artist culture in Brooklyn's coffee shops could be Haight-Ashbury in the Summer of Love.

Yet Henson's work suggests that it is possible to heal America's split personality. At the end of the *Dark Crystal,* the gentle race known as "the Mystics" leave their quaint reservation with its sand paintings and wooden bowls and return to the castle. They don't *displace* the power-obsessed Skeksis, they do something strange—they merge with them. This occurs at the same time the missing piece fits into the Crystal, which itself is "healed." The peaceful artists return to the castle, join with the cruel lords who are its current occupants, and the race returns to its proper form; they are whole.

What is a human being? Complex to the point of absurdity, a whole person is both greedy and generous. It is foolish to think we can't be both artists and entrepreneurs, especially when Henson was so wildly successful in both categories.

Since he was in college, Jim Henson was a natural capitalist. He owned a printmaking business and made commercials for lunchmeats. In the 1970s, he became a merchandising millionaire and made Hollywood movies. By 1987, he had shows on all three major networks plus HBO and PBS.[10] Though he didn't like to discuss his net worth, the price tag was revealed when he sold most of his characters to Disney for "nearly 150 million."[11] Of course, Henson was not just another Trump. *Believe* the beard.

The Dark Crystal, released in 1982, is an artistic masterpiece, which Henson himself described as "a rich fruitcake, full of different ingredients, and every bite you discover something new and delicious."[12] Its art-for-art's-sake–ness is undeniable. Muppets may at times be made of hardware-store items and discount-priced eyes, but when it came to creating the world of the Dark Crystal, it was impossible to do on the cheap. Henson was "notorious for going over budget,"[13] because he made it a point to hire and retain good artists. Unlike fur or doll eyes, that cost can't be skimped. If Jim Henson were *only* a shrewd businessman seeking nothing but licensing profits, he would have spent all his time and energy on the profitable Muppet toy lines. A businessman would never have made *The Dark Crystal*, a film that cost more to *create* than it made back in over a decade.[14] Such is the definition of a gift.

When Henson joined on to the experimental PBS show *Sesame Street* in 1968, he was underpaid for his services creating Big Bird and Oscar.[15] Yet he spent his free nights in his basement, shooting stop-motion films that taught kids to count.[16] If you watch these counting films, the spirit of Henson's gift shines through. I think any struggling artist today could count Henson among their ilk. He had all the makings of a tragic starving artist. The only difference between him and us is that he made *peace* with money. He found a way to make art and money *dance*.

"How," Hyde asks, "if art is essentially a gift, is the artist to survive in a society dominated by the market?"[17] It is a dance of timing, he answers:

> First, the artist allows himself to step outside the gift economy that is the primary commerce of his art and make some peace with the market. . . . The artist who wishes neither to lose his gift nor to starve his belly reserves a protected gift-sphere in which the work is created, but once the work is made he allows himself some contact with the market. And then—the necessary second phase—if he is successful in the marketplace, he converts market wealth into gift wealth: he contributes his earnings to the support of his art.[18]

The dance involves art and money, but *not at the same time.* In the first stage, it is paramount that the artist "reserves a protected gift-sphere in which the art is created." He keeps money out of it. But in the next two phases, they can dance. The way I see it, Hyde's dance steps go a little something like this:

1. Make art.
2. Make art make money.
3. Make money make art.

It is the last step that turns this dance into a waltz—something cyclical so that the money is not the real *end.* Truly, for Jim Henson, money was a *fuel* that fed art. According to *Fraggle Rock* producer Larry Mirkin:

> He viewed money as energy, the energy that makes concrete things happen out of worthy ideas. Money was not an end in itself. It could provide physical infrastructure or it could help him hire other artists and technicians to realize a nascent idea. I don't ever recall him being the least

> bit concerned or afraid of money or obsessed by it, which many people are. It just wasn't what drove him—at all.[19]

In Henson's creation mode—step 1—money was not a driving force. And once he had money, he used it to make more art—step 3. But step 2 is the hardest one for artists to negotiate, since it requires you make money without destroying your art.

Participation in the market is *tricky*, and Henson once told a Canadian reporter:

> Maintaining a balance between art and business has always been a part of what I do. You operate with as much honesty and integrity as you can afford. Success has brought the ability to pick and choose what we do.[20]

This balance is difficult to maintain. Yet, as Henson suggests, if you have no money, you cannot afford to be honest. Without step 2, you run out of money, and then you can't do step 1. Henson's legacy proves that there *is* such a thing as making an honest buck, and though it isn't easy, it gives an artist the ability to control his own destiny.

We may not want to run a business like Henson's, but we can take Henson's approach to money as far as we want—starting a video-game company or simply selling more sketches—becoming the most successful version of *yourself*. Whatever art you make, the first step to making money is an emotional one—to "make some peace," as Hyde says, "with the market." There is a time to eschew the market, and there is a time to join with it. There is no list of steps that can accomplish "making peace." But know that Henson *did* accomplish it, and because he did, you felt inspired by art throughout your childhood and perhaps through your children's as well. You know Jim Henson by name *because* he made peace with money.

You may not work in show business, but whatever your art, there is some business in which you participate. Scientists, inventors, and teachers all in some way resemble Henson in that they are professions of "the gift," of working for the benefit of others. If you simply want to do work of higher quality than business-as-usual seems to allow, you know the spirit of the gift, and you are not alone. It may be crazy to take turkey feathers, make them supple, cut their spines in half, bleach and clean them, dye the tips bright yellow, dye the bases golden yellow, adjust the tones so they look "gorgeous"[21] on both the US and British electron-firing color systems, separate them into five grades, take the top three grades, and have them ready at every shoot to replace anything that falls off of Big Bird. It might seem crazy, but to an artist like Henson, those are all necessary steps.[22] And if you are reading this book, you probably don't think it's crazy at all—intuitively we know that the magic of Big Bird depends on the spirit of the gift—in a *careful* dance with the market. It is the goal of this book to illustrate that dance. By closely examining Jim Henson's relationship with money, we can derive a philosophy that will serve us in our own careers—no matter what they may be.

In his office, Henson hung a "Shrine to the Almighty Dollar"—a comically large dollar bill with a small pyre at its feet. Decorated with paint and pennies, it may have been "tongue-in-cheek"[23] as the Henson archivist Karen Falk writes, but what is a shrine? It is a place—a physical object—upon which to focus one's thoughts. Like the restaurant owner who frames his first taste of success, Henson must have meditated on that shrine, thanked the dollar for its generosity, and hoped for more of its abundance. The dollar meant something to Henson—it meant more art. How might you make a shrine to the money that will fuel your art? A shrine may not actually *do* anything, but as artists, you know the value of focusing one's thoughts.

And what is a hero but a person upon whom to focus one's thoughts—to *imagine* one's dreams? I would not have written this book if I did not believe that a Henson-like path is possible for today's artists. In search of that path—for myself and all the artists I know—I've read everything I can find about Henson and money.

For simplicity's sake, here are ten Muppety lessons. Use them to develop your own ideas, to notice new ways to look at your own career; jot down things that you might like to try. Use this book as an object to focus your thoughts about art and money. And then go beyond it.

TEN LESSONS FOR ARTISTS

LESSON 1

FIND A GOOD REASON TO SELL OUT

The real breakthrough in Henson's career—the thing that would make him a mogul—was *Sesame Street.* It debuted in 1969, a good fifteen years into Henson's television career. Because it taught children across the country, Henson became a household name, and through *Sesame Street* toys, Henson became a millionaire. In short, merchandising is the "secret" to Henson's success. However, licensing toys, to Henson, felt like selling out. Before he became a mogul, he had to find a good reason to do so.

For Henson—like any artist—finding funding had always been a problem. From 1957 until 1969, Henson funded his workshop, his experimental television, and his films with commercials. This had been a "second job" as catering is to actors and teaching is to many poets. One of the virtues of the second job is that Hyde says it makes it easy for artists to "mark the boundary between their art and the market."[24] Henson didn't confuse his commercials with his shows—there was a clear boundary. And the money from these commercials insulated him from the market to a great extent. He could spend as much money as he wanted on his projects, using this second job for income. Similarly, Hyde notes that for many years Edward Hopper did commercial drafting for magazines before his real work became profitable. In the meantime, the magazine money allowed him to keep painting.

But with commercials, there *were* drawbacks. No matter how reputable the product or how honest the company, some part of Henson's content was always dictated by the sponsor. Later, he would look back on commercials and say, "It was a pleasure to get out of that world. If you've ever worked in commercials, it's a world of compromise and a world of . . ."[25] He trailed off midsentence in this interview, suggesting a kind of self-censorship—commercials were more than a *compromise* for Henson. They were something he didn't want to describe on record. Even when he was highly respected in the industry, he said, "The whole process is really not easy on a creative person."[26]

So, in 1969, Jim Henson decided to stop making commercials. He had a good excuse—he felt it was confusing to the impressionable viewers of *Sesame Street* to use his characters to both sell snacks and teach the alphabet. Artistically, this was a good decision, giving Henson more time to focus on *Sesame Street*. The only trouble was that Henson no longer had the buffer of commercial pay to keep his projects funded. Henson essentially cut a deal for the nonprofit CTW for his first-rate services on *Sesame Street*. As *Sesame* profiler Mike Davis wrote in *Street Gang*, his pay was "modest by show-business standards."[27]

To keep funding his high-quality work, Henson needed another option to emerge, and almost like karma, one did—merchandising. Davis writes that "within weeks of *Sesame Street*'s debut there was no shortage of opportunities. . . . [Co-creator Joan Ganz] Cooney began fielding cold calls from marketers eager to attach the likenesses of Muppet characters on to products, in exchange for a licensing fee."[28] Like commercials, toy merchandising offered Henson a way to be his own bankroller, and it would be better than commercials, because there would be no boss above his own creative vision; however, at first, Henson refused.

In 1970,[29] two years into *Sesame Street*'s production, Jim Henson argued the issue with his agent, Bernie Brillstein. In his memoir, *Where Did I Go Right?*, Brillstein wrote:

> Jim Henson and his wife, Jane, dropped by my house at 1240 Loma Vista. Soon we were pacing around the kitchen, arguing. If it was 110 degrees outside, it was definitely hotter inside.
>
> This was the problem: I wanted Jim and Jane to make a merchandising deal for the *Sesame Street* characters. They thought it was a bad idea. The Children's Television Workshop needed the deal because the revenue would ensure continued independent support for what had become a huge public television hit. But Jim and Jane owned half the rights, and *both* sides had to approve any arrangement.
>
> "You have to merchandise," I said.
>
> "No," said Jim and Jane at the same time. Jim hated the idea of selling out. . . .
>
> The Hensons were artsy-craftsy. They always wanted to do things for the right reasons. God bless them. They thought educating kids on public TV and then selling them toys based on the characters didn't mix. . . . [T]he whole idea of merchandising made them feel like sellouts. As artists, they couldn't live with that perception.[30]

But Henson, we know, came around. In 1970, he started merchandising the *Sesame Street* characters. He sold out—by his own standards. So what convinced him? Brillstein offered Henson three reasons. Brillstein told Henson::

> "Number one, you have every child in America watching this show, and one day it will hopefully be worldwide. You're educating kids better and more creatively than TV ever has. Shouldn't they have good dolls instead of the shit they're buying now? Shouldn't they have Kermit and Bert and Ernie? You can't not give it to them."[31]

As we will see later, Henson did, in fact, take great pains to make sure the products that made him rich were not "shit." But this reason was not alone convincing. So Brillstein assured him total veto control:

> "Second, you will have full control of what's done. Yes or no. You will kill anything you want to kill. You'll approve every license. Everything will be reasonably priced and above reproach."[32]

Sesame Street's *mission* was to educate poor kids. It was a philanthropically funded program that offered school preparation for inner-city and isolated rural kids—so that they might have a better shot at success. Because it was free, it was democratic; once it became priced, someone would get priced out. Moreover, Henson did not want to sell kids things that were bad for them—we can imagine Cookie Monster cap guns would be out.

Essentially, Brillstein was saying Henson would always control the merchandising; it would never control him. But this still wasn't enough. Brillstein continued:

> "Third, if what I believe will happen with this merchandising happens[,] . . . you will make enough money to have artistic freedom for the rest of your life."
>
> Artistic freedom. Those two words sold him . . . for an artist to imagine being able to do as his heart desired without asking anyone for money . . .
>
> Jim and Jane said okay.[33]

Henson spent much of his career asking moneymen to fund his work. Working in commercials had given him some barrier against it—after the pitch was secured and a commercial was made, he was free to use the money however he liked, no strings attached. But after giving up commercials, that monetary buffer against outside control had dissolved. It seems counterintuitive, but the less he engaged with capitalism, the more he needed to *beg*, and the more he was subject to the market's demands. It was the desire to be free from the market that ironically convinced Henson to become one of America's great merchandisers.

Framed as "creative freedom," merchandising was in fact an *ethical* system for viewers to pay Henson back—to repay his gift of quality—proportional to their own feelings of gratitude. If a child recognizes the art put into Big Bird—his glorious yellow feathers, the pantomime of the puppeteer with arm overhead, the humor of the invented voice—then as a reward, the company would receive money in proportion to how much children love the character. It was—in a positive light—a way to fund Henson's next project from the success of his last, the collection plate passed around after a sermon. At any rate, it was preferable to commercials, which by nature forced him to cede veto power to the client. Henson could refuse a job, but ultimately, the client was the final judge. Community Coffee, for instance, wouldn't pay Henson to make something that didn't at the very least say the name of their product. With merchandising, *Henson* had the veto power. He was the one in complete control of his art, and as we will see, he would ensure that the toys were more than commodities, that they would be art themselves, or at least approach it.

Another good reason to merchandise was for *Sesame Street* itself. Brillstein said in his argument that "Children's Television Workshop needed the deal."[34] Had it been only Henson's company at stake, he might not have done it. The partnership with CTW allowed Henson to see *his* needs through the unclouded mirror of *their* needs. Presented in this way, those needs became real. In *Street Gang*, Davis explains why CTW's funding was running out: "Foundations like Ford and Carnegie exist to seed projects, not sustain them . . . CTW needed a revenue stream."[35] This same revenue stream was necessary to allow Henson to stay independent.

The reason that *Sesame Street* became so lucrative for Henson was copyright and trademark—intellectual property. When he agreed to work with the show's co-creator, Joan Ganz Cooney, Henson stipulated that "the trademark for any Muppet characters created for the show would remain with his company," and that "any future revenues made from the licensing and merchandising of those characters would be split between him and CTW," according to Davis.[36] Copyright is a key to making money as an artist, because it allows a work of art to be made once at great cost—making it, in a sense, a gift—and then reproduced relatively cheaply, giving back to the creator infinite profits. Though commodities, these products still bear the stamp of the expensive original, reminding us of the gift.

Toy sales can be quite lucrative, especially with the rise of plastics, and by 1990, CTW and Henson split $15 million a year between them.[37] According to *Street Gang*, "both organizations depended on that revenue for survival."[38] This "revenue stream" allowed Henson to weather the ups and downs of the market relatively unscathed. You see, not *all* of Henson's projects made money. *The Muppet Movie* did, but *The Muppets Take Manhattan* didn't.[39] On the books, the original run of *The Muppet Show* just broke even; profit came in re-syndicating *The Muppet Show* to TNT, years later.[40] *The Dark Crystal* definitely didn't make a profit at the box office;[41] profit came with the invention of DVDs, years later.[42] These words "years later" are narrative consolation, but when a company must pay its yearly expenses, they can mean bankruptcy.

Yet, profit for art is *usually* a long-term prospect. It was artistic risk that made the Muppet "brand" successful, but that is a long-term approach to value that requires a steady and separate revenue stream—to continually invest in one's quality and to give, in the short term, more than one receives. To get to a point where he could afford to take a chance on *Sesame Street*, he first had to make commercials.

If commercials were the "second job" option, then toy merchandising was what Hyde would call "plac[ing] the work on the market." Hyde cautioned that it can be harder to keep a boundary between art and money in this option—but Henson at least had the distinction between puppet show and toy, right? He would not confuse a Fisher-Price Kermit for his palette. In a simple sense, toys make money and puppet shows spend it.

Yet, when characters become commodities, it can be harder to do things "for the right reasons."

THE SLEAZY TOYMAKER
AND HOW HENSON AND CTW ADDRESSED THIS INHERENT GROSSNESS

In our age, merchandising is so common we almost take it for granted. The merchandising for *Star Wars* allowed George Lucas to fund his own Industrial Light & Magic special effects, which spawned what is now Pixar Animation Studios. When Lucas took a financial hit in the divorce from his first wife, he decided to set Pixar free, and the company became independent. Pixar in turn made their first movie protagonists *toys*, which then went on to sell very well *as toys.* Cartoons today have toys built into their business plans. A walk through Toys"R"Us can make you dizzy with plastic wrap, TM symbols, and LED flashbacks, but at the heart of this "marketing scheme" is the simple act of making a child happy. The Hensons wanted to do everything for "the right reasons," in Brillstein's words, but what exactly is so *wrong* with selling toys?

In *Follow that Bird*, Big Bird is kidnapped by the owners of a carnival, Sid and Sam Sleaze. With their hats turned sideways, they charge a nickel to go up the Ferris wheel and a nickel to come back down. It's a racket. The fact that the kid—not a *child*, in their eyes, just some dumb *kid*—is vulnerable up there makes him an easy target. Kids' shows that make money off both commercials and merchandising are pulling this same double-dip. The kids are easy targets. Their parents use TV to babysit, and then they buy them cartloads of toys every December that were advertised by their babysitter. It's like shooting fish in a barrel. It's one thing if you're playing this game with adults—who might get what they deserve—but children don't have the experience with money to realize that their friends are only using them for profit. Sid and Sam Sleaze aren't in children's entertainment for "the right reasons," because they exploit kids for money without giving anything back. At night they count their money, while Big Bird sits alone in a cage, exploited for profit.

No one wants to grow up to be a Sleaze, and neither did CTW. *Sesame Street* may have needed toys for survival—because they *didn't* sell ads—but it still *looked* cheap to sell toys. Some in the CTW camp didn't want to. Gene Aleinikoff, legal consultant to CTW, reportedly said, "It's a whore's way of doing things."[43] Though it sounds vulgar, selling something that should be a gift is precisely what prostitution is.

To address this concern, CTW took a pedagogical approach. Initially, they made sure its toys were educational and, crucially, *perceived* that way. Karen Falk, the archivist for The Jim Henson Company, explains that CTW's press release "justified" the toys by "citing the education benefits of their products":

> CTW Marketing Director Jeanette Neff said that they did not want to be seen as ". . . exploiting this most precious and innocent of audiences, the children." Having already tested easily defended books and records, they entered the toy market as a means of ". . . extending the educational effect of the show." She also emphasized that ". . . all revenues from these and future commercial efforts are plowed back into Workshop educational projects."[44]

Feeling the need to "justify" what could be seen as "exploiting" children, CTW's first forays included books, records, a Spell-A-Phone, and hand puppets, which as Henson knew—from experience—encouraged the imagination. Of course, the toys had to be fun, too, but not look *too-* or *only*-fun. It was a fine line to walk. Christopher Cerf, the first head of the *Sesame* toy division, wrote in a press release: "We believe that only if our books and playthings are amusing will they be purchased and used enough to have educational value."[45] The superfluity of toys, Cerf explained, were an important part of the learning process—a spoonful of sugar to help the medicine go down.

The spin on the *Sesame* toys probably had more to do with CTW's curriculum department than it did with Henson, but in 1976, he would release a line of toys independently—in connection with the premier of *The Muppet Show*. Unlike CTW, he didn't market his toys as "learning machines." Jim Henson addressed the problem of toys his own way.

In 1976, for the first time, a child would be able to give Kermit the Frog a hug. According to Falk, "Kermit was considered a guest on [*Sesame Street*] and thus unavailable for consumers to take home. Fisher-Price was happy to exploit the pent-up demand and immediately began making products featuring Kermit."[46] A key word here is *exploit*. When Disney later agreed to buy the Muppet trademarks, one 1990 editorial noticed that Wall Street analysts explained Disney's motives "using the word exploit only twice."[47] If it was *only* twice, it must have been a good day on Wall Street. The fact is, when discussing business, it's perfectly natural to exploit *resources* and *markets*, unless of course what's being exploited is children and their innocent love and trust in us.

However, Henson dealt with the grossness of toy-making exactly the way an artist would. An artist can turn anything into art—even a commodity. Jim Henson did not simply take Fisher-Price's money—*kids'* money—and run. In fact, he didn't let Fisher-Price design the toys at all. Falk writes, "Jim's staff did the initial design work and prototypes (rather than leaving it to the licensee's research and development area)."[48] Henson approved every licensed product personally.[49] Even though he disliked making child-only fare and would likely rather be creating a Broadway play or a nightclub,

Henson gave his very *limited* time to design toys—so that they would be more than a simple economic exploitation. That *time* was a gift.

Fisher-Price's ad manager, Jerry Houle,[50] would eventually become the licensing director at Henson's company. He described going into his first meetings with Henson:

> The first thing I did was to study the industry to develop a strategy about how licensing would work and present it to Jim. His response was simple and elegant. He said, "We don't need the money, just make me beautiful products."[51]

For Henson, toys didn't need to be overtly *educational*, but they had to be gorgeous. Art, any artist knows, is inherently affirming, wondrous, and nourishing for the creative mind. It educates us without a curriculum. *Muppet Show* merchandise included snow globes, albums, dolls, notebooks, calendars, and teapots. They were not "teaching tools" or "learning machines," but they expressed *something*. If art *works*, it speaks to you about life. For Henson, that was enough—enough to make a toy no longer gross, no longer a commodity, but something *more*.

Muppeteer Steve Whitmire once explained Henson's *visceral* sense of taste:

> When we were doing *Fraggle Rock*, Jim was in Toronto, and I went out to lunch one day. I went across the street and someone had made these Muppet hot pads for your oven. And it was this knitted Ernie head. It was pretty terrible. And it was $10, so I bought it. I took it back and I said "I got you something over lunch," and Jim smiled and I handed it over to him, and the look on his face! It

> was really devastating to him. And he said "Do I have to take that??" And he was serious, so I said, "No of course not!" And I realized, he never had a problem, he almost let people rip him off if it was good. When people made things that he didn't feel were up to par, then it upset him. . . . [H]e wanted it to be at least complimentary.[52]

The *Red Book* is Henson's career journal, a careful record of his company's milestones and accomplishments, which has posted online by The Jim Henson Company archivist Karen Falk as a series of blog posts, many of which have been expanded with additional interviews, explanations, and photographs. On the blog, the first mention of Sesame Street merchandise is dated September 20–24, 1971. This is the week when Henson did what he told Brillstein he would never do—sell out.

Let us visually re-create Henson's entry, "Recording Alphabet album at night."[53] Now firstly, puppeteer Jerry Nelson said that "Jim loved to sing, as did we all,"[54] so picture that. He probably recorded the album at night because he was quite busy, but as he told Big Bird puppeteer Caroll Spinney when he hired him, he and Frank Oz would "get into a project and work all day, all night, all the next day, and sometimes the next night too. Do you like to work like that?"[55] Henson *liked* to work hard. And then picture that, in the seventies, Henson reportedly had a fridge in his office stocked with soda, beer, and cider.[56] Lastly, something recalled by Jerry Juhl:

> One of the images that I think we all have of Jim that we've seen repeatedly is Jim standing in the studio with his hand in the air and a puppet and he's laughing uncontrollably. Everything has come to a complete stop, and

> that kind of infectious enthusiasm kind of spread through all casts and crews.[57]

Now, with all that we know, let us picture September 1971's journal entry, "Recording Alphabet album at night." Joe Raposo's "J" song—a real *earworm*—paints the mood with a tongue-twister: "Hey Jim, he's tall and slim! He's got a jar of jam! Let's join with him!" This record album, made of plastic, may have been just *merchandise*, but one can imagine it as more of a joy or a party than a late night at the office, perhaps with a few of those beers from the fridge, really belting it out with Frank and the gang, and laughing to the point of tears when the last note goes hilariously off. Jim Henson countered merchandising's grossness by using it as an excuse to make more art.

And most importantly, Henson put the profits back into his art. This echoes CTW's stance: "all revenues from these and future commercial efforts are plowed back into Workshop educational projects."[58] And though Disney was much quicker to merchandise than Henson, Disney biographer Neal Gabler writes that he "continued to reinvest most of the profits back into the studio." As Hyde notes, it is a "necessary" phase for an artist existing in both a gift economy and a market economy: "If he is successful in the marketplace, he converts market wealth into gift wealth: he contributes his earnings to the support of his art.[59]

Larry Mirkin recalled:

> One time Jim and I were flying from Toronto to New York. I can't remember how it came up but we had this conversation about money which I think conveys well Jim's attitude about it, or at least my perception of Jim's attitude. He said, "How much money does someone

> need? $100,000 a year? $200,000? After whatever that number is, why do you need more?" As he pointed out, the question becomes: when you have more than whatever that "necessary personal number" (my phrase), what should you do with it? Jim usually decided to put it into the work if he had projects or ideas he really wanted to explore or develop. Now, I don't mean for a second that he was frivolous about this. He knew where every penny was being spent, but he had a Big Picture attitude that went far beyond the idea of "maximizing shareholder value." He was talking about deeper values, things (tangible and intangible) that last longer than money.[60]

For Henson, any work that bore his characters was an extension of himself—whether it was a show or a toy. He put greater effort into these toys than was required, and yet, this is not to say they were *pure* art, by any stretch of the imagination. About *The Muppet Alphabet Album*, Henson said, "I thought it would be great if we could just give a child something to remember—a handle, or a few clues that would make learning to read just a little easier and a bit more fun."[61] This observation—that people need a "handle"—was a key lesson for Henson in many ways.

PURE ART DON'T SELL
FIND A HANDLE

Because Henson fought so hard against toys in 1970, you might not expect that he'd actually licensed a line of toys four years earlier. Since this was two years before the idea for *Sesame Street*, there was no internal conflict. He was not even a children's entertainer in his mind, and in 1966, he was certainly no *educator*. He was a thirty-year-old artist with a family to support. It was also, like most of his actions in the 1960s, an experiment.

An interesting lesson came out of this foray into toys. Though Ideal Toy Company agreed to make three of Henson's puppets—Kermit, Rowlf, and Snerf—only two dolls ever made it to the store shelf. Kermit the Frog and Rowlf the Dog were manufactured, but left to obscurity was Snerf—the Whatever—an abstract creature resembling a pipe cleaner. Springy, wormlike Snerf appeared in some of Henson's bits on *The Ed Sullivan Show*. In that period, he was experimenting with trippy spectacles that made adults *think*. But these experiments only made it so far. In order to break out, Henson had to give the audience "a handle," as he called it.

But licensing Snerf wouldn't have made Henson millions. He couldn't license his creations the way they existed in 1966, as the abstractions in "Business, Business" or the dancing U-shaped tubes in "Java," another skit. These early "Muppets" were truly Henson's passion, his art in its purest form. But unfortunately, Snerf, as ingenious as he was, never made it past a prototype. The toy company, it seemed, knew what Henson didn't. Whatevers, Frackles, and Snerfs don't sell. Animals give people an easy handle. Dogs and frogs—that's what kids like.

This is unfortunate, because Henson the artist actually preferred the purity of the Whatever. In the beginning, he told Judy Harris, Kermit *wasn't* a frog.

> **Henson:** I didn't call him a frog.
> **Harris:** Right, he was just Kermit the thing.
> **Henson:** Yeah, all the characters in those days were abstract because that was part of the principle I was working under. . . . I still like very much the abstract characters and some of those abstract characters I still feel are slightly

> more pure. If you take a character and you call him a frog, or like Rowlf, our dog, call him a dog, you immediately give the audience a handle. You're assisting the audience to understand; you're giving them a bridge or an access. And if you don't give them that, if you keep it more abstract, it's almost more pure. It's a cooler thing. It's a difference of a sort of warmth and cool. . . . [I]n terms of going commercial and going broad audience, you want to reach the audience as much as possible, and you need those bridges.[62]

Although Henson spoke of the difference as merely interesting—with nice things about each—it would not be a stretch to say the "nice thing" about pure characters is the artistic game played with the audience—closer to approaching art—and the nice thing about the *handled* characters is their mass-market appeal—the money and ratings they can generate. The *Sam and Friends* characters in the 1950s were neither cuddly nor cute, and they wouldn't make great kids' toys. In fact, with Rowlf known only as a guest on *The Jimmy Dean Show* and Kermit being a character from pilots that had yet to be aired, even they couldn't earn Henson a great deal. It wasn't until these characters became known nationally (and internationally) on *Sesame Street* and *The Muppet Show* that their toys would blow up, as they say.

In order for Henson to get to do what he wanted, *he* had to change—he made his characters "warmer" than he as an artist would have wanted. Although I don't think Henson ever chased merchandising dollars, he *did* want to make a nationally broadcast Muppet show, and since TV executives wanted to program puppets only *for kids*—with potential toy-licensing splits—the more Kermit became froglike, the more likely it became that Henson's shows would air.

Artists may find this lesson depressing, yet without this initial "handle," Henson could never have made *The Dark Crystal* or *Fraggle Rock*, which were funded by Muppets money, green-lighted because of Muppets ratings, and ultimately reached closer to Henson's desired "abstract" principle. Warming up his characters, what we might call "selling out," allowed him to innovate, and he learned to accept that. In the sixties, Henson's projects were experimental—a documentary, a nightclub, and expressionist films. In the seventies, he did what worked: fairy tales, holiday specials, and kids' shows—TV by TV's rules. Henson may have *wanted* to make abstract creatures, but animals *sell.* This is very definitely connected to the shift in funding from commercials—a second job with a clear boundary—to toys, where the market has more power to change the art to suit financial needs. Yet the world loves the Muppets, and it could be argued they are *better* for having been "warmed." Jerry Seinfeld made the point that amateur comedians go out on stage thinking they'll tell the audience what's funny, but at some point, you learn that it is the audience that tells *you* what's funny about you. Because in show business the "market" is often the "audience," it is a blurry line between selling out and reaching many hearts with your gift. In my opinion, Henson was wiser in the seventies about what could be done with art on television, and though his work was perhaps not as *experimental* as it was in the sixties, it was, in a less pure form, more *watched* and more often green-lighted.

On *The Muppet Show,* the young and annoyingly earnest Scooter gets to have his way—because his uncle owns the theater. Kermit, in order to put on his show, must keep him happy. Scooter suggests a number with a dancing poodle.

Kermit says, "It sounds, said the frog, displaying his artistic judgment, sappy."

Scooter mentions his uncle.

Kermit adapts: "It sounds, said the frog, displaying his will to survive, wonderful."

In a sense, Kermit is lying, but more accurately, he is transparently expressing the truth of his situation—to the show's viewers. In order to have his show, he needs a theater. This seems a natural problem of selling one's work on the open market. The market can start to shape the work. Yet, *some* contact with the market will not entirely destroy a work.

The romantic image of the artist we have been given coyly ignores the fact that all artists are affected by the market—even Emily Dickinson, writing in her family's attic, might have used fewer long dashes had she been renting a basement apartment. *The Muppet Show* was an art that made clear compromises to conform to the market—having animal characters and, in its first season, employing traditional sitcom joke writers and using canned laughter. Yet, with all its compromises, *The Muppet Show* also raised the bar for what was possible on TV, by bringing more art to it than the medium required.

THERE ARE BAD TOYS WHICH MEANS THERE MUST ALSO BE GOOD TOYS

Henson's great genius lay in his ability to see the humor, the beauty, the *art,* in everything. His son said, "The same image that would depress somebody else was an image he could delight in. The same circumstance that would frustrate somebody would tickle him."[63] Henson's character Cantus seemed to believe there could be a song in *anything*, and Henson likewise seemed to be able to make art out of anything, even the crassest commodities. When Henson told Houle to make his toys beautiful, he was serious. He was asking

Houle to make toys in the same way he made toys for his own children. Falk describes his work for the *Sesame Street* "Number 8" counting film:

> Elaborate sets were built, and Jim hand-painted the large castle with windows that opened to reveal the eight Princesses. He was building dollhouses for his daughters at that time so his miniature abode-building skills were sharp.[64]

But, of course, to mass-produce toys this good, this "artsy-craftsy," would be impossible. As we know, the economic model of the toy *works,* because the toys can be mass-produced cheaply using a copyright that was very expensive to make. Toys are big profit because the original character can be a gift—a product of gift labor—and the commodity resembles that gift. To make each toy itself a work of art—such as a handmade dollhouse—would be totally unprofitable. On the other hand, to conform to the industry standard—to let Fisher-Price design his toys—would yield the *maximum* profits for Henson. Henson aimed for somewhere in between, to achieve a quality his fine taste would approve of. This extra overhead, of course, cut into his profits, but it was in this sense that the toys themselves could be *part* gift.

A downside to handling the licensing himself was that Henson had to add a new business arm to his company. When Pixar was faced with this proposition many years later, they instead negotiated a merger with Disney to let them handle it. Ed Catmull, Pixar's current president, who at the time was the company's chief technical officer, explained the danger of having to build a business arm quickly:

> All of a sudden there would be another two to three hundred businesspeople in the company, and that would be a risk to the culture.[65]

It was crucial that Henson's business arm respected the artistic process. Henson lawyer Al Gottesman explained how the company had to grow *carefully*:

> Jim was very concerned about quality control. . . . [A]nd he'd veto anything that he didn't like. When we went to license the *Muppet Show* characters, he wanted to approve everything himself, and that got crazy. We'd have a courier on the plane to London almost every day with a bag full of prototypes for him to look at. It wasn't that Jim couldn't delegate responsibility. I think it was just that he'd been used to running a very small company. . . . He would have to hire more business people and lawyers to take care of the expansion, but he would not fall into the trap of creating a company that broke down into two parts—the creative personnel on one side and the business people on the other. To avoid that schism, he tried to hire business people who would fit comfortably into the creative family that was already in place.[66]

When you add new participants to the Ouija Board game, the pointer starts to go in a new direction, and so Henson was most selective. Henson had famously waited for Frank Oz to finish high school so that he could hire this irreplaceable puppeteering prodigy, and with this same cautious precision, he hired businesspeople he had already worked with and knew he could trust. Houle had been working at Fisher-Price; Michael Frith, an illustrator, at Random

House. The licensing and publishing division of Henson's company grew in this way.

Henson had to make sure that every new person could "fit in comfortably to the creative family." Frith, who had worked with Dr. Seuss, fit in nicely. He explained that his first project as an official Henson employee was a day-and-night labor of love:

> *Sesame Street* licensing was just beginning to heat up, so there was a ton to vet and correct: much of the pile turned out to be artwork for a *Sesame* encyclopedia that was being produced in Japan. It was WAY past due—Jim hadn't been too concerned about their deadlines—and it was just . . . terrible. And it came with an extra dividend. Every morning when I arrived (and I was EARLY), there would be sitting in our little reception area a smiling Japanese man with a briefcase on his lap. Every night when I went home (and I was working LATE) he was still there. He never said a word. As far as I know, he never opened the briefcase. I labored on, sheet after sheet after sheet of reconceptions and corrections. Every now and then, usually late at night, our producer, David Lazer, would wander in, peer over my shoulder and murmur, "It'll always be a sow's ear."[67]

Frith was also responsible for *Miss Piggy's Treasury of Art Masterpieces from the Kermitage Collection.* Out of print, it now sells for about $35. It features full-page photographs of Miss Piggy as Whistler's mother, the Mona Lisa, a Rembrandt, a Vermeer. Frith described the idea's genesis:

> I began, in the rare spare moments the photo studio had, devising absurdly elaborate—and not inexpensive—re-creations of iconic works of art starring our (by now) much loved Muppet repertory company. I was determined to accomplish a couple of things, but most importantly to capture both the light and the composition of the originals (not easy when you're putting a short, dumpy pig in the place of a long, lissome Botticelli Venus), and to do it ALL in the camera—no tricks, no retouching. This, my dears, was pre-Photoshop. We had integrity then. And we were a little bit mad. Maybe more than a little.[68]

Here, "a little bit mad" seems to mean "willing to make art." Frith, with Henson's direction, took what might otherwise be a pure commodity and turned it into art—something that's more trouble than it's worth, but that one does anyway, in service of the gift. The saying goes that "You can't turn a sow's ear into a purse," but by hiring the right people to create his toys, Henson turned a commodity into something we might call "pop art."

In 1969, Henson published a *Woman's Day* spread with patterns that mothers could sew for their children's puppet shows. It seems like Henson hoped the whole world could be, in Brillstein's words, "artsy-craftsy." But what he found is that people want what they want, and as Brillstein said, "You can't not give it to them."[69] Postwar Americans don't make their own puppets; they drive to a toy store and buy them. Henson loved the handmade item—he filled his home with crafts while he sold their opposite, the mass-manufactured lunchbox. Yet, in a world filled with crass, cheap, gross merchandise, Henson's products often retained a glimmer of that "artsy-craftsy" feeling that made them, because he put more work into them than he had to. Though they may rightly be called commodities, they reminded us of something else.

PART OF THE PROBLEM TO BE PART OF THE SOLUTION

The TV special *The Great Santa Claus Switch* aired in 1970. As this was right around the time Henson decided to merchandise, it is unsurprising that the theme of his merchandising dilemma appears so clearly on the surface of the narrative. In the figure of Santa, it seems that Henson was debating the decision to use toys and, by extension, Christmas—the gift season—for monetary gain. Like the Grinch, toy manufacturers and network TV are *masters* at co-opting holiday generosity. And in 1970, Henson found himself right in the middle of the deception.

In the special, an evil magician named Cosmo Scam tries to profit off Christmas by kidnapping Santa and taking his sleigh. A small elf named Fred—Jim Henson's stand-in—works for Santa and tries to protect him, but unwittingly aids Scam. He promises Santa: "I wanna help help help, I wanna serve serve serve, I wanna do my duty faithfully and never ever swerve! I wanna do my best, I wanna serve with zest, I wanna help, I wanna help, I wanna help!" But unfortunately, Fred is so wrapped up in his pledge that he forgets to protect Santa. Henson's own zeal for art, like Fred's passion, led him into the exploitative world of merchandising.

In Cosmo Scam, we see an extreme capitalist whose only aim is money. His song explains: "I use my money to fulfill my plan . . . to make about a million bucks!" Scam is quite self-aware when he tells Santa: "I tell you something, the easy part about bein' a burglar is stealin' things, but the hard part is getting into people's houses . . . for stealin'. People just don't like burglars in their houses!

On the other hand . . . no one minds if Santa Claus comes into his house on Christmas Eve, follow me?" He continues, "So I gotta do just what . . . everybody would think that Santa Claus would do!"

In the puppet play, the evil wizard imitates Santa, and in the real world, the toy manufacturers imitate that famously benevolent, magnanimous toy manufacturer—Santa. They try to manufacture whatever everyone thinks Santa would make, not to give joy, but to "make about a million bucks." Scam tried to use Christmas to "get into the peoples' houses" through the chimney. The toy manufacturers get in through the television set. More precisely, they get into peoples' wallets through the eyes of the little tykes sitting in front of the *tube*, a conduit for gifts and thieves. As Scam sings, "Oh, there's a *bundle* to be made every Christmastime!"

None of this is news to us, but what strikes me is Fred's complicit role in the deception, and how he breaks free to redeem himself. Fred may have been guilty of letting himself be carried away while Santa gets kidnapped, but he was also a victim who was kidnapped himself. In the end, Fred *does* help Santa—using his creativity to free himself. After getting back to the workshop, Fred stows away on the sleigh and cuts the reins so Scam can't take off. We might call this strategy "changing the system from the inside."

In the end of the special, Santa's benevolence even turns the baddies off stealin' by giving Scam a gift. With Fred's help, Christmas is saved and the greedy wizard is converted. The world is *better* for what transpired. In real life, Henson used his merchandising profits to make twenty more years of art—art that tried to teach a worldwide audience to live together in peace. He used it to employ hundreds of artists and to inspire millions more. One could argue the world is a little better—*because* he sold out. If he hadn't, I don't know that we would be talking about him here today.

HOW TO
ENACT YOUR SELLOUT

We should never sell out to the extent that it would ruin our art or change our gift into an empty commodity. But artists today can learn from Henson's relationship with toys. By viewing them as "creative freedom," and then putting his effort into making them "beautiful," Henson seemed to sell out in a way that made us love the art no less, and possibly more.

All this is not to say that we should *all* sell toys. It's true that toys are lucrative, and you *could* try to copy his road map exactly—create copyrightable characters, promote them through a philanthropic teaching endeavor, and then merchandise—but such a plot would be soulless, and I doubt it would work, even if copied step-for-step. In fact, this is usually how *bad* toys are made. For one thing, such calculation tends to crowd into your ability to do things for "the right reasons." For another, Henson didn't calculate this path himself. It happened organically, because he liked the idea for *Sesame Street* and was in a place where he could afford to do something simply because it was a good idea. As we'll see in later lessons, his view of copyright wasn't about profit; it was about protecting the work.

You are not Jim Henson, and unless you are a puppeteer in show business, your career is unlikely to look much like his. Yet there are some universal lessons here. Your art may not involve characters or anything merchandisable, but there may yet be some way in which mass production or mass media can benefit you. This is the difference between selling a painting and selling a license to use the image of the painting, the difference between performing a live show and broadcasting a show. Copyright creates a nice loophole for artists in the law that says they must starve. If you can make a work once and profit infinitely—proportional to the amount of times the art is given—then you can beat the system. What are the options for mass production in your own art? How might you make a masterpiece once and sell it many times? Not just for profit—for the chance to make the thing great?

Regardless of what your art *is*, in the larger sense, there may be an option for revenue that you have closed off for moral reasons that, when seen through the right lens, could be the key to your artistic freedom. The trick is to be open to the possibilities. According to Frank Oz, "Jim always flowed with the river. He never fought very hard against it."[70] Yet, paradoxically, because of this strategy, Henson was able to blaze his own path. What would you *never* do for money? How could you convince yourself to do it—for art? Could you turn it into art itself? Know that making the choice *will* eat up more of your time, because as an artist, you will care about more than the business standard. However you choose to address the grossness of the problem will resemble the rest of your art—if you are an educator, you will turn the cash cow into a teaching tool; a scientist, into science; a philosopher, into philosophy.

Reconsider selling out as quite possibly buying you time later to be more pure. Know that in order to sell out, you might need a handle for the masses to grasp your idea, but once you have it, your audience will follow you into any strange and darkened corner of your imagination—into places you never thought possible. Because when you hit upon something as profitable as Kermit was, going with the market's demand can give you the artistic freedom to make your *Dark Crystal*, something the market doesn't know it wants until two generations in—when the children you taught to love it teach it to their kids.

Of course, if you do "cash in" on a big wave, it is "necessary," in Hyde's words, to funnel the profits back into the art. Readers who are artists, of course, will. There is always something bigger and better you want to make but just don't have the money for. What if you visualize your financial success as the funding for this massive undertaking?

If you've already dealt with selling out to some degree, how has it affected your career? Was it the easy money it promised to be, or did you work harder afterward? Did more money bring creative independence, more problems, or both? Would you do it again if it bought you more time to work? How did you come to the decision to do it? Do you have any regrets?

For myself, the switch from fiction to nonfiction is my sellout, but I came to it organically, at age thirty, out of personal necessity. I was spending hundreds of hours crafting my fiction, but the only place I managed to publish it was a very small press that didn't pay or have many readers. My master's degree qualified me to tutor online for $11 an hour, and if I'd had a PhD, I would have earned $12. Burnt out and confused, in the Christmas of 2010, I felt I *needed* the Muppets, and I began to watch them obsessively—for the reassuring feeling they gave me.

Since I am a writer by nature, I recognized this as "research." I wanted the kind of work Henson had—fun, difficult, rewarding, worthwhile. I started to study his business methods, because more than any other artist—the indie-rock dreamboats, the provocateur cartoonists—Henson's legacy is clearly one of benevolence, art, and giving, and it is *lasting*. If he could negotiate art and business, there was no reason why I couldn't too.

For me, writing a prescriptive book is a "handle" to get my ideas across. I used to think my novel would do that, but when an article I wrote about the Muppets struck a nerve online in 2011, I realized I needed to flow with the river, and to a greater extent, let the *readers* tell me what's working. Now, I have published my first book, and that is a dream come true. The fact is, I could not have learned so much about business from anyone else besides Jim Henson.

I would love it if you would add your thoughts to my blog at ElizabethHydeStevens.com. The questions in this book are not rhetorical—they are starting points for discussion and self-reflection. If you have ten minutes to think about the shape of your career, answer them. Tell us your story.

Truly, there is no one alive today who knows the way for *you* to become a successful artist. To find it, you'll need to imagine it. Lesson 1, selling out—the way Henson did—may be something to reconsider.

What would *you* do with artistic freedom?

LESSON 2

HOW MANY HOURS HAVE YOU PRACTICED?

IN SERVICE OF THE GIFT

It was the *Sesame Street* licensing bonanza that made Jim Henson rich, but that stroke of luck didn't appear overnight. Twenty years earlier, Kermit was "born" in 1955 when college freshman Jim Henson cut up his mother's coat and attached two halves of a Ping-Pong ball to it. The story goes back further still—in order for Henson to become the artist he was at age nineteen took nineteen years of evolution. And so to get Kermit to the point in 1976 when he was incredibly marketable, it took forty years—an entire *lifetime* of work.

We sometimes picture artists as people with leisure time, avoiding the hard work of the factory and cubicle, but art is *work.* And if you're wondering why, as the song goes, you haven't made it yet, perhaps you just haven't earned it yet. It's not the answer we *want* to hear. As artists, we desire nothing more than the freedom to work long hours on our art. Yet, if you have not already done so, you need to shift that freedom into its opposite form—total self-sacrifice and servitude. If art is a gift, then the way to create it is to sacrifice your life to it. You must give many hours to the work—hours that you do not *want* to give, but feel you *must* give.

The work of art that affected me most powerfully in my life was a blank canvas by Tom Friedman called *1000 Hours of Staring*. I stood in the Museum of Modern Art on a field trip thinking, *He didn't* really *stare at this for five years, did he? If he did, it left no mark, so what's the point? Aside from insanity, why would anyone do that?* The idea of that sacrifice stuck with me over the years, and I think it serves nicely as an image of what art is—a sacrifice of one's time, one's *lifetime*, to make others feel something. Every great work of art is, in some way, the equivalent of *1000 Hours of Staring*. A sacrifice, a gift, an object upon which people think in wonder, *Did he really give up his life for this?*

The amount of work Henson did to earn his success would probably be unthinkable to you right now. But working long hours, often without sleep, was a self-imposed sentence. And paradoxically, such an *insane* amount of work gave him time to experiment—to *play*. And herein lies the paradox. It is a special kind of work that artists must do, and it is a kind of work that sometimes looks nothing like work at all. Henson was always working, and because he was always working, he was always playing.

In many ways, Henson was a *slave* to his artistic gift—but to no one else. This is the ideal state for an artist. As we look at the many years Henson labored in service of his gift, labor that often came to nothing, try to picture yourself becoming more like this—like Sisyphus pushing a rock up a hill only to see it fall back down, knowing you will do this for eternity. Learn to work without hope of reward. That is, learn to push for the sake of pushing.

START WITH ANY ROCK AND PUSH
DO SOMETHING REPETITIVELY

As the story goes, Henson's career started with luck: When he was seventeen, producers from a local CBS channel, WTOP, approached his high-school puppetry club looking for puppeteers for a children's show.[71] Henson built a few puppets, auditioned with a friend, and got the job. As the club's set designer, had never actually puppeteered before, so he taught himself. *The Junior Morning Show* was Henson's start in television. Producers from another network saw his work and hired him. In time, they gave him his own show, and years later, he would be remembered as the premier creator of TV puppetry.

But the legend fast-forwards through the boring parts. If we take a closer look, we find that the real secret to Henson's success was *hard work*.

Firstly, Henson was already quite involved in the arts at his Hyattsville, Maryland, high school. He illustrated school publications, designed sets for plays, and attended a puppetry club though he didn't puppeteer.[72] And what can often go unsaid is that *The Junior Morning Show* wasn't a dream job—he got to be on TV, but he had to perform for kids and housewives. *The Junior Morning Show* was daytime filler. Moreover, it was cancelled almost as soon as it started, due to child-labor law violations.

Yet, by working, Henson got valuable exposure. It was lucky that a director from WRC-TV, a local NBC affiliate, happened to be on set to scout his talent, but he had to work a kiddie show to earn that luck. And the next jobs he got were still intended for young audiences, with names like *Circle 4 Ranch* and *Footlight Theater* and *Afternoon with Inga*. When you think of "crap jobs" we are forced to take, you might picture the clown hired to perform for kids' birthday parties, or, as in the movie *Scrooged*, on TV. Performing cowboy skits for the lunchbox crowd sitting cross-legged in the footlights doesn't exactly fit the definition of a "lucky break," but it was a start. If you've ever wondered why you've never seen any footage of *Afternoon*, it's because Henson didn't want you to. It's not the kind of work an artist is proud of. By admission he "refused to let the kinescopes out."[73] In a 1982 interview, he explained:

> Back in those days in television, most local stations had a midday show for housewives that had a series of things. . . . So we did a few little entertainment pieces on that show. . . . Basically, the work I did in those days is not stuff that I'm creatively very proud of. . . . That stuff was really experimenting and it was just stuff that I did as a lark. I was going to college and so I was doing this and it was a way of working my way through school.[74]

But the job was more than money. As he had learned, work was *exposure*. And in the summer of 1955, about a year into his TV career, the network offered him his own show. Archivist Karen Falk wrote, "Clearly he made an immediate impression—a May 15, 1955 article about the show quoted the producer Carl Degen saying of Jim, 'The kid is positively a genius. He's absolutely amazing.'"[75] We can think of this promotion as a result of paying his dues, but not in the traditional work-your-way-up-the-ladder sense. Henson was eighteen, just starting college. He didn't wait to advance, but rather created characters and bits as though he already had his own show. *Afternoon* became a stepping stone, a venue to give the *Sam and Friends* prototypes an audience.

Now, as the creator of *Sam and Friends*, Henson had artistic control of the whole show, five minutes of skits that aired twice daily on Washington, DC's local NBC affiliate, WRC-TV. Because it lasted for an impressive six years, it was here that Henson really got to serve his craft the way Sisyphus did. With a nightly show comes the kind of ball-and-chain the artist needs to evolve. Working every night is both the artist's dream and nightmare. Being locked in like this forced Henson to continually innovate, but he surely grew weary of it. He later said he wanted to quit after the fourth year, but the station convinced him not to.[76]

There were many benefits to pushing this rock, but money wasn't one. Henson said "there wasn't much money in TV at the time."[77]

He told Judy Harris:

> **Henson:** When I first started working, it was $5 a show; it was probably a little higher by the time I got to my own show, but I remember that they put me under contract at $100 a week, which to me was really an astronomical price.
> **Harris:** But didn't you have to create all the sets and the puppets and your props out of that money?
> **Henson:** Yeah, sure.[78]

With inflation, that's like getting $40 a day for your first job. It's not much, but then when he eventually got the raise, he was making the 1960 equivalent of $750 a week. Henson lived with his parents at the time. And if the shows were only five minutes long, that's akin to making $1,200 an hour, right?

Unfortunately not. Henson wasn't getting paid to work for the length of the five-minute show—*Sam and Friends* may have lasted only five minutes, but Henson worked all day. As he said, he had to make all the sets, puppets, and props out of that money. A hundred dollars a day is cheap when you consider the nature of an artist's work. It wasn't just writing the scripts; designing and building the props, sets, and puppets; and recruiting performers. It wasn't just the daily pressure to come up with new ideas. It was also the years of nurturing his imagination. How many hours a day does an artist work on his art? *All of them.*

But money wasn't what Henson was after, anyway. As Falk notes, having his own show was a technological training ground:

> It was his experience at WRC-TV that provided his professional training. . . . His time spent behind the scenes at the station gave him access to all the latest technology and a chance to watch the directors, editors and cameramen at work.[79]

Jane Henson said:

> In his spare time, he'd be in the control room trying to understand what was going on. And the technicians loved teaching him because he really learned his lessons well. He couldn't wait to try out the things he was learning on *Sam and Friends.* He would tell the technicians he would like to try this or that, and it would become a team thing.[80]

How else could Henson innovate in TV except by having the freedom to experiment with it on a regular basis? We might pause for a moment to picture this vision of Henson, holed up in the control room with the editors and tech guys, just learning, asking questions, throwing out what-ifs. It seems that he really wanted to know how television *works.* Henson's photo album from this time shows a montage of cameras, two men discussing a script, and a view of the audience from behind the scenes.[81] It was like the view from behind the scenes of *The Muppet Show*, except instead of a theater full of seats, you'd see cameras, booms, microphones, directors, and scripts—a crew of technicians.

This learning experience is what allowed Henson to develop his own system for performing with puppets on TV—an unnamed invention that was essentially a monitor feedback loop. Innovating the technology to suit the art was a key ingredient in the successes of Disney, Henson, and Pixar, as we will see in Lesson 5. Henson's innovative monitor system produced humanlike eye-lines and subtle expressions at the slightest tilt of the hand. And all of this stemmed from using his time on local TV to *experiment*.

Another benefit to the *Sam and Friends* grind was that it allowed Henson to see how his work played with an audience. According to Jerry Seinfeld, the only way to learn is on stage, for reasons discussed in Lesson 1. "Audiences will teach you what's funny about you,"[82] he told aspiring comedians, and this is true for any creative person, whether you want to be funny, poignant, or shocking. Though great art can surely be tainted by the marketplace, we must not go so far as to shut our work off from an *audience*. It is crucial for an artist's work to develop alongside viewers. Does this mean the artist must conform to what people want? Not at all. But it means that his style grows alongside their reactions to it, either to become recalcitrant and stubborn or to yield and give in—depending on the importance of the point and the human alchemy involved. Without *any* audience reaction, it seems impossible for one's work *not* to grow stale.

Sam and Friends was clearly a step up in Henson's career, and it was one he had been consciously working toward. Its timeslot was significant, because it was *not* daytime. The show aired at 6:25 p.m. and again at 11:25 p.m.[83] This meant he could catch the *whole* family. It preceded *The Huntley-Brinkley Report* and *The Tonight Show*. *Men* watched it. It won an Emmy for Best Local Entertainment of 1958.[84] Now Henson was experimenting in front of the *right* people—adults, his intended audience.

And yet, he said, it often felt like no one was watching. Fortunately for Henson, the network didn't ask him to rein in his weird ideas—they let him find the limit himself. Henson said, "We'd try some way-out things. . . . I was convinced no one else at the station ever watched the show because there was never a complaint or any attempt at censorship of any kind."[85] His wife and performing partner Jane said, "We had very sophisticated adult audiences right from the beginning, and I think it was very adventurous of the station to be willing to program our puppets at that time. They were—we were, you know, really pretty amateur, but always good. Jim's work was always good, even if it was a little rough."[86] When Jane Henson calls their audience "sophisticated," it brings to mind the viewers of *Saturday Night Live*, who can handle a few duds because of the payoff when the spontaneity really works.

Sam and Friends was often hilarious—two cowboys who can't get down from their horses, a spoken-word piece about late-night eating. But by today's standards, it was more than a little rough. Henson had no business manager. He was, in many ways, a college student trying things out. If he'd had his agent, Bernie, back then, he might've thought of doing different material. More commercial stuff like fairy tales and animals. But because it was not about maintaining a large business or maximizing profits, this was Henson's time to practice his art.

Over the six years of *Sam and Friends*, Henson got to see what worked and what didn't. For example, some characters were built with hard "dummy" heads, such as the ravenous Yorick. Though he embodied a specific kind of creeping terror, he had only one expression. Poor Yorick would disappear after the sixties. On the other hand, Kermit was a soft-headed puppet, and this allowed close-ups to show great subtlety of the hand underneath. As Falk puts it, "It's no surprise that Kermit, and a similarly constructed character Harry the Hipster, became the most visible puppets on the show and had the honor of starring in the final episode."[87] This is a very physical example of what it is to make a piece of cloth look *alive.* What it really takes, though, is six years of trying out every manner of subtle hand gestures you can come up with and seeing what they do. Through the monitor loop, Henson could instantly see the result of a tiny tilt in three dimensions, and could internalize it as part of his character's lexicon for expression. Ultimately, this sacrifice—years of giving his life away—is what makes Henson's characters seem *human.* No textbook or set of steps could explain this. It had to be learned through experience, through experimentation. By *doing.* For many years.

Now, as we will see in Lesson 10, this experimentation would not have been fruitful without copyright. It is crucial that characters can be copyrightable for artists to truly invest in them and make them human. There is something about a character that operates like a black hole—all the work you put into him stays with him. And because Henson owned the copyright to his characters from the very beginning, he was free to invest in them as much of his time as he could stand. It is for this reason that they went on to be worth millions—twenty years later.

Practice—it can be grueling, thankless, and unceasing—but in devoting oneself to trial and error, an artist is investing in the worth of one's name. It is possible that even if we did not honor copyright as a society, we would value the name of an artist whose name is synonymous with quality. Of the twenty-four hours of Henson's day, all of them went into his art in some way, eventually showing up as echoes in his characters, in an awareness of the world around him. From the outside, we often envy the artist sitting quietly in a chair dreaming about his next project, yet that artist does not experience his time as leisure. It's work, and it's work that's never done.

OTHER WAYS OF WORK
YOU MUST WORK TO FIND THEM

The twenty-four-hour days of artists can seem daunting. Duncan Kenworthy, a producer with Henson Associates, recalled Henson's Creature Shop as a "24-hour place." He said Henson would "wake up in the middle of the night and ring me up for my opinion on new ideas."[88] Likewise, Walt Disney's wife recalled, "Even in bed . . . he would usually toss and turn, thinking of studio problems, then rise early and declare, 'I think I've got it licked.'"[89] When you eat, sleep, and breathe your art, you never get a vacation, yet Henson and Disney chose it—willingly.

A good book is transformative, and the thing that has changed me the most from *The Gift* is Hyde's interpretation of "The Shoemaker and the Elves" as "a parable for artists."[90] In the old tale, the shoemaker is struggling—his business is failing, and he is tired. Though he knows he can't possibly make the shoes that night to save his business, he still cuts out enough leather and leaves the unsewn pieces on the bench. Magically, while he sleeps, little elves come and sew the shoes together far more masterfully than he ever could. When he wakes the next day, the shoemaker is overjoyed. He sells the shoes, buys more leather, and cuts out more pieces. This cycle continues until he makes a good deal of money. One night, he and his wife decide to stay up and see who is making the shoes. They hide in the corner and watch as the little elves—naked—work the night through. Grateful to the elves, the shoemaker and his wife make them clothing—including sets of tiny shoes. It is the first time he *himself* has sewn together the pieces, and that night the shoemaker leaves the clothes instead of the leather. The elves take the clothes and never return, but from that day forward, the shoemaker has learned to make the fine shoes himself. He runs a successful business from then on, cobbling beautifully with his own two hands.

Why is this a good parable for artists? For one thing, there are two types of work in the story. The shoemaker's work resembles a factory job—there is no art in such robotic tasks—tracing patterns, cutting them out. What the elves do, on the other hand, is more like magic. They are the artists. They sew in such a unique and gifted way as to produce quality—and not *everyone* can do it.

But in order for the shoemaker to get to a place where he could create art himself, he first had to cut a lot of leather. When artists speak of "practicing your craft" or "serving your gift," we might picture this kind of endless robotic toil. Yet the fully mature artist, the shoemaker at the end of the tale—*gets* to create art. For artists, there is nothing we'd rather do than this.

In *The Gift*, Hyde distinguishes the wage-earner's "work" from the artist's "labor." "Work is what we do by the hour," Hyde says, "it ends at a specific time."[91] You can clock in and out easily. On the other hand, "Labor has its own schedule. Things get done, but we often have the odd sense that we didn't do them."[92] With labor, it seems as though little elves came in the night and hijacked your hands. I have heard many similar stories by artists that their best work feels that it was done by someone else—that the power flowed *through* them. Henson himself said, "[W]hen I'm working well ideas just appear. . . . It's just a matter of our figuring out how to receive the ideas."[93] This does not require a supernatural explanation. To me, "The Shoemaker and the Elves" is the story of an artist and his subconscious mind, or perhaps, put a better way, his body.

So, Hyde says:

> Washing dishes, computing taxes, walking the rounds in a psychiatric ward, picking asparagus—these are work. . . . "Getting the program" in AA is labor. Writing a poem, raising a child, developing a new calculus, resolving a neurosis, invention in all forms—these are labors.[94]

And "labor," Hyde notes, "because it sets its own pace, is usually accompanied by idleness, leisure, even sleep."[95] Jim Henson's business was built on labor, not work. While the industrial revolution turned labor into a mechanical process, Henson's post-industrial, post-efficiency enterprise thrived on the principle that art does not happen by time clock. A labor, Hyde says, is "something that is often urgent but that nevertheless has its own interior rhythm, something more bound up with feeling, more interior, than work." It is ready when it is right. It takes as long as it takes. And unlike much work, it feels like a worthy use of one's time. Work tends to be paid by the hour, while labor is impossible to assign a fair wage to.

But when we dream of our masterpieces, we rarely picture the hard part. Elves do not come to a shoemaker who has not first cut out the leather. To get the elves to come, we must picture ourselves doing the work—purchasing the leather, tracing the patterns from books, cutting carefully day after day—a slave to these elves. It was only after years of service that the shoemaker was set free. This is the part of the story that changed my life. I realized that if I ever wanted to make magic, I would have to cut out many pieces of leather.

Hyde quotes the critic Erik Erikson, who noted the self-sacrifice of artists:

> Potentially creative men like [playwright George Bernard] Shaw build the personal fundament of their work during a self-decreed moratorium, during which they often starve themselves, socially, erotically, and last but not least, nutritionally, in order to let the grosser weeds die out, and make way for the growth of their inner garden.[96]

Jim Henson was rail thin. In 1979, a reporter described a conversation he'd had with Henson:

> "I don't drink *diet* cola," [Henson] informs [his secretary] with a smile. "Don't you have anything for skinny people?"
>
> Skinny? This fellow Henson is so thin he has to rent a shadow. He could be an advance man for a famine. If he were to drink tomato juice, he would surely look like a thermometer.
>
> "I am 6 feet 1 and I weigh 145 pounds, soaking wet."[97]

One would guess Henson worked too hard to eat much, and when he did, we know he drank soda—nondiet—and ate rich fruitcake—probably because he needed those calories to keep his body running. For an artist, there is nothing more fulfilling than making good art. Henson said, "The feeling of accomplishment is more real and satisfying than finishing a good meal or looking at one's accumulated wealth."[98]

Yet, the thing that saves the shoemaker from a life of toil is that he learns to make art himself, by clothing his elves. What does this mean for an artist? Essentially, observing the elves is the same as understanding the artistic process, even including the parts done by the subconscious. If you can practice your art enough to observe what your body does, you can learn to do it at will—with your conscious mind. "To put clothes on a thing is a kind of acknowledgement," Hyde writes, "like giving it a name."[99] The part of us that creates is often something we're ashamed of. Consciously, we ignore it. Society encourages this. Playing with puppets, for example, is *embarrassing* for a grown man.

The naked elves—our inner talents—are vulnerable. When the shoemaker makes the clothes, in effect, he protects his other self—the vulnerable or naked side of himself that truly creates—and validates it. He says it is a real, justified, valid thing. He sticks up for it. This means he can finally become that other part of himself—integrate it into his waking consciousness. There *are* other ways to work. Most of us do not think them valid, because they look too Fragglish.

In the ecosystem of *Fraggle Rock*, there are three main kinds of creature: Fraggles, Doozers, and Gorgs. The Doozers and Gorgs do a kind of work that is familiar to us. The Doozers are architects and construction workers. They are orderly, productive, and mechanistic. The Gorgs' job involves ruling the universe, farming, and various matrimonial duties. Doozers and Gorgs resemble familiar jobs of employees and bosses. They respectively toil and manage. As a society, we all respect their work.

On the other hand, the Fraggles dance their cares away. The ruling philosophy of their culture is, *When's lunch?*[100] They each have jobs to do for their thirty-minute workweek, but their work involves singing, dancing, swimming, and making the siren sound for the fire brigade. Our industrialized society tends to look down upon this kind of "work," and yet all three kinds of work—the Doozers', Gorgs', and Fraggles'—make the rock go round.

All three groups are interconnected, and it is likely that all three are necessary work for every working artist—cutting the leather, selling the shoes, and working the magic. That's a lot of work. Perhaps that is why it seems Henson never slept.

WORKAHOLIC NEVERBORED

Tales of Jim Henson's workaholism have a John Henry quality to them.

Dave Goelz:

> He once had surgery during his lunch hour and continued to shoot until eight p.m.[101]

Fran Brill:

> I remember once on the set I saw Jim's back was wounded. I said, "Jim, you're bleeding from the back," and he said, "It's no big deal."[102]

Frank Oz:

> I remember Jim—he had walking pneumonia, and we were shooting a commercial outside in a gas station 30 years ago, and it was five degrees, and he should have gone to the hospital, and he was still working.[103]

David Bowie:

> I just can't believe his capacity for work. For instance, he would finish shooting for the week on *Labyrinth* in London, catch an airplane to New York, work on a new production, TV series, or whatever over the weekend, then catch a plane back to London Sunday night, and be at the studios early Monday morning to resume filming.[104]

Caroll Spinney:

> He could get by on an hour or two [of sleep]. Once in London we left a party with him at 2:00 a.m. I was concerned about a nine o'clock call time that morning. Jim said that he'd be ready for it because he had a 5:00 a.m. meeting with Robert Altman first.[105]

Henson asked Spinney when he hired him:

> When I work with Frank Oz, we'll get into a project and work all day, all night, all the next day, and sometimes the next night two. Do you like to work like that?[106]

During his years with Henson, Frank Oz described himself as "a worker," "a drone":

> Going to work at 9 a.m. and getting back home at 9:30 at night, with time to eat, do some laundry and go to sleep.[107]

On Henson's lunch breaks from *The Muppet Show*, he would eat, conduct a writers' meeting, and field business calls.[108] When he took a cruise on the *QE2* with his wife, he took the whole company with him to work in London.[109] On his twenty-ninth birthday, he wrote a script for *Alexander the Grape*, an unpaid project.[110] The work was his cake and streamers. The work was his gift to himself. Henson turned forty on a plane trip[111] and spent his fiftieth on a "vacation cruise" with his agent.[112] Jerry Juhl said, "Year after year, we watched him push himself beyond what we could possibly imagine. You had to try to keep up."[113]

Henson himself denied being a workaholic. "I work a great deal," he said, "but I enjoy it."[114] Frank Oz has said, "It's hard for people to understand the reason Jim worked so hard is [that] he loved it."[115] This seems like a genuine sentiment, but what does it *mean*? What do you call someone who works all the time but is *not* a workaholic? And how would you ever distinguish one *from* a workaholic?

Henson said, "Perhaps one thing that has helped me in achieving my goals is that I sincerely believe in what I do, and get pleasure from it. I feel very fortunate because I can do what I love to do."[116] Now, that sounds very nice to most people. Most of us want *that*. But not at the cost of what workaholism really entails. Do you really want to work nonstop for the rest of your life?

For one thing, it takes a toll on family life. During Jane Henson's eulogy for her husband, she let slip a glimpse from the perspective of the famous man's family:

> Mostly, I just think now that it's only us, his family. These are only his kids, I'm only his wife. They had messy rooms, I burned the dinner. He didn't come home. The dog died. Whatever . . . all this stuff. It's only us."[117]

As Michael Davis wrote in *Street Gang*, "Jane was left abandoned in the suburbs while Jim Henson circumnavigated the globe."[118] In the boom period of 1980, the *Saturday Evening Post* reported, "Their marriage is one of show business'[s] more solid unions despite Jim Henson's absence from their Bedford Hills, New York, home for up to six months a year."[119] The Hensons officially separated in 1987.

Walt Disney's wife once described herself to a *Time* reporter as a "mouse widow."[120] In this sense, there were surely Muppet widows and orphans. Henson's son Brian said the children often visited Henson at work:

> He always had such a ball when he was at work, and that was one reason why we would love to go and visit him. And also, we were always welcome at work. No matter how young we were, we would hang around the shooting studio, and then the workshop, and even go to meetings and stuff, and be playing in the corner, and he was always fine with that.

One could imagine that another reason to visit Henson at work was that he was always there. A 1999 CNN profile compared interviews on the subject:

> **Cheryl Henson:** When we were growing up, we weren't very aware of my father being famous. That—there was much more of a sense that he was always more involved in his work, and he loved what he did, and always brought us into what he was doing.
> **Brian Henson:** He was also a very gentle and caring father. I remember even when he would work, sort of, endless hours, he'd pretty much always come home every

night at some point to, like, tuck us in.

Jane Henson: Whether or not he came home every night to tuck them in, I don't know. He certainly enjoyed being with them when he could. If they remember it as every night, that's nice, isn't it? I don't think it was every night.[121]

Henson gave what he could. Brian remembered him carving a turkey using the same voice he would later use for Link Hogthrob.[122] In his *Red Book* journal, family trips are often accompanied by the word "lovely."[123] In the early days, Henson's family and work were one; Jane would puppeteer with a bassinet next to her. When it became more difficult, Henson spent the whole month of July in 1971 on a western driving trip with the kids, visiting Muppets writer Jerry Juhl and stopping at Disneyland.[124] Henson loved his family. But it's not exactly the American dream—with picket fences or even simple cohabitation. This is not the work-life balance I'd want. I wouldn't want my husband to be a Henson, or to have to be that husband. It seems at the very least *difficult* to keep a family together in this line of work, and it seems to work best when the family *joins in.*

In Henson's TV movie *Emmet Otter's Jug-Band Christmas*, Emmet and his Ma both give up their family stability for the dream of making music. Ma hocks Emmet's tool chest, which he uses to do odd jobs, so that she can buy dress fabric to look good singing on stage. Emmet takes Ma's washtub, which she uses to do laundry, and puts a hole in it, turning it into an upright bass. They both believe they can win the talent contest, and once they do, they'll buy a gift for the other—a piano and a guitar. Both believe that music will *save* the family and provide for it.

Ma's friend points out how Ma's dream is jeopardizing her son's livelihood. "What if you *don't* win, Alice?" Ma shoots back without a beat: "*Got* to win. Why, Emmet's got to have a new guitar this Christmas." After the initial O. Henry tragedy, though, there is a touching victory. By performing *together*, Ma, Emmett, and his friends get a job at the hotel inn. The pay is "regular" and Ma says, "I sure enjoyed my first night's work."

Imagine that, *enjoying* one's work. But to *get* that, they had to give up stability of the other kind of work. For artists, like entrepreneurs, it seems, it's all or nothing—frequently poverty or riches—but a traditional middle-class life it's not.

This may look like sacrifice, and maybe it is, but remember what Henson said:

> I sincerely believe in what I do, and get pleasure from it. I feel very fortunate because I can do what I love to do.[125]

The thing that makes sacrifice worthwhile is that you *believe* in it. Walt Disney once said that a certain spirit prevailed at his studio. "I can see it in the guys," he said, "They have a feeling that it isn't a racket."[126]

WHAT DRIVES ART
PLAYFUL AMBITION

In *The Muppet Movie*, Kermit points out the similarities between himself and Doc Hopper, the fast-food magnate. Owning the most successful restaurant chain in the country is Hopper's dream. "I have a dream, too," Kermit tells him, "But it's about singing and dancing and making people happy."

Henson was a very driven man. In 1956, his older brother Paul died as a result of a car accident. Jane Henson recalled the effects of Paul's death on Henson, who was nineteen:

> They did things a lot together, and I think that he also felt that his parents had lost a lot by losing Paul. So I think that he felt he wanted to accomplish a lot because of that, but also because he always wanted to accomplish a lot.[127]

In Henson's journal, he used great emotion when discussing his work. "Met Trevor Jones—Loved him."[128] "Begin shooting The Great Muppet Caper!"[129] Career ambitions and life goals for Henson were one and the same. It was a rare moment when Henson was unsure of his destiny. But they do exist, and they are quite telling. In fact, it is likely that these moments of doubt cemented his resolve in the long run.

The first great moment of uncertainty came in 1958. After four years of *Sam and Friends*, the sudden death of his brother, and finishing college, Henson no longer wanted to do TV puppet shows. He wanted something more:

> I decided that what I really wanted to do was go off and paint. I was an artist, you see, so I was going to take the shows off the air—just quit for a while. The station prevailed upon me; they said, "Look, we'll pay you money and you can put somebody else doing the show."[130]

Michael Davis called this a "walkabout" in *Street Gang*—Henson traveled in Europe for two months that summer, visiting Germany, Switzerland, France, Belgium, and England, to ponder the question of what he should do next. He had enough money. He didn't even have to work anymore. What was *worth* doing? Surprisingly, he decided to do *more* TV puppetry—he returned and did three more years of *Sam and Friends*. What exactly had happened in Europe?

On his walkabout, Henson sketched French village streets and visited the World's Fair in Belgium.[131] It gave him perspective on his career. He remembered:

> I saw that puppetry was truly an art form in Europe. It was something that could be done artistically, with creativity. Back home, there weren't all that many puppeteers, but in Europe they are everywhere and everybody goes to puppet shows. It's an integral part of their lives and that was nice to see.[132]

Henson came back to the states, joined the Puppeteers of America, attended its festivals, and even became its president. Something had clicked for him—connecting what he had been doing with what he could achieve in the future.

In *The Muppet Movie*, when Kermit doubts himself in the desert, his inner voice reminds him: "I was wrong when I said I never promised anyone. I promised *me*." Joseph Campbell noted the way many mythic heroes "refuse the call" before ultimately accepting their destiny, and it has become cliché in films, yet clearly Henson had an epiphany in Europe. When he returned to his show, he had a new, ambitious idea about what puppetry on TV *could* be.

Years later, after the commercial disappointment of *Labyrinth*, Henson had another moment of doubt, recalled by his son Brian:

> It was the first time I ever saw him not want to work was during that period. There were a few months there that he

> didn't want to work. He wanted to travel, and stop, and think, and reflect a little.[133]

Some of the most mature Henson work came after this reflective period—*A Muppet Family Christmas* and *The Storyteller*, two enduring classics. It is refreshing to know that even someone as driven and ambitious as Henson had his moments of self-doubt, and to know that when he did, he didn't try to work against the doubt—he explored it. Perhaps that is the secret to his impressive resolve. In the *Fraggle Rock* episode "The Secret of Convincing John," Wembley learns that John's power stems from his "wembling" or second-guessing—after seeing things from all angles, he can be sure he has made the right decision. Self-doubt leads to self-knowledge, and these moments of contemplation likely allowed Henson to say, "I sincerely believe in what I do."

Apart from these moments of doubt, Jim Henson always seemed to *know* his destiny. He even said so:

> A driver was talking to me today asking, "Did you ever in your wildest dreams think you would have success like this?" The honest answer to this, which I do occasionally admit, is that yes, I've always known I would be very successful in anything I decided to do—and it turned out to be puppetry.[134]

To have a certainty in one's purpose is crucial, to feel that one is doing—as crazy as it sounds—exactly what one is meant to do. Muppeteer Caroll Spinney said the same thing: "People ask me, 'Are you surprised with the way your life has turned out?' No. I'm not surprised at all. I always believed that I would be doing this."[135]

I don't think that anyone can be certain of one's purpose without getting lost in the desert and facing self-doubt.

When Kermit says, "I promised *me*," in *The Muppet Movie*, out there under the endless stars, he is expressing his dream, his faith, and his doubt. When he sings, "Have you been half asleep, and have you heard voices? I've heard them calling my name. Is this the sweet sound that called the young sailors? The voice might be one and the same," Paul Williams and Kenneth Ascher's lyrics seem to express the same feeling of *destiny* that Henson felt.

Doc Hopper and Kermit are two sides of the same coin—both driven by an inner ambition, but Kermit's ambition seems to be a silly one, a childish or Fragglish ambition, sharing a laugh with friends, portraying a hopeful vision of humanity, inspiring change in the next generation without hurting anyone today. It's hard to put into words what Henson's dream *was*, exactly, but we know he was driven to see it realized.

And perhaps this is why "workaholic" doesn't exactly suit Henson. Jim Henson was atypically ambitious. A career like his takes a kind of devotion to play—one that is dead serious. Henson made play a kind of *duty*. Most of us do not grow up learning to operate this way. We are not taught that there are many kinds of work. Usually, we do not have artist parents. Few of us even have entrepreneur parents. Yet Jim Henson was a third parent to many of us. He subtly ingrained in us a strong capacity for laboring under a dream.

The Fraggles sing a song called "Workin'":

Wake up in the morning.
Get yourself to work.
Fraggles never fool around.
Fraggles never shirk.

Their duty's always waiting.
And duty must be done.
There's Ping-Pong games that must be played
and songs that must be sung.[136]

Henson seemed to have an unstoppable *drive* to make art. Part of achieving one's dreams rests in the feeling of duty to them. Yet, many artists are driven and still get stuck. What if Henson was just *lucky*?

COROLLARY TO LESSON 1
BE LUCKY

Henson was most certainly lucky. He was thirty-one in 1967—the perfect age to take advantage of that year's incredible cultural revolution. Because he was *over* thirty, he was taken seriously enough to sell TV shows. Because he was *only* thirty, he still "got" what the youth culture was doing. Even luckier, television—his chosen medium—was still an emerging technology. TV turned eighteen when he turned eighteen, which meant both were amenable to experimentation. While still in high school, Henson found himself in precisely the right time and the right place to change television history.

With all Henson's luck, it can give you the sense that *you'll* never make it. It's too late for most of us. We're too old. We didn't have early success and we missed our shot. I don't have six years to practice on TV—I don't have my own show. I am too busy working for a living. There are many advantages I just don't have.

Malcolm Gladwell states this argument very effectively in *Outliers*. Gladwell's "10,000-Hour Rule" is both an argument for serving your craft and a justification for why most people can't. Ten thousand hours is the ungodly amount of time it takes to become a genius at something. The Beatles, Gladwell writes, did their ten thousand hours in Hamburg strip clubs, performing "for 270 nights in just over a year and a half."[137] According to John Lennon, "In Hamburg, we had to play for eight hours, so we really had to find a new way of playing."[138] Pete Best said, "We played seven nights a week."[139]

Beatles biographer Philip Norman wrote, "They weren't disciplined onstage at all before that. But when they came back, they sounded like no one else. It was the making of them."[140] The formula seems to work for anyone. Gladwell tells us a study of elite violinists found they had each practiced for ten thousand hours.[141] A founding father of the Internet, Bill Joy coded in a computer lab for ten thousand hours.[142] Bill Gates hacked around in computer club for more than ten thousand hours.[143] It's empowering to think that hours of practice is all it takes to become a genius, but Gladwell notes that many disadvantaged people can't *afford* to spend ten thousand hours:

> Ten thousand hours is an enormous amount of time. It's all but impossible to reach that number all by yourself by the time you're a young adult. You have to have parents who encourage and support you. You can't be poor, because if you have to hold down a part-time job on the side to help make ends meet, there won't be time left in the day to practice enough.[144]

As a comment on the institutions of society, Gladwell's point is incredibly persuasive, but perhaps not on the level of *individuals*. Gladwell notes on his website that he doesn't mean to go as far as saying "success is something outside of an individual's control."[145]

"But I do think," he says, "that we vastly underestimate the extent to which success happens because of things the individual has nothing to do with."[146] Gladwell is entirely right that our systems should be fairer, and that class advantages play a part in the success of all of history's great men and women.

However, like Gladwell, I am a storyteller who is very interested in the way stories shape our lives. From that perspective, I believe it is possible for the individual to *will* the ten thousand hours *into existence*. Where might they come from? Well, some of them might already have happened.

In the 1972 TV special *The Muppet Musicians of Bremen*, a group of four animals escape from their terrible masters to become traveling musicians. Their masters embody every specter of the "bad boss." In a montage, you see them illustrated like a Bosch drawing of sin—one shows anger and poor communication, another sloth and gluttony, another is pathologically fearful and anxious, and the last is miserly and averse to work. The plight of their poor animals isn't so different from many of us today who are stuck in a job with a bad boss or, more generally, stuck in a life we didn't choose.

And when the animals escape, they don't immediately see it as a windfall. Leroy, the donkey, is nearly shot by his owner and just barely gets away. When he does, he has a heavy wagon tied to his back and a big tuba hung around his neck, the loot from the boss's robbery. The boss had cursed, "This junk ain't worth nothin'!" and so that is what Leroy believes. Chased from his home, Leroy finds himself alone in the world, pulling junk that ain't worth nothing. He doesn't seem very lucky at all. But he *can* be.

Enter the frog.

Leroy laments his condition to Kermit, who happens to be sitting on a fence. "I'm on the road to nowhere," he says. "I gave ol'

Mordecai eighteen years of hard work, and what do I have to show for it?"

Kermit points at the wagon.

"It's mighty hard pullin'." The wagon, he thinks, is nothing but a burden.

Kermit tells him he also has a tuba.

"You mean this big kinda twisty funnel thing? I don't even know what it's fer!"

"Oh, it's fer music!"

"Music? How do you play?"

Kermit teaches Leroy to play, and with stars in his eyes, Leroy sees a better future—as a traveling musician. "They'll just love me all to crazy!" he fantasizes. He changes his tune:

I'm on the road to somewhere.
Got my tuba all with me.
I'm on the road to somewhere.
It's a lovely place to be.[147]

Henson could have viewed his *Sam and Friends* work as a burden. In fact, when he left for Europe, he did. He had to create all the sets, puppets, and props himself. He had to write and perform sponsor promos. He had to hire people to help, and he had to do it daily, even when he didn't feel like it. After a while, he probably felt trapped, locked in. But his problem wasn't his life up until then—it was not knowing what his life had been *fer*. Or rather, for.

Everything that had happened before Henson's 1958 walkabout had been building to something. Henson had been learning to be a boss, he had been cultivating an intense work ethic, and he had developed a homegrown aesthetic. Henson's shoestring budget resulted in Kermit being fashioned out of fabric from his mother's old coat,[148] and that in turn spawned the look of a thousand Muppets. His work in commercials led both to a healthy workshop budget and eventually to *Sesame Street*, whose producers were trying to use the power of commercials to teach. It couldn't be predicted from the outset, but each part led to the next part, and eventually it added up to staggering success when Henson started to see the shape it might take.

Henson may not have chosen his career up until 1958, but he was able to turn burdens into strengths. "Take what you got and fly with it," Henson said.[149] Most of us simply don't know what we've got.

Rethink the wagon—your experiences that hold you back. The wagon might have been the last thing Leroy wanted, but he ends up pulling it the whole movie. He uses it to cart his new friends around, the fellow musicians that round out his band. Without them and their harmonies, he probably couldn't be a traveling musician. Likewise, Henson may not have wanted to be an employer, an adman, or even a children's entertainer, but these skills he turned into something truly beautiful—a career in art and a lasting place in history.

For our own lives, to counter the pessimism of Gladwell's ten thousand hours, we can look for individuals who turned burdens into advantages with a little art. Cheryl Strayed's career took flight when she converted her painful childhood into a kick-ass, no-nonsense voice for the column "Dear Sugar." She infused her advice with anger and shocked the world by openly talking about her sexual abuse and its effects, and strangely enough, that's when the world started to celebrate her work. She started to sell mugs bearing her slogan Write Like a Motherfucker, had two bestsellers, and is an inspiration for anyone who writes.

When used correctly, anything can be turned into music—anything can make us dance. At some point, we can see that what holds us back can also be a power, and it is at that point that we—like the Musicians of Bremen—sing the blues. Of course, it's hard to compare Henson's work to the blues since he was admittedly such a positive person:

> I know I drive some people crazy with what seems to be ridiculous optimism, but it has always worked out for me.[150]

At his own funeral, Henson requested a Dixieland band play "When the Saints Go Marching In" at a jolly, swinging pace. It is good to sing the blues, but perhaps it's even better to dance your cares away.

WHAT HAVE YOU *ALREADY* PRACTICED? PRACTICE IT *MORE*

Ten thousand hours, Gladwell says, is an unthinkable amount—too much for most of us. However, the hours don't have to be early or the result of random privilege. The first part of your ten thousand hours might have been forced on you—tedious piano lessons, a job with children that makes you hate kids, a history of colic. But the rest of the ten thousand hours you need to force on yourself, once you understand the power of your burden: a path to parody songs, artful puppetry, or imaginative writing. To everything, they say, there is a season. You don't have to be at the right place at the right time. You have to know what *your* time and place is good for. What ambitious story could you turn your life *into*? You can't start over. You have to use only what's in the toolbox—and make art out of it.

The thing is, Henson didn't grow up wanting to be a puppeteer. "It's surely not a career path that one would plan," he once said. "You wouldn't decide to become a puppeteer."[151] Puppetry, for Henson, was a means to an end. It was the raw material of his past, and he used it to create a job that didn't yet exist—the "Jim Henson" job—now cemented in history.

Part of the game of art is taking what *is*, playing with it, and seeing what *could be*. Henson became quite good at knowing "what it's fer." He wrote:

> When I was a child, my mother's family would gather at my grandmother's house. Fifteen or twenty people would be there, sitting around the dinner table, and my grandparents would have stories to tell—usually stories from their childhood. They would tell a tale and somebody would try to top it. I've always felt that these childhood experiences of my family sitting around the dinner table, making each other laugh, were my introduction to humor.[152]

Henson saw where his humor came from and where it could take him. But was it Henson's *family* that made him lucky, or was it Henson's *outlook* that made him see them that way? If he had bemoaned his "unserious" upbringing his whole life, then where would he be? To say that Henson was lucky implies something else, something emotionally worse, and that is that you and I are *not* lucky. Not *as* lucky. That's simply not true, because what I want to become, and what he became, are completely different destinations.

Think of all the ways you are unlucky. How might you play them like a tuba? As Kermit said, "Blow good and hard into the small end there." Play with it a bit, and try to figure out: what's it *fer*? We are *all* lucky for something. The trick is in knowing how you are *uniquely* lucky, and in turning that gift into something others can appreciate.

HOW TO MAKE YOUR OWN LUCK (HAVE A WORKSHOP IN YOUR BASEMENT OR GARAGE)

Much of success may be luck, but many people live their lives in such a tentative state that they never even roll the dice. Play and experimentation loosens our grip on life and allows for more chance luck to surprise us. The law of averages says that some of it will be *good* luck. But not if you don't play.

One way to allow surprises to happen in your career is to bring your work home with you, to let your work take over your life, to let it *become* your life. When Jim and Jane Henson were newlyweds, they bought a house together. On the lower level, they set up a puppet-building workshop.[153] Later, Henson set up an animation camera and experimented with stop-motion there. Disney also took his work home with him, setting up his first studio in his parents' garage, "roughly fifteen feet square,"[154] according to Neal Gabler. Creating a workspace in your home makes a space in your future for breakthroughs and epiphanies to exist—late night and early morning. It also just plain old means you'll work more.

Caroll Spinney wrote, "Someone once said 'the harder you work the more luck you'll get' and I've found that to be true."[155] In Henson's career, this was also the case. The things that look like luck—the Incorporated Television Company (ITC) producer writing to Henson out of nowhere to propose a Muppets show, for example—are the result of hard work. In reality, though Abe Mandell may have just "happened" to catch a Muppets special on

TV and sent a letter, the show he saw was a pilot made by Henson for the purpose of pitching it to every American network.[156] The ITC producer, like the magic elves, just seemed to appear, but Henson had to cut out the leather first. Behind Henson's stroke of luck lies a graveyard of TV pilots that were not picked up—countless TV specials made for exposure, a second job in commercials, and a twenty-year history of experimenting in television. Henson had worked *hard* for that luck.

To get your art to the level it needs to be, you must devote yourself for many years, doing work for its own sake. Take some time to think about your destiny. What is your true ambition? What could you do for the rest of your life that wouldn't be "a racket"? If you are not sure about what you were meant to do, set aside some time to think about it, so that you may become sure. What were you meant to do?

Where might your career be heading? Take some time to visualize the elements of your past and imagine how they might combine. Henson's career flowed organically from past to future. His high-school club led to auditions, which led to kids shows, which led to commercials, which led to *Sesame Street*, which led to *The Muppet Show,* which led to directing films. It started humbly, but built steadily. The key to your success may lie in something you already do, but do not yet see as your power, something you might not know yet "what it's fer." You may already be halfway to ten thousand hours and not realize it. Or you may already be there. You really can't know, so you must work all the same. Find the kind of work that you feel is worth doing. Do it *more*.

For myself, I am lucky that I failed at many practical career paths—engineering, web design, and information architecture. The only thing I did well—and helped people with—was writing, and I feel certain this is what I'm supposed to be doing. Knowing this, I feel fine sacrificing hundreds of hours to write a book on spec. Even if it's not published, it still counts toward my ten thousand hours, and if it's not good enough, it may help me to become good enough.

There was a point in my life when I didn't know if I *could* write because of a horrible shoulder pain that came on when I hunched over a computer screen. After reading *The Gift*, I made myself write *anyway*, and miraculously—my shoulders stopped hurting. Today when I clock five continuous hours in a chair, the feeling of accomplishment works better than an anti-inflammatory. Jim Henson's workaholism has inspired me; when I cultivate it myself, I become *more* the artist I was meant to be.

If you look back at the successes you've had with your art, can you remember how much work they took? It may not be easy to count the hours, but try to estimate. Were you repaid in full for your work, or was the work itself your payment? What compelled you to work when you didn't feel like it? Take some time to answer these questions, either in a journal or, if you like, on my website, ElizabethHydeStevens.com. In your own practice, what is the "work" and what is the "labor"? Which part could you do by will and which part seemed done by someone else? Really observe the way *you* work—even the parts you are ashamed to acknowledge. Validate your process by observing it.

In your own life, do you cut out the leather every night? How often do you force yourself to serve the gift, and do you think that frequency is enough? If not, why do you think you have refused the call? What didn't you want to give up—family, leisure, sleep, health? Could you imagine forgoing these things for *one day* in order to make a brilliant work of art? One day may not seem like much, but it is the start of a habit.

Make a challenge for yourself—do *x* by a certain day, or take an *x*-a-day pledge. Make a ball and chain to force you to work. You may not ever know if the elves will come, but you can at least cut out the leather, so that *if* they come, they can work their magic. How many hours did you work on your art today? How hard do you think Jim Henson would have worked on it? Now think about how much he *enjoyed* working. In an episode of *Fraggle Rock*, Mokey learns that all it takes to be a minstrel is "hard work." Henson's character, Cantus, says, "Yes, wonderful, isn't it? Being a minstrel is enough hard work to last your whole life!"[157]

Don't listen to your friends who tell you they like leaving their work at work. They don't have the same dream you do. They want the comfortable thing. You want the great thing. Take your work home. Longtime Muppet writer Jerry Juhl had a piece of paper above his desk at home that said, "Not writing is worse." I couldn't agree more.

There is nothing worse than *not* working on something you believe in.

LESSON 3

GIVE SOMEONE ELSE A BREAK

HIRE SOMEONE

Hard work is important, but even if you work every hour of the day, you can't create by yourself the kind of art Jim Henson made. Without *some* kind of collaboration, art just isn't as good, and it's definitely not as fun. A writer for *Fraggle Rock*, Sugith Varughese, said of his scripts:

> You feel like you were channeling something. It wasn't coming from me, it was coming from this collective funnel of creativity that came through because of the juxtaposition of real specific people like Jerry Juhl and Jim, and I was just lucky to be in the room. And it just passed through me.[158]

There is something about collaboration that encourages more play—the magic of the shoemaker's elves—that feeling of "channeling" something bigger than yourself. In collaboration between two people, credit is never clear-cut, and it can allow more of the "gift" feeling that art requires.

When should you hire someone else to work with you? As soon as you can. Hiring someone means you believe in your business. It makes you accountable to someone else, and it makes you work harder than you would if it were just your own neck on the line. There is power in numbers. Henson had great power, but it came from generosity. If you want a job like Henson's, you need to give *someone else* a job.

In *Emmet Otter's Jug-Band Christmas*, both Emmet and Ma Otter want to win the talent contest, but performing separately, they both lose to a group of hooligans—the Riverbottom Nightmare Band. In order to attain success—enough money and a job they enjoy—they must realize how their two songs fit *together*. Singing harmonies on their walk home, they are overheard by Doc Bullfrog, who remarks, "I thought you were missing something. Turns out, what you were missing was each other." It is only after they collaborate that Doc Bullfrog gives them a job performing nightly at his inn.

There is a lesson here specifically for artists. Art is often more interesting to the audience when artists collaborate. Collaboration makes an artist more successful, but that is not why artists should do it. For Emmet, his friends, and Ma, the reason to sing together was simply that they *enjoyed* it more. They were successful *because* they enjoyed it more.

The kind of art Henson wanted to make *required* collaboration. His crowd scenes celebrated this—the raucous audience of *The Muppet Show*, the rainbow shining down on two hundred Muppets at the end of *The Muppet Movie*, an entire species of Fraggles dancing, the whole Muppets family singing carols in *A Muppet Family Christmas*. Fiction mirrors the truth underneath the puppets—Henson said there were a "few hundred" puppeteers in the *Muppets Take Manhattan* wedding scene: "It's always fun to do those great big crowd scenes when we try to get everybody that works puppets that we know of . . . to come in for a shot or two."[159]

We feel the "fun" when we watch these crowd scenes. It's not about a certain number of puppets; it's more than that. What we feel as an audience is that a lot of people really enjoyed working together, something we don't get to experience very often in our own careers.

In a quieter way, the duos also show the alchemy of collaboration—Bert and Ernie singing "Have Yourself a Merry Little Christmas," Kermit and Piggy singing their marriage vows, Big Bird and Snuffy saying good-bye forever. Each duo was worth more together than the two alone. Part of the magic of the Muppets was in what happened *between* characters. Henson once said:

> I like working collaboratively with people. At its best, the film and television world functions creatively this way. I have a terrific group of people who work with me, and I think of the work we do as "our" work.[160]

This is a nice sentiment, and many companies say they *want* collaboration, but to truly co-create, to *share* your creations requires that you no longer know what you can take credit for. It is a pretty radical transformation of one's ego, and most businesses run on ego, from the top down. It is useless to ask employees to function collaboratively if that is not the way the leadership operates. Jim Henson thought of his work as "our work." This "us" mentality shows up in his *Red Book* journal, as he notes each time the company grew:

2/–/1957—Began working together. [Jane]
8/–/1961—Jerry joined us
7/9/1965—Olga Stevens comes to work for us[161]

The progression builds like a snowball, starting with Henson himself and growing beyond him. Olga Stevens was a secretary at Muppets, Inc., as the company was then called. But when Henson hired Stevens, she did not work for *him*, but "for us." It is a different—a radically generous—mentality.

THE SNOWBALL
HOW EACH JOINED THE GANG

This "us" feeling began with Henson's first employee—a woman who would become his business partner and eventually his wife. In 1954, Henson met Jane Nebel in his freshman-year puppetry class at the University of Maryland.[162] Falk says that "the class gave Jim an opportunity to assess the talent around him and he quickly saw that Jane had a lot to offer."[163] By the start of the next semester, they were working together at *Afternoon with Inga*, and that summer they launched *Sam and Friends*. This was the start of the snowball, but it was about to hit a bump.

As we saw in Lesson 2, Henson's 1958 trip to Europe was more than a vacation; it was almost the end of the Muppets. Three years into the show, Jim Henson left the show to go on a six-week summer trip in Europe—his "walkabout."[164] After experiencing bewildering success, the death of his brother, and graduation from college—in quick succession—Falk writes that "he needed a break."[165] Henson later said, "I was going to take the shows off the air—just quit for a while." He explained:

> The station prevailed upon me; they said, "Look, we'll pay you money and you can put somebody else doing the show," and so I realized I can get money and at the same time be off painting, so I brought in a friend of mine—an art student from the University of Maryland—and he worked with Jane.[166]

This summer hiatus—coming at the moment when the snowball was just staring to coalesce—would have a profound effect on the way Henson ran his business. Imagine for a moment that you built a television show based on your sense of humor, personality, and hard work. You kept it going for three years. What would it take for you to let someone else take over? In an era before e-mail and texting, Henson's trip to Europe meant that he truly *gave up* creative control. It certainly took faith in others.

When Henson came back, the show was still on the air and doing fine. Through stepping back, Henson learned he *could* step back, because the show was bigger than just him. This experience set the stage for a business that may have started with Henson, but became a powerful force of its own, made up of the collective creativity of all involved.

At the time of the walkabout, Jim and Jane were both engaged to other people. When Henson returned to the show, reenergized and sure of purpose, they decided they were meant to be together. Soon they made it official—they went into business together. Henson recalled: "Janie and I own the company. We set it up that way in 1957, before we were married. We were married in 1959."[167]

Henson's first employee became his business partner as well as life partner. This had the unique effect that the "us" of his company would resemble the "us" of marriage, another radical altering of the ego. Henson's marriage effectively set the tone for the kind of relationship he would cultivate with his next employees—that of partnership, family, and brotherhood.

In 1960, the Hensons attended their first Puppeteers of America festival.[168] The PofA and its festivals—like Henson's puppetry class—allowed him to scout and assess talent without a formal hiring process. In 1961, Jerry Juhl joined Muppets Inc. as a puppeteer, cowriter, and all-around collaborator. Something clicked between Juhl and the Hensons, and "Jerry jumped at the opportunity and moved to Washington to work with Jim that August,"[169] Falk explains.

By 1962, Henson had used the PofA to meet many talented puppeteers, and he had even become the president of the organization that year. One such "connection"—as we might call it today—was Burr Tillstrom, a friend who was at the time "the most successful puppeteer working on television,"[170] according to Falk. Tillstrom introduced Henson to Don Sahlin, who would become his next hire.

Sahlin was a puppet builder, and Henson first contracted him to build Rowlf in 1962 to use in commercials. The next year, Henson moved to New York and rented an office. With more business, Henson hired Sahlin on salary as a builder, designer, and general tech guy with expertise in stop-motion and explosions.

Next came Frank Oz. The *Saturday Evening Post* explained that Henson had met Oz three years earlier:

> Over the years, Henson has judiciously expanded his team, tracking down expert puppeteers in the manner of a major league baseball scout. In 1961, as an example, Henson attended the National Puppetry Convention in Carmel, California, where he spotted Jerry Juhl and Frank Oz working in tandem. With Jane Henson pregnant with

> their first child, Jim promptly hired Juhl, who was 23, to take her place with the Muppets—but Frank Oz, a prodigy among puppeteers, was barely 17.
>
> Henson exercised patience and waited for Oz to come close to majority. In 1964, he signed him as a puppeteer.[171]

At this point, with a master puppeteer on board, Juhl switched to writing—"for self-protection."[172] Each time someone new is squashed by the snowball, it seems, the mix changes. According to Juhl:

> In the beginning, it was just Jim and Jane and me and the three of us did everything. We all did a lot of writing together at first. Then Frank Oz joined later, and with this talented performer with us now, I could concentrate more on the writing which had been my strong suit. So the transition from performing to writing just sort of happened, I had no idea at the beginning that that's how it would turn out.[173]

During this time, Jane spent much of her time raising the family, which would eventually become quite large at five children. Roles were shifting, with work tending to find the person who was best suited to it. To picture the snowball in the sixties, it was part office, part playroom. Oz recalled:

> It was on 53rd Street and 2nd Avenue where the first New York City Muppets Studio would be. It was only two cramped rooms, one flight up, where Jim, Don Sahlin (the Muppets' puppet builder), Jerry Juhl, (the Muppets'

> writer) and I (the Muppets' performer), worked.
>
> In the front room, there was the counter where I would practice lip syncing day after day with a Muppet character; where Jerry would have his small desk pushed up against the wall working on Muppet scripts . . . where Jim would lie almost horizontal in his beloved Eames chair as he read and created. . . . The second room was the workshop where Don would work on making the Muppets and creating the special effects. The work was often uncomfortable, painful, exhausting, and intense. But we still had fun.[174]

The main feature of the office was not the Eames chair, Henson's Shrine to the Almighty Dollar, or the dartboard hung on the wall. It was the four exterior walls that created a space for these four men to work together. It made physical a kind of invisible glue holding the snowball together.

In the beginning of *The Muppet Movie*, Robin asks Kermit, "Is this about how the Muppets *really* got started?"

"Well, it's approximately how it happened," Kermit answers.

The Muppet Movie is a fable of the Henson's company's growth, but the true story has the same structure. For the Muppets, the road to Hollywood really did start with an agent named Bernie and ended happily with the beneficence of a producer named Lew Lord—or rather, Lord Lew Grade. Along the way, Kermit picks up other stragglers who share his dream—affectionately called weirdos. Kermit begins his journey alone in the swamp, and similarly, Henson grew up in Mississippi, playing in a swamp, an "idyllic"[175] childhood. In the movie, Kermit collects brothers and sisters everywhere he goes, until there are enough Muppets in the end to fill a warehouse.

One quality of a snowball is that the bigger it gets, the more internal cohesiveness— collective gravity—it possesses. When people worked well with Henson, he tried to keep them. Fifteen years later, that would remain true. Duncan Kenworthy explained, "At the end of *Labyrinth*, rather than laying everyone off, Jim wanted to start a permanent workshop, where research and development could be continued."[176] This became The Jim Henson Creature Shop. There, Anthony Minghella was brought in to write the script for *The Storyteller*. When it was finished, and Minghella started to pack up, Henson stopped him to say it "was no good reason to leave, just because the project was over."[177] If people worked well together, they should continue to work together—that was what Henson believed. Fortunately, he also had the means to keep them together: paying jobs.

There is a reason these movies touched us and continue to, because while the lines may be simple and sweet, Henson and his crew truly believed them. When Kermit sings "Getting there is half the fun, come share it with me," it's a basic sentiment, but one that was at the heart of the company's philosophy. More somberly, at Henson's funeral, all the people he had brought together and *kept* together sang "Just One Person," a favorite of his that says that if just one person believes in you, that's enough to make someone else believe it, and someone else, and so on. It ends with the poignant line, "When all these people believe in you . . . maybe even *you* can believe in you, too."

The collaboration at Henson's company came out in their songs, their plots, and every frame of their work. It's a big part of why we like the work. You may not know that Sprocket's head and his tail are two different people, or that Rowlf's head and right hand are two people, but you know that you like it. It's just plain fun to watch—because of collaboration.

FIND YOUR PEOPLE WITH A SILLINESS AUDITION

A snowball is indiscriminate, but Henson didn't just pick up *everyone* he met in his life. Jane was one out of a classroom of students, and Oz was one out of a festival of puppeteers. You need to find the *right* people, people like you.

Puppeteers Karen Prell and Dave Goelz once tried to put into words what it's like to "assist" or "right-hand" for another a puppeteer:

> **Goelz:** It's actually really fun to assist, because you have this exercise in just tuning in, it's almost like becoming a radio.
> **Prell:** And it was that way working with Jim, cuz you'd go to assist him, and you wouldn't know what was gonna happen. You just knew that it was gonna be fun and you'd just jump into it and explore and discover with him and the same way if you were just kinda open to the energy and went with it, you would surprise yourself. You would constantly surprise yourself performing, just to see what came out of two people at the same time.[178]

Not everyone would be able to "tune in" or "jump in" in this way. How did Henson know who could do this?

The nice thing about the PofA conferences was that it allowed Henson to actually watch other puppeteers perform—a kind of public audition that was more collegial than businesslike. Later, Henson held workshops—a sort of extended audition process lasting a week.

He explained that technical skill was just *one* of the things he was looking for:

> Generally we'll have a series of auditions. . . . We look for a basic sense of performance, a sense of humor. We look for the type of person who sparks to what you think everybody else would spark to. You have to find people who put their whole performance into their hand.[179]

Often, Henson hired people who had never puppeteered before. Terry Angus said that "some of [the new hires on *Fraggle Rock*] were just actors, jugglers, and mime artists and a few of them had never had a puppet on their arms in their lives."[180] When asked if puppetry could be taught, he answered yes:

> It can be taught if there's a basic kind of receptivity there. It's hard to know. I so often don't know myself and so usually what we do is after that first series of auditions, we go through a workshop period. . . . We'll work with all of them for a week. . . . [W]e basically know whether or not the person will become a good puppeteer or not. The whole process of learning our style and becoming good at it takes nearly a year, I would say, at least.[181]

One such trainee was Fran Brill, an actress who had done voice-over work. In 1970, she saw the call for a workshop in the want-ad section of a trade magazine:

> One day I picked up *Backstage* (every actor's favorite periodical) and there was an ad saying that Jim Henson was looking to train puppeteers for an upcoming Ed Sullivan

> Christmas special . . . and they were paying $75 a week to the attendees! On a whim, I called The Jim Henson Company explaining that I had no experience whatsoever with puppeteering but a meeting was scheduled soon after. I came to the company's offices and there was Jim Henson, Frank Oz and a trunk full of puppets.[182]

Henson first narrowed his search with that magazine, *Backstage*. Then, he winnowed them down further using that trunk of puppets. Karen Falk writes:

> Over a period of days, Jim could determine who had an aptitude for Muppet-style puppetry, a sense of comic timing, and, perhaps most importantly, got along with the team.[183]

Reading these accounts, it almost seems like the most *important* thing to display at the interview was an ability to have fun while working together. Brill said:

> [H]e made this "audition" feel relaxed and low-key and that we were collaborators already. We chatted for a few minutes, there were some scripts, I tried on a few puppets and miraculously came up with some characters. The three of us went off script and I remember that we laughed a lot.[184]

Of course, that became an increasingly tall order the more "crazies" the group had. Perhaps that is why, ten years later, Henson charged his most theatrical puppeteer, Richard Hunt, with making first contact with the junior puppeteers for *Fraggle Rock* in Toronto. Terry Angus, a high-school senior at the time, remembered the audition:

> [W]e were just sitting out in the hallway waiting to go in when this lady comes out. She was shaking her head and in complete shock. She came out saying "This guy's crazy! He's just . . . just . . . just . . . Crazy! I don't believe this!' So my mother turns to me and says, "Look, if they want crazy, you give 'em crazy." So I said, "Okay."
>
> . . .
>
> So I go in there and Richard Hunt barks off all these commands. "HEY, MY NAME'S RICHARD HUNT. HOW ARE YOU DOING? HEY, SIT DOWN THERE. OH YOU'RE FROM NOVA SCOTIA. OH THAT'S GREAT!" He was drilling them right off. And "OH, WE GOT TO GET A PICTURE OF YOU. JUST STAND OVER HERE AND LOOK INTO THE CAMERA AND SAY SMILE. WELL MAYBE NOT SMILE ANYWAY HERE'S THE PICTURE." He just keeps going on like that and sits me down, then goes, "OKAY, SO LET'S SEE WHAT YOU CAN DO."
>
> . . .
>
> I brought out Kermit for Richard somewhere in there and he got a kick out of that and was playing off it. He was very mean to the frog. I said in my best Kermit, "Ah, excuse me, Mr. Hunt, I *really* don't think you should be treating people like this." "OH YEAH? WHAT ARE YOU GONNA DO, FROG?" "Uh, err, *ahem* nothing."[185]

Working together is a crucial skill, because as Dave Goelz said, "Almost nothing in the Muppets is ever done in isolation. No one ever does anything really by themselves."[186] Puppeteers attended script meetings, and writers watched the tapings. A songwriter and lyricist played off one another, and off the script, which sometimes took its visual cues out of the song lyrics. As Goelz said, Henson's organization was "interdependent,"[187] just like the *Rock* itself.

Henson hired three mimes to perform the Gorg bodies in *Fraggle Rock*—Gord Robertson, Trish Leeper, and Rob Mills—who had already worked together for some time but who were, by their own admission, "kind of amateur."[188] Their audition was wild and a little alarming: they "smack[ed] the cane on [Henson's] table" and shouted "If you hire us, we'll make you money!"[189] Even though they were up against more well-respected mimes, Henson selected them. Robertson explained:

> The big advantage was, because they were auditioning in threes, all the other people who went in, they didn't know each other, so they were all trying to shine individually. And we went in—we're working together—we're working as one unit. And they were really looking for that. They were looking for a family unit already.[190]

These auditions may seem unbusinesslike, but Henson knew that his business wasn't like others. He knew what collaboration required, and he made sure to find it. In an episode of *Fraggle Rock*, Mokey auditions to join the "High Holy Order of Poobahs," a secret organization that is so exalted, no one even knows who's a member. To become a member, Mokey must endure trials like hopping on one foot, speaking "Oobidad," and juggling okra soup. When she finally laughs and calls them silly, it is Richard Hunt's theatrical character who says:

> Mokey Fraggle! You have told us . . . what you should tell us! We *are* kidding you. Yes, the High Holy Order of Poobahs isn't a serious group. It's a silly group. And now you're a member!

LAUGHTER
TENSION'S SWEETER SISTER

Christopher Finch—a writer granted an insider's look at *The Muppet Show*—described it as "a company with a built-in outlet for frustration."[191] What this means is that while workplace tension is unavoidable and potentially destructive, puppets can hit each other, yell, and blow up, and the puppeteers' tension disappears. You can see it in the auditions. The moment when aggression is alchemized into a shared laugh is the moment when Henson knew he could work with someone.

In *The Great Muppet Caper*, Kermit and Piggy break character during a fight scene to get into a real fight. "Piggy! You're overacting!" Kermit chides her. Seamlessly, they transition back into the fight "scene" and nail it. This scene isn't funny just because it is metafiction or breaks the fourth wall—it's funny because it describes the real process of puppeteering. It was an extra bit of honesty given to the audience about the process the performers were engaged in.

With a silliness audition, the release of tension in the form of laughter actually *rewards* crazy, neurotic, negative emotions. It converts them into comedy. But the raw fuel required to make this comedy is tension. Steve Whitmire describes a tense moment in his audition for Jim Henson when he had to work with a puppet that wasn't his own:

> So Jim's character said, "I notice that your head's flopping up and down a little. You might want to tone that down a little," and my puppet said, "Yeah, the inside of my head's not stuffed very well," and Jim's character said, "Don't talk back, kid. You're talkin' to the master." Which was a joke . . . I hoped![192]

Henson was joking—through the character's performance. Yet he really *was* the master, and Whitmire really *was* a kid. In some sense, the emotions were real, but they were also clearly fiction, converted into comedy for the sake of the scene. We see the same kind of channeling when Jerry Nelson auditioned for another legend of TV puppetry, Bil Baird:

> He said, "Okay, get familiar with it. I've got something to do. Call me when you feel comfortable and I'll come have a look." . . . I got familiar with the character, and eventually I guess he got tired of waiting for me to call, so he came over and sat on some steps and said, "Well, are you ready?" I didn't miss a beat. . . . I just pointed the gun at him with this character and said, "Listen here, Baird. . . . The mob thinks this kid Nelson's all right. They wants you should give him a job, okay? Think about it very carefully."[193]

Auditions are tense. There's a lot riding on them. No one would pull a gun on a potential employer, but many of us feel that desperate going in. But with puppetry—and many other arts—the more expansive honesty you put into the performance, the better it becomes.

Nelson would work as a puppeteer for both Bil Baird and Jim Henson. Neither one was territorial about it. Nelson said Baird "liked Jim a lot and respected his work."[194] The friendliness of the Puppeteers of America is similar to other guilds, but it seems to go one further. When Henson moved to New York, Burr Tillstrom set Henson up in an apartment in his building, let his builder be hired by Henson full-time, and even begged his own agent to take Henson on. Puppeteering, it seems, is a special kind of business.

In the 1980s, Henson let Steven Spielberg take a tour of his Creature Shop while they were making *The Dark Crystal* and *E.T.*, respectively. Kenworthy said:

> I was a bit panicked, because we were all concerned about people seeing our techniques. Jim was much less worried. He thought that everyone should share these new developments.[195]

Henson never seemed to worry about competition. That's because competition makes for great puppet scenes, when it's called "upstaging." In the play-full atmosphere of puppetry, the aggressive part of competition seems to fade, and the funny part of it remains, a gift to the audience—a hearty laugh.

Henson said in a 1982 interview with Judy Harris:

> There's not much competition between puppeteers in general because everybody's working their own style. I've never felt any sense of competition with anybody, and we're all friends; we're all good friends.[196]

In play, there is room for everyone, because there are infinite roles to play—you can change the game to make room. The conversion of competitive tendencies into play is truly the essence of Henson's work. Henson's relationships with fellow puppeteers is a model to follow in artistic fields where (1) tension can be channeled to serve to work, and (2) everyone's work is in its own style.

A HANDSHAKE MAN
NO HR PROFESSIONAL

Jim Henson was a handshake man. This would become evident in 1990, when he worked on a Disney World attraction without a contract. Henson worked on a handshake with Disney CEO Michael Eisner because, as a Henson lawyer said, he "didn't give a damn about legalities."[197] This was also quite evident in "the hiring process" as we call it today.

When Henson hired you, you probably felt like you were talking to a Muppet. Dave Goelz said, "He sounded like Ernie!"[198] Assistant Alex Rockwell recalled, "I picked up the phone and [someone who] sounded like Kermit the Frog was on the other end of the phone."[199] But, at the same time, you might not know you'd been hired. Henson tended to discuss creative matters—not business—with creative performers. This could be so extreme that it caused confusion.

Carroll Spinney recalled that it took two meetings with Henson to realize he had been hired:

> [Jim] said, "Why don't you come down to New York and we can talk about the Muppets?"
>
> I said that would be nice. . . . I had mistakenly assumed that he just wanted to chat. When I got to know

> him better, I learned that Jim Henson never wanted to chat. He almost always wanted to work. . . . Now, in Utah, he wanted to talk to me again. I had a sense that this time I had better find out what he wanted to talk about. I quickly stashed my show safely away and rushed to the lounge.
>
> "I saw your show," he said. "I liked what you were *trying* to do."
>
> . . .
>
> He recounted some of his own disasters, including driving a hundred miles to do a show and finding he'd left the all-important audiotape back in the workshop.
>
> Then he said, "Why don't you come down to New York and talk about the Muppets?"
>
> This time, amazed at this déjà vu moment, I asked him to clarify. "What do you mean by 'talk about the Muppets'?"
>
> "I mean, would you like to work for me?" he replied.[200]

Terry Angus had the same experience. After his audition, Angus explained:

> [Henson] brought out this book and started signing it and I thought, well, I'm being told very nicely with a little present "Thank you for coming, we don't need you" sort of thing. Or I got the job. I don't know what made me ask it right out, but I asked him, "Well, does that mean I get the job?" And he said, "Oh yeah, sure."[201]

Joseph Bailey had already worked on *Sesame Street* when he was asked to audition as a writer for *The Muppet Show*. He wrote a spec script, and was called in to meet with Henson:

> In his low key way, Jim told me he liked my material and we discussed the show for a while. When the conversation came to a close, he said to me, "Well what are you going to do now?"
>
> I told him that my wife and I were leaving soon for a two-week vacation on the Caribbean Island of Antigua. He said he hoped we'd have a good time and the meeting ended with no further discussion.[202]

Bailey didn't know he had a job to come back to until an urgent telephone message came in at his hotel: "Call Jim Henson immediately."

> "Where are you?" [Henson] asked. "We're having a writers' meeting for the opening show of the new season. Why aren't you here?"
>
> "Well, Jim, you see, nobody hired me."
>
> "Oh. (Pause) Well, how soon can you get here?"[203]

Henson's indirectness is extreme, and yet I would hesitate to call it a fault. If we try to imagine things Henson *could* have said to prevent these misunderstandings—"You've passed the audition," "You're hired," "Report to work at seven a.m."—he would be veering into the province of HR, into the realm of business and money. As we will see in Lesson 7, separating business and creative conversations is important; it creates a sense of play that is independent from economics. There is a time and place to discuss money matters, and in Henson's company, it was not when artists were discussing a possible collaboration.

For artists, money is often an afterthought, because the primary goal is making something good. Bailey recalled he had agreed to move to London before asking about pay:

> Jerry and I were standing at the elevators and Jim was striding quickly on his long legs toward the door on the other side of the lobby when suddenly I had a realization.
>
> "Hey, Jim!" I shouted across the lobby, "Who do I talk to about money!?"
>
> "Al Gottesman!" Jim yelled back before disappearing out the door.[204]

Earlier, when Bailey was hired for *Sesame Street*, Jon Stone had followed the same procedure:

> [Jon] dove in and started telling me exactly how he wanted the four pieces rewritten, which was his way of letting me know I was hired. He then directed me to "the sharks down the hall" in the Business Affairs Department to see about salary and contracts.[205]

To be fair, Bailey said that Al Gottesman was not a shark: "I never needed 'people' to talk to Jim's 'people.' I could talk to Al myself."[206] Yet the "sharkiness" of money negotiations was not something Henson wanted to engage in while he was working with an artist.

As a boss, Henson's hiring methods were quite *careful*, but they weren't exactly *professional.* They caused confusion, but they also created a lot of great collaboration, because decisions were based on criteria that had nothing to do with business, salaries, contracts, or per diem expenses. Michael Frith left his job at Dr. Seuss to join *Sesame Street* because he "wondered if there might be some synergy there."[207] When we navigate our professional careers, we tend to move toward quantifiable increases, greater money, and higher titles; we don't change jobs on the whim of some *potential* "synergy." But recall that Frith would spend many late nights working on a *Sesame Street* encyclopedia or a Miss Piggy photograph. For people who work day and night, the line between job and life is indistinguishable, and so is the line between coworker and friend. Most parents won't tell their children to chase synergy over salary, but the artists who worked with Henson did just that.

ADDENDUM TO LESSON 3

WHY PEOPLE WORK FOR YOU

The downside to placing synergy over salary is obvious. When Caroll Spinney left his job to puppeteer for *Sesame Street*, he didn't know what kind of money he was going to make:

> It was all settled except for one point—money. I asked him what I could expect to earn.
>
> Jim looked thoughtful and raised a finger. "We have a tradition," he started.
>
> I smiled. Who doesn't like a nice tradition?
>
> "What is it?" I asked.
>
> "You won't get paid much."
>
> That wasn't at all what I'd expected to hear. After all, I was joining the Muppets, the preeminent puppet troupe in the world. Wouldn't I get rich quick? His first offer was two hundred dollars a week. I was making almost that much a day in Boston on *Bozo's Big Top*.[208]

Because this was public television, even Henson made a "shamefully low salary"[209] according to Davis—not counting merchandising. At one point, Spinney even decided to quit *Sesame Street* because of the low pay. Puppet builder Kermit Love saw that he was frustrated and told him to give it a month. The next week, Big Bird was on the cover on *Time* magazine. This Spinney describes in the "Take a Pay Cut" chapter of his memoir. So why did Spinney, in the middle of his career, take a job for *less* money? He explains:

> The *Bozo* show paid well, but it got so that I hardly had to work. It wasn't the thing I had dreamed of as a boy. I wanted more, to educate, to do something artful, meaningful. When Jim offered me Big Bird, I knew that was it.[210]

What Spinney wanted was what every artist wants—a chance to be loved for the hard work that only *he* can do. To be rewarded for doing one's art. Not just a cheap, profitable derivative of one's art, but the real thing—the whole thing—what he was *born* to do, and do masterfully. Spinney was born to play Big Bird. Even down to his mild cerebral palsy (his unique postures and gestures undoubtedly translate into the distinctiveness of his characters) and the latent artistic aspirations of his mother, who sewed puppets for him. He developed an inimitable method involving reading glasses, tiny folded scripts, and roller-skating backward while puppeteering, seeing only through a miniature, reversed-image monitor inside his suit. No one else can play Big Bird the way Spinney does. That's why, today, the seventy-year-old earns over $300,000 a year.[211]

But in 1970, Spinney couldn't have known how much money the future would hold. Spinney took the pay cut because he wanted to do the best work he could. Because, in his own words:

> To me, that was the equivalent of—if I was a drummer, having some fellow say, "I've got a little band from Liverpool, then, would you like to be me drummer?" Because it was Jim Henson. Jim Henson and the Muppets to me were the Beatles, completely, of the puppet world.[212]

When you have a business like Henson's, people work for you for reasons that go deeper than money. Joseph Bailey describes in his memoir that he was "writing the TV show 10 hours a day."[213] Yet he was happy. "At thirty years of age," he wrote, "I got to run away and join the circus. The adventure lasted for 20 years."[214]

Dave Goelz was an industrial designer who showed up on set one day during his vacation. He also left a good career because he wanted something *better*. He relates:

> I started my own business doing industrial advertising. . . . Jim proposed that I keep my main industrial client, come to the Muppet Workshop as a designer/builder, and perform occasionally in specials. It gave me the Muppet work that I was passionate about and included several escapes to California each year. . . . How could I say no? So I did it.[215]

Karen Prell, in her own words, "bombarded Henson Associates [as the company was increasingly called from 1964–1990] with fan letters and inquiries about puppet building or performing work." In one such letter she introduced herself by saying, "I would like to work with the Muppets. Or at least attempt to." It goes on to explain why:

> I've gone through several jobs that offered security and dental insurance, but none that gave me an opportunity to become hairy monsters or singing animals.[216]

Joseph Bailey wrote in his "In Memoriam" chapter for Henson:

> I'll always remember him as the magical ringmaster who let me turn a quirky talent into a meaningful career and for letting me spend 20 fascinating years with his marvelous, mystical, magical circus.[217]

Artists work for artists for good reason. It is because they are "passionate," in Goelz's words, about art; they want to "become" something, in Prell's words; to have a "meaningful career" in Bailey's. To some people, that is more important than security and dental insurance.

On the other hand, it can be tempting to assume that *everyone* is, in some sense, an artist. Perhaps we are all born artists, but when it comes to finding dedicated collaborators, that simply isn't true.

QUALIFICATION TO ADDENDUM
NOT *EVERYONE* WANTS TO WORK FOR YOU

In 1980, a poll asked secretaries whom they'd most like to work for. In the poll, Jim Henson—at the height of his career—was just about as attractive to the secretaries as "the 'average employer'—3 percent." Many more women, it seemed, would like to work for Phil Donahue—the overwhelming winner with 18 percent. Other more preferable bosses included Erma Bombeck, Alan Alda, Dan Rather, and President Carter.[218] While it is notable to be on the list at all, it would be wrong to say that *everyone* wanted to work at Jim Henson's magical circus.

Some people will always want to work for someone more powerful, more handsome, or more charming. Not everyone, it seems, is a Fraggle. Not everyone wants to dance their cares away.

And perhaps that's the beauty of a nuanced phrases like "Why don't you come talk about working?" It's a quiet question that requires an overwhelming affirmative in order to truly connect. Not *everyone* wants to work for you. But some people really, *really* want to work for you. If Spinney hadn't really wanted to, he wouldn't have joined Henson. Prell had to write multiple letters to get in. Henson's quiet method effectively sought these people out and brought them into his group. And while Caroll Spinney could have begrudged Henson for hiring him at lower wages than he'd like, he didn't. Everyone who worked for Henson seemed to express gratitude for what they say was a positive experience. He let them create and achieve things, and it is hard to watch clips of Henson's funeral service without feeling this gratitude very deeply.

Muppet builder Caroly Wilcox later reflected on her time in the workshop, saying, "To be given the chance to create was something Jim did for all of us, and that was a great pleasure."[219] Jerry Juhl said of Fraggle Rock, "Jim had taken the show and taken this set of people and said you guys are gonna do this, and I've always been really grateful for it."[220] Not everyone wants to be an artist, and that's okay. It's not an easy lifestyle.

SIDEBAR
ON FREELANCERS

One of the drawbacks to working as an artist is the unpredictability of the freelance lifestyle. In the early days, Henson hired Don Sahlin and Jerry Juhl on salary. But as he built up his repertory company of puppeteers, many of them worked freelance, as members of a union, the American Federation of Television and Radio Artists.

> **Karen Prell:** Except for when I started out on *Sesame Street,* I was always a freelance performer, so I wasn't constantly on staff or anything.[221]
> **Steve Whitmire:** We're freelancers [with Disney], we're still freelancers, just as we were with Henson. And that's nice.[222]

With freelance jobs, work is done on a per-project basis. There is a start and end date. Because of the union, there were acceptable rates of pay set, and sometimes residuals. One reason Whitmire said "that's nice" is likely because trusted performers like him can negotiate their pay at the start of a project and choose to sign on or not. Freelancers tend to have more freedom in their lives, but the downside of flexibility is what it lacks—stability.

Jerry Nelson was hired to take over Rowlf the Dog's right hand when Frank Oz went to Europe. It was a great opportunity, but when Oz came back, Nelson was out of a job. Nelson told an interviewer:

> Well, Frank came back in '66, and up till '66 we did a lot of work, and then it kinda tailed off, and Jim said, 'Well, I don't have enough work for all of us, and you're the last one to have joined, so I'm going to have to let you go.'[223]

Freelancing has its ups and downs. Terry Angus, a puppeteer for *Fraggle Rock,* didn't go to Henson's funeral because when the show ended, "I was very much unemployed, had been for quite a while, and didn't have much money."[224] On the other hand, Caroll

Spinney could eventually renegotiate his contract up to what it is today—reportedly $314,000 a year,[225] in part because of the nature of freelancing.

Jerry Nelson appreciated the freelance system when he wanted to take time off from *The Muppet Show* to spend more time with his daughter. She would later pass away in 1982 from cystic fibrosis. Nelson explained:

> I went to Jim and I said, "You know . . . I want to go on, I want to work on the show, but I really think I have to spend this time with Christine." And he said, "All right." As a consequence, I had to give up characters like Statler, whom I had done in *Sex and Violence* and one other show . . .[226]

Nelson was able to have freedom when he needed it. But he had to give up something. He sacrificed a character and the money he would have earned. Some people can sacrifice money for time. Others can't. Hiring people freelance is not an easy thing to do because you have to let go of them. Angus's job at Henson Associates ended when *Fraggle Rock* did. But with the staff on salary, Joan Ganz Cooney said:

> He could never fire anybody, couldn't accept any plan for downsizing that was drawn up by one of his advisers. Jim feared he couldn't face people afterwards, so he just kept them on.[227]

Perhaps freelance hires were, in a way, easier on Henson, a way to let someone go without firing them. Still, as jubilant as the journal is when it says "Jerry joins us," Henson is equally sad to see people go:

2/–/1965 Carroll and Muppets parted
1/1/1968 Jerry Juhl leaves us
10/–/1976 Bonnie leaves us

Parting is clearly sweet sorrow to Henson in what might be to another boss mere personnel change. But though freelancing makes this situation habitual, it also makes it easy for people to return. Henson used an exclamation mark to note:

11/1/1981 Diana B. rejoins HA!

Collaborations formed with freelancers—while not constant—can be enduring. Many of Henson's freelancers returned to him over the years. Diana Birkenfield worked for a summer on *Time Piece*, then became a full-time producer for Henson in the sixties and seventies, and later returned to freelancing with the company in the eighties.[228] Michael Frith started out as a freelance designer for *The Muppet Musicians of Bremen* and later became the full-time Henson Associates art director.[229]

Though Jerry Juhl and Bonnie *left* Henson, they too returned. Juhl worked from home with the help of new computer technology. Bonnie Erickson left to start her own business, and Henson became one of her first clients. And Jerry Nelson may have been let go when Frank Oz came back from Europe, but Nelson returned to work on *Sesame Street* for the rest of his career. Getting to work for Henson once often meant the chance to work for Henson again. And from Henson's perspective, it was perhaps the longest audition process possible; he got to see over a span of years who would work out and who wouldn't.

Freelance work is risky because one doesn't know in advance one's yearly earnings, yet for many salaried employees, the ax can drop at any moment as well. There are really no days in the year on which we can wake up and be totally secure in our financial future. Working freelance simply makes one more aware of that reality.

It's also worthwhile to note that Henson's first work at WRC was as a freelancer.[230] It gave him exposure without being weighted down by what were effectively stepping stones in his career. It was likely he himself was a member of the American Federation of Television and Radio Artists union, and when he was working on such unambitious programs like *Footlight Theater* and *Circle 4 Ranch*, he was perhaps happy to know his job had an end date. During Henson's "very major big year"[231] of 1979, Henson had seventy-one full-time employees.[232] But he also had a wide net of freelancers, past and present, with whom he could potentially collaborate on future projects. Seventy-one is a *small* number for such a successful company, but even so, taking care of seventy-one people is a lot of responsibility for one artist to take on. It's not easy being a boss.

HERE'S ANOTHER OPTION
YOU CAN BE A HENSON OR YOU CAN BE A SPINNEY

Jim Henson and Caroll Spinney are both geniuses of puppetry who believed in the power of hard work. But they worked differently. Henson liked to work the whole night through and into the day and into the night again. He was willing to sacrifice family and a normal life for his work. Spinney wasn't, and he told Henson so. When Henson asked if he liked to work all night, Spinney recalled, "I should have been diplomatic and said that I did, but the truth was out. 'No way!' I said. I like a solid eight hours' sleep every night."[233]

Spinney was destined to be famous and successful, but he was not destined to be a boss.

Tellingly, they differed when it came to the way they treated *puppets*. Jim Henson believed that a puppet's personality came from what it looked like—down to every minute eye placement and seam. But he wasn't precious about the physical puppets. As we know, his first Kermit was made from one of his mother's old coats. He had to destroy something valuable to make art. On the other hand, Spinney's first puppets were sewn by his mother or bought from a store with saved-up money. They were precious to him.

Spinney describes the difference:

> Jim was never sentimental about the puppets. . . . Jim just started ripping Oscar apart to reuse the material, which actually came from a bath mat dyed orange. I was horrified. . . . Jim and Don didn't care. They had the puppet stripped down in a few minutes and were thinking about how to build another one. "Let's keep the eyebrows," I suggested.[234]

In another instance:

> Jim dropped the puppet on the floor. He had to get a prop, and since Ernie was in his way, he nudged him aside with his foot. I picked Ernie up and said to him, "Oh, Ernie. Jim didn't mean to do that."
>
> Jim said, "Yes, I did. He was in my way." Then he asked, "Do you really talk to the puppets?"
>
> I told him that I did. When I drop Picklepuss, I apologize to him.
>
> Jim smiled. He said, "To me, the puppets are just

> tools to get the scenes done. I'm not sentimental about them."[235]

The difference shows up in the shape of Henson and Spinney's careers. They are both great artists who can channel the forces inside their bodies, minds, and hearts into great performance. But though Henson was famously unable to fire anyone, he *could* hire people, which for many of us is just as hard.

Henson never kicked an employee or ripped one apart, but he had to tell Nelson there wasn't enough work to keep him. He had to lose good people and make hard choices so that the organization would stay afloat and people would get paid. The curse of the boss is often losing sleep over the responsibility that is yours alone. The beauty of being an employee is not having to take your work home with you.

In many ways, Spinney is truer to what we think an artist *should be*. He never had to fire anyone, ask anyone to give up a vacation or work for cheap. He has delighted children through the character of Big Bird for forty-five years without having to run a business. Clearly, there *is* a choice.

Michael Davis noted a similar difference between Henson and a predecessor of TV puppets, Burr Tillstrom:

> I don't think Jim ever thought the characters were too precious. That's why I did so much in the book about Burr Tillstrom. . . . [I]t's because Burr created a very different model about how he felt about those characters. He didn't want any commercialism at all. He didn't want a Kukla and Ollie in the stories. He felt that there was only one Kukla and one Ollie and those were the puppets on his hands. He felt that they had a soul and a life of their own.

> Jim didn't, he kept the puppets in a plastic bag, he didn't think that they were alive. He knew that the performers were the ones giving them life.
>
> [Tillstrom] could have been a gazillionaire. I'm old enough to remember *Kukla, Fran and Ollie* on television and they were it. They were it for a while. They could have been in every five and dime, every drug store, every toy store, but he didn't want it. And then here you have Jim who went about it carefully, cautiously, but he was interested in making money from the characters. Why? Because it gave him the freedom to do the things he really wanted to do like the *Dark Crystal* and *Labyrinth.* He wanted to expand and make sure that the people who worked for him made a good wage. It's two different ways of looking at the world.[236]

If one is too "precious" about one's art, one can't leverage its power as well to the benefit and survival of that art. And because he was not too "precious" about the characters, Henson was able to be a boss, to make tough decisions, to sacrifice one thing for another. Tillstrom succeeded on his own terms—he was the biggest thing in puppets in his lifetime. Spinney is also amazingly successful on his own terms, not running a business or licensing anything, but getting to create on a daily basis the work he was born to do.

It may be better to be a Spinney. It's *harder* to be a Henson. But who gave meaningful jobs to hundreds of creative artists? Spinneys have a boss they can trust. Hensons have to wake up and be that boss every day, rain or shine. It is difficult to say who had more of a lasting impact. I think there are kinder people walking the planet today because of the artwork of both these men. But every artist has a choice. You don't have to be a Henson.

But if you're going to be a Spinney, you need to *find* a Henson. It might not be easy—he might talk quietly or ask you to take a pay cut. But ultimately, his business could be the key to your career in art. Even Henson, in his early years, sought out a Henson. Henson didn't work for Tillstrom outright, but he attached himself to Tillstrom's mentorship, and it helped him to survive in New York City.[237]

Even if you plan to be a Henson, *finding a Henson* is a good start. You'll get a lot further than you could on your own. Reaching out is the first step to any collaboration.

HOW TO START A SNOWBALL

You would not be reading this book if you didn't dream of a career like Henson's, and the truth is that a great deal of his success came not from him alone but from the snowballing of a lot of creative artists working together. The first step toward harnessing that power is to hire someone—one person—right now. Hire someone *before* you believe in yourself. It is the kind of thing that will force you to believe in yourself, for their sake.

How can you guarantee paying someone when you're not even sure you can pay yourself? I think the better question is, what is *worth paying someone for*? If it has worth, it will accrue value, and it will get you more work. You might have to start with a freelancer—hire someone for a one-off project. Think of something that might be better with a new set of eyes. In turn, it will likely give *you* a new outlook on the work. When Jim Henson came back from Europe to see how *Sam and Friends* fared without him, he was surely surprised. Let other people surprise you.

Some artists—notably writers and painters—are known for their solitude, but we benefit from collaboration as much as anyone else. It was hard for me to ask an artist to illustrate one of my stories, frankly because I know that art is invaluable and offering any amount of money in return for it feels exploitative. But when you pay another artist to help you, you give them more than the check; you give them the message that good art is worth paying for. You also give yourself that message.

How have you added collaboration to your art? Did it cost money? Some people are able to form collectives tied together by common values instead of paychecks, and there are many good reasons we don't want money to enter into creative discussions. Yet oftentimes, without money, collaboration cannot happen. What are your strategies for handling the money aspect of your collaborations?

When you decide whom to hire, think about the skills you want them to possess, but more importantly, think about how they relate to you. What kind of humor is necessary in order to hang out with you for as long as it takes to get the job done? Because you may be doing just that—and at the end of as-long-as-it-takes, you will likely call that person a friend.

Please don't fall into the trap of becoming professional. Be yourself. Don't be "businesslike" because you think that's what business *is*. That's not what business is. The essence of business was what Henson was after. Not the suits, ties, and "best practices" of HR. Henson didn't need that. To him, business was a handshake—an acknowledgment that both parties were on the same page.

When you find good collaborators, you will do your darnedest to keep them around. Good people are worth keeping. What successes have you had with collaborators? What problems did you have? What kept you together? What kept you coming to work each day? Strangely enough, it's easier to go into work when there's a friend there to greet you. Lesson 9 will say more about Henson's strategies for managing collaboration, but the first step is very simple: reach out to other artists.

Take some time to find your people and reach out to them. They called Jim Henson "fearless leader." Imagine yourself as a "fearless leader" of artists, leaving a legacy like his. Even if you choose not to be the guy who writes the paychecks, you will probably have to be the guy who keeps everyone together. Money is just the best way to do it. Without that paycheck, family and life tend to get in the way—they tend to take groups apart. Picture money as the four walls of that little office on 2nd Avenue—as the thing that holds the snowball together. It's not the main reason we make art, but it helps keep pesky things like survival and supporting one's family from getting in the way.

When the right people appear in your life, they will have their own reasons for joining you. And it is usually because you, for whatever reason, can help them achieve their dreams. If you've already found collaborators, where did you find them? Do you feel you have enough collaboration in your work? These questions are worth journaling about. If you like, share your answers on my website, ElizabethHydeStevens.com.

Collaboration with other artists lightens the load for you. You don't have to do it all by yourself. What do you dream of? How can you find others who dream of that same thing? How will you know them when you meet them? How can you help them get there?

LESSON 4

MAKE COMMERCIALS FOR YOU

HIJACK THE AD

Henson's art relied on keeping a core group of people together. But to keep your collaborators with you long enough, you need to keep *paying* them. Without financial incentive, collaborators tend to move away, get families, get other jobs—ones that *do* pay. Art alone doesn't usually pay the bills, so what is an artist to do? Go where the money is. Jim Henson learned early that for his generation and line of work, that meant commercials.

Effectively, making TV commercials was Henson's second job to finance the rest of his artistic projects. In the 1950s and 1960s, he made hundreds of commercials, and was quite successful. As Henson put it, "At that point, I was making a lot of money."[238] Money is a good thing, and Henson himself admitted, "I rather enjoyed having money in my jeans."[239] But like most artists' "day jobs," it was not his passion. In fact, Henson felt ambivalent about commercials.

He explained to an interviewer that he decided to stop doing commercials in 1969, and didn't do another until 1981:

> **Harris:** You're not in the commercial business anymore, are you?
> **Henson:** Not really. . . . [I]t was a pleasure to get out of that world. If you've ever worked in commercials, it's a world of compromise and a world of . . .
> **Harris:** You're right. I used to think it would be fun to be behind the scenes and produce something like that, and I did work in an ad agency for a year, and I hated every minute of it. You're right about compromise. I was constantly told to talk down to people and pick the lowest common denominator, and it really made me grit my teeth. I was very unhappy.
> **Henson:** Yeah, it's interesting when you're working at the lower levels through agencies and that sort of thing, it's really quite difficult. . . . [B]ut even [when you're at the level where they respect you and your opinion] it's still a matter of every meeting is a meeting with a dozen people, who all have opinions and the whole process is really not easy on a creative person. So, anyhow.[240]

Henson's Vonnegutian so-it-goes signoff implies he was happy to leave his past—the frustration of commercial work—in the past. But commercials, as they say, *paid the bills.*

In Lewis Hyde's conclusion to *The Gift*, he explains that painter Edward Hopper's career required a "day job" for many years:

> For years before he established himself as a painter, Edward Hopper used to hire himself out as a commercial

> artist to magazines with names like *Hotel Management*. Hopper was an expert draftsman, and the illustrations and covers he drew during those years are skillfully rendered. But they are not art. They certainly have none of Hopper's particular gift, none of his insight, for example, into the way that incandescent light shapes an American city at night. . . . Hopper's magazine covers—happy couples in yellow sailboats and businessmen strolling the golf links—all have the air of assignments, of work for hire. Like the novelist who writes genre fiction according to a proven formula, or the composer who scores the tunes for television commercials, or the playwright flown in to polish up a Hollywood script, Hopper's work for magazines was a response to a market demand, and the results are commercial art. . . .
>
> In a sense Hopper's work for magazines should be considered not a part of his art at all but a second job taken to support his true labors.[241]

Hopper's career was split in two, and this allowed him to reserve what Hyde calls a "protected gift sphere" for himself, a space for his work to grow on its own terms, free from market demand. He spent half the week in this gift sphere, painting for its own sake, and half the week paying for that time with magazine covers. It wasn't until he was forty-one that his artwork began to earn him enough of a living to give up the second job.

The commercials Henson made for coffee and gasoline are like Hopper's magazine covers. It was a secondary career that helped him preserve his "protected gift sphere." It is no surprise, then, that the sixties—a time of heavy *commercial* work for Henson—was also the most *experimental* time in his career; within the gift sphere, money was not an issue and his highest boss was his own imagination. In this period, Henson made wild, out-there projects like *Time Piece*, a nine-minute film that used jazzy, music-timed cuts to convey meaning, in place of traditional filmic conventions like dialog or plot. *Time Piece* was nominated for an Oscar, but not because it was box-office successful—it is the kind of "short" that makes people think. Other projects Henson was working on at the time included *The Cube*, a teleplay about existential claustrophobia, and Cyclia, a nightclub that would feature projections of "light coming through trees" timed to music.[242] In the sixties, Henson also made the incisive documentary *Youth '68*, and a show for PBS called *The Muppets on Muppets*. These projects were all forward-thinking, independent-minded, and very much a gift to viewers. But one imagines none of them were all that profitable. These projects were "made possible" because of commercials.

Commercials protected Henson's art because they allowed him to do projects based on their merit, not for the money, until, of course, one came along that made its own money—the surprise hit *Sesame Street*. It seems advisable, then, for an ambitious artist to take on a second job like Henson did, in commercials. Yet Henson's relationship to commercials was complex. Years later, he advised his Creature Shop not to "get involved" in commercials. The Shop's creative supervisor said, "I think [Henson had] had one or two bad experiences with commercials early on, and decided he didn't like doing them, and he wasn't very keen that the Creature Shop should get involved."[243] Commercials can be good money, but they are not to be undertaken lightly by artists.

An episode of *Fraggle Rock* overtly criticizes commercials. In "Manny's Land of Carpets," the Fraggles find a radio that they believe to be transmitting wisdom from another world:

> "Manny's got everything you want. Manny's got everything you need. Manny wants you."
>
> "Me?"
>
> "Yes, *you* to get down here to Manny's Land of Carpets right now. Your happiness is guaranteed at Manny's!"[244]

The show parodies our relationship to television—and in particular—ads. Writer David Young explained it was "a show about the kind of delusional system that's projected by people's belief in the world that seems to be inside that box in the corner of the room."[245] The Fraggles almost abandon the rock to search for this land of eternal happiness, except that they begin fighting—some factions thinking they should travel instead to Bubba's Burger Barn, where they were promised something even more magical: all you can eat.

Television and its ads are a delusional system, and it takes a special kind of mindset to participate in them without losing your way as an artist. Henson had to be quite careful when treading these murky waters.

STRANGE BEDFELLOWS
IN BED WITH BAD COMPANY

We think of Henson as artsy-craftsy, philanthropic, and slightly revolutionary, so it is strange to imagine him making commercials for gasoline, banks, or junk food in good conscience. Part of the problem with ads is that when you endorse a for-profit business, you never really know who you're in bed with.

In 1966, Henson made commercials for prepackaged Wilson's sandwich meats that showed Henson enjoying perfectly folded bologna slices in a fluffy deli roll. Yet later he decided to become a vegetarian. Though this lifestyle didn't last, Henson's work expressed vegetarian leanings. A 1967 *Muppet Show* sketch parodies hunting, in which forest critters tell the viewers at home to "Stop, children," using a Buffalo Springfield song protesting violence. Later, in *The Dark Crystal*, the cruel, militant Skeksis are gluttons for roast "nebri" meat, a gentle creature that Kira is seen communicating with in the previous scene.

But if you make commercials, you don't get paid to express your reservations about the product. And though Henson was a strong conservationist in the 1980s, he nearly froze to death in 1968 for an oil company. He noted in his journal that it was "6 degrees" when they shot footage of a robot pumping gas for American Oil.[246] Frank Oz recalled that Henson "had walking pneumonia."[247] It is very strange indeed to think of Henson going to these lengths to promote an industry that we now associate with oil spills and wars in the Persian Gulf. But effectively, when you make commercials, you are often helping a for-profit company with a good deal of money, and often the reason that company has so much money is due to exploitation and disregard for humanity.

Henson seemed to be somewhat selective in the kinds of companies he worked for, and at the time, we perhaps didn't know how harmful oil dependence or factory farming could be. To see things from Henson's perspective, let us take a moment to go back to the 1960s.

Imagine a world without iPhones, without laptops or e-mail. A time before the mouse, before computer printers. Without GPS or texting. Nobody you knew had attention deficit disorder, and instead of checking Facebook, you would dial a friend for a long chat or take a walk down the street. You worked at an office with typewriters, a telephone switchboard, and a secretary pool, and a company called IBM was hoping you'd buy some of their new time-saving devices, a dictation recorder and a word processor that let you fix mistakes without x-ing them out. So they hired a man named Jim Henson to make an ad to convince you that your company was missing something.

In the 1967 commercial "Paperwork Explosion," IBM salesmen promise their machines will help you keep up with the stacks of paper that now plague your existence. We are told that "in the past, there always seemed to be enough time and people to do the paperwork." But today there is more paperwork than ever. IBM is here to help us. Henson ends the five-minute pitch with an inscrutable statement: "Machines should work. People should think." It's a nice idea, but computers didn't really solve the paperwork explosion; they merely moved it from filing cabinets onto servers. In the arms race of office technology, the company these new tools helped *most* was IBM.

Henson did even more for the growing technology company, creating entertainment for the salesmen themselves to watch for inspiration. In the late sixties, Henson made a series of "Coffee Break" films for IBM's "100% Club."[248] The idea is that salesmen would aspire to sell 100 percent of their yearly quota, and if they did, they would be rewarded with a trip, dinner, entertainment—including a humorous Muppet film—and recognition. One year, Henson performed live for this corporate event.

When IBM flew its "Golden Circle"–level salesmen to the Bahamas, part of their reward was a live performance by Rowlf the Dog. Henson, Juhl, and Nelson all earned a vacation to Nassau, where Henson was thrilled to win $75 at the casino.[249] For Henson, a puppet show is a puppet show, and a trip to the islands was surely appreciated, yet this is not the image we typically have of the bearded hippy, patiently laying out a shot. It is more like a puppet dancing on a string for a powerful corporation. One of the problems of work for hire like this is that Henson effectively affixed his name to IBM's, and their mission was quite different from his.

INTO THE LIAR'S DEN
HOW HENSON COULD BRING HIMSELF TO PROMOTE THIS JUNK

With everything that makes commercials worlds of compromise, and at their very *best* trying to take your money, how did Henson—an artist—convince himself to do them?

Henson's first true "commercials" were for Wilkins Coffee in 1957,[250] yet he had been doing something commercial-*like* before that. When *Sam and Friends* went on the air, it needed a sponsor to pay for it. With network television, since viewers didn't pay for programming, someone had to. So, like it or not, some of Henson's five minutes of airtime would be taken up by Esskay Meats. Henson had a choice—either air something the sponsor hands you, or do the spot yourself. If he used the sponsor's ad, he would be giving up a large chunk of his five-minute show. If he did the ad himself, he would be making claims about "quality chicken" and "tender, meaty drumsticks."[251] This seems—artistically—like a setback, but it wound up giving him extra time and control. Though it would seem like a hassle to have to read copy about juicy chicken wings, Henson created skits around these lines, often tongue-in-cheek.

So, in every episode of *Sam and Friends*, Henson's characters did a "brought to you by" spot. Henson's characters extolled how Esskay "combines the wonderful taste of pure pork sausage with the delicious flavor of hickory smoked quality bacon," how it "cooks to a tender, meaty richness, every time" how you should get some "soon, *today*!"[252] These ridiculous lines, when read with Henson's slightly off-kilter delivery, seem even more ridiculous. An early version of Kermit even sings a song about meat accompanied by his banjo.[253]

One commercial cleverly parodies Walt Disney's *Snow White.* When a housewife asks her magic mirror who's the fairest of them all, the spooky mirror extols the preeminence of Esskay's refrigerated chicken. There is a fun, ironic quality to it, almost like it is a spoof of the ad copy itself. In a sense, Henson was co-opting the sponsor spot and using it as his own airtime. If given the choice to cede some of your precious five minutes to a commercial sponsor or to use that time for an extra skit, it's easy to see why an artist might *choose* to do promos. If you watch this ad, you may notice elements of Henson's signature brand of humor that appear in his other projects that were more . . . art for art's sake. Though it is clearly work for hire, it is also, in a sense, a mini-show.

It seems only natural, then, that upon seeing these Esskay promos, other companies would start to ask Henson to have his puppets spoof their chicken, their coffee, their photocopiers, and so on. A great commercial advertiser, it seems, was born accidentally.

And to his credit, it is likely Henson *did* exercise judgment about what to promote, because most of the commercials he did were for wholesome staples of American life. There are ads for coffee: Wilkins Coffee,[254] Community Coffee, Martinson Coffee, Nash Coffee, La Touraine Coffee, Red Diamond Coffee[255]; ads for food: Wilson's Meats, Claussen's Bakery,[256] Southern Bread,[257] Taystee Bread,[258] La Choy Chow Mein, General Foods Canada's Wheels, Flutes and Crowns[259]; ads for household items: Aurora Bathroom Tissue, Linit Fabric Finish,[260] Pak-Nit fabric[261]; ads for business machines: IBM,[262] American Photocopy Equipment Company[263]; and other unassuming items: Canadian Purina Dog Chow,[264] Bufferin,[265] and the Easy-Bake Oven.[266] Besides Chase Manhattan Bank[267] and Getty Oil,[268] the most questionable of Henson's clients were Frito-Lay's Munchos[269] and Sprint candy bars[270]—processed sugary snacks, known even then to be bad for one's health. At the same time, Henson himself was rail thin and had no problem with enjoying soda or rich desserts.

These ads are wholesome—starching your shirts, cutting down on paperwork, alleviating a headache, taking out a mortgage, eating bread. It's hard to find fault with a man for selling bread to a bread-eating public. Yet Henson *did* have a problem with commercials.

In the late sixties, he made a parody ad for a fake product called "Flapsole Sneakers." If you watch it, you are promised in sing-song rhyme diapers that "never rot," and are then encouraged to "buy a pot" of Cavity Candies. A boy falls off a "Tipsy Toy" and a girl models a "Boo-boo Band-Aid" with a head gash still red with blood. The end of the commercial tells the endlessly credulous parent, "friend," if your kids *already have* all these products, buy them a mutual fund, "open end."[271]

According to Falk, Henson made "Flapsole Sneakers" to "play around."[272] But more than that, the fake ad displays Henson's obvious disdain for, and discomfort with, the job he was paid to do. "Flapsole Sneakers" is a parody of opportunist advertising, of selling unrealistic desires, and its complicit knowledge that products are not what they seem. At the end, it seems to say, none of these products will ever be enough, so when you've bought them all, we'll sell you imaginary financial "products," which, of course, will make the fund managers rich.

At its core, advertising is a game of con-artistry. At its most honest, it tells you where you can throw away your money on fleeting pleasure. And so, when you make a commercial for someone else, you are lowering yourself to become a puppet for someone else's greed. Ads trick us, making us think they're our friend, when they're really working for someone with interests that conflict with ours—put frankly, they want to take our money out of our pockets and make us believe we did it in our own best interest, which, by the laws of capitalism, can't be true in order for the company to profit. If you watch "Flapsole Sneakers," you get a sense that Henson is critiquing advertising in this manner—showing us that nothing "seen on TV" is something we really need.

And here is how Henson the artist managed to survive in the world of commercials for so long. Henson didn't just parody ads in this for-fun reel. He parodied ads in every one of his *for-real* commercials. The satirical streak we saw in the Esskay "Mirror, mirror" spot—a *knowingness* shared with the viewer—runs through all of Henson's ads.

PARODY THE AD WHILE STILL PLAYING THE GAME

There is a clear element of satire involved in all of Henson's commercial work. At a recent Henson exhibit, Karen Falk said:

> He was . . . making fun of Madison Avenue and the way things were sold, and yet he was very successful at it. He was much loved by the Madison Avenue executives. Maybe having it come from a puppet character made it O.K.[273]

Falk has described this kind of humor as "bit[ing] the hand that feeds you."[274] For example, when Henson did a private show for the salesmen of Thom McAn shoe stores, Rowlf sang, "Thom McAn, we love your credo, but we love the money even more!" He also did a "customized" version of Stan Freberg's "Money,"[275] whose original lines were "Give me buckets full of ducats, give me case-os full of pesos . . . money money money money money." Falk puts it best: "Typically, Jim was making fun of the capitalistic ambitions of the people that hired him."[276]

In a presentation film Henson made for the sales team at Wilson's Meats, the mouthy character Skip greets the audience, "Hi there, all you lovers of hot dogs and money!"[277] In another, he says, "Hi there, all you hot-shot Wilson's Meats sales-type people!"[278] They then go on to parody everything involving advertising. When doing customer "research," Frank Oz knocks over a customer's vase, candles, and books, until she chases him out of her house. One of the commercials they audience-test is described as using "a lot of filmic gimmickry," such as a shot of a hot dog thrown bowling-style at a stack of hot dogs. It has the same absurdist feel as a Terry Gilliam animation. Another "test" commercial is full of glasses-wearing lab coats using a machine labeled "smokeometer." The product doesn't look appealing and neither do the advertisers. The message underlying all these skits is that advertising is not a very helpful profession.

How did Henson get away with insulting his client, Wilson's Meats, and his partner, the Campbell Mithun ad firm? In these films, he showed them their *worst* selves—money-hungry, thoughtless to their customers, trying every stupid method of brainwashing there is. And yet, Wilson's Meats *liked* this film. They must have, because they contracted Henson to do a second round of commercials and another presentation film. In order for Henson to get more work out of them, he showed them just how recklessly he was spending their money—on silly skits and pranks. It's a pretty *crazy* strategy, actually. But it worked. Why?

Perhaps there is something, as Falk suggested, about puppets that makes it okay. Kermit, Henson once said, "can say things I hold back."[279] If a puppet insults you, you might be hurt, but you likely feel foolish for being angry at a puppet. Puppets are play things, so the insult is perhaps a play-insult. Perhaps it is all part of a game. Even so, the puppet has got your attention—has got you to engage with it. And for *some* reason, when working with puppets, negative emotions seem to be converted into play—into laughter.

Henson's strategy seemed to imply that people value laughter more than basically anything else—more, we see here, than their own pride. As a pitch reel, the film has done its job. The Wilson's Meats parody shows the client that Muppets can produce laughs. It shows them by making *the client* laugh. If Henson can make the client laugh, they know he can make their audiences laugh. Even as the presentation parodies the very idea of advertising, it is literally a demonstration of Henson's skill with engaging the viewer.

Henson's parody also worked in television ads. The over-the-top violent Wilkins coffee spots mock the very notion that ads can compel loyalty. A cowboy puppet shoots a prop gun at the character who doesn't drink Wilkins, then turns the gun on the viewer and says, "Now what do *you* think of Wilkins coffee?"[280] What exactly goes through a viewer's mind? *I should buy that coffee?* More likely something like, *Things I hear on TV can't really control me.* If it is true that people become immune to violence over time, perhaps these ads—by upping the ante to the point of ridiculousness—produce an immunity to the message of advertisers.

Henson even used this underlying message of skepticism in a commercial for his own line of Kermit toys in 1966. The puppet Kermits and Rowlfs sang in unison:

> Oh buy us, oh buy us, oh buy us we beg
> And if you don't buy us, we'll bite you in the leg.
> Buy us at once, we're a bundle of charms
> And if you don't buy us, we'll break both your arms.[281]

The ad essentially calls attention to the empty threats and promises ads wield. There is no real power behind their persuasion. His ads seem to teach young viewers the magic words of *Labyrinth*'s protagonist, "You have no power over me."

The ad for these trash-talking Kermits is *transparently* capitalist, and because of that transparency, not really very capitalist at all. In this way, Henson's ads functioned more like public-service announcements (PSAs), alerting the viewer to the motives and tricks of Madison Avenue. It was education, teaching anti-ad-literacy.

Henson occupied a complex position in the 1960s—one of being a successful advertiser while at the same time a very *skeptical* critic of the industry. We can see why Henson would give up ads in 1969, and yet, ironically, ads led him to the nonprofit stage of his career, *Sesame Street.*

AD VS. ART
AD *AS* ART

It is easy to see how the Esskay promos attracted the attention of Chicago ad agencies. If Henson could get laughs for Esskay, why not get Henson to do it for them? The same thing happened when the creators of *Sesame Street* saw Henson's ads. They realized that if he could make bathroom tissue irresistibly entertaining, he could probably do the same for the alphabet. In a strange way, Henson's "compromise" second job led to his first big chance to use art to change the world.

In *The Tipping Point*, Malcolm Gladwell explains that *Sesame Street*'s creators wanted to use the power of jingles to teach:

> Part of the appeal of Jim Henson and the Muppets to the show's creators, in fact, was that in the 1960s, Henson

> had been running a highly successful advertising shop. Many of the most famous Muppets were created for ad campaigns: Big Bird is really a variation of a seven foot dragon created by Henson for La Choy commercials; Cookie Monster was a pitchman for Frito-Lay; Grover was used in promotional films for IBM.[282]

Henson did retool his commercial characters in service of education, yet it would be quite wrong to think of Henson as an advertiser-*turned*-artist. He didn't get his start doing ads. He got his start doing puppets, and that just so happened to lead him into ads *and* education, not because he chose those worlds, but because they chose *him*. It's important to remember, Henson's mission—art—preceded both these pursuits.

It would be wrong to picture Henson as a "Mad Man" from Chicago or Madison Avenue. He was not *of* that world—he merely engaged with it. In Karen Falk's annotations of Jim's *Red Book*, the language makes it clear that Henson was never an *employee* of an ad agency. He would go to Chicago to work on ads for a day's shoot[283] because of "relationships"[284] with agencies, which he made ads "through."[285] Agencies like Campbell Mithun and companies like La Choy were both equally his "clients."[286] He had "contracts" with these agencies, but in at least one case, he bought that contract and produced commercials without the agency.[287] With his band of puppeteers simultaneously doing bits on *The Jimmy Dean Show* and dreaming up various pilots and projects, Henson was always a kind of outsider, having only one foot, so to speak, in the cesspool.

Jim Henson's company, called Muppets Incorporated—the name Henson continued to use for his advertising work[288]—was not a subsidiary of any advertising company. It was both its own advertising company *and* its own production company. Because of that, Henson wanted much more than a typical advertiser wants.

One Muppets writer, Joseph Bailey, *was* a self-proclaimed Mad Man at one time. His memoir shows a picture of him clean-shaven in a slick sixties suit and tie. "I'll admit it," he writes, "Being a Mad Man on Madison Avenue in the 1960s was fun. . . . Advertising was challenging, creative, glamorous, sexy and lucrative."[289] Later, when he joined the Muppets in the 1970s, he looked very different—in a photo taken at the time, he sports a dark turtleneck, hippy beard, and a matching mop of long hair.

In contrast, Henson never donned this glamour or anything like a sexy image. We can see him in the presentation film for Wilson's Meats, acting in a behind-the-scenes re-creation of the commercials. In it, Henson's team appears as fun-loving, zany man-children, and the employees of advertising agency Campbell Mithun appear as buttoned-down suits, almost like parents. Campbell Mithun staff all seem to wear the same suit and haircut. Each Muppets Incorporated member wears a different outfit—white shirt, suit, work jacket. Jerry Nelson wears paisley with sunglasses. Henson dons a beard, and his hair is overgrown on top. Jerry Juhl displays the affectation of a smoking pipe.[290]

What made Henson different from the Mad Men was that Henson's enthusiasm in his ads came from an honest belief that he had something to offer viewers. And what he had to offer wasn't bread or coffee or gasoline at all. It was his art. Henson pitched his commercials the same way a playwright would pitch his play to a theater—giving it *everything* to get to make his art.

By the time Henson started college, he already had an innate sense of commerce. At the University of Maryland, he ran a "poster business."[291] Making illustrated bills for plays and concerts, Henson used advertising quite well in these posters:

POSTERS
Silk screen process
for information
• call Jim Henson WA 7–0351.
• Inquire at S.U. cigar counter.[292]

2 colors, 30 posters: $25
3 colors, 50 posters: $35[293]

It's a classic up-sell. Who wouldn't go for the option with more quality and quantity for less money? We can see here that Henson was already thinking like a salesman. He was also thinking like a signmaker. His posters display the design abilities he promises—lettering that is slick, yet has a personality, an abstract three-tone print of a jazz band, described as "reminiscent of a famous Picasso painting" by Finch.[294] The poster itself is pretty nice. That is because a person who makes art and *also* sells art thinks in a very *uncommon* way.

Henson's "second job" did more than pay the bills. If you want to go from being an artist with a day job to being an artist whose work pays for itself, exposure is the key. With enough exposure, an artist can *find* his market, or perhaps *create* it. Henson's commercials were, in a sense, a lot of free exposure. Shifting the lens a bit, they were an ad for his own work. Every time Henson displayed his puppetry, whether it was for love or money—no matter whom the ad was technically *for*—it became an ad for Jim Henson's Muppets. His distinct look—a look of quality—was one that people began to crave more than sugary soda.

There is a simple joy in humanity that runs through all Henson's projects. The knowing *positivity* of Henson's Muppets is just as strong in the ads as it is in *The Muppet Movie*. I would not go so far as to say that the ads themselves are what one would call "art" proper. Yet they certainly grew out of art.

We can think of it like this: In *The Muppet Movie*, Kermit becomes an advertiser by accident and definitely by necessity. At the El Sleezo Cafe, Kermit and Fozzie are trapped onstage and told to dance at gunpoint for the crowd of drunks. Doc Hopper's underling sees his performance and recognizes its money-making potential. If Kermit can console a barroom full of thugs with his frog legs, he can surely hypnotize viewers into buying a carton of frogs' legs, deep-fried. Like Kermit, Henson had to do ads for *Sam and Friends*, and the Doc Hoppers of the world begged him to dance for them.

Kermit loved to dance and sing for the joy of it. The agent, fast-food magnate, and Hollywood producer each see dollar signs in Kermit's work, and while he does work for some of them, his dance and song, like Henson's puppetry, has its own raison d'être. More than the usual con-artistry of commercials, there is art *in* the ads.

UNCOMMON ADMAKING
WHAT IT LOOKS LIKE

We hate ads because they are false, because they lie to us. But I will give you two examples of ads Henson took out in major periodicals that were truthful communication and hopeful promotion of art.

In 1968, Henson took out a full-page ad that said:

> The Muppets are very happy to be represented by the
> Bernie Brillstein Company.
> 144 South Beverly Drive, Beverly Hills Calif.[295]

This ad had a picture of Rowlf, who was performing regularly on *The Jimmy Dean Show*, and an assortment of monsters and creatures. But to understand why Henson paid for this ad, we must consider the context. Henson's manager, Bernie Brillstein, had just left William Morris and moved to Los Angeles to start out on his own. Out of loyalty, Henson stayed with Brillstein, even though striking out as an entrepreneur made Brillstein much more small-time in terms of connections: people looking to book Henson would not necessarily know whom to contact.

To clear up confusion, Henson paid for this ad, giving Brillstein's start-up some much-needed publicity. When you see ads like this one in the newspaper—expensive full-page spots that have the feel of a want ad—you think of marriage proposals towed by an airplane or missed connections on craigslist. It changes the way you think of advertising. It becomes less like a scam and more like communicating something important to a large number of people.

Henson took out another ad from that same year that filled the entire back page of *Variety*:

> GOOD THINGS
> by henson associates
> YOUTH '68 [Inset: beautiful hippy with round sunglasses]
> TIMEPIECE [Inset: Henson running with top hat]
> MUPPETS [Inset: Rowlf the Dog]
> TV Commercials [Inset: Wilkins and Wontkins][296]

Through positive reviews and description, this ad explained that these seemingly unconnected projects were brought to us by one company, Henson's, so that viewers and industry people would understand his work. Why might viewers need clarification? Well, Henson's was a company with diverse interests—commercial work, certainly, but also narrative puppetry shows, and even stranger still, avant-garde thought-pieces like the existentialist anti-drama *The Cube*, the experimental film *Time Piece,* and the rock-star-laden, trippily edited, literature-quoting documentary *Youth '68*. This clever ad positioned Henson as a force in entertainment—one page in a national newspaper turned twelve years of commercials into ads for Henson Associates, a name that would become official at this time, signifying the company was much more than Muppets. It was not so much a call for more commercial work, because that was the year he was began to consider leaving the ad business. This full-page message to the public seemed, then, like a call for more *experimental* challenges, demonstrating what he, as an artist, was capable of.

And this is how Henson *hijacked* the ad. Today, Henson's name is world famous, but I can't find Wilkins Coffee *anywhere*. Henson's ads for Wilkins were memorable—just about every single one of 179[297] spots featured injury for refusal to drink the product—"Wontkins" is stabbed in a knife-throwing routine, threatened with trampling by wild horses, drowned in a swimming pool, nearing a throat-slitting by a barber's straight razor, branded by a cowboy, thrown off a plane at five miles up, and flat-out executed with a big prop cannon. The humor in them is infectious, but while it may have helped people remember the name "Wilkins" and associate it with laughter, they more effectively helped people remember funny-faced puppets on TV with goofy voices telling jokes. Just as Henson's print ads merely stated that he made art, the commercials, with their mini-puppet shows, demonstrated what he did. While the ads were ostensibly for various purchasables, they more effectively advertised something intangible—Henson's potential.

When CTW's Joan Ganz Cooney put together *Sesame Street*, she was told they *had* to get Jim Henson. Then she remembered she had seen Henson's work before, in a theater:

> When I was doing the study for Carnegie, my friend Edith Zornow called me and said, "Joan, I want you to come with me to the Johnny Victor Theater to see a screening of the commercials done by a guy named Jim Henson." I went to the . . . theater and was on the floor. I couldn't believe puppets could be so hip and funny.[298]

I would ask you, how many times have *you* been to a theater to watch a screening of commercials? Ever? I haven't. That's because they don't have screenings of commercials at theaters. Theaters show *art*.

For a second job, Henson made commercials *work* for him. Yet as Hopper and Henson both show, when you can afford to give up your day job, artists do—and should. Although commercial work may have given Henson some of his ten thousand hours of puppetry, eventually day jobs tend to drain energy away from one's art. In 1969, Henson quit the ad game, and his move suggests that in the long run, it is a game an artist really can't win.

STOP AS SOON AS YOU CAN

SAY NO TO ADS WHEN YOU CAN AFFORD TO

The Muppet Movie's Doc Hopper, like many Muppet villains, is an exploiter. As the owner of a fast-food franchising operation, he wants Kermit to dance in his commercials promoting fried frog legs. He wants to steal Kermit's gift and use it for profit.

The Muppet Movie was Henson's very first movie. This choice of antagonist shows he was keenly aware that his skills at advertising were a threat to his art. In the end, Kermit refuses to cede to commercialism. This is not simply a good ending for a film; it represents, as Kermit tells Robin at the beginning of the film, "approximately" "how the Muppets really got together." Throughout the sixties, there were times Henson had to say no to commercialism.

His agent Bernie Brillstein recalled:

> When we were first together, I'd get offers of fifty or sixty grand for him to do a commercial. Jim needed the money, so I'd say, "Let's do it to pay the overhead." Sometimes he'd agree, but usually he'd pass. "Not this one," he'd say, "because they want to own the character." Jim's rule was simple: Don't sell [the copyrights to] anything.[299]

Even early on, when he arguably needed it most, Henson *refused* some money. If inflation calculators can be trusted, that would look more like $400,000 today. When Hyde talks about "making peace with the market," it is at the same time a "peace" with barriers, with reservations and refusals. In 1969, he put up a great wall.

Sesame Street gave Henson the excuse he needed to refuse commercials altogether. We can forget today that there was a time before the government required networks to air educational content for children, now that *Sesame Street* has been on the air for over forty years. In the 1960s, there was no program on TV with a "curriculum." There was no *Sesame Street*. The first nonprofit public television stations were beginning to emerge. Idealistic minds were starting to get excited about what could be done with television. *Sesame Street* was born of 1960s idealism, and it was revolutionary. Henson signed on to the project before anyone knew that *Sesame Street* would be a success, because he believed it had a mission worth supporting.

According to its website, the Sesame Workshop's mission is "to use the educational power of media to help children everywhere reach their highest potential."[300] Originally, *Sesame Street*'s goal was to reach poor children who might fall through the cracks. It was pitched as potentially cheaper and more effective than a preschool Head Start program.[301] Its founders convinced the Carnegie and Ford Foundations to give them a million dollars each[302] to try this grand experiment, to educate kids where they lived—parked in front of the TV.

When Jim Henson signed onto *Sesame Street*, he took the responsibility very seriously—being an educator meant he had to change. If a child saw his friend Cookie Monster (or a close cousin) selling cookies in an ad, it just wouldn't be right. With *Sesame Street* came a firm *moral* reason for Henson to quit his second job.

One company, Frito-Lay, didn't take no for an answer. Wanting Henson to continue making ads, their legal department sent a proposal in 1969. According to Falk, it acknowledged that Henson's agent Bernie Brillstein had "advised that Jim Henson, in an effort to avoid commercialization of *Sesame Street*, and also because of a demanding schedule, is not interested in making new commercials."[303] As a work-around, they proposed Henson somehow *oversee* the work done by a puppet studio—no doubt erasing all appearance of wrongdoing by removing his name. Falk says,

> After much discussion, Jim's lawyer crafted a response that underlined Jim's high regard for Young & Rubicam while also turning them down. Jim was determined to leave advertising behind to protect the young viewers of *Sesame Street*.[304]

Henson couldn't make commercials *and Sesame Street*, because he was channeling the power of advertising now *for good. Sesame Street* was, in fact, *all* ads. There were no commercial breaks, but every episode was brought to you by letters like W and T or by the number 4. The flashy colors, animation, and quick-cut bits were designed to look and feel like commercials. This is Gladwell's point when he says *Sesame Street* grew out of commercials. The creator-producer of *Sesame Street*, Joan Ganz Cooney, explained in her research:

> Parents report that their children learn to recite all sorts of advertising slogans, read product names on the screen (and, more remarkably, elsewhere) and to sing commercial jingles.[305]

Sesame Street, on purpose, used what was already transfixing young minds to their TVs. Michael Davis put it best:

> If the neurotransmitters in their little brains could *snap, crackle*, and *pop* for a cereal commercial, couldn't similar electrical activity be duplicated by teaching children the concepts of *over*, *around*, *under*, and *through*?"[306]

The segments on *Sesame Street* were ads—ads for literacy, good behavior, number skills, peace, and love.

If Henson were to continue making commercials, it would be damaging to his credibility as an educator. In fact, that is exactly what *New York Times* television reviewer Jack Gould criticized him for after the 1970 airing of *Hey, Cinderella!*—a television special Henson had made with Jon Stone a few years before. When it aired on commercial TV a year into *Sesame Street*, something looked quite amiss. Gould panned the show:

> Kermit the Frog, one of the deservedly major attractions of "Sesame Street," was more or less the host. One of whose functions was to introduce the commercials. Apparently the Children's Television Workshop, producer

> of "Sesame Street," is not adverse to cashing in when success strikes. Whatever television may be called, public or commercial, sooner or later the compromises start if the ratings are right. "Sesame Street" last night lost a little of its luster as Kermit broke the faith and became one more pitchman.[307]

Gould had a point. According to an advertisement, one of the show's sponsors was RJR Foods, a subsidiary of cigarette manufacturer RJ Reynolds. It would look terrible if Kermit told viewers to watch the commercials for a cigarette company. However, commercials are an unavoidable part of commercial television. And from Henson's point of view, it seems strange that the type of work he had been doing for the past ten years was suddenly reprehensible. For someone who had recently refused incredibly well-paid commercial deals, it would be a very hard review to read. In Henson's defense, Gould didn't know that *Hey Cinderella!* predated *Sesame Street.*

Henson's response says a good deal about the way he felt about commercials:

> April 13, 1970
> Dear Mr. Gould:
> In your April 11 review of our special, *Hey, Cinderella*, you made an erroneous assumption, which I believe it is important to correct.
>
> Because there were several people from the *Sesame Street* staff involved in the production of the special, you inferred that they, and Kermit, the frog, who is very close to my heart, were capitalizing on the success of *Sesame Street* and had sold out to commercialism.

> Kermit, the frog, is a Muppet I made over ten years ago and have used on many network shows and commercials. For the past ten or twelve years, approximately half my income has been derived from producing Muppet commercials. . . .
>
> However, since the advent of *Sesame Street*, and my own interest and concern for children's television (I am an enthusiastic member of Action for Children's Television), I have become a great deal more selective, and have turned down many lucrative offers that seemed to be trying to capitalize on *Sesame Street*. . . .
>
> The Children's Television Workshop is a very dedicated group of people who function with the highest sense of integrity. To mistakenly attribute a motive of exploitation to these people is not only insulting but potentially quite damaging to the job they are doing.
>
> As for myself, I don't intend to leave commercial television. This is where the Muppets and I have worked for many years, and it is the income from commercial TV that makes my participation in educational TV possible.
>
> What I will try to do is what I have tried to do on *Sesame Street* this season, that is, to work with a degree of integrity and responsibility to the children of the country.
>
> Yours truly,
> Jim Henson[308]

Henson kept a copy of his letter to Gould, which implies it was sent, but there is no evidence it ever appeared in print. One can imagine it was a personal sting to have his integrity questioned like this. Yet, for Henson, compromise had actually *led him* to integrity.

In his own words, "it is the income from commercial TV that makes my participation in educational TV possible."

When *The Muppet Show* aired in 1975, Henson could have used the characters—who were in no way educational—in commercials, yet he did so only sparingly. At that point, his business generated enough money on its own that commercials were not necessary, and Henson could afford to be choosy. Throughout the seventies and eighties, Henson only made a handful of commercials, according to archivist Falk, "where he felt the situation and product was particularly appropriate."[309] This included a Polaroid commercial, since the camera "held a special place in Jim's memories."[310] In 1975, he made a commercial for a soft drink that Pepsi promised not to air in the United States, so that it would not confuse young PBS viewers.[311]

He appeared in a 1977 ad campaign for American Express, saying, "When I travel, I take the American Express Card."[312] Falk notes, "For the record, he even signed an affidavit confirming that his experience using the card matched his statements in the commercial."[313]

And quite often, Henson used his Muppets to make public-service announcements, in essence commercials for cherished causes. In a 1988 PSA for The Better World Society, Kermit and the Muppets asked "What if everyone in the world lived in one house? . . . We do."[314] Henson made one called "Food" and another on "Bombs."[315] In a 1988 PSA for the National Wildlife Federation, Kermit says, "Our forests are in trouble. They're being threatened by development and people who don't treat 'em with respect!"[316] Henson saw commercials for what they are—tools. And tools are neither good nor bad; it's what *you make* that is.

Muppet heroes stand up to Muppet villains who want to use their powers to do unjust things. In the showdown at the end of

The Muppet Movie, Doc Hopper threatens Kermit one last time: "Are you gonna do my TV commercial live or stuffed?" Kermit refuses to be extorted: "If what I'm saying really doesn't make sense to you, then go ahead and kill me." A Muppet protagonist would rather die than be the puppet of an unjust cause. The Muppet musicians of Bremen leave their thieving, abusive owners to make music "for folks." Santa Claus breaks free of Scam's prison and delivers the toys to everyone—even Scam. The happy ending in a Muppet story involves breaking free of exploitation. But it doesn't mean the Muppets stop performing. They don't stop *dancing* with frog legs or making music or delivering presents. Their power, their *art*—which makes them attractive to advertisers/exploiters in the first place—is theirs to use. To their own ends.

As we've seen repeatedly in Henson's career, one thing led to another. *Sam and Friends* led to commercials. Commercials led to *Sesame Street. Sesame Street* led to licensing. Licensing led to *The Muppet Show*, and *The Muppet Show* led to movies. Henson made art make money and then made money make art. And though it was right for Henson to quit ads when he did, they were an important step along the way.

THE ONLY WAY TO STOP IS TO (FIRST) START
RETHINKING THE AD

Jim Henson will be remembered as an innovator in both television and movies, but he was far more *financially* successful in television. Part of that is because of something TV has that movies don't—commercials.

His assistant Alex Rockwell explained:

> Jim had not been able to make a successful movie in a long time. There was a chunk of time there where it wasn't quite working.[317]

The chunk of time in particular included the box-office disappointments of *The Dark Crystal* and *The Labyrinth*. Brian Henson recalled:

> When *Labyrinth* was not a commercial success, that, I think, that was quite a blow to him. At that point, I think he was starting to feel like, "I love the Muppets, but I have more in me. Why did this not work? How could this not have worked?"[318]

Today, these works are considered classic fantasy films. They've been criticized for their scripts, but a good deal of box-office *hits* have scripts that pale next to David Odell's and Terry Jones's.

Unfortunately for Henson, whose dream was to make big-budget movies, there is a fundamental difference in the economies of movies and television. And it is especially important for an artist, whose work operates in a gift economy. Movies, by nature, are less *gift* than TV. With TV, fans don't buy a show—advertisers do. By the time the fans see it, it's like a free lunch. Moviegoers don't get a free lunch. They get the lunch they've paid for. Though movie theaters increasingly show ads before the film, they don't require you to sit through them mid-film, and they do require a ticket for *each* film. A world where you had to pay for each individual show you watched on television would create very different programming—it's a very different sales model.

And perhaps this is why it didn't quite work for Henson to make the shift from television to movies. It seemed like it would when *The Muppet Movie* made $76 million, but perhaps that was because it was a first, a novelty. Once Henson started to rely on the fans *themselves* to pay for his gift to them, the system—built on giving more than getting—fell apart.

The truth is that ads are not just thievery. They are also benefactors. Because of network TV, viewers who buy a TV once can be given gifts. TV directors can give the viewer more than he expects, and it's paid for by a sponsor. In this way, we might rethink the ad. Ads can be exploitative and obnoxious, but if you're smart enough to ignore them—if you're happy with your life and aren't tempted to buy other people's lives—what ads really do is facilitate the consumption of *free art*. In Henson's lifetime, TV, of all the available mediums, had the most potential for art—because no other medium had as many ads.

A test case is *Fraggle Rock*, which aired in the United States on HBO, a subscription-based network without ads. HBO has been an amazing benefactor to the arts—and *Fraggle Rock* was its first original series—starting a legacy that would go on to include *The Sopranos* and *Girls*. HBO's strength is that it doesn't let commercial sponsors call the shots, but that's also its weakness. Because it doesn't have commercials, viewers must pay to subscribe to the channel. It becomes more like the movie economy.

Most Canadian children of a certain age equate Fraggles with childhood. There, the show aired on the government-subsidized CBC and was free to all. But in the US, *Fraggle Rock* is a gem that was enjoyed by a precious few. Had it aired on a national US network, commercial sponsors would have made it available to all. The two countries saw the same show, but in a slightly different economic model. Unlike the CBC, HBO was not free to view.

The Muppet Show was. And it was a smash hit in the US, as much as it was abroad. Aired right before prime-time network TV, it had ads. Free to view on CBS, it was, effectively, a gift. Hyde writes that artists have historically found "patrons" to support them and today that often takes the form of grants.[319] But it could also look like a TV commercial. *Time* magazine called Big Bird "TV's Gift to Children." The Ford and Carnegie philanthropic foundations and PBS gave us Big Bird. But Henson's characters were also a gift—ads' gift to everyone.

For Jim Henson, working in television commercials was a *complex* second job, to put it mildly. He was participating in an ethically dicey line of work. But ads are themselves tools—exposure—that can be used for various purposes, including good ones. In *The Great Muppet Caper*, it is telling that both the crooks *and* Kermit break into the museum. They both have tools—glass cutters and whoopee cushions, respectively. The crooks were there to steal the jewels. The Muppets were there to catch the crooks. The Muppets' break-in is designed to alert the police to the identity of the real criminal. And Henson's commercials seem to aim at this, too—to get the viewer to *wise up*.

It's ethically confusing, and that is why most idealists don't participate in advertising. Yet, without the big heist scene, there could be no movie. Yes, Henson ultimately had to refuse commercials to protect *Sesame Street*. But without Henson's participation in commercials, there would be no *Sesame Street* to protect.

HOW TO HIJACK YOUR DAY JOB

As artists, how can we learn from Jim Henson's complex relationship with ads? So much has changed: today, corporations can sponsor a human being and his car with a tattoo and a paint job. At the same time, regular humans resent ads even more than they did in the sixties. Still, that makes a particularly gift-like ad all the more appreciated. Filmmakers Errol Morris and Christopher Guest both make television commercials as a source of income, and their "gift" makes TV a little better than it might otherwise be.

Where might we hijack advertising? Product placement is perhaps the worst ad of all—because it is so insidious, exploitative, and sneaky. But what if it weren't? It is entirely *possible* to Henson-ize the product placement. A video game could feature a side game for Pepsi that is more fun, self-satirizing, and inventive than the rest of the game. It could wind up becoming an ad for the full-length game you're going to make in ten years. It could be the exposure you need to get people interested. I'm not saying this is *your* answer, but it's an example of the type of thinking that could lead us to our own answers.

For myself, my second job is teaching, but I am keenly interested in the ways advertising factors into my writing and how it is read. An essay on a website like *The Awl* has the potential to go viral and reach readers everywhere because it is funded by advertisements, whereas currently, the *New York Times* is locked behind a subscriber paywall. From a certain point of view, an artist might *rather* publish a free *New Yorker* blog post than a proper *New Yorker* feature, which you can't send a friend, even if you really love it. Interestingly, wherever we place ads, we are given a gift—a cat video on YouTube, a game of Words with Friends, a show on Hulu. These experiences of art are free to view and free to share. When my Kindle Fire goes to the lock screen, it shows an ad for a television show or a book, and honestly, I enjoy them, because I know they're subsidizing my tablet experience.

I'm the kind of person who despises billboards, brand names, and the Home Shopping Network, but when I see a good commercial, I will tweet it. For artists who came of age as the Internet did, there are many new places to put an ad, and we might think of these as *places to put your art.* Think of the places where ads are most annoying, where you groan and curse the company for their shortsighted idea of "monetizing"—the shameless interruptions to your Facebook and Twitter feeds. These are the places that need a little more of the "gift" spirit of art. If Jim Henson had been born a little later, perhaps he would be making us laugh with Promoted Tweets and Suggested Posts.

Where is the money right now? Where are the thieves? Where is the most potential to impress people with a little art? Where might you come in?

If you do use commercials for a second job, be *very* careful. Refuse anything that is not consistent with your vision. Make money with ads, by all means, but if you *do* go into advertising, *hijack* the ad. Make it an ad for *you*, for your continued work, for your idealistic worldview, for the smart viewers you *want* to have. Don't talk down to people. Don't say anything you don't believe. If you think something is bogus, say so. Parody it. See if they pay you anyway, as long as you produce work according to your own standards. Don't fall into the trap of becoming jaded, of becoming a liar—remember, one foot in the pool only.

Just as Henson reserved a separate "gift-sphere" for his art, make the time to work on your non-paying projects. Reserve hours or whole days that are just for art. Don't let your day job take over your life simply because it has a more immediate payoff. Never forget why your second job is there: *to support your art.*

What is your day job? Does it help your art? Does it hurt your art? In what ways is it a complex relationship? How might you make it work better *for you*?

Hijack commercials and commercialism. Use it to create ads for you. For your continued creativity. For you to get to keep making art.

LESSON 5

GROUPS AND OUTSIDERS

INVITE THE OUTSIDE IN

It is no easy task to be a part of the commercial world and yet be above it. Plenty of our finest creative talents have entered the advertising business only to be exploited and burned out. The key for those of us who would follow in Henson's footsteps is not simply how to *enter* business. It is how to conceptually rethink the relationship between ourselves, our group of likeminded people, and those outside that group.

The world of advertising, for example, is a group. Henson was able to permeate the boundary of that group while not becoming trapped. What artists of today need, then, is not a push to the dark side—as it were—but a reimagining of the nature of that boundary.

Advertising was just one extension of Henson's work, and we can wonder how he was able to work for hire even while it was "not really easy on a creative person."[320] The answer is that he had a very uncommon attitude toward this group. Henson didn't assimilate to advertising culture, or to network executive culture. He didn't want to destroy them, but he didn't want to join them, either.

He wanted *them* to join *him*.

This is one of the big conceptual shifts an artist must make in order to achieve Henson-like success, and it requires a change in the relative size of what we would think of as our territory. Your world is limitless. If you don't see eye to eye with someone, invite them into *your* world.

THE REAL JIM HENSON
WHICH ONE WAS HE?

Henson demonstrated an ability to glide between modes, like business and art, with ease—to put on a pitchman hat and then a replace it with his groovy beaded headband. In his *Sell, Sell, Sell* film, his character Leo says archly, "I won't apologize for this great democratic free enterprise system of America. We're here to make an honest dollar!"[321] Yet, in the *Youth '68* documentary, Henson uses a very different quote from Reverend Coffin: "If we don't learn to be meek, nobody is going to inherit the earth."[322] There is always a resonant *honesty* in Henson's voice, even in a character we *know* is lying, such as his ironic narration in the Wilson's Meats spoofs—and even when his various characters contradict themselves. It can lead us to wonder, who was the *real* Jim Henson?

Henson's 1980s assistant Alex Rockwell remembered Henson switching back and forth:

> He'd be doing Kermit the Frog, come off stage and I'd fire some random deal-making question at him that our business guy needed the answer to and he would respond to that and then he'd go back and do Kermit brilliantly.[323]

Henson could glide between roles, but notably, when he was an artist, he seemed to be *all* artist. When Henson made a deal, he surely had to consider how it would affect the art. Yet when he performed a character, I don't think a deal—money—was allowed into his mind. *Muppets Take Manhattan* actress Juliana Donald remembered:

> Henson was crazy busy with a number of other projects. . . . We were shooting the jogging scene in Central Park and there were a few camera problems which caused a delay. Before Jim's assistant could whisk him away to the awaiting car a little boy walked up, his mouth agape at the sight of Kermit the Frog. The little boy started talking to Kermit, totally oblivious to Jim's arm coming out one side, wide eyed to the wonder of the moment. It was so memorable to me because time just stopped; Jim started interacting with the little boy oblivious to all the commotion around him. Before long other kids walked up and soon Jim was entertaining an entire group of kids. It was a wonderfully magical moment where you experience someone's true joy with their work."[324]

This idea that "time just stopped" would feel familiar to artists who often lose track of time when they work. In truth, they lose track of much more than time—they often forget hunger, cleanliness, money, and other worldly preoccupations while "in the zone," the saying goes, or in what Hyde might call the "protected gift-sphere where the work is created."[325]

The scene in Central Park might lead us to believe that Henson's "true" self was a children's performer. Though he could certainly put on that hat, it was just another extension of Henson's career—not the real core of him. In fact, even though *Sesame Street* made Henson famous beyond belief, he reportedly called up the show's co-creator, Joan Ganz Cooney, and told her, "You have ruined my life. Why did you have to be so successful? I am now living my worst nightmare."[326]

Though *Sesame Street* jump-started Henson's career, he was now pigeonholed as a children's entertainer. Henson did not want to be stuck working for just *one* group of people. Just as his true calling was not commercials, neither was it educational TV. Henson wanted to entertain *everyone*.

Jim Henson clearly understood how to talk to different audiences, whether it was a group of kids in the park or a group of IBM salesmen in Nassau. He spoke each's language. For the businessmen, he spoke business-ese. The pitch reel for *The Muppet Show* explained to CBS executives that the show's great ratings were going to make everyone rich. Henson promised it would be:

> A show that will be loved and adored by every Nielsen home in the country. Small children will love the cute, cuddly characters. Young people will love the fresh and innovative comedy. College kids and intellectual eggheads will love the underlying symbolism of everything. Freaky, longhaired, dirty, cynical hippies will love our freaky, longhaired, dirty, cynical Muppets. Because that's what show business is all about![327]

Was Henson "on the side" of the CBS executives who wanted Nielsen ratings or "on the side of" the longhaired, dirty, cynical hippies? Like a double-agent movie, do we know where Henson's loyalties really lay? The answer requires us to do away with this concept of being on one side. Henson said in 1979 that the Muppets "transcend all age groups. Their satiric comment on society seems to delight all ages."[328] Henson's satire—like the gentle mockery of Don Quixote—parodied everyone. He didn't just parody the businessmen for the artists or the artists for the businessmen. He parodied all of us for all of us.

Henson wasn't lying to the executives when he said he wanted his new show to be a hit across all demographics. He truly wanted the ratings that they wanted, but for a different reason. In *Street Gang*, Michael Davis explains that Henson and *Sesame Street* director Jon Stone had a very specific idea about entertainment, one that many of us today do not:

> Because Henson and Stone were children of radio's golden age, in adulthood they sought ways to provide contemporary families with a reason to sit around and be entertained, just as many once had in front of a full-throated Philco floor model.[329]

This calls to mind that image of Henson's whole family gathered together at his grandmother's house: "fifteen or twenty people would be there . . . my family, sitting around the dinner table, making each other laugh."[330] Was Henson's a family of storytellers because they listened to the radio, or did they listen to the radio because they were a family of storytellers? Whichever the case, this image of a whole family gathered in one place—grandparents, adults, children, laughing at the same thing—seems to be at the core of Henson's artistic mission. He didn't want to entertain only the men, only the housewives, only the children. Henson's happy memories of his whole family coming together as a child and laughing—it seemed to give him hope that differences could be overcome. Even serious cultural conflicts.

Fraggle Rock doesn't seem like a place for war, but in the episode entitled "Fraggle Wars," Mokey is kidnapped by a group of stranger-Fraggles. The World's Oldest Fraggle then tries to convince his people to hate them: "They're not the same as you and me. Their kind just lives for cruelty. They never laugh. They never even smile."

It is clearly a Cold War satire with McCarthyism overtones, since Mokey is forced to repeat, "My name is Mokey Fraggle. I am not now nor have I ever been a member of the enemy Fraggles." With a little laughter, Red Fraggle and Beige—one of the enemy Fraggles—diffuse the conflict: the other Fraggles think that the funniest thing about throwing a pie in someone's face is getting to clean it all up. While they have different senses of humor, they *both* think pie-facing is good fun. Red and Beige count to three and pie-face their leaders, which causes everyone to laugh at the same time. When both armies devolve into laughter, the war ends.

This seemed to be Henson's great wish for the world. Like Edgar Bergen on the radio making dad and son laugh at the same time, Henson believed that puppetry could help the world overcome cultural conflicts. *Fraggle Rock* was designed, in fact, to be shown in many countries all over the world. Henson's shows, he hoped, could be that pie in the face.

In recalling the origins of the show, creative consultants Jocelyn Stevenson and Duncan Kenworthy explained that a business advisor had pitched to Henson the idea of an international kids' show, a business idea:

> **Stevenson:** Jim took that and sort of thinking, okay international co-production for children, that means we can reach a lot of children around the world. . . . Hmm, why don't we do a series that will help stop war?
> **Kenworthy:** And we all I think separately had this same reaction where we all like laughed at him, because it was like how are you going to make a children's series to stop war in the world, it's such a—on the face of

> it—impossible, enormous, grandiose sort of idea. But . . .
> **Stevenson:** That's how he was.
> **Kenworthy:** That was how he was.[331]

Most of us would feel foolish for thinking we could stop war in the world. And most of us wouldn't even try. But Henson thought differently, as he always seemed to. Part of this difference was that he wasn't deluded by the thinking of any particular group of people. He didn't think about groups in the way that we do. A pie in the face reminds us not to take anything or anyone too seriously.

Henson's experience led him to think this way. His work in puppetry opened doors and helped him transcend his country and class. There is a picture of Henson shaking hands with Vice President Nixon when he won a local TV award at age twenty-two.[332] On one visit to the Nixon White House, Caroll Spinney "ran to the top of the stairs and slid all the way down the banister."[333] Through puppetry, Henson performed for Queen Elizabeth II,[334] for First Lady Rosalynn Carter at the White House,[335] and had the honor of screening *The Labyrinth* for Princess Diana.[336] The laughter that his characters inspired was able to break down barriers, proving that even queens, presidents, and all other manner of Poohbahs are just *people*, and their humanity is evident when they share a moment in laughter.

It wasn't as crazy as it sounds for Henson to think laughter could stop war, because in his experience, time and time again, laughter brought dissimilar people together. In 1976, Henson performed on Japanese TV in Kyoto. His producer was worried the humor in his script wouldn't work. But, Falk writes:

> Much of what was scripted was physical, slapstick comedy—and it turned out to work well for Japanese

> audiences. When they watched the playback, the Japanese crew practically fell out of their chairs laughing. Sensing an opportunity to rib his producer, Jim snapped some pictures to show her in New York.[337]

Shared laughter breaks through barriers of language, culture, and prejudice. Puppetry can do the same. Like math and music, puppetry is a universal language. Art scholar John Bell wrote that puppetry is "the material world in performance."[338] Puppets, he explains, can "articulate essential elements of modern life."[339] We learn about ourselves through puppetry. Puppetry—like the pie in the face—has historically has been used for political activism, Bell explains, as with the Bread and Puppet activist movement of the 1960s and the Little Theater Movement of the 1920s. Going back further than that, puppetry seems to have a strong effect on people of all cultures. At the funeral for ventriloquist Edgar Bergen, Henson said:

> It's interesting to note that there have been puppets as long as we have had records of mankind. Some of the early puppets were used by witch doctors—or for religious purposes. In any case, puppets have often been connected with magic.[340]

I do not think Henson is naïve to call puppetry "magic," because if something has a ceremonial role in bringing people together, and we don't really know how it works, and it's of demonstrated value to a group of people, "magic" seems like an appropriate label for such a thing.

We might look back on Henson's work as frivolous kids' stuff, and yet, to some extent, his work carried out a kind of international diplomacy whose effects have never really been measured. In his essay "Muppets and Money," Andrew Leal points out:

> As proof that differing socioeconomic systems do not deter the Muppets, in 1983, Big Bird starred in the first co-production between a U.S. television network and the People's Republic of China. *Big Bird in China*, which aired in both countries, had the bird functioning as a goodwill ambassador, learning about China. . . . A year after *Big Bird in China*, Jim Henson made the first of many visits to the Soviet Union, performing Kermit and meeting with noted Russian puppeteer Sergei Obratzov . . . culminating in the Muppet involvement in the first joint co-production between the Soviet Union and the United States. This project was the 1988 special *Free to Be . . . a Family*, broadcast in both countries through a satellite hook-up. . . . The purpose of the special was to emphasize the fact that kids in the U.S. and Russia are much the same and can relate to one another, in hopes of bringing peace between the two nations. Coincidentally or otherwise, the Berlin Wall collapsed the following year, and the Cold War officially ended.[341]

Frank Oz once said, "Jim didn't think of it in hit terms."[342] So when he told CBS that his show would be watched by "every Nielsen home in the country," that it would have a "forty share" of the ratings, he had a different *reason* than the TV executives. Brillstein said the Hensons wanted to do everything "for the right reasons."[343] And so whether you want to enchant a huge number of people for the ratings dollars or for your ego or, as Henson did, for the togetherness it can inspire, the result is ironically the same—you can earn a good deal of money.

Many artists today refuse to aim for a broad audience, because they feel it will water down the quality of their work. If you seek to please everyone, the saying goes, you will please no one. There is wisdom to this—often times the more "pop" an artist gets, the less they actually have to say, the more hollow the work becomes, and the more beholden to market demands. Yet Henson's message did not seem to turn hollow even while it became more expansive to attract more audiences—to get closer to "everyone." It's impressive.

To answer this question of the *real* Jim Henson, let us return to "Business, Business," the 1968 skit on *The Ed Sullivan Show*. Ed Sullivan was shown in prime time to a "family" audience, and that makes it more properly Henson's ideal stage than a corporate or educational show. It's getting closer to the "everyone" that was Henson's intended audience. In "Business, Business," the puppets were abstract, but the message was evident: idealists were a threat to the business establishment, the youthful idealists would win, but they would in turn become businesslike. And then when it cut to a commercial break, the camera showed the audience. Remember that businessman without any hint of a smirk? Many men's wives around him were happily clapping, and his own wife turned to him for a reaction. Instead, he sat stoic, unamused.

Now, skip forward nine months to November, when Henson has returned to *The Ed Sullivan Show*. He performs a nearly identical sketch about the conflict between two groups of long-necked puppets. But this skit is called "Sclrap Flyapp." They are now clearly aliens on another planet, and instead of "Business, Business," the first group says "Sclrap Flyapp." A new species comes up and says something different, "Merp." He even gets the younger Sclrap Flyapper to say it. A nearly identical fight happens, but this time when the young innovator wins, he says "Merp." The idealistic innovator *didn't* change his tune.

Ending aside, the premise is the same as "Business, Business," but Henson altered the details so that it could be a more accessible comment on society. The eggheads in the audience could still sit and ponder the "underlying symbolism of it all," but it was no longer simply about the conflict he was in. "Sclrap Flyapp" wouldn't offend businessmen. It was about a broader human tendency to distrust those in new groups. By making "Business, Business" into "Sclrap Flyapp," it became more abstract and more universal. Perhaps, Henson likely hoped, that unamused man in a suit would crack a smile.

With "Sclrap Flyapp," Henson invited the outside in. The real Henson started as a young idealist artist, and he remained an artist throughout his career. But he cultivated a universal appeal in order to try to bring the whole world into *his* fold, as it were.

In *Fraggle Rock*, the minstrel's goal is to "unite the rock with music." In the *New York Times*, Henson said, "I want to unify everybody," referring to a spiral staircase in the center of the new offices. Unification was so deeply embedded in his mentality that it became part of his business's architecture.

If we are looking for a way to become more successful, more *Henson-like* in our own careers and lives, we might start by trying to see beyond our own culture. Each one of us, whether we like it or not, is entrenched—stuck—in our own place and time. We speak a certain language, operate under a certain economic system, have a certain idea of what is and isn't cool. And to see *around* our culture, it makes sense that we must first see ourselves clearly—to picture ourselves, perhaps, as aliens on a strange planet, or silly puppets.

THE PARADOX OF OUTSIDES AND INSIDES

Watching these *Ed Sullivan* appearances from the late sixties and early seventies, we can see many specters of "Sclrap Flyapp." In "The Wild String Quartet," a jazz drummer comes into conflict with classical musicians. "Man-Na-Ma-Na" is similar, but with pop instead of classical. In one skit, a giver—Santa Claus—encounters takers, a band of thieves. In "The Art of Visual Thinking," a hip Kermit meets a square, and optimist meets pessimist in "The Happy Girl Meets a Monster." It starts to become apparent that a recipe for a Henson-like skit is to put two different worldviews together, and to let the ensuing conflicts turn into comedy. This trend can be seen throughout Henson's career as it built to the grand proportions of species such as the Mystics versus the Skeksis, or a whole ecosystem with the Fraggles, Doozers, and Gorgs.

Like a clam worrying a piece of sand into a pearl, Henson seemed to be constantly turning over this problem—the paradox of outsides and insides—in his work. Each of us can see only so much of the world, and others see a different chunk than we do. It's something we really can't avoid, and it causes conflicts in all of our lives. If you hear your friends laughing, it brings you joy, but if you hear a group of strangers laughing, it makes you insecure. Are they laughing *at you*? This inclusion/exclusion feeling holds us back. But if you closely watch Henson's works, they seem to offer a way out, especially *Fraggle Rock*, as the DVD interviews with the show's writers and producer make clear:

> **Kenworthy:** Underpinning it all was this idea that as Jocelyn said Jim wanted to stop conflict. So it was a sort of layered approach. That if you want to stop war in the

> world, well how do you do that? Well, it's about conflict resolution. And how do you teach people to resolve conflicts amicably? And obviously, adults are somehow lost causes so let's approach the kids . . . so then this idea I think about different perspectives got incorporated, so that the notion that everyone looking at the world from their own point of view had a particular perspective, and then if you somehow reversed the perspective and were able to take on other peoples' perspectives and see that in fact even though if it was opposed, it was very similar to your own, maybe that would loosen those conflicts. The Gorgs think of the Fraggles in the same way the Fraggles think of the Doozers, that came from that.
> **Juhl:** And all three of these species, they are interdependent in various ways. They really need each other and have no idea why they need each other.
> **Stevenson:** The kid was the only one watching who could see all the inner relationships, which we were hoping would make people go, oh wait a minute, so they could understand the Gorgs, they could understand the Fraggles, and they could understand the Doozers, and see why they couldn't understand each other.[344]

In short, *Fraggle Rock* showed kids how the paradox *works*. A group is called a cult from the outside. From the inside it is called a family. The key is to be able to see it from both sides—to understand that it, truly, is both.

The paradox applies to any group of humans you can name—families, religions, colleges, political parties, countries, ethnic groups, subcultures, economic classes, corporations, start-ups, bands, high school cliques, gangs, and professions. They look one way from the inside and another way from the outside. The paradox of outsides and insides seems to show up thematically in Henson's work, and always with a sort of lighthearted positivity. To me, that suggests that Henson believed there was a way out of society's perpetual conflicts.

Henson's puppetry was able to rise above the paradox—to break free of commercials or the stigma of children's TV. Part of his ability to garner universal appeal was that he looked within each group to find that which was human. You might say he spoke to the wise "inner child" in us, and perhaps this is why his work was so often misunderstood as being childish.

ADULTHOOD IS ANOTHER CULT

Muppets writer Jerry Juhl once said the success of the Muppets "has something to do with the fact that it crosses over generational lines. It reminds adults of childhood and innocence. There's a sweetness we get away with without being sentimental."[345] By seeing the good people inside all of us, Henson treated his audience as innocents. This wasn't childish of him. But to the cult of adulthood, it seemed like kids' stuff.

Children, it should be noted, exist almost 100 percent in the gift economy. Children do not have jobs, money, or transactions with their friends and family. Their meals are given to them, and at Christmas, they are bestowed mountains of gifts. They give their parents back affection, but for the most part, they are given far more than they have any hope of repaying. If karma works, then they will go out into the world and behave generously, perhaps to their own children one day. Someone once said that all children are artists, but adulthood avails us of this habit. It makes sense, then, that while art tends not to pay, children's books, toys, and television is a huge market. Adults, it seems, are far more willing to buy art if it is a gift for a child.

But Jim Henson was determined to make art for *adults*. Muppets writer Jerry Juhl remembered: "Jim would pound on the desk and say, 'We are not doing children's puppetry here!' . . . He wanted to make puppetry for adults."[346] So, in 1975, six years into *Sesame Street*, Henson joined the original cast of *Saturday Night Live*, creating weekly skits where he puppeteered a group of unhappily married aliens. It was not out of character. In 1971, the Muppets had performed in Nancy Sinatra's Las Vegas nightclub act in an attempt to escape puppetry's G-rated stigma. Henson said, "I don't particularly like people to think that's all we do. We have always worked in the realm of adults."[347]

Yet, even though Henson pitched a prime-time Muppet show to all three major US networks, they had no interest. "Why would adults want to watch puppets?" the networks asked. Henson said in the *Saturday Evening Post*, "It's something I've always faced, this slight condescension toward puppets. I think of Edgar Bergen, a very sophisticated man, who always worked to an adult audience—in theaters, vaudeville, nightclubs, radio, movies, TV. But it's always been practically impossible to talk the networks into any kind of puppet show for adults."[348]

Although ABC did not pick up *The Muppet Show*, they did pay for a couple of pilots in addition to what they really thought Henson should do, an Afterschool Special. In classic irreverent style, Henson gave them a raucous special called "Out to Lunch." Henson explained the premise:

> The entire staff of ABC-TV goes out to lunch, and all these wild people break into the studio and take over. It's really a parody of commercial television.[349]

The pilot Henson gave them was even wilder. Falk writes, "It was titled 'Sex and Violence with The Muppets' (Jim's effort to make it clear that he could work for adult audiences), but researchers at ABC got negative reactions so the show was promoted as *The Muppet Show*."[350] In the CBS pitch reel, a salesman promises that God will bestow ratings upon the show. Kermit's reaction to this spiel was quite adult: "What the *hell* was that all about?"[351] It's a word you don't see in children's television, but strangely, it sounded innocent coming from Kermit.

What unites all adults? The fact that we were all once children. Uniting adults is a very wise thing for a self-supporting adult to do. Trying to be edgy and hard as so many "serious" artists do prevents them from reaping the benefits of a truly *universal* audience. In exposing that *everyone*, deep down, is childish—is meek, innocent, and goofy, and has a sense of wonder and a capacity for joy— Henson's *Muppet Show*, when it finally received funding from London's ITC, broke down the barrier between adulthood and childhood.

Alex Rockwell recalled:

> When it came on, I had that very common experience for the whole family sitting down and watching. And I can remember laughing at jokes and then turning and seeing my father laugh at the same time, and for some reason that's what made it this very special show, that was very different from other television that was out there.[352]

What is so different about that? It's not that TV could make a teenage girl laugh. Or that it could make a middle-aged father laugh. It's that something could make them *both* laugh at *the same time*. Today, even films like *Shrek* and *Toy Story*, which aim at universality, tend to make adults and children laugh at different times, with physical humor for the tykes and innuendo for mom and dad.

The Muppet Show actually achieved what Henson couldn't in that early *Ed Sullivan* skit—he made that woman's husband laugh. It took years of insistence that his puppets could work for adults, but eventually the grown-ups gave in. At the height of *The Muppet Show*'s popularity, *Time* magazine wrote, "Stop giggling and pay attention, because we are going to discuss what may be the only adult show on television."[353] Not only was it an adult show, it was *the only adult* show. The *Saturday Evening Post* said 75 percent of its audience were adults.[354]

The *Post* continued:

> These little open-bottomed sacks with outrageous expressions have taken on genuine personalities and are much more humanly genuine and complex than the stock police, hospital and soap opera series which clog our networks.[355]

In those days, *Sesame Street*, too, had a large adult viewership, including my own grandfather, a retired textile salesman in his fifties. Going back to watch *Sesame Street* "Classic," as it's now branded, it rather resembles MTV's Liquid Television cartoons—clearly made with adults in mind. Originally, as *Sesame Street* writer Joseph Bailey put it, "an effort was made to make the show fresh and entertaining to adults as well as children so there would be less chance of adults changing the channel."[356] *Sesame Street*'s first head writer, Jeff Moss, said, "I used to say to the writers, 'You've got two jobs. One is to do a television show that a four-year-old wants to watch. The second is to do a show that you want to watch.'"[357] Today, because of the Barney-driven nineties, much of this spirit has been lost, which is a shame, because without Henson's and Stone's vaudevillian sense of humor, *Sesame Street* is just a philanthropist, a room of child psychologists, and Elmo. Most adults would turn down such a dinner party.

On the other hand, in 1983, none of the creators of *Fraggle Rock* seemed to think it was a children's show at all, and in fact, the Canadian Broadcasting Corporation, which funded it, put it in the "Variety" department, not "Kids." Producer Larry Mirkin said, "Because it wasn't a sitcom and it wasn't a kids show we could just tell whatever story we wanted to tell."[358] Netflix may categorize the show today as "feel-good" and "family-friendly" and certainly children watched it, but according to one director it was too intelligent to be a children's show. Co-creator Jocelyn Stevenson disagreed: "It was *exactly* as intelligent as it needed to be to be a kids' show."[359]

Henson's "family programming" was not lobotomized or candy-coated, because he didn't see an insurmountable difference between adults and children. Jerry Juhl explained:

> We the adults [at *Sesame Street*] doing the show were entertaining ourselves. We knew that it wasn't going to work for the four year olds and five year olds if it didn't work for us too. And that was a basic attitude of Jim's that permeated everything he ever did. . . . By the time we got to *Fraggle Rock*, . . . we didn't pick an age group, we never thought about it. We knew that this would be children's entertainment, but it was a view of the world and a philosophy of looking at the world that was important for us and we thought kids could grasp, and get something out of.[360]

When choosing the songwriters for *Fraggle Rock*, Juhl choose Phil Balsam and Dennis Lee, "because it just did not have the sensibility that this was for little children. It had the sensibility of having innocence and yet a kind of perceived wisdom."[361]

And though Henson was at one time mad at Cooney for *Sesame Street* "ruining his life," it was, perhaps, an advantage to be underestimated. Universality is rare, which is often why it is misjudged as simplistic or watered down—things that are much more common. It takes courage to stand up for something dismissed as childish, and that again makes Henson rare. Rarity in business is quite advantageous—it means there will be less competition for your profits.

Working in what is considered a children's medium gave Henson the element of surprise. So, when he made a pitch reel for *Sesame Street* to be shown to adults, it was a pleasant surprise. In one skit, Muppet execs "boardroom" the title. One suggests a tongue-twister: "The Itty-Bitty, Farm and City, Witty-Ditty, Nitty-Gritty, Dog and Kitty, Pretty Little Kiddie Show." Another Muppet interjects: "Hey. These Kids can't read or write, can they? Then how about we call the show . . . 'Hey, Stupid!'"[362] This pitch made adults laugh because it put kids on the same level as adults—as being strong enough to take a joke. We could imagine that a child watching this clip today might even laugh at its unexpectedness.

MAKE A JERK LAUGH
WHY PUPPETS CAN SAY WHAT WE CAN'T

If children are innocent and wise, then what does that make adults? The cult of business is made up of adults whose primary mode of interaction with others is capitalism—buying and selling rather than giving and receiving gifts. We often call adults "hardened," but Henson's parodies of the business world seemed to get them to soften up a bit.

Though Henson stopped making commercials in 1969, he struck upon another side business that was somewhat similar: Muppet Meeting Films. Because Henson had been so successful with his own presentation films for the Wilson's Meats sales team and promotional films like "Paperwork Explosion" for IBM, it gave David Lazer, IBM's audiovisual program manager, an idea for a new venue for the Muppets: boring meetings. When Lazer left IBM to become a producer for *The Muppet Show* in 1975, he also organized a set of short films that companies could buy or rent in order to add liveliness to the normal workday. Karen Falk wrote that the Meeting Films were designed to counteract "the stupor of technical language and diagrams."[363]

These films were sold to businesses, yet they poked fun at businesses. In an "inspirational" film for the 100% Club, Rowlf reads IBM's "golden words in the sales manual . . . thou shalt conduct IBM's business in a responsible and ethical manner." He then loses all his sales by being too ethical. The scenario is ridiculous, but it discloses a fundamental paradox of business ethics. How do you run a business with honor, ethics, and integrity when you're competing to out-sell, under-sell, and ideally obliterate the competition? It's a dicey thing to say in an IBM meeting. Yet, in the Muppet Meeting Films this kind of conflict turns into absurdist humor.

It goes back to Bell's definition of puppetry as "performance of the material world."[364] Puppetry is an art that shows the world to itself, shows it how it moves, and makes that movement (which is terrifying, dangerous, and larger than any of us) small, nonthreatening, and funny. In revolutions, puppet effigies of leaders are burned, and in therapy sessions, puppets are used to speak true feelings. Henson said in an interview that puppetry is "a part of theater in which small wooden figures serve to represent things. With puppets you can deal with subjects in a way that isn't possible with people."[365]

There is an interesting effect when people perform with the Muppets or any puppet—we can't help but react positively toward them. The incredibly serious Morley Safer of *60 Minutes* cracked up hysterically when he got pulled into talking—really *interacting*, instinctually—with a stuffed pig. We see it with the child in Central Park who knows Henson is there but ignores him. We also see it when tough-guy actor Arthur Godfrey performs as Santa with a group of Muppet monsters on *The Ed Sullivan Show*. One can imagine that Godfrey must have refused to wear an itchy beard, because he makes for an odd, beardless Santa. And when the monsters surround him and sway, he looks slightly uncomfortable with all the grown men puppeteers so close to him. Yet, when a proto-Grover character leans in to make eye contact, Godfrey instinctually nuzzles Grover's nose.

There is something about the diminutive size of a puppet that gives us fond feelings—the kind we would have for a child or a pet. For children, this quite closely resembles their feelings toward a doll or stuffed animal. There is something about a small being that is harmless and almost irresistibly lovable.

This is exactly the way that Muppet Meeting Films seemed to make adults laugh by insulting them. Falk describes the song "Money," which Rowlf performed for both television and corporate audiences:

> A send-up of the money-hungry, it was a great song for Jim as he enjoyed parodying the business world and the quest for the almighty dollar.[366]

In it, Henson sings Stan Freberg's ode to "mazuma, el dinero, wanna be a millionaire-o." Falk notes: "Rowlf . . . would become expert at poking fun of corporate America."[367] These puppet performances showed the salesman to himself in puppet form. Puppets can do what people can't; they can show a jerk how he's funny, how he's human. It is an example of inviting the outside in.

Boring business meetings were the perfect place to invite the outside into Henson's way of thinking. We might picture two framings of the Muppet Meeting Film. First, imagine a room full of men in suits, sitting at a table with a pitcher of water, and a dozen legal pads. You are Jim Henson and you walk into this room, contracted to perform a puppet show to entertain them. You are on their turf. How do you feel? When we enter someone else's turf, and we are outnumbered, we tend to feel defensive. It's a tough crowd.

Now, let us back up and reimagine this interaction in a new way. Picture instead sitting in a room full of men in suits. You are one of them, and your suit is uncomfortable. You have a strong urge to see what the guy next to you has written on his legal pad, but you know you will be judged if you do. The guy next to you won't stop doing that annoying thing he always does, tapping his foot and clearing his throat. Your boss announces a short film. On a screen, a Muppet cracks jokes about the seriousness of your job. You find yourself laughing out loud. How do you feel? Maybe like you don't want it to end. Maybe like you'd rather go into the world of that screen than stay in that boring meeting.

We can walk into the world of business feeling we are on the turf of strangers, possible enemies. Or we can enter that world in a way that brings our own turf with us, so that we no longer feel defensive but expansive. With the realization of the power our art wields, we can become generous. When we do, we become compelling, enviable, *impressive*, and we have the ability to change things.

Henson truly felt this largeness of spirit. Puppeteer Dave Goelz said: "There's a philosophy I think Jim started out with—that people are basically good, life is to be enjoyed, take care of other people, there's enough for everybody."[368]

This feeling that "there's enough," is actually not as common as you'd think in a country with such wealth and opportunity. In *The Gift*, Hyde writes, "Scarcity and abundance have as much to do with the form of exchange as with how much material wealth is at hand. Scarcity appears when wealth cannot flow."[369] That is to say that, with any given amount of wealth, one can either feel abundance or scarcity, and it has less to do with amount than it does with whether we trust that wealth will come and go when we need it. Modern capitalist societies, Hyde explains, tend to operate on the principle of scarcity. The idea is that we should hoard whatever we have because we might not get more. Hunter-gatherer tribes, on the other hand, eat the entirety of what they catch, stockpiling none, and trust that three days later, they can go out and catch another boar. For one who trusts in nature, there is an abundance of natural wealth.

What does it mean to feel that "there's enough for everybody" as Henson did?

Well, as we have seen, it meant Henson giving Steven Spielberg a tour of his Creature Shop when he was developing *E.T.*, even though he was technically Henson's competition. Kenworthy said:

> I was a bit panicked, because we were all concerned about people seeing our techniques. Jim was much less worried. He thought that everyone should share these new developments."[370]

Henson invited Spielberg—the outside—in. The laws of a market economy would tell you to protect your secrets from the competition—especially given the fact that Spielberg's *E.T.* would in fact go on to win most of 1982's box-office dollars while *The Dark Crystal* foundered. Yet Henson didn't see movie tickets as a scarcity, but rather an abundance, infinitely renewable. And today both films are enduring classics.

Henson similarly felt unthreatened by George Lucas, another possible competitor. Henson chose to collaborate instead. Industrial Light and Magic produced glass paintings for *The Dark Crystal*, and then Henson let Frank Oz create Yoda for *Star Wars*. Because Henson felt magnanimous toward other fantasy filmmakers, he gained allies in Hollywood. George Lucas, for example, went on to produce Henson's *Labyrinth*.

With Meeting Films, Henson came onto business's turf and yet felt that *he* was the one who was at home. When the Muppet Skip says, "Hi there, all you lovers of hot dogs and money," to Wilson's Meats executives, and the shock of a puppet's insulting you makes you laugh, it is effectively like saying, "Come on in, sit down, take your shoes off. Stay awhile."

The insults Henson's puppets wielded were so effective in changing people's minds because they weren't meant to hurt. They were meant as a gift.

PARODY AS GIFT
GIVE GREED A MIRROR

For Henson, parody was the gift that could bring disparate groups together. It allowed him to enter the business world as an artist, and to have members of the business class engage with his art. If you saw yourself or someone you knew puppetted on *The Muppet Show*, you received a gift. Someone had taken the time to study your features and how they moved. It was like being shown a mirror, but one that took exorbitant effort to make—in effect, a portrait that wasn't commissioned. By seeing people as basically good, Henson's caricature started to resemble something more like flattery. It seemed to encourage its recipient to go out and do the same for someone else—to pay close attention to their uniqueness.

If Henson's parody was a gift in the Hydian sense, then it contributes to the feeling of abundance that characterizes a gift economy. Conversely, if Henson refused to give any gifts to the business world, it would further the feeling of scarcity. In the *Fraggle Rock* episode "The Perfect Blue Rollie," Wembley gives Boober a shiny pebble that's a real honey, but being a worrier, Boober decides to hoard it in a museum he's made. Not allowing the gift to move isolates him and nearly kills him in a rock slide. He's saved by his friends and then decides to give the pebble to them. Boober finally learns what Wembley said in the beginning: giving makes you feel really good.

It was telling that Henson's plots never ended in revenge fantasies like the vultures in *Snow White* eating the evil queen. In Henson's worldview, the villains are always given a gift in the attempt to invite them into the Muppets' way of thinking. For instance, Larry Mirkin said of *Fraggle Rock*, "Most of us—certainly Jerry and I and I think Jim and Jocelyn—we really didn't believe in the idea of good and evil as I think sometimes it's handled in different shows, and the conflicts in the show are usually because of people's misunderstanding—conflicts of interest rather than one character is good and one character is bad. We just didn't think that way about the show."[371]

That is, the dragon is never meant to be slain. He is meant to be transformed, and he is transformed when he is given a gift and he chooses not to hoard it. The gift melts the dragon's heart—or more accurately, melts the distinction between outside and inside—and it effectively invites the dragon, the fearful hoarder, into the gift economy. It shows him the benefits of the gift and shows him that, in order to enjoy them, he can't sell them for profit. He has to keep the giving cycle alive. And give back.

In *The Great Santa Claus Switch*, Santa turns the oversized henchmen Thig and Thog over to the good side by giving a gift. Confused, they ask, "Why are you always giving stuff to people?" Santa tells them, "because giving makes a person feel very very good." On *The Ed Sullivan Show*, a bunch of monsters think Santa's toys are "worth quite a lot," and plan on "selling them at a fantastic profit."[372] They sing, "Come Christmas tomorrow, we'll make a fast buck."[373] Arthur Godfrey as Santa tells them, "You can't steal it because I'm *giving* it to you." Godfrey tells them, "There are plenty of toys to go around,"[374] because when gifts are allowed to move and not hoarded, no matter how many gifts there are, it will be an economy of abundance. Everyone will get a chance to experience them. In echoes of Seuss's Grinch, the monsters who are outside the gift circle aren't meant to be beaten or killed, but rather, brought into the inside group of the Christmas gift exchange.

The Muppet universe is one of inclusion, with striking echoes of Hyde's book. In fact, "The Perfect Blue Rollie" episode of *Fraggle Rock* was written by David Young after reading *The Gift*, which had been given to him by Margaret Atwood. The Song "Pass It On" from "The Perfect Blue Rollie" was later used in *A Muppet Family Christmas*, when the Fraggles give a ceremonial Fraggle pebble to *The Muppet Show*'s Robin, who then gives it to *Sesame Street*'s Grover. Gobo Fraggle said, "That pebble's been given thirty-seven times." Similarly, in the early eighties, Atwood gave out copies of *The Gift* to every artist she knew.

In order to turn a stranger into a friend, a gift is given. Nearly all children's stories tell us this; however, it is deceptive how many adult conflicts stem from the outside-inside paradox, and how many could actually be resolved through the giving of a gift.

The kind of parody that Henson gave hardened adults was to see themselves clearly for their faults and offer them an invitation to be innocent once again. It is the gift Kermit gives to Doc Hopper in the showdown scene of *The Muppet Movie.* A Disney hero might duel with Hopper to the death. Instead, Kermit reaches out to him:

> Even though you've been greedy and vicious, you are still a man with a heart and soul. . . . I don't think you're a bad man, Doc. But if you look in your heart, you'll find you really want to let me and my friends go.[375]

Henson once said, "I try hard not to judge anyone."[376] This is interesting from a man whose puppets could be incredibly satirical. But the kind of parody Henson gave people who were different from him was the kind of mirror that does not lie, but offers a chance to join "us."

Henson himself said:

> Even the most worldly of our characters is innocent. Our villains are innocent, really. And it's that innocence that I think is the connection to the audience.[377]

In 1986, Jim Henson was asked what his underlying message was. "It's basically just a sort of positive approach: taking the attitude that life is good and people are good."[378]

It is my belief that the successful people in this world who, like Henson, achieve universality, are almost always those who truly *want* to—who want to talk to everybody and bring everyone together. Their staggering reach can give them great wealth and power, but in some truly beautiful cases, it's done "for the right reasons."

And who knows, the next great universal voice could be yours.

HENSON'S UNIVERSALISM
REFUSING TO FALL INTO SUBCATEGORIES OF HUMAN

Henson was able to reach diverse groups of people so effectively because he himself refused to be categorized by any one group. As a result, he had a very enigmatic personality. Let us look at some of the boundaries Henson transcended.

BETWEEN HIPPIES AND SQUARES:

Of *Youth '68*, Karen Falk writes:

> The show attempted not to editorialize but to demonstrate the juxtaposition of different value systems within the context of a changing world. Because Jim was young but also professionally established, he felt like he was a part of both generations. By contrasting the different viewpoints and attitudes of each age, Jim created a portrait of society as a whole.[379]

One viewer called it "the best TV show I have ever seen."[380] Another letter to the network read: "*Youth '68*!?! Where on earth did they get those awful creeps? From old hippie pad? What is their contribution to this country other than peddling marijuana?"[381] Henson kept the negative letter. Someone else might have thrown it away as an unnecessary voice. I don't think Henson thought such a thing existed.

BETWEEN AMERICA AND THE WORLD:

Henson was born in Mississippi, but he traveled often beyond the United States, and lived in London for many years. *The Muppet Show*, at the time the most watched show on earth, was "broadcast in over 100 countries to over 250 million children and adults."[382] Tellingly, a 1984 article reported that "the [*Muppet Show*] characters most popular in the United States are the most popular everywhere."[383] Every nation, it seems, fell in love with the singular Miss Piggy. Henson's global view is evident in his public-service announcement that suggested we imagine everyone on earth living in "One house." In it, Kermit adds, "We do!"

BETWEEN POSITIVISM AND REALISM:

David Odell wrote of Henson, "He was wildly enthusiastic and tended to ignore obstacles. . . . [A]t the same time he was very practical and realistic and able to laugh at his excessive flights of fancy."[384] Although Henson was very idealistic and positive about humanity, he was very aware of how the world *actually* worked. Henson's realism is what allowed him to *market* his idealism, leaving the world a little better than he found it.

BETWEEN VIOLENCE AND PACIFISM:

Henson said in a 1986 interview, "I am certainly quite strongly against violence on television. It is near criminal what the networks are doing."[385] Yet, at the same time, his own early commercials featured a revolver aimed and fired at a Muppet. His Creature Shop even made the turtle suits for *Teenage Mutant Ninja Turtles*. Brian Henson said:

> *Turtles* was pushing the edge of what my father thought we should be doing because it was violent. He was always worried that it was glamorizing violence for kids, but Steve Barron convinced him that the violence was very cartoonlike.[386]

It is a narrow line between cartoon violence and being mistaken for condoning violence. Henson drew a line in the sand, and yet, when given the right reasons, he crossed that line. Eschewing absolutes in favor of his own judgment, it is possible that nothing was considered truly "off limits."

BETWEEN HIGH AND LOW:

Jim Henson promised in *The Muppet Show* pitch reel his work would appeal to both eggheads and families, and like Mark Twain, he always seemed to combine the common with the intellectual. This was also part of the beauty of *Sesame Street*'s workshops.

Throughout the show, there was a balance between the practical knowledge of the director and puppeteers and the book smarts of the curriculum specialists, Rhodes scholars, and child psychologists. As *Sesame Street* research director Dr. Lewis Bernstein described:

> We bring in the experts to allow the writer to soak in expertise. We in Research bring in people to provide the

> information, and then the artistry of the writer takes over, as they integrate what they've heard.[387]

If we picture Jim Henson and Maurice Sendak doodling in the back of the classroom at the *Sesame Street* teach-ins in Cambridge 1968, we have the right idea. A mix of high and low culture is what made *Sesame Street* a classic.

BETWEEN RICH AND POOR:

Caroll Spinney wrote:

> "[Jim Henson] told me that as a kid he'd wanted something of the good life. Like me, he wanted things that he saw but couldn't have, and he decided that one day he'd get them. . . . He loved tuxedo nights and limousines, and it was thrilling to be included in an evening with Jim."[388]

Yet, Henson's business manager, David Lazer, recalled that he found the moon's reflection to be more enchanting than the stars of Cannes:

> The evening ended with a party on a private yacht loaded with stars and movers and shakers. We left the yacht at one o'clock in the morning and walked along the dock. Even the moon seemed to do a shimmer dance on the water just for Jim. He was mesmerized by the beauty, the serenity, and the nurturing power of Nature. None of the glitz of Cannes or all the accolades he received had this effect on him.[389]

Lazer noted:

> His values were not materialistic. Even though he liked to dress up and eat in nice places, he was one with the universe. He could look at a sunset and it would feed him. It was as if someone else got a million-dollar check.[390]

Yet, Henson enjoyed sports cars like a Jaguar XJ6 and a BMW. According to Spinney, "Jim would walk across the set, and Richard would say out loud in front of me, 'Here comes that rich bastard millionaire.'"[391] Hunt was joking, but Henson *was* a millionaire. Still, Henson seemed to enjoy sharing his wealth and threw lavish parties yearly for everyone in his company. Spinney wrote, "Jim never scrimped when he entertained, and there was caviar and hors d'oeuvres and lots of champagne."[392]

BETWEEN BUSINESS AND ART:

Let us come back to the topic that started this book. Caroll Spinney wrote, "Business suits were not for Jim. He'd wear "cool" clothes, peasant shirts and one-of-a-kind items he'd find in his travels."[393] Yet when it was good for the art, he'd dress up. In one interview, the reporter said that except for his "wearing an understated club tie speckled with Kermits," he "could pass for a stockbroker."[394] In *The Muppets Take Manhattan*, Kermit dresses up like an agent in order to trick a Broadway bigwig into producing his show, saying it's "Boffo, Lenny! Socko, Lenny! . . . Let's do lunch."[395] Later, he thinks he's an advertising executive and comes up with a brilliant slogan for soap: "It gets you clean."

Yet, it is important to remind ourselves here that as much as Henson permeated the boundaries between business and art, the driving force of his life was art. He called himself a "purist,"[396] described puppetry as his "palette,"[397] waxed "performance is where the humanity is, where the relationship is,"[398] and described how difficult it was to make Big Bird look "gorgeous"[399] on TV sets. A 1990 interviewer said of Henson, "If I spoke business with him, he was friendly but matter-of-fact. On the subject of puppets, his voice lit up, with Kermit's looping tones detectable somewhere beneath the enthusiasm."[400]

In the TV special *The Muppets Celebrate Jim Henson*, made just after Henson's death, Rizzo finds Henson's name written on a paycheck and Gonzo says: "That must mean he was . . . an accountant!"[401] Yet accountants are often the butt of jokes in the Muppet world—in *Dog City*, they say being the child of accountants is worse than being an orphan. Harvard Business Scholar Clayton Christensen, the author of *The Innovator's Dilemma*, has said, "God doesn't employ accountants or statisticians. God doesn't aggregate. God doesn't count."[402] Meaning that, when you decide how to *live your life*, numbers shouldn't really come into it. And that includes money. In *The Gift*, Hyde warns that "[w]ealth ceases to move freely when all things are counted and priced."[403]

THE ONLY BOUNDARY YOU NEED CANNOT BE TORN DOWN

As we saw in the filming of *The Muppets Take Manhattan*, Henson could become Kermit, arrange a business deal, and go back to being Kermit. But if a child walked up to him in Central Park, he would lose himself completely in the performance, for the joy of it. He was a businessman and an artist, and he proves that these roles can coexist in one person.

But there are two things that could have destroyed Henson's art if he had not maintained *some* boundary between art and money. The first would have been if had truly forgotten art when he came off the stage with Kermit on his hand to answer deal-making questions—if he had lost himself in business. The second would be if he had been considering deals and dollar signs when he was performing for the little boy in the park. The boundary between art and business *should* be uneven. When you pass into business, the boundary should be porous, but when you are in the gift-sphere, the boundary should be thick as a wall. The strength of this wall is what allows you to do what Henson did—invite the outside in.

How much of a boundary do you need? Just enough so that they don't convince you to join *them*. Enough so that you're on the inside wherever you go. When you find yourself walking into a business, do you find yourself feeling like you're on someone else's turf? Or do you feel that you bring your own turf with you?

Jim Henson liked to transcend barriers between groups and invite *everyone* in. So how will you invite them in? Start by noticing the uniqueness of your enemies. Who don't you see eye to eye with? Critics, corporations, squares, hippies? Who are they exactly, and what do they want? Study these people, and look for ways in which they are really not all that different from you.

Show them there is a way out—show them, with your art, that the line is permeable. Make them laugh. Puppet them. Spend some time really studying them and do an impression. "Boffo, Lenny, Socko, Lenny." Speak the way they do, but turn it into a song—"Money, money, money, money, money." Whatever your art, your calling, you can integrate a bit of parody into it. How might you think of parody as a gift? Dale Carnegie once said that the most beautiful word to any speaker of English is his own name.

When you understand your outside, give them a gift, but what kind of gift? Something you like or something they like? How might you translate your goals and gifts into their language? In my writing career I have learned to code-switch between my aim—sharing my ideas around the world—and the things that matter to publishers: the numbers. Page views, Twitter followers, and community members mean profits for the business side of writing, and luckily for me, I want those things, because to me, it means I get to engage readers to discuss things that matter to me. How do you code-switch in your art? In what ways do you actually see eye to eye with the accountants? If you want to explore this idea further, then share what you think on my website, ElizabethHydeStevens.com. Who are the "enemy Fraggles" in your life?

Never forget that you're more than any one group. You're more than your country, your church, or your family. Even though we all stick to our little cults, try to see yourself from the outside and to speak from that wisdom. If you truly *want* to include everyone, I think you can. You're a human being, and all human beings start out as artists. If you've chosen a life of art, well then, that's the only boundary you can't transcend.

If you are always an artist, and you experience the abundance of the artistic gift, you are always on your own home turf. When you truly feel this way, when your ego is expansive enough, they'll all line up to join *you.*

LESSON 6

ALWAYS INNOVATE

ON TECHNOLOGY AND ART

Many of Jim Henson's early *Ed Sullivan Show* sketches demonstrate what happens when someone comes along who thinks *differently*. So it is fitting that Jim Henson, his predecessor Walt Disney, and our modern day visionary—Pixar—each pioneered an emerging technology to make art. These artists—or in Pixar's case, a group of artists and engineers—did the impossible: they all turned their fringe art into a bona fide, full-length Oscar-worthy Hollywood hit. As technology companies know, innovation is not possible without R&D—research and development—and if we rewind the story to before *Toy Story*, *The Muppet Movie*, and *Snow White*, we see that all of these innovators gave themselves ample time to *play* with the "new media" of their day. For Disney, it was film; for Henson, television; and for Pixar, computers. When you compare the three, it almost feels like the same timeline has been transposed three times over the years 1937, 1979, and 1995.

In the 1937 full-length *Snow White and the Seven Dwarfs*, Walt Disney convinced the world that hand-drawn animation could *feel* just as real as live action. The emerging technology of Disney's day was film, and the first narrative films appeared around 1901, the same year Disney was born. When Disney was nineteen, he began working on them—producing short animated reels for theaters. We could say the technology emerged when he did, and it was ripe for experimentation in its late teenage years, which were Disney's teenage years as well. After years of playing with film, at the age of thirty-six, Disney made his first feature film. We would never forget it.

About forty years after *Snow White*, Jim Henson showed the world puppets could sustain a full-length Hollywood movie with 1979's *The Muppet Movie*. But the real emerging technology in Henson's career was television. Television was where Henson developed his art, and even in his movies, he would work with a closed-circuit television monitor at his feet, showing him what the camera sees. Similar to Disney, Jim Henson was two years old when cathode-ray-tube TVs became available to the public. He was twelve in 1948 when commercial network programming began. CNN noted in its profile of Henson:

> **Willow Bay:** The television age was new [when Henson was a boy]. In 1946, right after World War II, there were 7,000 television sets in the United States. One year later, the television audience had grown to 1 million. Jimmy desperately wanted his family to get a TV, and in 1950 [when he was fourteen], they finally did.
> **Jane Henson:** "It was the new media and the new, the new and exciting media on the scene."[404]

Four years later, Henson was *on* TV. And he was still only eighteen. The medium of television was ripe for innovation, since it was about sixteen years old, and Henson was at a good age to do it. The television "tricks" Henson learned at local TV studios would lead to a mastery of the medium, and at the age of forty-three, Henson brought his Muppets to Hollywood, to the delight of critics and families across the world.

Sixteen years after *The Muppet Movie*, our modern-day source of magic, Pixar, proved that computer animation could make us *feel* with its full-length *Toy Story* in 1995. Pixar's success can be traced back to the invention of computers. In a familiar narrative, Pixar's chief technical officer, Ed Catmull, was born in 1945, a few years after the first program-controlled computer appeared. By the time the first mouse appeared, he had graduated college and started working on computers, around age twenty-two. Catmull's dream at Pixar was to make movies, and with the addition of chief creative officer John Lasseter and investor Steve Jobs, that dream came true. By age fifty, Catmull saw his company make it to the silver screen. It is striking that Disney, Henson, and Catmull each used a technology that emerged around the time of his birth and matured at the same time he did—around twenty—when he began toying with it. It seems like a pretty good formula for artistic and financial success.

We call men like these "innovators." Yet it is not enough to simply *use* technology. Each of us uses a personal computer and, for the most part, our days are wasted by checking Facebook and e-mail. Buying an iPhone or using Twitter isn't going to turn you into an innovator. We have plenty of new technology today, and people can look pretty silly flashing hashtags trying to keep up. New technology isn't *always* innovative. It's how you *use* the technology.

As Myspace users used to say, it's complicated. For one thing, quality is relative, and when you create something new, it has no competition. If something has never been done before, there is no measuring stick for it. How do you know if your innovation is *good*?

QUALITY IS NOT PERFECTION

The Muppets are undoubtedly remembered for their quality. When you think of puppetry, Henson's name is the first one we remember, because truly, he did it best. In comparison, most other puppets on TV look cheap. This is because Jim Henson was demanding, but surprisingly, he was not a perfectionist.

Walt Disney *was* a perfectionist. In the making of *Snow White*, he would micromanage his animators, saying "[The dwarf's] fanny in the last half of scene is too high," or "Have hummingbird make four pick-ups instead of six."[405] And in order to get greater realism in his cartoons, Disney started driving his animators to art classes and picking them up at night, to show them, in Gabler's words, "the effect of gravity on mass, and how flesh and muscle move."[406] This attention to verisimilitude reminds us of Pixar's realism—art that sometimes feels scanned or photographic. Both contrast sharply with Henson's work, which while *lifelike*, was not *realistic*. It sought to represent, to suggest reality, but not to copy it.

In *Snow White*, Walt Disney used the modern-day equivalent of motion-capture—animators drew the fair princess by tracing photographs of a real actress. Similarly, in *Toy Story 3*, Pixar re-created an incredibly believable scene above the ceiling panels in a daycare, replete with wiring and appropriate lighting. The details are immaculate, but they are often ordinary—even dull. We can contrast this with *The Dark Crystal*, in which Henson created the *feeling* of reality by creating from scratch a *new* reality, one more fantastic than the one we live in. Henson explained:

> There's a wonderful texture and depth of this world and if you went to photograph it . . . in the background there would be all these sort of edges of things, parts of life, that

> you don't know about, but it indicates a depth that's there, so in creating the world, we had to create all that depth from the beginning. And so we went into a great deal more work than we probably needed to, to have thought out the history of all the people and the buildings and the plants.[407]

For *The Dark Crystal*, Henson's artists created new languages, new species, a new map, new plants, new cultures with their own new folk-art traditions. In short: a new reality. While Disney and Pixar seemed to be trying to escape being cartoonish, meticulously re-creating a woman's dimensions or the space above a ceiling panel, Henson's work always seemed to delight in how unreal objects—the dime-store doll eyes of the Muppets or the impossible flora-fauna hybrids of *The Dark Crystal*—could *suggest* reality.

One effect of Walt Disney's perfectionism was that in order to get exactly the image he envisioned, he unfortunately suppressed the creativity of the artists he worked with. One writer remembered:

> God help you if you took his idea and ran with it in the wrong direction. . . . If you did, one eyebrow would rise and the other would descend, and he'd say, "You don't seem to get it at all."[408]

Disney animator Wilfred Jackson said, "It is my opinion that if Walt had started in some different place at the same time with a different bunch of guys, the result would have been more or less along the same lines."[409] *Snow White*, it seems, would have looked the same no matter who worked for Walt Disney. His artists were not there to make *their* art. They were there to make *his* art.

Henson was not a perfectionist in this sense, because his version of "quality" required not just his own creativity, but the creativity of those around him. Steve Whitmire explained what was most important to Henson: "seeing to it that this person does what they need to do well."[410] Henson's conception of "quality" was such that it allowed for others to co-create his worlds, which meant that he did not know in advance what those worlds would look like. If Henson had started with a different bunch of guys, *The Muppet Movie* would look completely different.

Henson cared a great deal for *quality*, but that was defined as the best each person could do, and when the voices came together in harmony, in an organic—but not random—creation, the outcomes of his projects must have been a constant surprise to him. This is no typical perfectionism, because it is *accepting* while still being *demanding*. Dave Goelz said:

> He on one hand was intent on refining every take, every subsequent take, but at the same time, he enjoyed every one for what was good about it.[411]

Henson knew that allowing others to truly create—not to blindly re-create his ideas but to add to them and imagine their own—would make his projects better than anything he could have imagined alone.

Wendy Midener remembered that she was not told exactly what the gelflings in *The Dark Crystal* would look like in three dimensions—she had to find it herself, by creating them:

> I would just keep sculpting them, turning them out. And Jim and Brian [Froud] would come by and say, yes well I like that, but change the eyes, change the mouth. And

> we went through a whole series of developments . . . and finally it seems like after years of this, I did get two heads and Jim and Frank and Brian came to look at them and finally said, yes I think that's it. I think that will be the gelflings.[412]

Henson was truly *demanding*, as when one shot of a rolling drum in *Emmet Otter* took 233 takes.[413] He had a long patience, and this inspired those around him to also have a long patience—for quality. According to Jerry Nelson:

> If he could see it happening in his mind's eye and knew that it would work, he would *dog* it until it worked. . . . We always wanted to give Jim exactly what he was looking for. We didn't always know what that was, but we were willing to try until we found it.[414]

Yet, as frustrating as it must have been to get the shot right, if you watch the outtake reel, Nelson and Oz, the performers in the scene, seem incredibly good-natured about it, extending Henson the time to achieve his vision, perhaps because he would have done the same for them.

Henson was *like* a perfectionist at times, because he took the time to get something right. He said of *The Dark Crystal* that they "went into a great deal more work than we probably needed to." Similarly, the rig that made the Muppets ride bicycles in circles for *The Great Muppet Caper* was more trouble than most people would go to:

> Part of the challenge, he explained, was that, ". . . the puppet's feet on the pedals had to turn in time with the

> beat of the music and both to be in time with each other and travel at realistic speed." He went on, describing that there were three different types of platforms rigged to the crane. When Miss Piggy and Kermit rode side by side and then turned in two circles, the marionettists worked on two circular platforms. As the bicycles went into their circles, the crane stopped moving and the momentum was carried on by the puppeteers who worked around the outside of the platforms. Once the puppeteers got back to their start position, the crane started up and the bicycles continued on a straight path. Several additional paragraphs detailed the use of radio control for the heads, and the use of a tow rope from a large tricycle and variously sized trolleys for the group shots.[415]

It seems crazy to go to such lengths, as Rowlf sings in *The Muppets Take Manhattan*, "There'll be plenty of people saying forget all about it, it ain't worth the trouble, all the trouble that you're going to."[416] Why would anyone go to such lengths? When asked why Henson made movies, Frank Oz once said:

> Jim didn't think of it in hit terms. He got to have control and play. And create whatever he wanted; and that was a joy, and he loved it. He always pushed the envelope. He just loved breaking barriers. He just loved breaking barriers.[417]

Oz repeated it twice for emphasis. Henson just *loved* breaking barriers. It wasn't about creating the most perfect example of a thing—because there is no surprise in that. For Henson, it seemed to be about *the surprise*. Doing something truly *new*.

It is this innovator's temperament that made Henson change the beloved intro on *The Muppet Show*—from Scooter in the star's dressing room to Pops at the door. What worked well for four seasons would have been fine for most people, but for the last season, why not try something new? Nelson explained the reason Henson changed a proven formula: "Jim liked to change things around on the show to keep it new. And he liked to change the look of the show, slightly."[418]

In fact, Jim Henson was continually changing small things as well as the overarching style of his work. Many times, he changed the look of his characters by bringing in new designers. For *Fraggle Rock*, Henson asked Michael Frith to create sketches for the characters and their world. Previously, Frith had been a writer–illustrator with Dr. Seuss, and his design gave the show a particular Seuss-like quality. For *The Dark Crystal*, Henson asked Brian Froud to create the sketches, and he gave it a kind of Celtic, Tolkeinesque look. Bonnie Erickson is responsible for the look of the masklike faces in *The Muppet Musicians of Bremen*. Henson seemed to love seeing what other people could come up with—to surprise him.

Ron Mueck, a sculptor, remembers being picked as the conceptual designer of the unfinished series Henson called "Rocket Ship Show":

> A memo went around inviting everyone to contribute ideas toward the design of the characters. . . . Jim liked the sketches I sent through to him and I was assigned to the project and spent the next five months churning out sketches and models. Jim was always very enthusiastic and encouraging when he came to see my latest batch of drawings or sculpts. He wasn't exactly sure what we were aiming for, but he seemed to know when we weren't there

> yet. And so I would launch into a new batch of variations. Eventually we arrived at a group of characters he liked the look of. . . ."[419]

If Henson had been a perfectionist, he would have been able to tell Mueck or Midener *precisely* what he wanted and saved them a lot of trouble, but since Henson wanted the best that Meuck was capable of—a product unique to Meuck and different from what Henson could imagine—he could only encourage more experimentation.

Innovation requires experimentation. But this leads us to a hard reality: *playing* with your medium costs an enormous amount of money. *Fraggle Rock* producer Larry Mirkin compared this expense to R&D in any industry:

> If you want to put a "business plan lens" on it—and I don't know that you should—I would argue that [Henson] understood how "Research and Development" works in the Arts. Everyone in the sciences and many people in industry understand the value of R&D, but in the Arts, spending money on "experimentation" or on something that has no concrete "end user" in sight is often considered wasteful, when it's absolutely essential to innovation in the arts (just as it is in the sciences or in industry). On a deep artistic level, Jim trusted the process of creating art and he had the economic means (derived from other artistic efforts) to support that process. He really did put his money where his mouth (or his artistic soul) was.[420]

In fact, Henson put his own money—millions of it—into *The Muppet Show*, *Fraggle Rock*, *The Dark Crystal*, and almost all of his other projects, *before* he found a financial backer. But here lies a major problem for artists.

THE (FINANCIAL) TROUBLE WITH QUALITY
IT'S PROFIT-LESS

Innovation is expensive. The way to get it—experimentation—tends to cost more than it has to, making it a kind of gift. But giving gifts, as Lewis Hyde illustrated, does not make artists rich and seldom makes them break even. *The Muppet Show* in its fifth season cost $250,000 *per episode*—bankrolled by British producer Lew Grade.[421] To shoot an innovative spot like "In the Navy" with Muppet Vikings, the crew spent a whole day to get two minutes of film.[422] According to *Time* it was "listed on the books as making no profit, in part because Henson keeps putting money back into the program. . . . 'The long-range profit for this show is down the road, when it's syndicated and sold to the stations,' says Henson. 'It's a couple of years away.'"[423] It seems strange that Grade, a savvy businessman, was funding something that made him no profit.

But this isn't entirely true, because toy sales—split with Grade—were most likely left off the books. If toy sales made Henson's agent rich—15 percent of Henson's split, then Grade's percentage was surely substantial. Just as toy sales made Henson's gift of *Sesame Street* possible, they allowed *The Muppet Show* to be profitable, even while making no profit. In this way, innovation often tends to yield profit in the long run. *Time* explains:

> Lord Grade adds with satisfaction that the take from this "strip syndication"—the sale of a show for the same time slot several days a week—will be split equally between

> HA! [Henson Associates] and his ACC group and will mean "millions of dollars."[424]

Because it was innovative, *The Muppet Show* was syndicated on TNT in the 1980s. At that point, people still loved the Muppets; the name was synonymous with quality—*because* Henson kept feeding money back into the show. This is how thinking long-term can turn an unprofitable business model profitable. The show itself was a gift—it did not make a profit. Its investor was repaid with toy sales, and then, years later . . . they hoped its quality would lead to an increase in value. Ironically, when Henson finally saw the profit from the show, he would use it for an even bigger project.

To short-term thinkers, as many managers and executives today tend to be, it seems crazy. Feeding the quality-monster is a circular and paradoxical way to run a business.

Emmet Otter points this out to his mother in *Jug-Band Christmas*, who, like the shoemaker in the fairy tale, funnels all her earnings back into raw materials for more work:

> Good thinking, Ma! Now you can knit more socks to buy more pumpkins to sell more pies, to buy more wool . . .

It's a circular business model that traps workers in infinite work. Profitwise, you'll never get ahead. *However*, if you are an innovator who absolutely *loves* what you do, this is actually the most ideal, satisfying, and self-sustaining business model you can adopt. *The Fraggle Rock* minstrels sing about their lifestyle:

> What we are is what we play
> never get a holiday

> ecstasy's the only pay
> music makes us roam.

The Minstrel Cantus tells Mokey, "Wonderful, isn't it? Being a minstrel is enough work for your whole life!"[425] This is the business model in which an artist and innovator can thrive—one with enough (art)work to last a lifetime. To the average businessman, it's a gamble—there's too much risk involved, there's no end game, and what will we tell the shareholders at the quarterly meeting?

You'd have to tell them to *wait*. Sinking money back into *The Muppet Show* meant the show could get better and better. The higher the quality of the show, the more likely it would endure in the affection of viewers and the more likely it would earn a lot in syndication. It was a long-term strategy very different than the one used by the fly-by-night entertainment shows we usually see that lure with suspense, don't deliver, but get out in enough time to take their ad profits to the bank. Making something with quality requires a different business model. Innovation requires patience—years with zero dollars on the books, a separate revenue stream if possible, and very often investment of one's own money.

In *Of Muppets and Men*, Finch wrote:

> Puppet shows on television have generally been characterized by a minimal expenditure on sets and production values. Where *The Muppet Show* is concerned, though, the opposite is the case. If an elaborate set is needed, it is built no matter what the cost, and the cost of the set is just the beginning.[426]

Whereas a typical businessman would spare this expense, Henson wanted to create something *new*. We see the same attitude with Walt

Disney: "He admitted to one reporter that after *Snow White* 'he was afraid he could not equal it in other endeavors'—an attitude, the reporter observed, 'quite in reverse of the Hollywood philosophy of coasting as long as possible on one successful film.'"[427]

But Hollywood has its reasons. I can imagine the venture capitalists on *Shark Tank* laughing at Henson's business model, which permits eight hours of shooting to get two minutes of film—as it did when Linda Ronstadt performed "Blue Bayou" on *The Muppet Show.* How expensive is it to shoot eight hours on set at Elstree Studios, paying cameramen, lighting crew, puppeteers, a director? And that doesn't include the man-hours of set builders or even the hours spent recording the song in the studio. Nor the hours spent conceptualizing it. The two-minute "Blue Bayou" sketch is the result of more like a hundred hours—like years of pressure compressing carbon into a diamond. "Blue Bayou" is effectually a two-minute *masterpiece.* It didn't need to be that good or take that long. Perhaps that's why it felt like a gift. Thirty years later, the show is still selling as a DVD. And one thing the venture capitalists forget is that when you blaze a trail with (expensive) quality, you are unlikely to have much competition.

On *60 Minutes*, Morley Safer said,

> One reason the show has not been copied the way everything successful in television is copied, is that it's so expensive to produce. *The Muppet Show* has set such a high standard for this kind of work that a cheap version of it would just be unacceptable.[428]

This same effect is noted with Disney and Pixar. Their quality came from an expense too great for any sane business to undertake. Both these businesses were notorious for *draining* capital in their early years.

In the 1930s, Walt Disney borrowed close to two million dollars from the Bank of America for *Snow White.*[429] The budget started out as only $250,000,[430] but as filming went on, Walt and his brother Roy O. Disney took out three more loans. At each step along the way, Disney lured Bank of America in deeper with promises of *Snow White*'s success—and he was right. These loans were completely repaid when *Snow White* dazzled everyone who saw it. Of course, this didn't end Disney's debt—it just allowed him more credit to borrow for his next films. As soon as he retired his debt, Disney opened a revolving million-dollar line of credit. Borrow-and-promise had been Disney's business strategy from the very beginning. Even before he got to Hollywood, he was perpetually borrowing money from friends and family and even declared bankruptcy in Kansas City.

With greater expenses than Disney's cameras and hand-drawn cels, the Pixar studio needed to develop hardware, software, *and* trained computer animators to make its first movie. Their angel funder, Steve Jobs, essentially bought a stake in the company for $5 million, but reportedly sank $55 million into it over its first five years, when he saw essentially no profit.[431]

For innovative companies, it is not surprising to see periods of money-sucking while a masterpiece is in development. And it is the rare funder who can stomach such an investment. It is likely Bank of America didn't know what it was getting into with *Snow White.* Steve Jobs likened his gradual-but-hefty investment to a frog being heated up in water: "If somebody had come to me and said, I want you to invest $55 million in this company, I would have said, 'No!'"[432] We might see this stringing-them-along strategy in Henson's initial deal with Grade for a single season of twenty-four episodes.[433] That one season of investing turned into five seasons, plus *The Muppet Movie* and the fifteen-million-dollar *Dark Crystal*.[434]

To get funding, Henson had to convince Grade to share his long patience. Grade was once an artist himself—a dancer—turned mogul. Compared to Disney, Jim Henson started out with more capital of his own—profits from commercials and then *Sesame Street* toy sales—but in order to make a prime-time puppet show and then a full-length puppet movie, Henson *needed* angel funding from Lord Grade. Movies are just plain expensive, and as Davis said, Henson was "notorious for going over budget."[435]

It's hard to say whether Grade was ever repaid for his investment, because, like Henson, he was also funneling his own profits back into art. Grade loved to fund expensive projects like the lovely and enduring *The Last Unicorn*, but in 1982, financial trouble forced him to sell his company off. It leads us to wonder, do the angel funders in art ever get to see their imagined profit?

We all know the factoid that says it was Pixar—not Apple—that made Steve Jobs a billionaire. Yet, to get that, he had to agree to a merger with Disney, to essentially be *bought out*. Similarly, the supposed $150 million value of Henson's company in 1990 was not necessarily a real accounting of profits, but rather "Disney dollars," the amount Disney was willing to pay in stock to get Henson. Disney's own company was unsuccessful for long after his death, which is why his nephew Roy E. Disney installed Michael Eisner's aggressive—and arguably anti-artist—business team in the 1980s.

While artistic businesses can get going to a good financial clip, they require more and more funding as time goes on, and bigger and better projects. I don't know that there is ever a time when the money-suck *ends* and there is plenty of cash left behind. In *that* sense, I don't know that art is ever truly "profitable." *The Gift* certainly implies it isn't:

> Each of the paths I have described is a way of getting by, not a way of getting rich. . . . No matter how the artist chooses, or is forced, to resolve the problem of his livelihood, he is likely to be poor.[436]

In the final accounting, Hyde seems to say, art will always cost more than it makes. And unlike the investor, it seems the artist can't ever stop creating, take his profits, and live on vacation for the rest of his life. Yet, Henson's career shows us that while he was alive and *working*, an artist—while not technically profiting—can *thrive* when capital is flowing. Jerry Nelson explained that Lew Grade was quite happy to spend money on *The Muppet Show* so that his studio would have something to do. This demonstrates a certain way of thinking about money, an accounting that values *flow* more than the bottom line:

> He said, "I'll put up [half] the money, provided you do it in my facility. That'll do two things," he said, "that'll get your people busy, and it'll keep my people busy." Lew Grade was great at that . . . the art of taking money out of one pocket, giving it to you, then taking it back with the other hand and putting it in the other pocket. That's big business, man. Thank God for him. He was one of the true showmen. He and his brother. They used to be hoofers.[437]

There seems to be some sleight of hand involved in making art pay, almost like the creation of a market bubble whereby the value of your work increases consistently over time because of people's belief in it. It's the difference between real dollars and "Disney dollars." Companies like Pixar, Henson, and Disney built their reputation based on quality that they had to *borrow* to pay for. The value of the company rises, and often makes back more money in the long term with toy sales, resyndication, or video recordings. But the value of the reputation demands even greater expenses, and so the bubble grows only as long as there are passionate artists working at its behest.

And then sometimes you get lucky. Legerdemain aside, Henson *did* earn millions with *Sesame Street* and *The Muppet Show*, because of their quality, and because of the continuous evolution of technology. In both cases, Henson didn't earn money based on the show *itself*; he earned money *after* the shows were made—almost karmically because it would have been hard to predict at the time. In the days before VHS and Betamax, Henson could sell only music records to fans who wanted to relive a show. But then in the late seventies, home video came along and opened up a new revenue stream. It's luck, but it's luck you can't capitalize on without quality. If a show is cheap, it's not worth watching once, but if it is *quality*, it can be rewatched, sold, and rented again and again. Today, the Sesame Workshop sells full episodes of *Sesame Street* "Classics" for $1.99 on YouTube. I don't think that anyone in 1969 could have predicted that—not even the forward-looking Jim Henson. But it's just the kind of luck innovators tend to hit upon.

WHAT WAS SO INNOVATIVE ABOUT *SESAME STREET*? EVERYTHING

One of the most innovative works in Henson's career was *Sesame Street*, a show many of us take for granted. Looking back, he took an extreme gamble in 1968 joining up with the Children's Television Workshop to change the face of children's television, especially when he was making a pretty good living at the time and just starting to break into experimental film. Looking back, few of us could imagine it. Here was an established entertainer, famous for commercials and late-night acts, who could sink his time into anything—documentaries, a nightclub, a Broadway show—and he ended up doing exactly what he said he *didn't* want to do—children's puppetry. Not only that, but joining *Sesame Street* required him to give up his commercial revenue in order to do something that paid quite little—nonprofit television. Why?

His agent, Bernie Brillstein, saw it as a natural fit: "It seemed perfect for him. He always did odd and unusual projects and this seemed to fit the mold."[438] Put simply, *Sesame Street* was innovative. The never-before, the what-if, the why-not, *Sesame Street* was more experimental than anything else Henson had done in the sixties, and that was saying a lot. A collaboration between Madison Avenue, Harvard curriculum experts, nonprofit television, and network comedy writers, *Sesame Street* took a technology—television—and asked, what can we do with it to help people?

Today *Sesame Street* is an American institution, the longest-running children's show in history. In order to be part of this moment in history, Henson relaxed his stance against making kids' TV, and he didn't negotiate for a big salary. Davis wrote that his "compensation was modest by show-business standards, perhaps an accommodation made to the fledgling nonprofit enterprise."[439] Henson stood to gain very little financially from joining *Sesame Street,* since, according to Brillstein, he never intended to license toys. Despite all the obstacles, the appeal of *the new* was so strong that Henson decided to not only provide the puppets for the show, but to create many of its original animations.

His daughter Cheryl recalled, "He used to stay up almost all night, painting each and every little stroke for the numbers that would go, you know, count up, and then count back down again."[440]

The number films were some of *Sesame Street*'s most iconic bits—and because they are works of art, they are still exciting to watch today. Henson also made stop-motion films using pebbles—they demonstrate three ways to cross a pond or stack themselves into the number twelve. He said it "took about eight hours to shoot these little rocks."[441] Henson clearly did this work not expecting profit. You can't license a stone. But I think any artist will agree: getting to do a project *worth doing* is actually a very good deal.

Jim Henson joined *Sesame Street* because, as Oz said, he loved breaking barriers. It was a first—a show devoted to social justice that used television in a *new way*—as a tool for change. Michael Davis writes, "Never before had anyone assembled an A-list of advisers to develop a series with stated educational norms and objectives. Never before had anyone viewed a show as a living laboratory, where results would be vigorously and continually tested."[442]

Innovation is not the *easy* path. It's not the road to short-term financial profit. It's the never-before. The miracle of creation. The first. The first full-length animated movie, the first full-length puppet movie, the first full-length computer-animated movie. When you're working on the never-before, your employees feel exhilarated and invested in their work, and so do you. Everyone does their best, and in that sense, it is of quality. If you create quality, you create value.

Like Henson, *Sesame Street* used an existing technology, television, in a new way. But it's important to note that it is possible to innovate even with technology that is very old. Do not overlook the potential of old technologies—puppetry, writing, a tribal drum. Innovation is not just about using the latest tools; it's an itchy temperament that is always looking to surprise itself.

Not a new technology at all, puppetry was many millennia old by the time Henson came along. In 1979, the *New York Times* wrote: "If it's possible with puppets, Henson will probably try it. 'His passion,' said Jerry Juhl, 'is to push the art form as far as he can.'"[443] And while our image of "innovation" often looks like a gadget described in *Wired* magazine, innovation at its best looks timeless, such as the way Henson "pushed the art form" of puppetry. The *New York Times* noted: "Miss Piggy's emotional range may be the broadest of any puppet in history. In fact, at her best, she may be the first round character in puppet history."[444]

Frank Oz was an innovative puppeteer. His technology was little more than human ingenuity, play, and the tilt of his own hand. Innovation is experimenting, seeing what is possible, using whatever is at hand.

TO REMEMBER IS TO MISREMEMBER, THAT IS, TO IMAGINE
CHANGE THE PAST

When we praise Henson with words like "imaginative," "creative," "original," and "innovative," we are misrepresenting what it actually means to do something *new*. Creation does not resemble the fiat "Let there be light" out of darkness. Those things that are really and truly new are so unrecognizable to us as to be invisible. Just as it takes a baby a while to see shapes in the shadows, new things confound us. "Creating," for artists, is then a process of making incremental changes to the familiar in order to let us see—to learn—the new. There is great footage of Henson playing around with googly eyes, shifting the angle a little wider from the nose and looking at the result to determine how it affects the puppet's personality. He is not inventing eyes; he is more like the "tweaker" that Gladwell describes Steve Jobs as in his 2011 *New Yorker* profile. To be original, you *must* play with the familiar.

Copying is the start of any artist's style. In his first TV show, *Sam and Friends*, Jim Henson regularly lip-synced to other people's records, and this continued even when he went on national TV, for instance the Rosemary Clooney recording, "I've Grown Accustomed to Her Face." In one famous story, a peeved Stan Freberg called Henson up, complaining he hadn't gotten any credit for the use of his songs. Freberg recalled:

> He said well you want some credit? Come on to the show tonight and I'll give you credit. I came down to the show and he said just stick your head up there any time that you want. . . . So I said excuse me . . . my name is Stan Freberg and I'd like a little credit once in a while since you seem to be doing all my records on the Ed Sullivan show . . . and so Kermit said you want some credit? I said yeah. Well here's a little credit! And he has this big mallet and they're pounding me on the head, pounding me down out of sight.[445]

Today, this would be seen as copyright infringement, since Henson didn't ask for permission or pay for it. Copyright lawyers have conditioned us to think that artists create something out of nothing and then retain full, exclusive rights to that something. This version of art makes the lawyers and entertainment companies a lot of money. But the truth is that all artists borrow from the work around them, which often contains someone else's tweaks.

Henson added to what Freberg had done, and his effort and spirit determine the novel-ness of what is now *his* intellectual property—the lip-sync. This is never a clear-cut line, though, and the way it is settled is usually very similar to the Freberg case—by a gentleman's agreement. In questions of copyright, courts tend to ask, is anyone hurt by the borrowing? Is it profits, potential profits, or simply hurt feelings? Can this damage be assuaged? Artists might ask themselves, does the borrowing hurt or help the person being copied? Arguably, Henson helped Freberg's career with this exposure.

In the current climate of copyright litigiousness, many artists look to the public domain for raw material. Copyright, according to Hyde, was intended as a way to speed works *into* the public domain where they are free for all, originally lasting only fourteen years, renewable only once.[446] Today, companies like Disney have lobbied for copyright to include the author's lifetime *plus* seventy years. For that reason, smart artists tend to tweak the uncopyrightable—works like Shakespeare and the Bible that are so old their copyrights have clearly expired—or tropes from the never-copyrighted: folktales, fairy tales, and legends.

Henson avoided copyright problems by writing many parts for witches, princes, and kings. Early in his career, many of his shows drew on fairy tales: *Tales from the Tinkerdee*, *Hey, Cinderella!*, and *The Frog Prince*, much like Walt Disney before him. Even in the last years of his life, Henson drew on folktales to make "The Storyteller," recombining Russian Cinderella tales with Celtic myths. Folklore allows an artist to play with *what's there* without getting sued.

Both Henson and Disney also drew on an American theatrical tradition—the vaudeville variety circuit. In the thirties, Walt Disney hired vaudeville comedians to perform silly gestures for his animators as inspiration for the seven dwarfs. Many *Sesame Street* comedy routines were adapted from vaudeville by director Jon Stone and "reinterpreted for our young audience,"[447] according to writer Joseph Bailey. In *The Muppet Show*, "Lydia, the Tattooed Lady," was a song popularized by Groucho Marx. Kermit sings it with a hat and cane, jacket and bow tie, the same ones used for "Simon Smith and

His Dancing Bear," to give it the feel of the variety-act tradition. English dance hall numbers were also used, such as "Waiting at the Church" and "Any Old Iron." These tongue-twisting audience sing-alongs used traditional songs that were considered "standards." The songwriters likely copyrighted them, but it was harder to prosecute infringement when a musician moved his act from theater to theater each night.

We might think of all those egghead writers who draw on Shakespeare as pale-faced grammar-dusters, but many times, they're doing it out of economic necessity. You can't play around with David Foster Wallace's or Jonathan Franzen's characters, or a lawyer may issue a cease-and-desist letter. Cinderella, a folktale, you can always play around with. No one can own her.

Doing a new take on an old tale is something Henson did throughout his career, from *Hey, Cinderella!* to *The Storyteller*'s "Sapsorrow," from *The Frog Prince* to *Hans My Hedgehog*. In fact, he used these old standards many times over, creating multiple versions of the tales. Much of Henson's style as a creator can be linked back to his love of jazz, and its theme-and-variations approach.

Jerry Nelson was asked how he invented the voice for Pa Gorg. He answered:

> My bad impression of Wallace Beery. If I did a good impression, people would say, "Oh, he's just doing Wallace Beery, or Jimmy Durante." Doing bad impressions makes it seem like I do all kinds of characters. Shh, don't tell anyone.[448]

Many artists will recognize this process—doing an impression so badly people hear it as new. By copying, the flaws in our copy often alert us to the skills that are uniquely ours. Like dreaming, art reassembles the familiar into something new. It is in the *misremembering* or the *reimagining* that the actual "creation" occurs.

REIMAGINING TELEVISION
BECOME BOTH PERFORMER AND AUDIENCE

Henson didn't invent puppetry. He was certainly aware of his place in a long-standing tradition. He noted in 1979, "Puppetry has been around for thousands of years."[449] Henson brought the ancient art of puppetry to a new medium and, better than anyone else, adapted it to look good on TV. But according to Henson, "When I started out, I didn't know that much about puppets, and not having seen that many, I wasn't overly influenced by what had gone before."[450]

We think of originators as sui generis bootstrappers, blazing their own path. A lack of education can be a boon, forcing an artist to make it up as he goes along. Yet, it would be unrealistic to think of anyone cutting an entire path in the Amazon alone. There is much talk of influences on Jim Henson—so who really *was* and who *wasn't* an influence?

Articles often cite a walkabout to Europe in 1958 as instilling in Henson the appreciation for fine puppetry, yet Henson discredits this in 1982:

> Andrew Terhone is a very good French puppeteer, does some marvelous things, and I'm sure I picked up some things from him but that was, as I say, three or four years into my work at least.[451]

Other journalists note his similarity to Edgar Bergen, the radio ventriloquist. Henson recalled hearing Bergen's characters as a boy: "I tried to imagine how they all looked as they made their jokes, but I don't remember ever thinking of them as one man and his puppets. To me, they were all human."[452] While there is no doubt that Henson learned much about humor from Bergen, he also learned more. Perhaps listening to the radio is what taught Henson to be such a "visual thinker," as is often said of him.

Henson spoke at Bergen's funeral. His speech was described in the *New York Times*:

> Certainly, Edgar Bergen's work with Charlie and Mortimer was magic. Magic in the real sense. Something happened when Edgar spoke through Charlie—things were said that couldn't be said by ordinary people. . . . We of the Muppets, as well as many others, are continuing in his footsteps. We're part of the cycle."[453]

But though Henson's characters similarly "spoke through" him and said what "couldn't be said by ordinary people," ultimately, Henson's puppets were different from Bergen's dummies in that they were far more visual, and part of that was an innovative camera trick he devised.

Henson describes the difference:

> The ventriloquist is out there facing the audience. The puppeteer works below. In that way, on television, I can watch the monitor and see how my own performance is going. No actor can do that. It's an eerie feeling but a great one because you become both performer and audience.[454]

This innovation was revolutionary, yet has no name. In behind-the-scenes footage of the Muppets, you can see each puppeteer looking down at their feet at a monitor, performing, almost as though in a mirror. But the television monitor is more than a mirror, because left and right are reversed, and so using it tends to take up a lot of focus. When Henson says "you become both performer and audience," he is implying that though you yourself are moving your hand, you might be surprised by what you see on screen, being from a different perspective than your own. For this reason, watching the Muppet performers backstage has the funny look to it of dancing while being *tethered* by the constant eye contact with a TV monitor. A *New York Times* reporter described Henson watching a monitor "as if he were waiting with some vague hunger at a microwave oven."[455] It is an intense focus.

For Caroll Spinney, his monitor is tiny and sits inside the belly of his Big Bird costume. What this does for the performer is to allow him to become a director of the scene—to position his character in the frame in a deliberate way—and to use the subtlest of head tilts to convey emotion. More than that, it functions much like Errol Morris's Interrotron, a camera system set up so that a person can be interviewed while looking into the eyes of an interviewer. Both Henson's monitors and Morris's function in essence as eye-contact-creating machines, because when Kermit is looking out into the audience and it feels like he is looking at you, that is because he really *is* looking out *at Jim Henson*, who was watching the performance on his monitor. The puppet and puppeteer are locked in eye contact through the monitor system, just as Morris and his interviewee really *are* making eye contact, and empathizing—as humans do.

It's easy to miss how incredible this invention was. Adding a screen into the equation is key. It means the puppeteer is actually performing gestures for himself to delight in. The real innovation is in using TV to watch *yourself*.

Journalists often portray Henson as being influenced by Burr Tillstrom of *Kukla, Fran and Ollie* or by Bil and Cora Baird's *Life with Snarky Parker*. Tillstrom and the Bairds had cut their teeth in live puppet theaters, where the performer crouches behind a wooden puppet stage, performing by feel, not really able to know what the audience sees. Both outfits televised puppetry before Henson, and he would eventually become friends with them. At a Puppeteers of America gathering, they can all be seen sitting around a table together, smiling. However, neither of these forbears used an extra monitor the way Henson did, and as a result, they didn't discover the need for softer puppets that gave Henson's Muppets their incredibly subtle expressions. Henson explains:

> A painted expression on a doll is all right when the audience isn't up too close, but on television it's very important that you put life and sensitivity into a puppet's face. I learned early on that the Muppets would have to have a flexibility.[456]

Tillstrom helped Henson find an apartment in New York, an agent, and his first tech guy, Don Sahlin. Tillstrom even used a backstage monitor in his show. However, according to one archive, it was used to watch other performers, not his own performance:

> [Tillstrom] operates standing erect, behind a translucent screen, resting his puppet-clad arms on a ledge and keeping his eyes to the right, watching a tiny monitor-screen that shows him what the kids and Fran are doing out front.[457]

Even so, by the time Henson met Tillstrom in 1960, he was already five years into his work, and had already developed a monitor system of his own. Likewise, the Bairds may have given Henson the idea to lip-sync to records on TV, a staple of his *Sam and Friends* work, but he was too old to have been influenced by their puppet show *Life with Snarky Parker*. Essentially, Henson learned a little bit from many people, but avoided being *overly* influenced.

Henson's humor was influenced by listening to Bergen and *The Shadow* on the radio as well as many visual artists. Falk notes, "Jim loved comics and cartoons and collected books of Pogo, Peanuts, Dennis the Menace, Li'l Abner, Charles Addams, Jules Feiffer, Roger Price, James Thurber, and Johnny Hart."[458] Since his empire was often compared to Disney's, especially in the later period, Henson was asked whether Disney was one of his main influences. His answer is clearly measured but declines the invitation: "Ah, I love Disney's stuff, you know all of his early animation stuff in particular, I always enjoyed very much. I don't think there's any main influences on me."[459]

When asked if he resisted the comparison, he said, "Yes, I do."[460] An eternal pluralist, Henson seemed more influenced by artists *working for* Disney than by the man himself. Nelson recalled Henson's excitement over a balloon-animal performer from Disneyland named Wally Boag.[461] On his first trip to Disneyland, Henson bought an animation stand and camera and played around making a cat-and-mouse film.[462] Henson was especially interested in a few of the animators who *left* Disney—the creators of Pogo and Mr. Magoo.[463] But Disney changed the face of popular entertainment, and Henson acknowledged that Disney's "big fantasy films, animated films that he did over the years were certainly an influence on me."[464]

Though influenced by many, Henson didn't live in the shadow of anyone. He gave this advice:

> Many of the things I've done in my life have basically been self-taught . . . if you learn too much of what others have done, you may tend to take the same direction as everybody else.[465]

Perhaps the way around the anxiety of influence is to combine as many good things as possible into your style. You cannot help but draw on the past if you wish to innovate. Henson describes his innovation of TV puppetry modestly: "I made extensive use of the mouth, and combined a lot of technology other people were using."[466] It sounds simple: combine a lot of technology. And yet buying the latest iPhone or tablet won't turn you into an innovator.

When we look at the technology developed by Disney, Henson, and Pixar, we start to notice that, like the puppeteer, it seems tethered to something. When Disney developed the multiplane camera, a ten-foot-tall contraption that pointed a camera down through five panes of glass, he did it in order to make *Snow White*, a story he told and retold to anyone who would listen.[467] When Pixar created the RenderMan program that made computer graphics *move*, they did so to achieve their dream of making the first full-length computer-animated film. When Henson invented the monitor-feedback system, he did it in order to make his characters look more alive on TV. All of them invented new technology, yet none of them did so for the sake of technology; they did it for the sake of art. They invented a technology that would help them achieve their narrative needs. They were working on art *first*.

For artist-entrepreneurs, technology—when it is innovative—grows in tandem with the needs of the artist. Tech follows ideas. It *hugs* them—closely.

USING NEW MEDIA
WITHOUT LOOKING LIKE A CHUMP

When Henson was in his fifties, he made *The Jim Henson Hour.* In its "Inner Tube" segments, it featured a computer-generated backdrop that was quite new for the time in order to create a control room filled with TVs. Looking back, it appears to work a lot like the Internet does today—Ted Danson magically appears on a TV set and converses with Kermit in real time, erasing distance and reveling in simultaneity. But in hindsight, it's pretty schlocky. It uses technology in a way that calls attention to itself—it's almost a celebration of technology for technology's sake. And the trouble with technology is that it keeps changing, so what's super cool and new today might just be old hat tomorrow. More than any other genre, futurism dates itself quickly.

What made "Inner Tube" schlocky? Henson was trying too hard to *keep up* with the times. The Electric Mayhem were updated to a slick MTV-looking crew whose futuristic keyboardist was named Digit. They're totally unlikable and less interesting to watch than a real music video from the era. "Inner Tube" is reminiscent of executives today who suggest a "social media initiative" headed by an intern. It's using technology when it doesn't fit a purpose—just for the sake of keeping up with the Joneses.

In the same year, Henson also made *The Storyteller*, which used music video production plus magic-lantern storytelling of folktales. This combination of old and new was graceful, beautiful, and enduring. Today, it still looks fantastic. But Henson used a digital "paint box" here, too. What makes *The Storyteller*'s technology good?

The Storyteller used technology to service the story. The good use of technology had to evolve to an end. The "Inner Tube" segments of *The Jim Henson Hour* had no story—the story was just a demonstration of the technology. The technology was its own empty achievement. To be fair, "Inner Tube" didn't have much R&D time to find a story before being hurried onto *The Jim Henson Hour. The Storyteller*, on the other hand, had Oscar-winning screenwriter Anthony Minghella. It won BAFTA Awards and an Emmy.[468] One gets the sense that Henson used flash-in-the-pan technological tricks for "Inner Tube" mainly in order to appear attractive to Disney to give him the deal he wanted for their impending merger. It was almost as though Henson knew that what many large, well-established corporations value is the *appearance*—not the reality—of innovation.

TO CGI OR NOT TO CGI

Since the 1995 hit *Toy Story*, there has been a great shift in animation to computer-generated imagery (CGI). In order to "catch up" with Pixar, competing animation companies have diverted their resources from analog to digital, a shift that has turned hand-drawn animation into something of a lost art. *Toy Story* was an amazing film, but sadly, after its box-office success, Disney—under Michael Eisner—"shut down hand-drawn animation at the studio" and started their own secret computer lab in an attempt to keep up with the times.[469] It's a classic wrongheaded business move. Because Pixar and digital animation were beating Disney at the box office, they decided to stop doing what Disney does best and start trying to copy Pixar. Similarly, Ray Katzenberg left Disney to found DreamWorks, and made *Shrek* using another California CGI studio. It's typical competitive thinking.

But Eisner's decision failed to consider that it wasn't Pixar's technology that was beating them; it was their story. Disney's animators complained of their management in 2003:

> The unique traditions of visual storytelling, humor and personality animation on which the Walt Disney Studio had thrived, gave way to politically correct sloganeering, stale one-liners and film seminar formulae to which audiences have failed to respond."[470]

In short, it was the stories of Disney's films that should have been improved, not the technology.

With the exception of "Inner Tube," this is absolutely an un-Henson-like approach. Henson's relationship to digital technology was decidedly pro—he delighted in tinkering with cameras and toys—but again, it's not about the technology you use, but in how you use it.

Henson's "Monster Eats Machine" bit is a classic that he did on *Ed Sullivan*, *The Muppet Show*, and a Muppet Meeting Film. A state-of-the-art piece of office gadgetry has a built-in tape recorder that explains all its features. As it describes them, a monster gleefully rips it off and eats it. This is, at its best, Henson's attitude toward technology. A monster knows tech is there to be eaten. Technology lives and dies by its *people*. But after the monster has devoured the entire machine, including the tape player, the machine explains its own self-destruct mechanism, and that destroys both it and the monster. The technology has been destroyed in irreverent glee. But what remains is the intention of the inventor, another *person*. Machines are just pieces of junk, we see, but the true players in this drama are the monster and the voice on the tape recording—the person who made the junk.

Eisner's mistake was that it wasn't the technology that made *Toy Story* great—it was the people who could use technology to suit their artistic goal. If Disney truly wanted to compete with Pixar, they should have increased funding to their hand-drawn animation studio. But by fetishizing the *effects* of innovators, Disney defunded innovation. Today, Pixar president Ed Catmull has taken over Disney Animation Studios, in part because his idea of how to run a creative company worked much better than Eisner's. In an article published in the *Harvard Business Review*, he argued openly that it is more important to find good people than to find good ideas. About 50 percent of businesspeople he's talked to think that ideas—something created by people—are more important than people. "It reflects a profound misunderstanding . . ."[471] Catmull writes. According to its president, the most important part of Pixar was its people.

Many exalt technology, but the monster is irreverent, as is the inventor. All technology is a mechanical embodiment of someone's dream. The machine can be destroyed, taken apart, and *used* to create something new, but the voice of the inventor is what endures. Henson's attitude toward technology resembles this gleeful monster—he was excited to be on the cutting edge of digital technology, but his excitement wasn't about the technology itself, it was about how he could eat it.

Henson would undoubtedly be creating in digital media today. In 1988, he pronounced that high-definition TV was the future.[472] He said he would have used digital video effects on the ending of *The Dark Crystal* if the resolution had been high enough at the time.[473] As early as 1970, he visited the Scanimate computer image software lab and experimented with its graphics—glowing green circles resembling primitive screen-savers.[474] In 1990, working with Pacific Data Images—now DreamWorks's studio—Henson made the world's first computer-generated puppet character, Waldo C. Graphic.[475]

According to Falk:

> Jim was always interested in the next technological advancement to further express his creative vision, so it's not surprising that he would seek out the earliest innovations in computer animation. . . . It's unclear how Jim learned about Scanimate, but he had been interested in electronics in general and had used his Moog synthesizer to great effect on numerous projects. His colleague, Jerry Juhl, was an early adapter of computers and would have been intrigued with the process as well.[476]

Steve Whitmire perhaps put it best in a fan interview when he said, "Whatever the new technology there was, he always wanted to jump right in the middle of it."[477] Digital was certainly where Henson was headed.

Yet I don't think Jim Henson would be thrilled about some uses of digital technology. Today, the Disney Company scrubs the arm-rods out of every shot in which a Muppet arm rises into the camera frame. Whitmire explained to a ToughPigs interviewer:

> One of the things that Disney wants to do, and it's very expensive, but they do it on virtually everything we do, is they digitally remove the rods. You see Piggy sitting in a chair on that special and motioning, and there's no arm rods. It throws me sometimes, I expect to see the arm rods, but they removed every one from that piece, so Kermit's just leaping through the air.[478]

Although Henson loved "to jump into the middle of new technology," he jumped in to *experiment*, to *play*, not to perfect. The kind of perfection Disney gives the Muppets—erasing flaws—is not at all thrilling. It asks graphic artists to work for hours with a little "erase" tool on their console. What's fun or interesting or new about that? Nothing, except more cases of carpal tunnel syndrome. This is not the kind of thing that Henson would "spark to," to use his phrase.

Even Pixar, which has not been without its "repetitive stress injuries,"[479] is run with the philosophy that "[t]echnology inspires art, and art challenges the technology." Catmull writes, "Walt Disney understood this. He believed that when . . . technology and art are together, magical things happen."[480] Scrubbing rods out of film frames is technology without the art.

Frank Oz once said of Henson, "He pulls together technological elements in such a way as to achieve an artistic end."[481] Not to achieve a seamless, flawless, perfect end—an *artistic* end. Art *isn't* perfect. It's human. It's about expressing something about life, and if it doesn't do that, it's not art.

When creating his lush, expensive *Muppet Show*, sometimes Muppets were improvised from items bought at the hardware store.[482] We know Muppets have been made from bath mats and coats and some seem to resemble toilet scrubbers. For the fan, their do-it-yourself spirit makes the Muppets even *more* magical. Knowing that someone scrubbed rods off film for hours doesn't. It's depressing to picture. The poor technician who had to do that didn't get to play, to build, or create. He was essentially an in-betweener, like in the days of Disney's first factory studio, the grunt workers who filled in the cels between major gestures, essentially RenderMan programs. In 1941, Disney's in-betweeners went on strike, one holding a sign that said, "1 Genius Against 1,200 Guinea Pigs."[483]

In contrast, Henson's workshop sounds more like the kind of place an artist would enjoy working hard. In the eighties, Finch described the Henson Creature Shop boldly: "Such a seething tide of vitality . . . the Muppet universe is infinitely protean."[484] It's hard to imagine such energy in a room of rod-scrubbers or in-betweeners. There is technology that enlivens the soul and technology that dulls it.

This is how *Henson* removed the rods from his characters. In 1980, *The Muppet Show* did a Pinocchio number. It used a new technology called Chromakey to remove the puppeteers' heads—which were covered in the same blue as the backdrop. Henson effectively CGIed them out, but at the same time, he *added* strings—fake strings from which Pinocchio broke free. Henson used the CGI to do something surprising, showing a Muppet moving in a new way, to make a joke *about* puppetry, not hide it. When you hear this, it makes the scene even more magical. The how'd-they-*think*-of-that factor is high. Henson always seemed to be aware that how he used technology would be—or would eventually be—part of the story, part of the act. It was Henson's job to hide the rods, and it was our job to find them. It was our job to wonder, *how'd they do that?*

Disney's rod-scrubbing is by contrast a simple deception. It's trying to make puppetry resemble animation, which of course, it isn't. Our job as audience members is to not think too hard about how they did it.

It is perhaps unsurprising that Karen Prell, the puppeteer who performed Red Fraggle, later went on to work at Pixar. So did her husband, another Henson puppeteer. Prell told a fan interviewer, "I think Jim would have loved what Pixar is doing. The exciting, creative atmosphere there is very similar to that at Muppets when they were doing *Fraggle Rock*. Maybe that's why I've been able to fit in so well at Pixar and feel at home."[485]

With the experience of working as both a Muppet performer and a Pixar animator, Prell describes the difference:

> There's such a joy in spontaneous performing and expression in puppeteering that I miss very much and hope I can get a chance to do again sometime. There's such a totally different mindset with animating. You're able to get a lot more detail and flexibility in the movement and able to revise and revise and revise, and really able to get things perfected a lot more than you can with live action. Still, something about the energy and spontaneity of performing live puppets brings its own flavor to characters and storytelling. . . . [With animation] there's a lot of planning, a lot of working with numbers. I equate it to performing while doing your taxes.[486]

Animation and puppetry are different, and one should not try to be the other. Both Pixar and Henson valued *people* as the creators of both art and innovation. Pixar was able to achieve great technological feats because it kept a core group of talented people together—from the days of Lucas to Jobs and now Disney. Henson created the Creature Shop as his in-house technological lab for engineers, machinists, and builders, because, "By keeping a group of people together . . . you can make it better every time and build on your past work."[487] For Henson, it was important to bring together the *people*, not the technology itself. That would be stupid.

One of Henson's most important tech guys, Faz Fazakas, made "mechanicals." He was a machinist—a lost art in our age of computers, but many of his rigs look better on film today than your average CGI-scape. That's not because he used radio control vs. a computer—it's because he was a person who really *cared* about doing his job well. Prell explains what made working at *Fraggle Rock* great: "Everybody wanting to do it well and not wanting to compromise and cut corners.[488] The message that great technology conveys is this: there are people in this world—tinkerers—who will work on things until they get them to work. That's what's so exciting about Pixar and Henson Associates. With these companies, it's not the medium; it's the message.

Henson is quoted in the *New York Times*:

> "I like mixing all things together," says Mr. Henson, as if all the assembled flesh and blood, ingeniously hinged creatures and colorful electronic stuff were troughs of finger-paints for squishing and smiling over. A tall, thin, bearded man, he often speaks of his work: "One technique doesn't negate the other. It becomes more exciting. You can do almost anything in terms of image."[489]

Henson seemed to "spark to" technology used like finger-painting. He used it to cut corners or to cover up, and he wouldn't use it when it became too robotic, like the robots in the Hall of Presidents at Disneyland. "The automated shows very often look incredibly wooden to me because it's that sense of performance that's not there," Henson said.[490] Technology is not across-the-board innovative. He told Judy Harris in 1982:

> [It] always has to be a key thing to us: that all of the mechanical things and all of the radio controlled stuff is always at the service of the performer in order to try to get a more complete performance . . . the performance is where the humanity is, where the relationship is and I think that has to stay at the heart of it all.[491]

If a technology didn't express "humanity," Henson wouldn't use it.[492] Waldo C. Graphic—the computer-generated Muppet created in partnership with Pacific Data Images—clearly wasn't yet good enough yet to use for any length of time. Still, it was fun to tinker around with, and maybe that's the point.

THE SCHOOL OF FAILURE
THE ONLY WAY TO LEARN WITHOUT COPYING

Henson was careful not to copy other artists. On *The Muppet Show*, he rejected one bit in a writers' meeting for being too similar to a Mel Brooks movie. "I think," said Henson, "the idea is just too close."[493] This was not an issue of copyright. While expressions can be copyrighted, no one can own an idea. It was more like a professional courtesy. Innovation tends to lead to differentiation, which is good for the whole guild. It makes room for everyone.

But if you don't copy someone, how do you know what works? Trial and error.

Henson saw it as a "good thing" that he had learned in this manner:

> I think we, as the Muppets, broke new ground because we approached puppetry from a different angle. I had never worked with puppets when I was a kid, and even when I began on television, I really didn't know what I was doing. I'm sure that this was a good thing, because I learned as I tackled each new problem.[494]

Though Henson did earn a college degree at the University of Maryland, his path was incredibly self-directed. Irreverent about peoples' opinions, he took classes in the "Home Ec" department, traditionally a women's major, in order to practice the skills like sewing and puppetry that he needed. Falk also notes of his first puppetry class, "According to [Jane] and the professor, Edward Longley, the freshman Jim was the star and practically taught the course."[495] Henson graduated in six years because he was a part-time student. For the most part, he was learning by doing at the local TV station. There, he learned about cameras, drawing and photographing them.[496] He said he wasn't "creatively very proud of" that work, but it was "really experimenting."[497] The best way to educate yourself is not necessarily to enroll in school, but to learn by doing, learn by trying, and often learn by *failing.*

You do not need to go to school to be successful. Bill Gates, Steve Jobs, Mark Zuckerberg, and Walt Disney did not have college degrees, and certainly not MBAs. They learned by doing, and often by failing.

Yet while these entrepreneurs didn't get MBAs, they did read books. According to Falk, the teenage Henson "checked out some books from the public library for instruction—one was Obrtazov's 1950 book, *My Profession*."[498] Walt Disney took night classes on animation, picked the brain of an animator he knew, and may have taken a correspondence course. He also took out the only book on animation from the Kansas City Library, *Animated Cartoons: How They Are Made, Their Origin and Development.*[499] Pixar also looked to a book, when they incorporated. *To Infinity and Beyond* explains:

> The executives then running Lucasfilm, [Smith] said, didn't seem to realize that the true value of the computer division was the talent that had produced the technology, not the technology itself. So Catmull and Smith got a "How to start a business" book, drew up a plan for a

> 40-person company . . . it was agreed—the Computer Division would strike out on its own.[500]

Many careers start with a library book, because self-directed learning is the kind that really sticks. More valuable than an MBA—which might indoctrinate you to think in a business-as-usual state of mind—are the cheaper tools available to anyone: library books, an adult education classes, joining a guild, or engaging with a community of other entrepreneurs.

Of course, these things will not protect one against failure. Bill Gates's first business, Traf-O-Data, failed. Disney's Laugh-O-Gram Studio declared bankruptcy. Is it risky to go it alone? Yes. But that is the only way you will truly learn. Business school only hedges you against failure by delaying the inevitable. And in the meantime it perniciously indoctrinates you to the common way of doing something. To go "the same direction as everybody else." There's a reason business-as-usual is so competitive and cutthroat; there's a lot of competition in that pool.

HOW TO INNOVATE FOR THE REST OF YOUR LIFE

It is the uncommon entrepreneur who can make her own market. Though she may be unready at first, trying and failing is the only way to learn. To be uncommon, avoid being overly influenced by what has come before. Use your influences promiscuously—appreciating what is good about each one. Put many technologies into your toolbox and start finger-painting.

Do not fetishize a technology just because it is new. Use whatever works well. Think toilet scrubbers, not rod scrubbers. Henson would use any technology—any trick would do, even something as simple as a well-placed mirror under a stool in one *Muppet Show* scene, to create an elegant illusion of Kermit sitting on a stool with no puppeteer beneath. In *The Dark Crystal*, Henson had a Lucasfilm artist paint on glass for one backdrop, a trick dating back to the earliest days of cinema. It didn't matter what the technology was, but it had to work toward making the characters and story feel *alive*. For Henson, that came from performance, something that comes out of a human being in a state halfway between work and play.

Quality is not perfection, as Disney believed. It is not achieving exactly what you envisioned, everyone else be damned. It is not asking people to erase mistakes or to do the work of robots. Quality is asking for one more take, getting everyone to focus and work well together, helping others to co-create and achieve their own personal best.

Pay attention to the emerging technology of your time, because it will become the newest ingredient to your mix. The emerging technology in Henson's time was television. For many of us, the emerging technology will involve the Internet. You might look at what innovations happened at the time of your birth. Video games? Streaming videos? Texting? Word processors? What technology has fascinated you? How might you combine that tech with something very old?

Be on the lookout for all that is uncopyrighted, or uncopyrightable. Folktales, well-worn comedy setups, and very old literature. What is in the public domain belongs to everyone, especially artists. But when you try to copy your heroes, do it as a tool for self-exploration. Notice the flaws in the copy. They are uniquely yours, and they may not be flaws at all. How might you use them to open up a space for yourself?

Think of innovation not simply as doing something new, but as doing something amazing. Many rush to copyright their work in order to keep up with the Joneses, but this is a small way of thinking. Copyright is merely a legal restatement of the artist's creed to not copy one another. Think not about how to register your work, but rather how to use the power of innovation to make people trust your name, which is naturally your trademark and no one else's.

Realistically, file sharing has erased the twentieth century's copyright goldmine for artists. It is almost as though we are going back to the performance-based economy of vaudeville and dance-hall—with DJs, lectures, and appearances meaning more than the songs, words, and recordings that can be duplicated. With the *Billboard* Hot 100 now counting YouTube views in their rankings, it seems that recordable material has a different role in the artist's ledger than it did before. "Likes" don't earn you money, but they earn you exposure, which earns you performance gigs. Notice how technology plays into your work, because we cannot help but be affected by it.

The concept of the Internet was born around the time I was, 1980, and I've been playing around there since high school, when I made websites and used the message boards of indie rock labels. Going back earlier than that, my dad instilled in me a love of video games and keyboard typing. I could probably *live* online. New technology is great. This book wouldn't be possible without Twitter and Facebook sending my work viral. But the truth is that my most clutch technology is ten years old—Microsoft Word for Windows XP. Having a flip phone is also critical for my art; it gives me the ability to turn off my connection and *focus*. And I still marvel at the old technology that works like magic: pen and paper.

Continue to invest in your own R&D, to innovate your art with technology old and new. Henson didn't wait for a network to fund him; he put his own money into the development of his projects. Innovation costs a lot—not because of technology but because of man-hours. And yet, even if your work doesn't earn you profit for the time being, its quality is what can earn money down the road—sometimes years later. Karmically, Henson, Disney, and Pixar were rewarded financially for their costly artistic risks. This does not mean a payday is inevitable, but it means it is worth trying. As new technologies are being developed faster than ever, it makes sense to trust that if you make something of quality, it could increase in value. Hollywood insiders thought Henson was crazy to spend so much money on his films, twice as much as Disney was spending at the time.

Now, thanks to DVDs and Blu-ray, we will pay to watch Henson's most glorious scenes remastered: the pool number with Piggy in *The Great Muppet Caper*—a tribute to 1940s Hollywood, Piggy, in a couture ball gown, underwater, with synchronized swimmers; the crumbling tower in *The Dark Crystal*—filmed once and months of work actually destroyed on camera; and that "Couldn't We Ride" bike reverie in *The Muppets Take Manhattan*—each of these was a one-of-a-kind first, never to be copied. They give Henson's work a timelessness—his projects can be rewatched many times and continue to earn well beyond their one-time budgets.

As an artist, you probably aren't thinking of an endgame in which you get to quit art and just enjoy life. And so, the ever-increasing cost of quality should not be depressing to you as long as you can find a way to get money to flow long enough for you to make your quality projects. The worth of your company—the final tally—isn't your ultimate goal. It's the ability to keep making great art. The next lesson recommends you hire someone to keep watch on the numbers for you. Because in order to leave a lasting legacy, you don't want to die with the most money in your account; you want to leave behind pieces of work that feel as alive as you once were.

The work environment for Henson's projects was one in which artists really *cared* about what they were doing, and the amazement audiences feel correlates directly to the glee felt by Henson and the people who worked with him. Get out of companies that don't value people and that don't let them innovate. When you are ready, start your own company that will.

LESSON 7

BRING TOGETHER A TRIAD

SEPARATION OF ROLES

As we have seen, both Disney and Henson were innovators, and yet there have always been key differences in their companies—one being scale. In 2012, the Disney Company employed 15,600 people while The Henson Company (as it has been known since 1997) employed only 300.[501] Much of the size of Disney today can be attributed to the eighties-era expansion by the team of Frank Wells, Jeffrey Katzenberg, and Michael Eisner, who saved a company that was essentially failing.

Yet the difference goes back further. Though they each started with just one person, the most telling comparison would be when each company made its first movie.

To make 1937's *Snow White*, Disney's studio grew from 300 to 1,200 employees.[502] At the time of 1979's *Muppet Movie*, "between 1975 and 1980, the company went from having 30 people on the payroll to employing over 130."[503] And discounting freelancers, in 1979, Henson's *full-time* employees were numbered at a meager 71.[504] Movies require many hands; however, the Henson and Disney companies differed by an order of magnitude.

Though it was compared to a college campus in the thirties, Disney has always been a *huge* corporation, and by contrast Henson has always had "a very fuzzy, Grateful Dead kind of sensibility,"[505] according to one *Sesame Street* writer in 1990. The same year, *Newsweek* called Henson's a "family-run . . . shop."[506]

Over the years, more than a few journalists have made comparisons between the companies, implying Henson would eventually grow to match Disney's scale. He chose not to, for very good reason. But with this key difference set aside, the *structures* of Henson and Disney's companies look similar. They started, respectively, in a basement and a garage, and they each had a triumvirate.

A TRIUMVIRATE

In a 1979 *New York Times* article, John Culhane noticed the appearance of the triumvirate:

> Walt Disney Productions in the 1930s was only a little company in which Walt Disney ran the creative end; his brother, Roy, ran the business end, and an attorney named Gunther R. Lessing did their legal work. Henson Associates, too, is run by a triumvirate. Henson is free to control the creative end, he said, "because of working with lawyer Al Gottesman and producer David Lazer," a former I.B.M. executive. "The two of them run the business side. It's wonderful for me."[507]

Culhane gives us a good picture of the business side of both Disney's and Henson's operations. Yet this is not the full picture. Both Gottesman and Lazer are responsible for the business side of Henson's company, and to this list, we should add Henson's agent,

Bernie Brillstein, and—for a while—producer Lew Grade. Though they are not technically part of the company, Henson's business couldn't run without them.

But in my mind, there is also a second triad structure at play. The real triumvirate that we see at Henson, Disney, and even Pixar contains three necessary ingredients for success: business, *tech*, and art.

We might think of it as the three species in *Fraggle Rock*: Gorgs (business), Doozers (tech), and Fraggles (art). The Gorgs own a castle, wear crowns, and think they are royalty. The Fraggles love to play, sing, and dance all day. The Doozers enjoy building, preferring to work their cares away. Each one of these groups made Henson's company successful—businessmen, artists, and engineers. But they have very different modes of working, and though they are interconnected, it is very important that they sometimes be kept separate.

Perhaps the most similar of the groups are the builders and artists. Art and technology are both innovative, and Pixar's head engineer, Ed Catmull, went so far as to call his work "art."[508] In Henson's company there was much overlap. Dave Goelz started at the company as a puppet builder, but decided he wanted to puppeteer. He went on to create the character of Gonzo by adding an eye-opening mechanism to an old Frackle puppet that was lying around the workshop from 1970's *The Great Santa Claus Switch*. Similarly, the engineers at Pixar dabbled in animation. Catmull's senior thesis was a graphic of a moving hand. And at Disney, animator Ub Iwerks's tinkering led to both the multiplane camera *and* the first sketch of Mickey. And yet technological innovation is very different from artistic innovation. In *Fraggle Rock*, Cotterpin Doozer envied the exciting lives of Fraggles, but ultimately decided she wasn't one. There are things that Doozers hate—such as swimming—and those are some of the things Fraggles love.

Though a famous animator in his own right, ultimately, Ub Iwerks decided, after developing the first multiplane animation camera, that he would rather work on technical problems in Disney's studio. Similarly, Ed Catmull and his fellow Pixar engineer Alvy Ray Smith decided to bring on a true "artist," CalArts-trained John Lasseter, in order to give their technology beauty and pathos.

In Henson's company, there were many non-performing builders in "the shop." Don Sahlin rigged explosions and built Rowlf from one of Henson's sketches. Faz Fazakas built radio-controlled puppetry systems for Doozers and Gorgs, and the puppet builders in Caroly Wilcox's workshop sewed puppets together that brought storybooks like *Emmet Otter* to life. Together with Henson, costume designer Bonnie Erickson discovered a new way to create puppets by sculpting foam and then electrostatically "flocking" it, so foam Piggy has the same fleece look as cloth-covered Kermit. Builder Kermit Love designed marionettes as well as Big Bird and Snuffleupagus. None of them performed on-screen. Their work was art-of-a-sort, but art that was decidedly backstage and, for lack of a better word, *impersonal.* What I mean by this is not that the builder didn't leave his mark on the puppet, because great craftsmanship always retains a trace of a human touch. What I mean by "impersonal" is that the work could be easily removed from its person.

By contrast, performers and other artists create things that are more *personal,* in the sense that their developments can be used by them alone, and cannot really be transferred. Artists can't tell someone else how to do what they do. In the artist category, Henson had himself, his puppeteers who performed characters (Oz and Nelson), his writers (Juhl and Stevenson) who imagined scenarios, and his conceptual designers (Frith and Froud) who sketched people and even worlds. These are the people who get to dream up intangibles that others are tasked with building. And in many cases, *figuring out how* to build. I do not mean to imply that the builders' work was easier or less important, but that it didn't require as much of an ego.

Like the dwarfs in *Snow White,* the tech side spends all day digging for jewels, but when they leave the mine, they leave the key hanging right next to the door, not seeming to bother with ownership. The Doozers spend all day building constructions out of radishes, only so that the Fraggles can eat them. The "art" of engineers is a kind that is meant to be used by others. It doesn't bother with displaying the mark of its inventor, working best if it looks like whoever is using it. On the other hand, the dance of a Fraggle is distinctly *personal*; it resembles that Fraggle and that Fraggle alone. Red and Boober move nothing alike. This is art in the more traditional sense—writers, painters, and performers, makers of intellectual property that feels decidedly *human*.

This is something we all acknowledge, because we treat copyright and patents quite differently. With the patent, the inventor registers clear instructions at the Library of Congress for how to make the invention. With a copyright, the work itself is registered and the "how-to" is left an object of wonder. Many artists don't know *how* they do what they do, let alone how to teach someone else to do it. Patents last only twenty years before the product enters the public domain, much less than the seventy-plus years of a copyright. The implication is that a tech advance is meant to be used by all; an art advance is meant to be used by the artist. In practice, this means that the names of tech developers are often left to obscurity.

We all know the names Walt Disney and Jim Henson, but few of us know the name Ub Iwerks, who gave Mickey his iconic circles-and-ovals shape, a true pioneer of animation and Disney's first partner. Disney biographer Neal Gabler explains:

> Iwerks's remoteness and social awkwardness . . . made him a perfect complement for Walt Disney, which is no doubt why Iwerks sought him out. While Iwerks, who was diligent, meticulous, and extremely facile with the brush, stayed at his drawing board, Walt could talk up customers and hustle business.[509]

History has not immortalized Ub Iwerks for creating Mickey Mouse. Likewise, we don't know the name Larry Jameson, an electro-mechanical tinkerer for the Henson workshop, but we know his woodworking—Kermit's banjo, for instance, and the intricate replicas of a Les Paul guitar and Fender bass we see in *The Muppet Show*.[510] These technicians contributed to the quality of the art, and yet the credit seems to go elsewhere.

This may be less exploitative than *symbiotic*, as some prefer to work in obscurity and avoid the anxiety of the limelight—the way notoriety tends to isolate a person from his peers. In an episode of *Fraggle Rock*, the Doozers don't understand the concept of "taking credit." They build "for the joy of building." When two Doozers named after tech devices—Flange and Modem—fight over who is to get credit for a particularly good tower, Cotterpin tells them, "You two are acting like a couple of Fraggles." For Doozers, the work is its own reward and credit; jealousy and competition are un-Doozerly.[511]

The relationship between art and technology is mutually beneficial. The art that builders make is impersonal—it can be used by others to make *their* art. When Fraggles eat Doozer constructions, far from upset, the Doozers are *happy*. It means they get to build even more the next day. It goes without saying that artists are excited about new technology—it gives them more opportunity to dream up something never seen before. As Catmull said, "technology inspires art, and art challenges the technology."[512]

Disney was fascinated by the multiplane camera that Iwerks built when he was running his own company, and had his engineers make one for *Snow White* to give it the depth of background movement that we see in real life. John Lasseter used Pixar's RenderMan system to turn everyday objects like desk lamps and plastic toys into characters that are fully human. Jim Henson, fascinated by television cameras, set up a monitor feedback system to give puppets microexpressions like real people. He used Sahlin's explosions to express hard truths about humanity in a way that makes you laugh out loud. And he used Faz Fazakas's radio-controlled puppets to make surprisingly big puppets, surprisingly tiny puppets, and puppets rowing downstream with no puppeteers drowned underwater.

Each of these technologies became art, but notably, each was developed *alongside* an artistic goal, hugging it like a double helix. The tech guys—Pixar's Ed Catmull and his team, Disney's Ub Iwerks, and Henson's special-effects guys—all had artistic aspirations in mind, developed technology to suit artistic aims, and *then* handed off their creations to artists who could truly make those tools *sing*. We have seen with Henson's "Inner Tube" what happens when technology becomes disjointed from art: it dates itself quickly and it lacks heart. The relationship between art and tech is thus one that works best when the two work *closely*, with constant cross-pollination.

While the combination of tech and art is crucial to Henson's success, it is a relatively uncomplicated relationship. Those who like to tinker get to, and are happily paid to do so without stamping their personality on it. For Sahlin, perhaps, it was enough to create an explosion; he didn't need to trademark it "A Don Sahlin Production." Artists tend to understand inventors. The artist recognizes the glee the techie feels making a device as the same high he gets from making stories and characters. As a boss, the artist perhaps implicitly understands how a techie thinks—he loves to tinker, just like the artist.

On the other hand, the relationship between the business side and art is *hard* to get right. Moneymen tend to treat technology and art in the *same* way—at worst like commodities and at best like talent. In his *Harvard Business Review* article, Pixar's Catmull notes in a section titled "Power to the Creatives" that the creative power in a film *has* to reside with the creative leadership, not with the corporate executives. So, at Pixar, the development department's job is not to tell the artists what to do, but to "help directors refine their own ideas" and "give them enormous leeway."[513] Yet, Catmull says, most companies aren't run this way, because most executives want to minimize the financial risks of art. It a rare businessperson who can stomach artistic risk. This is why Jim Henson carefully selected the right kind of businesspeople for his organization, and trained them over the years—the way he trained his creatives—to understand the process.

While art and technology have a nice way of feeding off each other, there are so many ways that art and money can come into conflict. Businesspeople often fail to understand how art works. Henson's agent, Bernie Brillstein, once tried to convince him to do a remake of *Gigi* with the puppeteer as the romantic lead. Henson wasn't interested. Later, Brillstein successfully convinced Henson to make the cheaper-looking-than-usual *Muppet Babies* series in order to get exposure. There were times when Henson had to say "no" to his businesspeople, and because of the way he built his company, he could.

On the other hand, we can understand *why* businesspeople have problems with artists: art leeches money. Financing high-budget films may have led Lew Grade to lose his media empire. Art requires a large investment in money that may not be repaid—essentially a gift. Any business professional will tell you that doesn't make business sense. There are many ways the relationship between art and business can go very wrong. It's only natural, since each has its own ends, yet when art and money can work *together*, they tend to create the greatest art the world has ever seen.

The primary reason Henson, Disney, and Pixar were able to achieve symbiosis with their business departments rested in *who* those businesspeople were. Walt Disney's brother Roy, Pixar's majority investor Steve Jobs, and Henson's business guys—agent Bernie Brillstein, lawyer Al Gottesman, manager David Lazer, and producer Lew Grade—all had a *personal* connection to the artist and all valued the art as the thing that made the money possible. More than that, these uncommon businessmen were able to function—in a way—as a barrier, keeping art and money separate.

Walt Disney found the keeper to his purse strings in his own family—his brother Roy, whom Gabler called "his guardian angel."[514] This fraternal connection turned out to be crucial to the success of the business, because Walt could more easily fend off Roy than a typical manager. Gabler explains:

> Dave Hand recalled a meeting where Roy complained, as he often did, that the pictures were costing too much. "There was complete silence," Hand related. "Then Walt's loose eyebrow shot up at an unusually sharp angle, and turning to Roy in an uncompromising matter-of-fact straight-from-the-shoulder answer, said quite simply, 'Roy, *we'll* make the pictures, *you* get the money.' That was that."[515]

For Henson, finding the right business guy started with a friend.

YOUR AGENT WORKS FOR YOU BUT YOU ALSO WORK FOR YOUR AGENT

In 1960, Jim Henson attended the Puppeteers of America Festival and met television puppeteer Burr Tillstrom of *Kukla, Fran and Ollie*.[516] Tillstrom's agent was a young man named Bernie Brillstein at William Morris, and Henson had no agent. To help out a friend, Tillstrom begged Brillstein to meet Henson. In Brillstein's words, "He said please, for me, do me a favor, get him off my back."[517] Serendipitously, three things came together to secure Henson's agent—his friend's endorsement, a mystical connection, and a stroke of luck, as Brillstein recalled:

> "You'll like him," said Tillstrom. "He's funny. See him."
>
> I didn't want to, but I said okay.
>
> When the friend showed up, I couldn't believe my eyes. In walked this guy who looked like a cross between Abe Lincoln and Jesus: six three, hippie arts-and-crafts leather suit. . . . He'd brought a big box of puppets. When he put them on his hands, it was magic. . . . For some mysterious reason, although I'd never met anyone like Jim before, when Jim performed I *understood* it. I got it. Instinct told me what to do.
>
> After Jim left, my boss [at William Morris] called and said, "Bernie, have you ever heard of Jim Henson and the Muppets? Someone wants to book him into Radio City Music Hall."
>
> "Heard of him? I said. "I just signed him!"
>
> We were together thirty years, until he died.[518]

One gets the sense that it was fate, and yet I've never heard that Henson actually performed at Radio City Music Hall that year. It's more likely that Henson himself arranged for William Morris to get a call about him on the same day he auditioned—maybe saying they were already his agency, or maybe getting a friend to call as a publicity stunt. Whatever the case, Henson got to Brillstein, through enough friends that it appeared he was everywhere.

But more importantly, Henson's *work* got to Brillstein. Laughter is a magical thing. According to Brillstein, "Jim appealed to my perverse sense of humor."[519] Henson and Brillstein didn't see the world the same way: "I don't think we ever completely understood, in our guts, what the other did,"[520] Brillstein said. Though Brillstein didn't "understand" how the artist worked, he "understood" the art, "for some mysterious reason." The relationship between an agent and an artist is a very strange one—and that is the nature of the job.

Although Brillstein worked hard for Jim Henson, he was not a Henson employee. To be technically accurate, Jim Henson was Brillstein's client. In practice what this means is that both of them worked for each other. Either one of them could fire the other. The best comparison might be to business partners or husband and wife. Henson was already familiar with this kind of relationship because he and his wife, Jane, incorporated a business partnership in 1958.[521]

Before finding an agent, Henson had already been doing *Sam and Friends*, commercials, and television appearances. Then in 1964, he moved his family to New York City and signed Brillstein as his manager.[522] It is telling that Brillstein's business logo when he started his own company was a turtle[523]—Henson was known for his long patience, and any businessman who worked with him probably had to have an even longer patience. Henson paid homage to Brillstein on-screen—he named the agent played by Dom

DeLuise in *The Muppet Movie* Bernie, and any time Piggy calls her agent and gives him a mouthful, it's also Bernie.

Agents typically take 15 percent of an artist's deals. That may seem like a lot for someone who doesn't perform or share in any of the work—an agent's work tends to reside in phone calls. So why did Henson need a 15-percent man when he was clearly so good at networking himself? Brillstein did indeed get Henson more commercials and appearances, including a weekly gig for Rowlf on *The Jimmy Dean Show* that significantly increased his national exposure. But Brillstein's value went beyond the actual jobs he was able to get Henson. More philosophically, an agent is someone who makes money *when you make money*. In effect, an agent makes you make money. If you don't, your agent leaves you. The nature of the relationship is such that, in many cases, a person with an agent will earn more than a person without one. He has two people looking out for his financial health.

In business, the client is always right, but if agent and artist work for each other, who has final say? When it came to what work Henson would do, it was Henson who had the veto power.

Brillstein tried to convince Henson to do many things that he refused. If we revisit an earlier quote from Brillstein, we notice the balance of power favors the artist in the agent-artist partnership. According to Brillstein:

> When we were first together, I'd get offers of fifty or sixty grand for him to do a commercial. Jim needed the money, so I'd say, "Let's do it to pay the overhead." Sometimes he'd agree, but usually he'd pass. "Not this one," he'd say. "Because they want to own the character."[524]

Of course, Henson was not a despot. He could be reasoned with. As Brillstein explains, it was often more of a dialog, as when Jim and Jane debated his idea to merchandise:

> I completely understood their hesitation, but as Jim's manager I was paid to have my own long-term vision. Fortunately, Jim was not the kind to act stubborn and say, "I just won't do it." If I had a counterargument, he always listened and considered it fairly.[525]

Perhaps the nature of the agent-artist relationship makes open dialog like this more likely. As in a marriage, either party may walk away at any point. If either side can leave, both sides can have a say. But this marriage of equality requires the artist to put his foot down more than he may like. There is a reason that 85 percent of profits go to the artist, and that is because an artist can make art without an agent, but an agent needs an artist to make money. There are times when an artist needs to just say no.

The agent is a gentle reminder to make more money, but not from a boss, and not at all costs. The relationship between Brillstein and Henson was in many ways like the relationship between Roy and Walt Disney. Both Roy and Brillstein looked out for their artists in a paternal way—letting the artist have his way more often than not, but quietly steering him to financial solvency.

Sesame Street profiler Michael Davis said:

> I know they weren't separated by age in that many years, but [Brillstein] took on a more paternal role with Jim as his son, and I really do think that Jim's death was not unlike when a parent loses a child."[526]

Neal Gabler notes a similar paternalism in Roy Disney: "He admitted that he was afraid that without his protection, his "fervent protection," Walt would have been taken advantage of."[527]

In fact, Walt had been. When he got a contract to make Laugh-O-Grams, he asked for "thirty cents a foot,"[528] which was at cost, meaning he worked for free. His business strategy, Gabler wrote, "was excellence," not money. Gabler often notes Walt Disney's "disdain,"[529] as he called it, for money:

> "If you want to know the real secret of Walt's success," longtime animator Ward Kimball would say, "it's that he never tried to make money. He was always trying to make something that he could have fun with to be proud of."[530]

This led to great art, but it didn't *always* lead to staying in business, and so it was important to the Disney studios that *someone* be good with money. Snow White needed her prince to come and save her, and so did Disney. Time and time again, Roy got Walt the money he needed to make his masterpieces.

Yet Roy knew that his brother's talent was something special, something he did not have himself. For that reason, he became his brother's keeper. Similarly, Brillstein wrote:

> I called Jim Henson and his band of puppeteers "the arts and crafts set." They wanted as little as possible to do with the money-first, deal-making, soul-killing aspects of show business that I confronted every day. Jim didn't want to ignore reality, he just didn't want any contact with the parts that were pollutants and alien to his company's creativity. It was better, Jim believed, to live in a fantastic world of creatures and characters that tried to speak to the

> humanity in us all through magical performances. He was a hippie. That's why he had me.[531]

The "moonbeam" aspect of Henson was precisely why Brillstein *needed* Henson, because his art was what people lined up to pay for. And so it became important to a show-businessman like Brillstein that he *not kill* the innocence of his client. In a sense, the agent is ambidextrous—he can be tough as nails when talking to a TV executive, but he must be soft as lace when dealing with the artist. The business partner must truly value the art. He must trust that your hippie attitude is what makes you profitable to him. You can't have a business partner who doesn't see your value.

Brillstein saw Henson's value, though in some ways it baffled him. He wrote,

> If you could pick the most illogical pairing the world, it would have been Jim Henson and me. . . . Our bond was the unspoken certainty that we belonged together. We were who we were and it just worked.[532]

It is a delicate, almost familial relationship. In a sense, the more fraternal the relationship, the more it allows the artist—arguably the more delicate of the brothers—to have sway. "You never win with bankers," Walt said once of his lenders at Bank of America.[533] On the other hand, when Walt was able to get around Roy's austerities, he bragged, "I beat Roy in this one."[534] Having Roy as an intermediary between himself and the bankers was crucial. Disney could win with Roy. But without Roy, it's an uneven fight—in the end, you never win against bankers.

In his early days in Kansas City, Disney borrowed heavily from friends and neighbors, declaring bankruptcy in his early twenties.

This is not so with Henson, who drove a Rolls-Royce to his college graduation. Henson came to his projects with his own money pile from his advertising work, whereas Disney was constantly borrowing, first from family, and then from banks. Yet while Henson didn't have as much "disdain" for money, he still remained above it. A 1990 article explains that he did pick a side:

> Like other artists who have become hugely successful entrepreneurs, Henson had a decision to make: Was he a businessman or a creator? Despite media interests all over the globe, he leaned toward the creative, remaining fascinated with little cloth creatures and what they could do. If I spoke business with him, he was friendly but matter-of-fact. On the subject of puppets, his voice lit up, with Kermit's looping tones detectable somewhere beneath the enthusiasm.[535]

Both Disney and Henson valued being kept separate from the money, as would Pixar's Lasseter and Catmull with their unlikely angel funder, Steve Jobs, taking on the lion's share of the fierce negotiations with Michael Eisner at Disney. Going back to Hyde's theory, these moneymen intermediaries serve to do something very necessary for successful artists, to "mark the boundary between their art and the market."[536] They are a permeable barrier through which the artist can both enter business and then retreat into the "protected gift-sphere in which the work is created."[537] While Hyde beautifully describes the need for this barrier, Henson's life can be seen as a modern-day example of how such a barrier can allow an artist to *thrive*.

WHAT THE AGENT KNEW
HOW BERNIE KEPT HENSON A HIPPIE

To understand Henson's relationship to money, one of the key scenes we need to picture is that heated argument between the Hensons and Brillstein in his kitchen over merchandising *Sesame Street.* That scene showed us that selling out gave Henson a lifetime of creative freedom. It also cemented Henson—with his own words—as an artist and not a businessman. But Henson wasn't always described as so "artsy-craftsy."

When Henson agreed to work with the Children's Television Workshop on *Sesame Street,* he made sure to keep control of the copyrights and a good percentage of the merchandising profits for himself. Jon Stone, *Sesame Street*'s original director wrote:

> Ever the businessman, Jim made sure up front that his interests would be protected and drove a hard bargain with the Workshop's lawyers regarding ownership of his characters.[538]

Could Henson have anticipated the commercial success of toys? It almost seems that way. Davis writes that though Henson's "compensation request was modest by show-business standards," he "insisted that any future revenues generated by the licensing and merchandising of those characters would be split between him and CTW."[539] This, according to Davis, would "fill Henson's coffers for twenty years."[540] Stone writes that "[friendship and respect] never got in the way of The Deal. Jim was a killer businessman."[541] But if Henson was indeed a "killer businessman" at the table with CTW, then why did he put up such a fight about merchandising in Brillstein's kitchen? How do we reconcile Stone's version of Henson the hard bargainer with Brillstein's "artsy-craftsy" puppeteer, doing everything "for the right reasons"?

Now we are told by Brillstein that Henson did not do *Sesame Street* with the intention of making millions off toys—that he never even thought he would "sell out," until Brillstein convinced him. But let's not forget that Brillstein was a Hollywood agent who had a vested interest in keeping Henson's image family-friendly. When he sat down to write his autobiography, it's possible he played up the integrity of Henson—his most famous client—to secure himself a place in show-business legends. Brillstein himself wrote that representing Henson gave him "legitimacy in the family and children's market, the equivalent of the Good Housekeeping Seal of Approval."[542] It leads me to wonder, could Henson have harbored a "long-term vision" of his own involving profit splits?

We can't know the answer to this question, but perhaps we can try to get closer to it. Using what we know about Henson at the time, let's re-create that scene at the negotiating table with Henson and CTW's lawyers.

Not too much earlier, Joan Ganz Cooney saw Henson for the first time at a large meeting. She remembered, "this bearded, prophetic figure in sandals walks in and sits way at the back, ram-rod straight, staring straight ahead with no expression on his face." Someone called him "the hippy back there."[543] The actress who played Susan on *Sesame Street* remembered meeting Henson in 1969:

> Everything on Jim's body was buckskin and it was lashed together with rawhide. I mean his wife made his clothes and his sandals were handmade and he had this long brown hair and this benign peaceful face, and I said who in the world was that, and then he had these crazy

> puppeteers with him. It was like Robin Hood and his Merry Men came out of Sherwood Forest. I had never seen any guys like that before in my life.[544]

This is the Henson that we should picture in the scene, the Henson of 1968 to 1969. Now Jon Stone may have marveled at Henson's business skills, but the first time *he* met Henson, he was told by a CBS vice president, "Friday morning we are going to meet with Christ and his dog."[545] Though he may have underestimated Henson, this TV executive didn't see him as a "killer" businessman. The final piece of the puzzle comes from Stone's unpublished memoir, described in *Street Gang*, which gives us a vivid picture of the negotiation for *Hey, Cinderella!*, another deal Henson made in the late sixties:

> Lean, bearded Jim Henson . . . listened to the pitch Stone and Whedon had prepared. . . . "Jim nodded characteristically and hmmmmmed as we talked, then gently began to explain to us why realistic animal puppets are not nearly as easy or effective as more abstract puppets. Tom and I glanced at each other. 'He doesn't like it,' we thought. 'We've lost him.' And then, softly, suddenly, Jim said he liked the idea. Count him in."
>
> "No sooner had Jim nodded than the door bust open and an army of suits filled the room," Stone said. Among them were Bernie Brillstein, Henson's agent, and Al Gottesman, the puppeteer's business manager. "All were suddenly at the table, machine-gunning demands of a hundred percent of merchandising, percentage of gross revenues, percentages of ownership, residual control, and

> a hundred other demands. Tom and I watched in amazement. . . ."[546]

In this earlier deal, it was Henson who decided whether he could do a project based on its artistic merits, and it was the moneymen who—after bursting in the door—machine-gunned demands. This is the version of the scene that makes the most sense, because as Brillstein said, "As Henson's manager, I was paid to have my own long-term vision."[547]

Brillstein's account—that Henson never intended to cash in on *Sesame Street* toys—seems plausible. From this angle, Henson's obsession with owning his trademarks and copyrights is an issue of artistic survival—he wanted to *protect* his vision, to not let anyone else dilute his quality, and to be free to build upon anything he creates. It seems likely, then, that while "merchandising" rights were important, Henson took "merchandising" to mean records and the soon-to-come videos that would *themselves* be art—not toys. At this stage, I take Brillstein at face value that Henson participated in the CTW deal as an artist, never thinking that he'd get rich off toys. Jon Stone wasn't wrong to say Henson was a "killer businessman," but perhaps it gives us the wrong impression. Part of Henson's brilliance at business was in employing people like Brillstein and Al Gottesman, whose first priority was money, which freed Henson up to focus on *his* first priority—art.

As an artist, with few exceptions, Henson took projects that he thought would be interesting, not projects that would make the most money. Yet, karmically, *Sesame Street*—"a fledgling nonprofit" in Davis's words, made Henson rich. Brillstein wrote:

> The merchandising bonanza surprised even me. After a couple years my end of the first royalty check was nearly six hundred grand. This went on for five years."[548]

If Brillstein made the standard 15 percent agent's cut, this means that Henson made $4 million a year on kids' toys. Even assuming his wife (who technically owned half the company) received her fair share, that's $2 million a year. Depending on the split, another couple million went to CTW. Toys were an unexpected bonanza for Henson, but not for Brillstein. Let us look closely at what Brillstein said—the scale of the money "surprised *even* me." What that means is that he was expecting to earn a lot of money from toys. Just not $3 million.

Brillstein knew what was at stake with *Sesame Street*, even if Henson didn't. Re-creating this scene tells us a lot about the way an agent and artist symbiotically operate through business. Like a Ouija board, each party leads the partnership on its course. Likewise, this scene shows another clear Hydian boundary between the spheres of art and commerce—in the literal door that the managers "bust" through. In determining whether Henson would *take* the project, the "army of suits" are kept outside. When it is decided how much he will *earn* for the project, the barrier becomes permeable and art and money are allowed to interact.

When we picture the "army of suits" invading the room, it calls to mind the image of Buzz Lightyear in *Toy Story* landing in Andy's bedroom. In many ways Buzz resembles the strange new bedfellow Pixar had encountered, Steve Jobs, who became the studio's majority investor after George Lucas's divorce led him to sell it.[549] Like Buzz, Jobs became part of the team, and yet was himself a ruthless crusader. Pixar needed someone like Jobs to negotiate with Disney's lawyers for favorable distribution terms. Having a businessman like

Steve Jobs ensured that Michael Eisner's Disney would not exploit Pixar's artists and engineers.

A decade earlier, Jim Henson could've used someone like Jobs when he negotiated with Michael Eisner. In 1990, Henson himself arranged for a deal with Disney for funding, which ended in "invective-filled" lawsuits.[550] In arranging the details of the Henson–Disney deal, one Henson source called Eisner's lawyers "overzealous robots."[551] According to *Newsweek*, Henson said "he found Disney's negotiators offensive."[552] Ironically, Henson didn't have a clear barrier to protect him or negotiate for him, because he was in a sense trying to *replace* his business side with Disney. Brillstein couldn't shield him from Disney's lawyers, because Henson's goal was to get Disney to *take over* his business operations, to replace his agent, his merchandising department, and his marketing department. Henson's quote at the time is telling: "eliminating the dealmaking, administrative aspect of what I did was attractive."[553]

In 1990, Henson could have used someone like Buzz Lightyear—an arrogant captain to wrestle Disney's lawyers into a favorable deal. Steve Jobs may have been famously hard to work with, calling Atari engineers "moronic,"[554] for instance, but he fought for Pixar in his negotiations with Disney—ensuring the name Pixar would be featured prominently on all branding, and brokering for years in search of a fair 50–50 split of profits. But as much as artists need someone to fight for them, that "fighting" spirit is often detrimental "in the play room." In *Toy Story*, Buzz Lightyear had a hard time fitting in, and according to Pixar's Pamela Kerwin, it was a "relief" for Pixar when Jobs left Pixar alone:

> There was a little bit of tension in that he had more to give Pixar than Pixar actually wanted. . . . So when he went back to Apple, it was great because that could absorb

> his passion, and Steve could still do the stuff that Pixar really needed Steve to do, which was managing Disney, getting Pixar better distribution terms.[555]

Jobs's true value to Pixar seemed to lie not in his famously obsessive perfectionism, but in his ability to negotiate with Disney—to *be* the barrier that protected the artists from money. The tough guys who are good at business, many times, need to wait outside the door to let artists do their thing.

THE VALUE OF SEPARATION
LAWYERING THE LAWLESS

One reason to have a legal department is so that artists don't have to discuss money with one another. When writer Joseph Bailey was hired for *Sesame Street*, he recalled:

> [Director Jon Stone] then directed me to the "the sharks down the hall" in the Business Affairs Department to see about salary and contracts. . . . It was then I learned that 'creative' people don't discuss business with each other. We have our 'people' to do that."[556]

What is so uncreative about money? Well, even though money sometimes rewards innovation, it more typically rewards a sure thing—whatever your audience currently pays for. The money side *usually* tells you to make what it knows will be profitable, such as the direct-to-video *Cinderella II*.

Then there is the issue of copyright. It is *uncreative* to sue people. Artists need to build upon the work of the past in order to make something new. But sometimes, a copyright can act as a *barrier* to the marketplace for an artist. It can be part of what protects the gift-sphere in which the work is created. Copyright, for example, protected the La Choy Dragon from being used by La Choy after Henson stopped making their commercials, and it allowed *him* to tweak that character until it became Big Bird. Copyright prevents the art—while in a nascent stage—from being traded freely according to laws of supply and demand. If an artist's work is constantly evolving, as Henson's was, then copyright, in a sense, kept it in a protected sphere where it could grow according to its own demands, and be "given" to the world and market only when it was for artistic purposes.

Pixar could have used a copyright clause like Henson's when they made *Toy Story*, because unfortunately, their deal gave the copyright of the characters over to Disney. This gave Disney the upper hand in negotiations, since, as David Price wrote in *The Pixar Touch*, "the idea of Disney cranking out [sequels] drove Lasseter to distraction. . . . Disney-made sequels under Eisner, it seemed, would be objects of commerce above all. 'These were the people who put out *Cinderella II*,' Lasseter later said mordantly."[557] In *To Infinity and Beyond*, Lasseter said, "Steve Jobs stayed at the negotiating table with Disney about two to three years longer because of me. Because I wanted our characters."[558] For the time being, Pixar had to walk away, leaving their characters behind.

Legalese is of critical importance to artists. Whitmire said of Henson, "I don't think he took a lot of legal action [against copyright infringement]."[559] Yet Henson acknowledged in 1979, "We do have copyright lawyers who try to prevent the name *muppet* from becoming generic. That would not help."[560] Henson needed lawyers to negotiate contracts with toy companies that wanted to license Muppet characters. His lawyers arranged clearances for *others* to use his work, but they also arranged clearances for *Henson* to use his own work. For example, When Henson hosted *The Dick Cavett Show* in 1971, he showed clips from *Sam and Friends*, which aired on another network.[561] Legally, Henson had to clear the rights to air those clips. In this case, lawyers secured Henson the ability to build upon his earlier work in a natural way.

Another role for Henson's lawyers was to foster collaboration. In most cases collaboration costs money. In order to make the film *Emmett Otter's Jug-Band Christmas* based on the book by Russell and Lillian Hoban, Henson made a deal with the authors to use their intellectual materials. Lawyers are of great value, not just because they are experts at contracts and legalities, but because their work means that artists don't have to be. Henson and the Hobans most likely did not bicker in person over the price of adapting their book. Can you imagine what kind of movie it would have been if Henson had been resentful of his character's authors? Or if he thought of each quotation as a sum of money?

Jerry Juhl parodied this attitude in a greeting card that went out to his friends. A disclaimer warned the reader to read the fine print before opening:

> The Muppets© "TM" are trademarked and copyrighted properties belonging to The Muppet Studio LLC (TMSLLC). The project herein described is independent of TMSLLC, The Sesame Workshop, and/or The Jim Henson Companies ("Organizations"). The pig-like, bear-like and other anthropomorphic images on the inside of this card exist as an attention-getting device only and in no way implies an endorsement by the Organizations.[562]

This was a *Christmas card*. And while it is clearly is a joke, there very often must've been warnings such as this on scripts, treatments, and communications. The parody and frustration with such requirements is understandable to any artist—legalities are decidedly uncreative, or more accurately, un*pro*creative.

So, legal counsel, while serving as a protective barrier, can also go too far. For that reason, Henson was as picky about his lawyers as he was about his puppeteers.

After hiring writer Joseph Bailey, Henson referred him to talk to Al Gottesman, "the head of the Muppet legal department . . . about money":[563]

> I was to get so much per script plus appropriate Writers Guild residuals, so much per diem expenses; a certain number of trips home from England and first class travel. . . . Al Gottesman is such a decent, straightforward guy that I never needed "people" to talk to Jim's "people." I could talk to Al myself.[564]

It is essential that the lawyers for a creative company understand how to work with artists. How did Henson secure such "decent" legal counsel? It begins with Henson inviting the outside in, as Gottesman literally met Henson for the first time in Henson's own offices:

> I had never before been in such a remarkable place. On the lower floor was the pure fantasy of the company's workshop with its several designers and builders (one who looked like Santa Claus) surrounded by colorful costumes and puppets. I soon learned that these were hallowed premises that you did not enter unless you were invited. However, each time I passed them in the next few years, walking up the carriage-house stairs, I'd steal a look,

> which always made me feel good and reminded me that I was in a very special place.[565]

There are lawyers who go into the profession for the money and there are lawyers who go into it for other reasons. Not everyone in Gottesman's place would have found Henson's workshop "special" in the good sense. Yet, as he recalled:

> I knew pretty much then or shortly afterwards that I wanted to work with this man. I could sense his essential decency and his desire to produce, with his puppets, only, engaging, meaningful and quality entertainment. And I was right.[566]

It is telling that Gottesman noted Henson's "decency" and was himself called "decent" by Bailey. It is nice to think of a marriage between art and business—show business—as running smoothly, but we can't forget that the executives at Goldman Sachs famously called their clients "muppets." For *some* corporate professionals, "muppet" is a pejorative, and for the ignorant Gorgs, Fraggles are dirty pests. Sometimes, though, there is defection—a Gorg can become a Fraggle.

On *Fraggle Rock*, Junior Gorg rejects his father's tradition when he has the courage to blow the royal kazoo. While his father never tried—for fear of failure—Junior, with the minstrel Fraggles' help, succeeds merely by *trying* to play. While the prince of the Gorgs is still ten times the size of the Fraggles, he has a newfound appreciation for them. Perhaps the way for businesspeople to truly appreciate artists is to try to make art themselves, and to see—usually—that artistic talent is actually quite rare, and so it is something worth protecting.

By taking a chance and joining up with "muppets" in the Goldman-Sachs sense, Al Gottesman was able to make real change in the world by helping to "produce . . . meaningful entertainment." A few years later, another businessman would become a muppet.

HIRE A BOSS

When asked about his workaholism, Henson once told a magazine, "I hired a boss," and then chuckled, "a business affairs manager." It's unclear whether this was David Lazer, but he said it "lessened his load."[567] Henson had met Lazer in the sixties when he was a manager at IBM and had arranged to have Henson do Meeting Films for the electronics company. According to Brillstein, Lazer "thought Jim was brilliant and approached him with funding."[568]

In 1975, Henson hired Lazer as the executive producer of *The Muppet Show*, where it was Lazer's job to interact with all the show's guest stars. Once he joined Henson Associates, Lazer truly *enjoyed* working in show business, describing his trip to the Cannes Film Festival by saying, "What a thrill!"[569] Lazer would become instrumental in developing Muppet Meeting Films and producing Henson's big Hollywood movies. But was Lazer Henson's boss? Sort of. David Lazer described his role like this:

> Jim's an astute businessman and he knows everything that's going on in this company but he just doesn't have time to attend to everything personally so it's up to me to give him the breathing space so he can run the creative side of the operation.[570]

In many ways, he took over for Diana Birkenfield, who had worked on *The Jimmy Dean Show* before becoming Henson's producer for various television projects.[571] Why was "breathing space" important for the creative side?

Well, for one thing, Bailey recalled a time at *The Muppet Show* when the walls were too thin and he could hear Lazer's phone calls. So Bailey put up a sign explaining that for a few coins, the employees could listen in to "HEAR YOUR SALARY AND RAISES DISCUSSED!"[572] Lazer learned to make his calls quieter. It is hard to imagine what a totally transparent business–art relationship would look like, but I can imagine there would be a lot of unhappy artists and not a lot of productive collaboration.

There seems to be overlap in Henson's business department, as Brillstein, Gottesman, and then Lazer all have been referred to as Henson's manager. It is likely that, as Henson hired each new businessman, the roles became more specialized. When it came to firing someone, for instance, one would think Lazer would handle it, but in one case, Henson asked Brillstein to do it, since he also represented the employee in question. Brillstein explains:

> Jim was patient and rarely raised his voice. He didn't like confrontation, so he usually gave me the unpleasant jobs. I know it was dead serious time when he told me to fire his head writer, Jack Burns, who was my good friend and client. The way Jim did it was perfectly Jim. He called from London and said, "Hi, Bernie, how ya doing?"
>
> "Fine. How does everything look?"
>
> "Fine," he said, and paused. "You know something, Bernie? Jack Burns gives me a stomachache."
>
> I knew exactly what he meant. Time to make a change. "How soon?" I asked.
>
> "Soon," he said.[573]

Although he didn't always renew every freelancer's contract, Henson was known to avoid firing employees. Recall Cooney's statement:

> Jim didn't run his company like a good businessman. He could never fire anybody, couldn't accept any plan for downsizing that was drawn up for him by his advisers. Jim feared that he couldn't face people afterward, so he just kept them on.[574]

The fact that Henson kept Brillstein (agent), Gottesman (lawyer), and Lazer (producer) all on the payroll rather than having these managers replace one another demonstrates this. And, in fact, when Diana Birkenfield returned from her other projects in 1981, she too rejoined Henson's business team as vice president of television production.[575]

Henson was a collaborator. In a business where collaboration is more important than minimizing overhead, where hierarchies dissolve, and people often come to work with one another again and again, it does not make sense to burn bridges by firing.

Luckily, Henson didn't even have to express his wish to fire someone before Brillstein said "How soon?" *This* is how Brillstein kept Henson a hippie, and how the businesspeople that Henson selected insulated him and his artists from the market economy, from *money*. Yet they alone were not enough for Henson to make movies. Film, like Broadway, is incredibly expensive to produce. For that, Henson needed an angel.

FIND THE ANGEL FUNDER
LORD LEW GRADE

The academic William Wetzel used the term "angel" to refer to a rare kind of investor. Borrowing from a Broadway term, an angel funder is one who takes on great risk for a start-up for reasons besides pure monetary reward. Henson found his angel funder in the British entertainment mogul Lord Lew Grade, without whom there would be no *Muppet Show*, no *Muppet Movie*, and no *Dark Crystal*.

Throughout the sixties, Henson attempted to sell American television networks on a Muppet series in prime time. In the seventies, using *Sesame Street*'s cache, he produced two pilots that aired on ABC and a pitch tape for NBC, but no one in the US wanted a puppet show for adults. Watching both the pilots and the pitch tape on YouTube today, it is evident how much *work* went into Henson's bid for a network show. Yet it came to nothing—in the US.

However, because of Henson's hustle, his pilot *The Muppet Show: Sex and Violence* had been seen by the public, and it was strong enough to convince an angel funder in the UK to invest in it. According to Finch:

> In the summer of 1975 . . . Abe Mandell—head of ITC Entertainment, the American division of ACC, Lord Grade's entertainment corporation—wrote an enthusiastic letter to Jim Henson, expressing great interest in the potential of the Muppets. As Lord Grade himself recalls, Mandell had seen the second of the ABC pilots and had advised that ITC should make every effort to sign the Muppets for a syndicated series.[576]

Though it wasn't technically "prime time," but instead the syndicated lead-up at 7:30 p.m., Grade's London-based ITC had "the same kind of production facilities and financial backing that could be expected from a major American network." Finch continues:

> Henson Associates' business arm—headed by David Lazer, Al Gottesman, executive vice president of Henson Associates, and Bernie Brillstein of the Bernie Brillstein Office, Henson Associates' management company—began serious negotiations with ITC. The one thing they were after, above all else, was an assurance that they would not be underfinanced. Lazer and Brillstein visited Mandell in his home and asked for a guarantee of a budget that would ensure high production values, along with a promise of creative independence.[577]

They would get both generous funding as well as creative freedom from Grade. They also argued for more—as with *Sesame Street*, Henson's suits ensured a favorable merchandising split, seeing that Henson Associates was already reaping the benefits of Bert and Ernie toys. According to a 1979 *New York Times* article, Henson's company split the licensing revenue for *The Muppet Show* "on a 50–50 basis" with Grade's ITC company.[578] The article points out, though, that Kermit was not included in either deal. Those profits went entirely to Henson Associates.

Grade's 50 percent deal *seems* like a lot, but it was Kermit that the kids really wanted, since they already knew him from *Sesame Street*. Piggy and Fozzie were new in 1975, and when Fisher-Price released the *Muppet Show* character toys, one can imagine Kermit was the bestseller. Henson's "people" drove a hard deal with Lew Grade to keep Kermit off the table, and here we see another instance where *they* were tough so that *Henson* didn't have to be. What Henson received from Lew Grade was a gift, a generous funding, and so if Henson had had to negotiate with his "angel," it would have been a different relationship. With the barrier in place, Henson was able to receive the gift of "creative independence" and to truly experience it *as a gift*. As Finch wrote:

> It may well have been a blessing that *The Muppet Show* was not picked up by one of the major American networks. Had [Henson] found himself working in Hollywood and answerable to network executives, the pressures might well have made it impossible for him to sustain the atmosphere that now exists in the Muppet world. Lord Grade's hands-off policy has been vital to the success of the enterprise.[579]

This "blessing" was another sense in which Lew Grade was an "angel." *The Muppet Show* wasn't just a risk, it was also one he couldn't manage—he had to trust in Henson's vision. Moreover, it was expensive, costing $250,000 an episode by the fifth season. It was said the show didn't make a profit on the books in its original run. Rare indeed is the investor that can stomach an arrangement like this. Brillstein notes Grade was a "robust entertainer and one-time champion Charleston dancer." Perhaps Grade's own history as an artist is why he invested the way he did. As we know, he "spent a bundle" on a terrible flop, *Raise the Titanic*, according to Brillstein.[580] That film effectively ended his movie-making career.

According to Brillstein, when Grade ordered a twenty-four-episode season, "My packaging fee would be $4000 per show, or ninety-six grand. I managed to keep the merchandising for Jim, but gave 10 percent of the net merchandising profits to Grade."[581] This was perhaps renegotiated up to the reported 50–50 split later, or perhaps one source has misreported the split. But either way, we see that Grade essentially agreed to fund a show that would only make him money if the toys sold well *or* if they re-syndicated a few years later—making *The Muppet Show* a wildly expensive project with only a dream's hope of returning on his investment.

And once Grade was in, it seems his generosity kept going. Brillstein writes:

> When Jim was ready, David Lazer and I sold Lord Grade on the idea of making *The Muppet Movie* . . . the budget was $9 million. A couple studio heads I told thought Grade was a moron because Disney was making kids' movies for a million and a half. Grade, God bless him, believed in Jim—and not only because he made millions from *The Muppet Show*. Jim had proved himself. Grade . . . said, "Here's the money. Go do it."[582]

From there, Henson made a movie twice as expensive. According to Brian Jay Jones, the budget for *The Dark Crystal* was initially $16 million, and later David Lazer was able to get Grade to raise that to $25 million.[583] On *Dark Crystal*, Grade *still* didn't ask a thing of Henson's art. Henson said:

> There was no pressure from anyone but ourselves [on creative decisions] because we were the ones doing this from the beginning. Lew Grade, who financed the film, never put any pressure on us, which was very nice.[584]

This "angelic" belief-in-art philosophy can be contrasted with the entrepreneur who bought out Grade's sinking movie business in 1982. Sir Robert Holmes à Court was, according to Wikipedia, "one of the world's most feared corporate raiders." This put *The Dark Crystal*, set to release that year, in jeopardy. Brillstein recalled:

> Jim didn't like the way Sir Robert was handling the film, so he called me and announced he wanted to buy back the movie. . . .
>
> "I'll control its destiny," he said. "I love it."[585]

Henson had been incredibly fortunate to have an angel funder like Grade. Letting the average corporate raider control Henson's masterpiece was unacceptable. As with Pixar and their *Toy Story* characters, Henson couldn't stand to have his masterpiece reside in the wrong hands.

The Dark Crystal is Henson's masterpiece, and it could not have been made without an angel funder like Grade. In a way, Grade found Henson, yet in another, Henson's incredible work ethic helped him find Grade by putting enough work out there for Grade to stumble upon. Grade is immortalized in the end of *The Muppet Movie* as the character Lew Lord, played by Orson Wells. It is he who calls in his secretary to say, "Tracy, prepare the standard rich and famous contract."[586]

Angel funders are anything but standard. And while our cynical age has come to distrust the Hollywood happy ending, Grade really did give Henson the ticket to achieve his dream.

HOW TO GET THEM ALL TO WORK TOGETHER

As we see, it is very advantageous to have business guys. Especially if you wish to *remain* an artist—a hippie, a moonbeam, or a "muppet" in the corporate sense of the word. You have to partner with someone who understands business and can shield you from it. It should be someone you trust, a brother (Roy Disney), someone who gets you (Brillstein), someone who respects your creative freedom

(Grade). The relationship should in no way resemble "professionalism." It should more rightly resemble a matrimonial, paternal, or fraternal relationship. You must trust your businesspeople, but that does not mean you should trust *any* businessperson.

Michael Eisner, Steve Jobs, Robert Holmes à Court—as successful businessmen, they have great power to help art and great power to hurt it. The words *raider*, *egomaniac*, *robot*, and *shark* describe some of the most abrasive kinds of business guys. The best relationship to have with your business people is *distant*. You can be personally "close" with your businesspeople—Henson vacationed with Brillstein—but the business side needs to respect your "magical space" in Gottesman's words, and give you "breathing room" in Lazer's. They need to wait outside the door of the creative collaboration before rushing in and turning it into negotiation. Henson selected his "people" well so that they would not damage the spirit of his enterprise. The first step was to invite them in—into his world—and make them *want* to be a part of it, to share his dream.

If you have an ambitious goal—to win an Oscar, to get to Broadway, or to make a video game—you need to find your angel funder. There are organizations of angels that an artist might look for; however, they are more likely more interested in technology rather than art. Patrons for the arts are often just normal people with money to spare. To find someone who *loves* your work, you might have to let your benefactor find *you*. But in order to be seen, put out all the work you can. Henson's Muppets were on television for twenty years before Grade saw them. Let your entire body of work be your pitch to your imaginary angel funder.

The complex triad that Henson brought together can be recreated on any scale you wish—Disney's massive scale, Henson's more homespun scale, or your own one-person start-up. Even the most solitary of artists, the writer, employs business partners—an agent, financial advisors, and publicists—or sometimes a *cloud* of investors through Kickstarter crowdfunding. The writer may also employ artists like a photographer or illustrator, and tech people—a web designer, copyeditor, or e-book maker.

If you already engage with the parts of the triad, what conflicts have you encountered in their differing points of view? The relationships between the three groups—the Gorgs, Fraggles, and Doozers—are not equilateral, though they are interconnected. While tech and art should work together *closely*, business should protect art and tech with *distance*, because in essence, their role is to be a barrier, a silent Ouija-board collaborator.

The right business partners for artists are indispensable. While many artists write off all businessmen as heartless suits, Henson understood the debt he owed to them. They, too, participate in the gift cycle of art. And in 1982, he tried to pass along the gift they had given him.

In his forties, Jim Henson started a foundation for puppeteers. The Henson Foundation "has awarded over 600 grants to more than 250 American puppet artists for the creation and development of innovative, contemporary puppet theater,"[587] according to Falk. Among the grant recipients was Julie Taymore, who went on to directing the Tony Award winning musical *The Lion King*. With this foundation, Henson gave artists something indispensable that had been given to him—funding. In essence, a grant could take over the money arm for another artist, sit in for Brillstein, Gottesman, Lazer, and Grade, and allow the artist money to play with. Whether it is a grant or a business investment, funding is truly a gift.

Your masterpiece may be years away still, but it makes sense to start thinking today about how you could combine business, technology, and art to give the world something it's never seen before. Do the successful artists in your medium know any good tech guys and money guys? Maybe you should know them, too.

LESSON 8

PITCH, PITCH, PITCH

AND THE INEVITABILITY OF FAILURE

When you hear the story about how *The Muppet Show* came to be, it sounds like a deus ex machina. Lew Grade went looking for Henson and gave him a show. Not only that, he said Henson could use his ATV station studio in London to film the show, and he would broadcast it all over the UK and US through the ITC network of stations. Brillstein's breezy style certainly makes it appear that it was easy:

> A little guy named Hal Huff, working out of a back room at the local CBS station in New York, got the idea that the Muppets might make a great syndicated show. . . . ITC's president, Abe Mandel, heard Huff's idea and went looking for me. . . . I explained what we wanted to do. . . . Mandel was sold.[588]

Most of us have never thought about what it took for Henson to get his shows and movies made—we were given the story in *The Muppet Movie*—Orson Welles playing Lew Lord says, "Prepare the standard rich and famous contract,"[589] and that's that. Yet the truth is that Henson had been pitching this show for years prior to Mandell's offer. This windfall—the angel funder Lord Lew Grade—would never have come had Henson not cultivated his inner preacher, his inner pulpiteer.

It is something that separates the successful artist from the starving artist—the ability to sell oneself effectively. Walt Disney was "quite a salesman," according to his animator Rudy Ising.[590] In his essay "Muppets and Money," Andrew Leal named one section "P is for Pitchman."[591] Watching Henson's pitch reels on YouTube today, it is clear he, too, could sell his socks off. And while many social marketing "experts" tell us to "self-promote," bad preaching is more likely to turn audiences off. So how did Henson, an artist, hustle *effectively*? How did he become a pitchman for his art?

Partly, it must've helped to have a manager who could see the steps it would take to get a major network interested. Brillstein urged him to take as many TV appearances as possible, saying, "I feel you need television exposure,"[592] and "We needed to create some media momentum."[593] In many ways for Henson, the late sixties and early seventies were all one big pitch—leading up to *The Muppet Show*. The fact that Mandell happened to see Henson's work on TV was not luck; it was the result of throwing hundreds of darts at the board. After long enough, one of them has to hit the bull's-eye.

What Mandell saw in the Muppets was precisely what Henson *wanted* a network to see. The ABC special *The Muppet Show: Sex and Violence* clearly outlined the show Henson wanted to make[594]—a quick-moving variety show with an at-the-dance number, the Electric Mayhem band, a backstage section, and even Sam the Eagle. This ABC special was essentially a pitch tape proving that puppets could work in prime time, telling whoever was willing to listen exactly what Henson wanted to do.

ARE PITCHMEN BORN OR MADE?

Jim Henson performed two characters on *Fraggle Rock*. One was Cantus, the wandering minstrel. Cantus could play every song in the rock on a mystical pipe, because he spent most of his time *listening*. It was hard to get him to make a concrete statement at any time. He preferred to ponder life's mysteries rather than endorse any message. He was a bit of a mystic.

Henson's other character was Convincing John, who could convince anyone of anything. One of the most powerful and dangerous Fraggles in the rock, Convincing John spends most of his time *talking*. He is almost manic in his "preachification," so sure of his opinion he can convince anyone of it, even if it is something as ridiculous as insisting everyone wear cups on their hands. Jerry Nelson said these rather *opposing* characters shared something: "The intensity of Convincing John or Cantus the Minstrel always had a kind of intensity that kind of was Jim."[595]

Both these characters show Jim Henson in partial relief, because they are two of his modes. A good artist is likely already skilled at listening, learning, and appreciating. These traits fit well in the gift economy that is art. But going beyond *The Gift*, Henson shows us that it is possible to channel one's inner Convincing John in the service of one's inner minstrel. Quite often, financially successful artists resemble con artists. This is not always a good thing, as the con-man persona often seems to take over and suppress the minstrel. However, when kept in check—in the service of the art—channeling one's inner fanatic can break the artist out of his self-imposed poverty.

It is hard to say whether pitchmen are born or made. It is my suspicion that they are grown. Was Henson always fervent and outspoken? Hardly. He described himself as shy. At his funeral, Brillstein said, "Henson rarely spoke above a whisper. You had to lean in to hear him most of the time."[596] And yet, in spite of his quietness, Henson can be seen on camera working up a sweat—pitching as though his life depended on it.

If you want to find your inner pitchman, I would recommend getting ahold of the Muppet Meeting Film *Sell, Sell, Sell.* In it, a character named Leo—puppeteered by Jim Henson—works himself up into a frenzy trying to inspire you to go out and sell whatever it is you sell:

> For the sake of free enterprise, for the sake of the company, for the sake of the family, for the sake of the children, for motherhood, for apple pie, for puppy dogs and kitty cats, for everything that is near and dear to us, I ask you to remember just one word, and that word is *sell*! I want you to get out there and sell, sell, *sell*! I want you to sell your socks off! I want you to sell! Sell![597]

Leo's bit started as an outgrowth of what was really going on at Henson Associates in earnest. As Jerry Juhl explains, "This was in the early days before the shows were taped. We were pitching ideas to networks."[598] As we saw with Henson's work in commercials, no matter what Henson was selling, he was *really* selling the Muppets—and more work for them.

Specters of the "frenzy" bit can be seen in many Henson productions. The song "I Wanna Help" from *The Great Santa Claus Switch*, and *The Muppet Show Pitch Reel* both feature characters who work themselves into a state of manic preaching, just like *Fraggle*

Rock's Convincing John. Juhl said of the pitch reel that it "started out quietly and just built and built and BUILT where it ends up with a shot of the heavens."[599] He said that Leo became "more frantic" with time.[600] This tendency of enthusiasm to *build* upon itself suggests that you can *teach* yourself to pitch; you can work yourself up. The skill can be *grown*—for the right reasons.

Henson was different from your average salesman. When you have the gift of the pitch, you can sell as many vacuum cleaners or financial derivatives as you want. But Henson didn't sell products for profit; he pitched his heart out for Cantus, that is, for the music, the dance, and the art. What is the difference between a salesman and a pitchman? A salesman sells a commodity. A pitchman sells his own future work.

This starts to resemble a gift more than a real "sale." Hyde writes in *The Gift*:

> It is the cardinal difference between a gift and commodity exchange that a gift establishes a feeling-bond between two people, while the sale of a commodity leaves no necessary connection.[601]

When a product is sold, it means the salesman can go home and have no further contact with the buyer. When a pitch is sold, it means the pitchman must to work for the buyer—*gets* to work for the buyer. A bond is formed.

Becoming a pitchman was instrumental in getting Henson's work aired and funded. He started pitching early in his career, and though he might have liked a break, he never stopped. An examination of his journal shows that the ABP lifestyle—Always Be Pitching—held true in every era of his career. Except, perhaps, one.

THE CONSTANT PITCHMAN

Searching for the word "pitch" in the Henson Archives' *Jim Henson's Red Book* blog, the word comes up often. If we start at the very beginning and work through some examples, we see a narrative emerge that helps us think about cultivating our own ability to pitch.

WASHINGTON 1954–1962 AT THE BEGINNING, PITCH LIKE HELL

When my students read that Henson's career began with a stroke of luck—a visit to his high school puppetry club by some producers at WTOP-TV[602]—they tend to think he had it easy. Yet, as all the articles made clear, he still had to *audition* for this first job, and that audition required that he make his own puppets. When this show was cancelled, Henson worked on three more shows before he was given his own show, *Sam and Friends*. Even then, it was only five minutes long.

And even when *that* show had run stably for six years, he still had to pitch commercials. A good illustration of this is his behind-the-scenes film showing the Wilson's Meats sales team how his company worked—which suspiciously involved a lot of lunchmeat. Though much of it is parody, Henson says incredibly *pitchy* things like, "In short, the Jim Henson Muppets have become famous as a delight to children all over the world." The implication was that since everyone loves the Muppets, Wilson's Meats should keep paying them to make commercials.

What is surprising about these meeting films is that they essentially promote a set of commercials that have *already* been made for

Wilson's. Henson already had a contract with the company. But even then, he couldn't stop pitching—he had to pitch for his *next* set of commercials with them. He did, in fact, produce a second meeting film for Wilson's a few months later. When you look at the long list of companies Henson made commercials for, you can imagine an equally impressive list of pitches.

At the end of this era, beginning around 1961, agent Bernie Brillstein started helping Henson pitch his work.[603] Falk writes, "Brillstein spent the 1960s marketing the Muppets to variety shows and pitching other projects developed by Jim and Jerry Juhl that ranged from experimental television specials to live-action feature films."[604] It would be nice to think that Henson could stop pitching now, once he hired a pitchman to do it for him.

Yet, as we will see, the opposite is true. Even with an agent, Henson still had to hustle. Even if it was Bernie who made initial contact, sussed out deals, or delivered the pitch, it was Henson who had to provide the material to be pitched. He seemed to pitch even *more* after Brillstein joined him, likely due to the growth of the company.

And to get that agent, what did he have to do? He had to walk into Brillstein's office with a bag of puppets and make a pitch. In the last lesson, we saw that getting an agent was a combination of using connections, performing, and someone calling William Morris asking to book Henson—some stroke of luck or cunning. It took a great pitch to win over Brillstein—who was not very interested in puppets. And once Brillstein was on board, Henson had to pitch even more, because Brillstein got him more auditions and urged him to get more "exposure" and "media momentum."

NEW YORK 1963–1969 THROWING A LOT OF DARTS IN ALL DIRECTIONS, THEN ONE BIG PITCH

New York in the 1960s was a period of experimentation for Henson. Energized by the possibilities, he came up with wildly varied new ideas—PBS specials, a nightclub, a short film. He was simultaneously doing commercials, talk-show appearances, film-festival fare, and a documentary, and was developing work for NBC's "Experiment in Television." He was going a long way to achieve what Brillstein wanted—"media momentum"—however, in this period he did not have a long-running series, which was not for lack of trying.

In 1964, Henson made a pilot for a puppet series called *Tales from the Tinkerdee.*[605] Containing clever wordplay, original music, and broad appeal, this is some of the best and most timeless work that Henson, Juhl, and Jane ever did. The music is eerily good and the wordplay funny. A foot—played by Henson—misinterprets "a diamond-encrusted, hand-cut crystal, delicately fashioned, Italian birdbath" as "a bird-headed, delicately dashing, bath-cut diamond, hand-encrusted Italian."[606] Falk writes, "Despite Jim's best efforts to sell the show, it never aired."[607] Why did the show fail? Perhaps it just took time for Henson to find the right funder. Or perhaps it was because he had too many eggs in different baskets. This period of diffused dreaming may have been busy for Henson Associates, but it didn't yield a long-running show, unfortunately.

At this time, Henson was also pitching a line of toys. When Ideal Toys made puppets of Kermit and Rowlf in 1966, Henson's ad pitch was aggressive, as Falk notes:

> Given the great care that was later used when marketing *Sesame Street* toys, it is amusing to see how the Ideal Toys spot was much more like the Wilkins commercial in its use of the hard sell. This is the only time you will hear Kermit saying, "Oh, buy, oh, buy us, oh, buy us, we beg. And if you don't buy us, we'll bite you in the leg! We're loving and cuddly—we're a bundle of charms. And if you don't buy us we'll break both your arms."[608]

Not only was it Henson's job to pitch to the public, but to the company's salesmen as well. Falk describes Henson's visit to the Ideal Toys sales team:

> After a bit of shtick, they introduced Kermit, and they practiced some sales techniques together, skewering Ideal with jokes about rival Mattel. Finally, the toy versions of Kermit came out and made their pitch. They were a hit. In an appreciative letter, the Director of Sales Promotion Bill Reese wrote Jim, "Not only were you entertaining, you created an attitude and environment for our friends, The Muppets, that is bound to influence every single salesman who was a witness to the show. They now have 'a feel' of the characters and the merchandise, which should send them on their way well motivated toward successful selling."[609]

This only furthers the idea that there is *no* good time to stop pitching. Even when Ideal Toys had salesmen to do Henson's job *for him*, Henson still needed to prime those salesmen to understand his ethos. But with such a wide range of projects Henson was involved in, we are starting to see a *split*—a growing apart of ads and art.

Because on the one hand we have something quite commercial, toy licensing; and on the other, we have his experimental film, *Time Piece.*

Time Piece went on to garner an Oscar nomination, and yet, just because it was artistic, abstractly symbolic, and without a clear "message," does not mean Henson was freed from pitching. Even when he became an auteur and "authored" an art-house film, Henson had to hustle. Falk writes:

> When Jim completed production on his short film *Time Piece* in early 1965, he . . . invited his friends and colleagues to a private screening on May 6th at the Museum of Modern Art. He sent prints of the film to potential distributors, underwriters, and clients. Copies went to the U.S. Steel Corporation's Applied Research Laboratory . . . [who] offered to show it at the Industrial Audio-Visual Association meeting in Boston. . . . Through the William Morris Agency, he sent a print to Eastman Kodak. . . . Jim submitted the film to festivals in Germany and Italy where it got much recognition.[610]

For noncommercial works of art, *distribution* makes all the difference, and often, indie artists have to do the distribution themselves. When you look at the work Henson did sending his film out, it starts to become clear that when you are promoting your art, it's no longer a con. At least it doesn't feel that way. When you've put so much of your time, effort, and passion into something, it is hard *not* to feel like proselytizing.

And yet, in this 1960s period, Henson promoted both this art film *and* kiddie toys. This period of experimentation seemed to create a split—on the one hand Henson Associates made the documentary

Youth '68, juxtaposing quotes from the founding fathers and revolutionary rockers of the youth culture; on the other, they made commercials for products like Wheels, Flutes, and Crowns—Bugle-like snacks that weren't exactly nutritious.[611] Brillstein wrote, "It was as if the guy had two careers: one public and successful, the other personal and noncommercial. They fed each other."[612]

It is my hypothesis that this period allowed Henson a crucial realization: it is easier to pitch something that is *both* commercial and good than it is to pitch either alone. From all this unfocused dart-throwing, we see that neither the film project nor the toy brand led to anything long-lasting. Henson didn't continue to make art-house films, and he likewise stopped making commercials. But Henson's longest-running project to date marked the end of this period, when he found something truly worth pitching—PBS's great experiment, *Sesame Street.*

SESAME STREET 1969–1975 BULL'S-EYE: PITCH TO FIND A HOME, THEN PITCH TO FLY THE COOP

Although Henson was always working on multiple ideas at once, the *Sesame Street* era brought stability to his company. The network PBS gave his characters a home that allowed them to grow and allowed the public to grow fond of them. Part of the beauty of *Sesame Street* was that it was perfect for Henson—it combined both his commercial, persuasive skills and his philanthropic, artistic skills. Henson was able to harness his Convincing John powers in service of a good cause: to sell kids on reading. So, when it came time to pitch *this* project, Henson was all in.

It is strange to think of anyone needing to "pitch" *Sesame Street*, and yet that is precisely what happened. First, CTW needed to win over the press. So Henson and director Jon Stone made a "sales film" for a press conference. Though it was clearly an educational show, in the film, a Muppet boardroom spit-balled titles like a commercial network would, coming up with the "Itty-Bitty, Farm and City, Witty-Ditty, Nitty-Gritty, Dog and Kitty, Pretty Little Kiddie Show" or simply "Hey, Stupid!"[613] Even when the show aired, it needed to win over parents and teachers—the guardians who could control whether children watched or not. NBC aired a "preview" called "This Way to Sesame Street" meant to bring parents on board.[614] *Sesame Street* was a new idea, and its premise—using commercial techniques to lure kids into learning—could have backfired. It is in great part due to Henson's pitching prowess that *Sesame Street* won the country's hearts.

Yet a moment of stability, like every other period of time, is not a good time to stop pitching. When *Sesame Street* made Henson a household name, he felt that it had "ruined [his] life" by barring his career from ever taking an adult route. Since he'd never wanted to relegate himself to the role of children's entertainer, in this era, Henson pitched all the harder, this time to escape the pigeonhole he'd found himself in.

He continued to pitch work for adults like the existentialist anti-drama *The Cube*, and a pilot for *The Wizard of Ibid.*[615] And now, as a reaction to the squeaky-clean *Sesame* stigma, Henson ramped up his adult content. He cheekily titled a pilot for ABC *Sex and Violence*. Brillstein got him a spot on the first season of the edgy night show *Saturday Night Live* with a race of puppet aliens with very *adult* marital issues. Sample sketches were called "Scred and Peuta's Affair" and "Scred's Sex Device."[616] These projects seemed almost designed to question Henson's kids-only image. What strikes me in examining this period is that Henson was driven to pitch more in this period in order to *avoid* something. His characters already had a home on TV, but it wasn't his *own* show—on *Sesame Street*, he had to answer to curriculum specialists. It wasn't quite the Muppet series about which Henson had been dreaming.

And yet, in order for Henson to get to the place he wanted—a show for adults *and* children—he had to achieve media momentum, and since the only exposure the networks wanted to give him was predominantly light "family" fare, that is much of what he pitched.

He aired an hour-long special called *The Great Santa Claus Switch* on *The Ed Sullivan Show* in this period, in 1970 after seven years of pitching. It was closer to his own show, and yet the holiday theme seemed something the market wanted, not something the artist wanted. When you watch the skits on *The Ed Sullivan Show*, Sullivan seems most delighted when he can say the puppets are "for the kiddies." When he says they are for adults, he seems uncomfortable. This stigma was something Henson fought his entire career.

So it is strange to read Falk describe the lengths Henson went to pitch *The Great Santa Claus Switch*: "In order to sell the show to executives, Jim created watercolor illustrations to accompany a written proposal.[617] For someone who did not want to be known as a children's entertainer, it seems incongruous to work *that* hard—painting watercolors—for a special that was clearly for "the kiddies." Yet here we see Henson's long patience embodied, and we also see something else: an uncommon kind of pitchman.

Typically, we may think of a pitch as a bit of fast-talking, the forked tongue of a televangelist or a snake-oil–selling carpetbagger. Yet for the kind of pitching artists do, we ought to replace that image with one of a man sitting down to paint a watercolor—careful, meticulous artistic creation. Since the "pitch" was for someone to fund Henson doing more painting and puppetry, it seems less like a con and more like something any of us can do. The only difference between painting and pitching in this case was that the watercolor was *purposed* toward future artwork. The art promised more art. In that, it was a pitch. When used strategically, art can *be* a pitch.

Perhaps the holiday specials made sense to Henson, since they were to be aired at a time when the whole family was apt to watch TV together. David Lazer said in *Of Muppets and Men*:

> Our pitch for presenting the Muppets case to the networks was that this was a family show, a show that would appeal to all age groups. The network didn't feel that it was possible for us to reach both children and adults.[618]

At Christmas, families were supposed to spend time together, so parents were forced to watch with children, and perhaps Henson thought this exposure—even if it seemed like moving backward—could help him get to his dream. Falk writes of a shift in focus:

> Around 1968, . . . Jim started to seriously pitch his idea for a regular variety show hosted by the Muppets. Building on ideas from his guest appearances on *The Ed Sullivan Show*, *The Tonight Show* and the like, Jim created numerous proposals illustrating his concepts which he circulated to the networks, producers, and via his agent Bernie Brillstein. There seemed to be little interest in a full scale series, so Jim switched gears and started trying to sell Muppet variety specials themed around holidays.[619]

Henson made compromises in order to be on television. His shows from this period included *The Muppets Valentine Show* with Mia Farrow and an ABC Afterschool Special called *Out to Lunch*. In these instances, Henson seemed to be giving the networks what they *said* they wanted—tame kiddie fare—but also gave them what he *knew* was better—anarchic adult glee. In the Valentine's Day special, we learned that some people can love objects like a mop and women love mice with motorcycles. There is innuendo that delivers a shock today, forty years later. In the Afterschool Special, Henson explained, when the network goes "Out to Lunch," "all these wild people break into the studio and take over. It's really a parody of commercial television."[620] Henson pitched and made these shows because the perfect is the enemy of the good. A gooey Valentine's Day special became a stone on his path to what he *did* want. Yet it didn't happen right away—it took a few more pitches.

When ABC ultimately passed on *The Muppet Show*, according to Falk, Henson was "undeterred" and "continued to try to sell the show and Jim continued writing up ideas."[621] In 1975, he made a *Muppet Show* pitch reel for CBS with a Muppet who looks just like Leo from *Sell, Sell, Sell.* We have seen a quote from this speech before, but Henson's over-the-top pitch goes on for nearly three minutes:

> In conclusion I would like to point out that it is time for a revolutionary new look in prime-time variety television. . . . And what is this fusion of creative juices called? *The Muppet Show*! A show that will be loved and adored by every Nielsen family in the country! Small children will love the cute, cuddly characters, young people will love the fresh and innovative comedy, college kids and intellectual eggheads will love the underlying symbolism

> of everything, freaky longhaired dirty cynical hippies will love our freaky longhaired dirty cynical Muppets, because that is what show business is all about! Yes, and when this show hits, the careers of the men who made the decision to put this show on the air will skyrocket. . . . Friends, the United States of America *needs The Muppet Show*! And you should buy this show! Now, we're not pulling any punches here, I mean there's nothing subtle about this pitch! So buy the show, and put it on the air, and we'll all be famous. The Muppets will be famous, and CBS will be famous because we'll have a hit show on our hands, and we'll all get temperamental and hard to work with, but you won't care, because we'll all make a lot of money![622]

This pitch also failed. And yet now we are caught up to the moment when ITC's Abe Mandell "just so happened" to see *Sex and Violence* on TV and wanted to give Henson a syndicated show. Far from a deus ex machina, *The Muppet Show* had been pitched seriously for about six years before the angel funder came along. And even then, it had to be pitched—to him.

Falk writes, "Jim was ready with his presentation film."[623] Physically, Brillstein said, it was he who "flew to New York with my twelve-minute Muppet presentation. I took a car to his house in Scarsdale. . . . Mandel wore an eye patch. His den floor was flooded." This does not seem like a simple sell. Just as ABC had done, ITC wanted to evaluate a pilot, so Mandell offered Brillstein a hundred thousand dollars to make a pilot. "You don't have to spend a hundred thousand," Brillstein told him. "I have the pilot in my pocket."[624]

At what point was Mandell sold on *The Muppet Show*? When he called up Henson's people trying to court him? When Brillstein arrived? When Brillstein had the tape in hand already? When he watched the pilot? This deal may seem like a gift from on high—and surely it was—and yet the pitch was ongoing, like a fish on the line that could still be lost at any moment. It is likely that Mandell saw many things that day that his basement flooded—Henson's eagerness to work with ITC, Henson's vision for the show, and how easy he would be to work with.

Even though it was Mandell making the "overtures,"[625] in Falk's words, Henson *still* had to pitch to get *The Muppet Show*.

LONDON
1975–1979
THE WORK ITSELF CAN BE A PITCH

When Henson had finally got his dream—a national nighttime series for the Muppets, he was funded for only a single season. In effect, that made the success of the first season the pitch for next year's renewal. As we've seen, the quality of the series was directly related to its expense—with each show's profits being pumped back into the next show. Each season was a pitch for an even bigger season, and then for the next step in Henson's career.

With a few years of *The Muppet Show* success behind him, Henson started to set his sights on the next target—Hollywood. In January1978, he noted in his journal, "trying to sell Emmet Otter."[626] A made-for-TV-movie, *Emmet Otter* was a classic work of art, but it was also itself a pitch—a pilot showing that he could sustain an entire movie with puppets. Nearly two years later, he noted, "Bernie calls—sold Emmet Otter to ABC for next year!"[627] This entry shows that even though Bernie was doing much of the legwork, having an agent didn't free Henson from the emotional effects of pitching. Here, it was Henson who created the pitch *material*, and it was Henson who surely held his breath whenever the phone rang. We can picture the miracle of "Bernie calls" as pure joy but more realistically as the cessation of pain. In fact, with the pitch out of your hands, the process can often be even *more* emotionally taxing, because there is nothing you can do.

Yet, because *The Muppet Show* and *Emmet Otter* were, in effect, pitches for renewal and a movie deal, there is little mention of pitching in this period of Henson's journal. Perhaps it is because he was relatively happy: he had achieved fame in 105 countries, as well as the satisfaction of knowing he was right—that puppets could work for adults. But more likely he was *busy* with an intense show-a-week schedule on *The Muppet Show* in London for months out of the year, the yearly few weeks he put into *Sesame Street* in New York, and then *Emmet Otter*, a movie made in Toronto. Things were about to get even busier. Dave Goelz once said, "I always think of TV as calisthenics and movies as craftsmanship. You get in shape with TV, because you do so much material so fast. . . . Then you go shoot a film, and you get the luxury of doing it right."[628] The shift to movies required more time and more money, but a little less pitching.

HOLLYWOOD
1979–1982
THE WORK THAT IS NOT A PITCH

Luckily, Henson didn't have to look far to find his funding for *The Muppet Movie*. He simply had to convince his angel funder, Lorde Grade. The quote we've seen from Brillstein's memoir makes this clear: "Jim had proved himself. Grade . . . said, 'Here's the money. Go do it.'"[629] During Henson's boom years, pitching seemed easy. And for as long as he was on top, it was.

The Muppet Movie did very well at the box office. It was the seventh-highest grossing film of 1979, and the most successful Muppet movie until 2011. Henson had been dreaming of something even grander—an entirely new world made out of puppetry. A puppeteer's love song to Hollywood. But that seemed to require even *more* distribution than Lew Grade's ITC alone could handle. In 1979, he noted in his *Red Book* journal, "Fly to NY to pitch Dark Crystal,"[630] and pitched the film to Paramount, although Universal ended up being the distributor. Lew Grade's ITC funded the movie, which eventually cost $15 million. Everything Henson had done thus far in movies and television seemed, in a way, to be a pitch for this one great film.

In the meantime, Henson made *The Great Muppet Caper*, and it is arguably the loveliest of the Muppet movies, because Henson himself directed it, composing painstaking artistic shots. *The Dark Crystal* was even more artisanal. It really didn't seem to be a pitch for anything—it is the thing itself, everything Henson wanted it to be.

Perhaps this is why *The Dark Crystal*'s poor reception was such a blow to Henson. It wasn't a failed pitch that he could dust off and try again. The movie took five years to make, and it was made exactly the way Henson wanted. It must have been *confusing*. In some interviews, he refused to call it a failure: "Some people like it very much; those with good taste. Some didn't care for it at all or missed the point."[631]

Frank Oz spoke about the moment when movie executives previewed the movie: "The lights went on, and they stood up and they walked out. And Jim was so depressed from that, and he was depressed from some of the reviews."[632]

What does depression for Henson look like? Well, Brian Henson recalled a similar depression five years later:

> When *Labyrinth* was not a commercial success, that, I think, that was quite a blow to him. . . . It was the first time I ever saw him not want to work was during that period. There was a few months there that he didn't want to work. He wanted to travel, and stop, and think, and reflect a little.[633]

If we apply this kind of stop-and-think moment to 1982, when Henson's masterpiece was not universally applauded, we can see Henson—the pitcher—at a crossroads.

PRODUCERMAN 1982–1989 PITCHING MORE TO GET AWAY FROM PITCHING SO MUCH

While Henson was making *The Dark Crystal,* he was also letting his core creative team from *The Muppet Show* develop the kind of show they'd like to do next, which became *Fraggle Rock.* We can imagine an alternative eighties in which *The Dark Crystal* had been a box-office smash, and in that universe, perhaps Henson would have made two more five-year fantasy films and had two long-running series, *Fraggle Rock* and *Sesame Street.* He could have been intimately involved in every second of shooting for all these projects.

Yet the perceived failure of *The Dark Crystal* seemed to cause Henson to reevaluate his strategy. Since masterpiece movies did not return the investment,[634] Henson took a step back and began to throw more darts at the board again. In his journal, we see a big spike in pitches in the eighties. Henson probably didn't record half the pitches he made in these years. It would be as unnecessary as writing "I drink water."

Around 1984, Henson started telling interviewers, "I think my own strengths are in television production."[635] He pitched a great many TV shows in this period—*Fraggle Rock*, *Puppetman*, *Starboppers*, *The Ghost of Faffner Hall*, *A Muppet Family Christmas*, *Muppet Babies*, *Little Muppet Monsters*, *The Storyteller*, and more. There is "pitch material" for an unrealized *Muppet Institute of Technology* collaboration with *The Hitchhiker's Guide to the Galaxy* writer Douglas Adams.[636] Henson had varying degrees of involvement in these shows, but in general, he was not very involved in the day-to-day production of them. It is almost as though Henson the auteur filmmaker had been burned by putting all of his eggs into one basket and here shifted to coming up with great ideas, getting the ball rolling, and letting others take the helm of a fleet of Henson-produced television projects.

As the granddaddy to these projects, Henson seemed to take on more of the business side of his company than ever, leaving much creative direction up to others. Frank Oz was given the role of director for the movie *The Muppets Take Manhattan*. *Fraggle Rock* was largely left up to writers Jocelyn Stevenson and Jerry Juhl, producer Duncan Kenworthy, and the veteran performers Richard Hunt and Jerry Nelson. According to Whitmire:

> He was not there very much. . . . It was kind of left in our hands to be the authorities about what we do on a daily basis on all sides of this, performing and writing and everything, you know [the Fraggle-building] workshop was similar, he wasn't overseeing things as he had been in the past. He left it up to us, and we sort of had to rise to the challenge for that.[637]

Jerry Nelson said, "It was the first production I had ever been involved in at Jim Henson's company where he was not directly involved all the way through."[638] Yet he told an interviewer, "[Henson] didn't leave until he had worked with enough directors with correct focus to make the show work in a seamless way. And of course, he came back from time to time to join in the fun."[639]

In the 1980s, producerman Henson launched many ships with others at the helm, and let them take their own course. Few were long-sailing—*Fraggle Rock* being perhaps the most successful. And it is telling when Nelson says he would come back to "join the fun from time to time," because this implies that most of his life was spent not joining the fun. Henson was no longer a puppetman like the eponymous character in that short-lived sitcom he pitched. As producerman, his life took on more tasks, as his 1988 journal entries describe: "At Warners—Show piece of film to get more money"[640] and "In LA—selling the Witches to Lorimar."[641]

Duncan Kenworthy recalled pitching *Fraggle Rock* to HBO:

> The evening before I was supposed to go in and pitch it to whoever it was, the top brass of HBO, we had a little celebration at Henson's as somebody was leaving, and the next day I somehow didn't quite feel up to it, and Jim rather bad-temperedly said, "Okay well I'll do it then," so he went off and did the pitch and of course did brilliantly and HBO bought it.[642]

Henson, who had been at the same party, made the pitch to HBO. At this stage of his career, one would think Henson would developed and proven his business. Wouldn't his work ever be funded without having to pitch?

Sadly, no. At the age of fifty-one, Henson *still* had to pitch. And his bad-temperedness suggests he was starting to tire of it. The lifestyle of a producerman may have seemed at the start of the eighties like the best way for Henson to keep making art, but at the end of the decade, it seemed like another thing to work *away from*. Though he pitched more furiously than ever then, it seemed to be in order to escape pitching.

In the *Sesame Street* period, Henson pitched kiddie shows in order to escape kiddie shows. Similarly, in the eighties, Henson pitched an empire's worth of shows so that he could once again become a hired performer. As we will see, Henson's long-view gamble was that by saturating the media, he would become an attractive purchase for Disney.

It has been said that Henson was a man of a million ideas—he was always thinking toward the *next* project. This could explain his life of constant pitching, and yet I don't think Henson was happy to merely hand off his ideas to others. *The Dark Crystal* resembled the *Sam and Friends* days, because Henson got to *do* everything. A movie director may have more people helping him than a puppet show creator has, but they both get to create an entire world from scratch, and, with both projects, the artistic control rested with Henson. For an artist like Henson, this artistic work was "the fun" to be joined in. The stories of Henson working through the night with Oz, or cracking up singing with Nelson and Hunt—they convince me that Henson really wanted to get back to "work." To *art*work.

In this view, Henson's furious pitches in the eighties may have been an attempt to get away from the whole endeavor of pitching altogether.

DISNEY 1989–1990 APPEARING HOT IN ORDER TO COOL DOWN

If Disney were to buy Henson's Muppet business, they would become his new angel funder—promising to green-light any expensive project he wanted, because he would work exclusively for them. For an artist, that's a very attractive proposition—it would mean Henson could spend less time pitching and more time *creating*.

In 1990, Henson finally made the sale he'd really been pitching—himself to Disney.

According to Brillstein, there had been talk since the early eighties of a Henson/Disney "pairing":

> I called Eisner and pitched him on the idea. He was interested. A couple weeks later, David Lazer, Katzenberg, Eisner, and I met in the private dining room at Chasen's restaurant. The Disney team . . . told us what we already knew . . . the Muppets weren't exactly hot. *The Muppet Show* was over and except for the movies, not much was happening. Even the Muppets merchandise wasn't selling well. *Sesame Street* merchandise did, but *Sesame Street* was untouchable . . . Disney passed and Jim went back to work.[643]

In the early eighties, the Muppets "weren't exactly hot" in Eisner's acquisitive eyes, but by 1988, Henson had Muppets on all of the five major networks—ABC, NBC, CBS, PBS, and HBO. It could not have been a coincidence. All that producerman pitching in the eighties starts to seem like a deliberate strategy to attract Disney's interest. In 1989 Brillstein writes, "By 1989 The Henson Company [as it would become known] was in better shape. They had more cash and exploitable material, so Eisner's interest didn't surprise me."[644]

Though the 1990s that Henson imagined—a ten-year contract with Disney to fund expensive projects like 3-D movies and theme-park rides—would never materialize due to his untimely death, we can see his motives for the Disney sale clearly. As Brillstein wrote, Henson wanted to "get out from under the organizational albatross that drained his creative energy. . . . With Disney's money and machinery, Jim could be fully creative."[645] As a funded artist at Disney, Henson could stop being a producerman, and he might not even have to be a pitchman.

The noteworthy part of this period, to me, is that if Brillstein's version of history is correct, Henson was *sick and tired* of pitching. If he had been a natural salesman—born to love pitching—I don't think he would have traded his licensing to Disney for promised funding. If he wanted to make a big project like a 3-D movie, he could've pitched it to enough companies to get it funded. He may not have loved to pitch, but it was always a necessary part of the job.

My view of Henson is that, from the start, he cultivated the skill of the pitch in order to achieve *artistic* aims. And if a shy creator like Henson could do it, anyone can.

FAIL, FAIL, FAIL
PITCHING IS THE EASY PART

If we try to cultivate our own ability to pitch—to *preach*—we might start by getting wrapped up in the *good* things in others' work, then really working to appreciate and revel in the *good* things in our work, until we finally get obsessed with convincing others of what *could* be. Henson was a teenager in an optimistic period of American history—the postwar fifties. It likely made him a very positive person.

Yet, with pitching, failure is inevitable. To become pitchmen, we are going to have to find a way to deal with failure. Expressing enthusiasm for your work is, in fact, the easy part of pitching. The hard part is all the failure.

One consolation for this is the adrenaline rush of *selling* a project. Henson uses exclamation marks in his *Red Book* journal when a movie sells. It's the same kind of jubilation when he writes "New Central Park Zoo opens!"[646] Pitching and selling gives you an innocent, childlike high, such that when one is suitably addicted, it offsets the pain of failure.

When I was a student, I used to watch struggling artists fail, and I'd think, *How can I avoid becoming like that?* I thought people who failed must've made some mistake that I should avoid making. Successful people like Jim Henson tend to keep their biographies positive—all sales and no fails—because it is good PR, but when you dig deeper, you see that everyone successful fails in monstrous proportions matching their success. It's just that they promote the success louder than the failure. Now that I'm older, I watch struggling artists fail, and I think, *How can I become more like that?* How can I summon the courage to fail like that? How can I learn to survive failure *for a living*?

Ironically, the road to Henson's success is a string of failures, and this was as true for Henson as it is for anyone else. As we look at Henson's three biggest failures, take heart knowing that you are fully capable of failing *this much*, brushing yourself off, and trying again.

JOHNNY CARSON AND THE MUPPET MACHINE NEVER MADE

For my research, I've tried to watch every project Henson ever made. Wandering the Henson exhibit at New York's Museum of the Moving Image, I was excited to see a promotion for a special with the Muppets and Johnny Carson. From the drawings—pen and ink in Henson's own hand—it looked so imaginative, like a Rube Goldberg mousetrap. The style is gorgeously intricate, yet freewheeling—a comic strip with swirling borders presents a story of mayhem: monsters in chef's hats, a box with a note that says "RUN!"[647] The machine explodes in the next doodle, and Johnny Carson is spit out of a theater onto the street. A janitor with a wry smile cleans it all up.

I went home all ready to watch what might have been my new favorite Henson project. But there was no Carson special to watch, no Muppet machine, no trippy new gags or allusions to Henson's business. The Carson pitch was great—but it was rejected. In polite industry terms it "wasn't picked up," but in an artist's estimation, it was *wasted.* Those lovely drawings made—for nothing.

Can you imagine spending a day drawing the specs and being rejected? You should, because as an artist of the gift economy, your faith in art—despite its risk—is what can turn a commodity into a gift. Picture yourself spending a day in wasted art, because that is what the labor of a successful artist looks like.

If you go to The Henson Company's *Red Book* blog, you'll see that Henson's doodles from this pitch were adapted as wingdings—a search box, a footer, and bookends for a navigation tool. It seems that somebody wanted this art to be *seen.* Karen Falk, the Henson archivist, presents projects like this from Henson's files, precisely because so much of Henson's work, like the iceberg's underwater majority, remains unseen.

CYCLIA NEVER MADE

It's fun to imagine what the world would have been like if Jim Henson had become a nightclub owner—going out dancing today might include more rustling leaves and the sound of flowing streams. Jim Henson's planned nightclub, Cyclia, would have given the late sixties a truly fantastic experience of rotating polarized disks, imagist film "poetry" timed to the music and projected onto all the furniture and people in a geodesic dome.[648] Falk writes:

> In the descriptions of his nightclub project Cyclia, Jim hoped to match quieter music with filmed depictions of nature—light coming through trees, reflected off water, and changing over time. His 1974 pitch for a television special called *Reflections* suggested, ". . . an hour of visual poetry. It is an affirmation of our sense of wonder."[649]

Henson scouted locations in New York and Los Angeles.

> As his vision expanded to giant geodesic domes, Jim made inquiries about a vacant lot on Second Avenue that now houses the base of the Roosevelt Island Tram. In an empty space like that, there were practically no design limitations. By 1970, however, the Cyclia Corporation was dissolved, and Jim's energies went into *Sesame Street* and his quest for a Muppet series.[650]

The idea was dropped. So was the *Reflections* TV special. Henson had already shot test footage. The good news is that the planning of this nightclub likely honed the directorial skills that he would later use in *The Dark Crystal*, *Labyrinth*, and *The Storyteller*. Yet, with the exception of the Henson Archives blog, there is nowhere you can go to see this Henson project. You have to imagine it. Henson's Cyclia club was never made.

As Falk said, Henson's "energies" went into other things—he gave up on these particular projects and moved on. But there was one idea that Henson refused to truly forget.

B'WAY
THE DESTINY OF GREAT PUPPETRY, BUT NOT FOR HENSON

It is not surprising that Henson refers to Broadway in his *Red Book* as "B'way." Nicknames are for friends—and Henson's fondness of theater is clear. If he saw a show, he carefully marked if it was "Off B'way."[651] The abbreviation was deeply ingrained, so he even wrote, "Museum of B'casting."[652] Broadway is, of course, the highest echelon of live theater. Puppetry, as old as any brand of live performance, seemed like a natural fit for that hallowed venue.

And while *Warhorse* or *The Lion King* have foregrounded puppetry in the world of high theater, Henson never made it. Part of the problem was that Americans looked down on puppetry. Henson explained:

> I saw that puppetry was truly an art form in Europe. It was something that could be done artistically, with creativity. Back home, there weren't all that many puppeteers, but in Europe they are everywhere and everybody goes to puppet shows. It's an integral part of their lives.[653]

Broadway may have occupied a place in Henson's mind as the site where critical success and respect would finally be afforded to his work, even if it was only a lowly puppet show. If a puppet show made it to Lincoln Center, maybe then the "slight condescension toward puppets" he noted would cease to follow him.[654]

When asked about his work with Nancy Sinatra in Vegas, Henson said, "I have in mind doing a stage show, a full Broadway show with puppets."[655] The way he says "a full Broadway show with puppets" he might as well be saying "a legitimate puppet theater." So Henson began pitching the show, and by the end of 1971, he was "in discussions with Lincoln Center." Falk describes what might have been:

> An ambitious piece was meant to give a capsule history of religion, falling into chaos and ending with a lone flower. A flock of birds in the trees provided a comic moment, and the joyous ending featured all the puppeteers taking off their costumes and puppets, singing "We are all just people underneath."[656]

Two years later, Henson signed with two producers, Manny Azenberg and Eugene Wolsk. Four years on, Falk writes:

> Azenberg and Wolsk were still selling the show. . . . By then, however, Jim was getting real interest for *The Muppet Show* and began appearing on *Saturday Night Live*. The Broadway Show project was set aside."[657]

Whether it was "set aside" or "fell through" is unclear. His writer, Larry Gelbart, left the business to make *M*A*S*H*.[658] Henson noted, "Gelbart out of B'way." Falk writes:

> After Jim's deal to create a live show at Lincoln Center featuring an array of specially designed puppets fell through, he continued to pitch his idea. He had developed a script with Marshall Brickman called *The Muppets Get It Together* and a related script for a companion television special called *An Evening with the Muppets*, and Jim was eager to try again. While the records are thin, it is apparent from Jim's journal that he gave this idea another chance by auditioning for the Shuberts, the renowned Broadway producers.[659]

It may be true that if Henson had not been so busy working on TV projects—*The Muppet Show* pitch, *Saturday Night Live (SNL)*, and *Sesame Street*—he might have made it to Broadway. Or maybe the world was simply not ready. But as it was, the closest Henson ever came to Lincoln Center was as a museum exhibit, not a Broadway show. In 1979, he noted: "Lincoln Center Library—Party exhibit of The Art of the Muppets (runs thru Aug.)."[660] And in 1982 his film masterpiece *The Dark Crystal* followed: "D.C. Exhibit opens Lincoln Center Library."[661] At Lincoln Center, fans could marvel at "all the spectacular craftsmanship"[662] of the movie, including costumes, jewelry, musical instruments, and cooking utensils. The Muppets may have made it to Lincoln Center, but they never really made it to B'way.

But there was something about B'way that made it different from Cyclia or the Carson special—it was an elusive goal that lingered. So, after he made his essentially prime-time series and his Hollywood films, Henson returned to the Broadway failure in the eighties, hoping to turn it into a success. How did Henson deal with failure here? He refused to call it quits.

Henson's tenacity with Broadway starts to resemble Kermit's indefatigable scheming to get to Broadway in *The Muppets Take Manhattan.* Falk writes of this failure's long history:

> Jim had started on a project for the stage written by Hugh Wheeler called Bodo featuring medieval characters, some designed by Brian Froud. The day before his talk with Gelbart, he noted in his journal "Drop Bodo." Clearly, he was not giving up on the Broadway Show idea, but wanted to do something different and thought Gelbart might be a good collaborator. In July, he and Gelbart met with Brian and Wendy Froud and started discussions about a new project for the stage that would also feature medieval characters. Over the next year, a writing deal was negotiated with Gelbart for what was then being referred to as the Medieval Show, but by 1983, Jim was looking into other writers, including Neil Simon.
>
> Nothing came of the Medieval idea, but in 1985, Jim began developing a different idea for a Broadway Show, this time in a more contemporary world. With a working title of "The Puppet Show," it was to be an array of performances with a variety of music loosely strung together with a behind-the-scenes storyline focusing on the puppeteers and their personalities and relationships.[663]

Henson wrote in his journal, "10/26/1982 Lunch with Neil Simon—B'way." Whatever it was—other projects in the way, people backing out, or perhaps not enough lunches in the day, Broadway never saw a Muppets show. Brillstein wrote, "My one regret is that I never got him to do *An Evening with the Muppets* on Broadway. I believe if he had, it would still be running today."[664]

With all the dealing, planning, and failure of the never-made B'way show, it is hard to picture myself doing something like this—trying and failing for two decades to make something happen. B'way was a failure every year of Henson's career. But it was also a possibility every year of his career—because he refused to close the door on something just because it was difficult to achieve. Henson's long view is an attitude any artist can benefit from. Remember what Jerry Nelson said of Henson: "If [Jim] could see it happening in his mind's eye and knew that it would work, he would *dog* it until it worked."[665]

In *The Muppets Take Manhattan*, Rowlf sang about failure. When the Muppets tried to get their Broadway show produced, doors slammed in their faces. Yet, in spite of rejection, Rowlf sang, "You can't take no for an answer. No no no." The theme of that song, and that movie, is that artists—like you—*need* to be able to fail *this hard* and to be able to get back up and try again.

Some doors are closed permanently—but if you look at it another way, they're not really closed—they're just angled to lead somewhere new.

REUSE, REPURPOSE, RECYCLE

Since Henson owned his copyrights, nothing was ever truly *wasted*, even if it seems like it came to nothing. We see elements from *Johnny Carson and the Muppet Machine*—a janitor with a broom, an exploding machine, a world of cave dwellers, a labyrinth rooted in the explorer's fears—in many later Henson works. The spectacle of Cyclia reappears in Henson's lavish masked-ball scene in *Labyrinth*. And though Henson never made a Broadway show, the Muppets did, fictionally, in a movie.

Time called *The Muppets Take Manhattan* "a lullaby to Broadway." The Muppets endure relentless failure with agents, producers, and other B'way types. But they succeed in the fictional film when the son of a producer falls in love with the novelty of their idea. Though we might see this as Henson's swan song for his B'way dreams, in a way, the movie was *also* a pitch for the B'way show that might *yet* be made—by the next generation of angel investors. As a pitch, the big wedding at the end—a masterful song and dance number—showed any producers watching that it could *still* work.

The beauty of turning Henson's Broadway failure into a Hollywood love story is that he was at once accepting defeat in the present and holding onto the possibility of success in the future. If he never made a B'way show—which he didn't—then the film would recycle many of his ideas and make them bear fruit. People saw *The Muppets Take Manhattan*. It has a Wikipedia page. That's something. The B'way project doesn't.

Another recycled "waste" is Leo from *The Muppet Show* pitch reel. Henson reused Leo's pitch as the meeting film *Sell, Sell, Sell.* Even if it didn't work with CBS, it did work as a business-to-business rental. This DVD is still for sale for $445, or for rent for $250 a week.[666] Recycling made Leo bear fruit—meaning money to fund projects—but also more. Leo gave Henson exposure in a new market. Though *The Muppet Show* pitch reel was seen by only a handful of CBS executives, the *Sell, Sell, Sell* film was seen by many employees at companies like IBM—adults—who probably became more likely to become fans of *The Muppet Show*, once it was put in an adult context.

Exposure is always a good thing. And then there is the lucky-devil possibility that one of your rejecters will change their mind. In 1966, Henson noted, "Wrote 'The Cube' with Jerry—NBC rejected."[667] According to Falk, NBC sent a "warm" rejection note:

> The producer described Jim as "one of the most brilliant creative artists of our time," but that he saw "no hope for it at any domestic network unless CBS Playhouse turns out to be far more courageous and experimental that I expect them to be." As it happened, in 1967, the NBC television network began a series of one-hour Sunday afternoon programs under the heading NBC Experiment in Television, conceived as an opportunity to develop new television formats and concepts. In 1968, NBC bought *The Cube* and Jim produced it for the series to air the following February.[668]

Rejection letters often contain the polite phrase "not for us," but sometimes, a rejection is the first step to a relationship. Henson was ahead of his time. When NBC caught up and became more experimental, they remembered Henson's pitch. Had he not subjected himself to failure, he would not have been forefront in their minds. We might picture it as a blessing to be defined as "not for us," when an executive thinks, *Oh where was that thing that was not for us? It would be perfect for* this.

Henson's pitch—though technically a failure—actually primed NBC to be more aware of experimental content and its value to their changing audience. It makes sense to keep in touch with warm rejecters, and to never be less than warm back, no matter how much rejection may sting.

When we look at Henson's disappointments with NBC, the pitch reel, and *The Cube*, failure almost starts to seem like getting a free distribution deal that no one took a cut of. Pitching your idea is free, and it's a free form of exposure. You take up the industry's time by pitching, and getting an audience with a network turned out to be incredibly valuable to Henson, even if the pitches were met with "sorry, not for us."

In many ways, a life of constant pitching is a life of constant failure. The next time you watch *The Muppets Take Manhattan*, know that the kind of dogged, naïve enthusiasm that the Muppets display when trying to get their Broadway show made was exactly what enabled Henson to make his ideas *real*. When you watch an artist struggle and fail, think to yourself, *How can I do that? How can I keep failing and keep pitching?*

RE-SYNDICATE, CO-FUND, RE-PROFIT

Another benefit to pitching widely is that it tends to create more offers to fund your work. And if no one funder can offer enough to make your project, Henson realized, you could get *two* people to co-fund you. With some clever sleight of hand, giving the same thing to multiple people yields a higher amount of funding.

Usually, it is only prime time series that get picked up for syndication. *Seinfeld*, for instance, started in prime time on NBC and was then licensed to smaller networks to fill their odd daytime timeslots. *The Muppet Show* was never prime time. It came on at 7:30 p.m. on most CBS affiliates, and because of that, most people *thought* it was prime time. Because no one could tell it was syndicated, it could later be re-syndicated as reruns by the TNT network. As we saw, the show made no money when it first aired and became profitable only after it was re-syndicated. In this sense, from the point of view of a historian, TNT and ATV effectively pooled their resources so that the show would make a profit for Henson.

Brillstein wrote, "Most people then didn't know the difference between a network show and a syndicated show, so it seemed like we were on CBS proper."[669] Henson would later use this same trick with *Fraggle Rock*.

In 1982, Henson needed more funding than he could get from one network for *Fraggle Rock*. So he pitched it to both CBC and HBO to co-fund. According to Duncan Kenworthy:

> The deal was that CBC were going to provide all the facilities, so the crew and the studio and things that didn't actually cost them hard cash . . . And then we had to pitch it to HBO . . . to get the cash . . . . It was probably one of the only times...where we managed to get two countries to pay for the entire show and then . . . we were able to then sell it and coproduce it and adapt it around the world.[670]

Most people in the US thought *Fraggle Rock* was a US show made by HBO. In Canada, you'd think it was a Canadian show made by CBC. And with the coproductions, you might think it's a British, German, or French show, depending where you live, because you would see a different wraparound—a "Doc" who lived in a Scottish lighthouse and was a captain, or who lived in a bakery and was a French chef. The money came from many hands, but the show stayed in Henson's. To this day, it is The Henson Company that can sell DVDs of the show and produce sequels.

One problem with co-funding is that if one backer backs out, you have to stop. You now have to worry about two funders. Jerry Nelson explains why *Fraggle Rock* ended:

> HBO, at that time, felt that they were over-extended and needed to cut back. . . . CBC would have been perfectly happy keeping it, and in fact, they tried to find some

> other way to carry on with it. Another season would have been ideal.[671]

Co-funding, like crowdfunding, has its drawbacks, but it can also lead to greater quality—while it lasts.

Because of co-funding, *Fraggle Rock* had a generous budget. It gets expensive to have writers watch tapings and performers attend writing meetings, or to pay for overtime when a writer wants to flood the Gorgs' basement, yet the "cash" from HBO, as Kenworthy put it, made such a collaboration affordable. "We had plenty of money," said producer Larry Mirkin.[672] Designer Michael Frith wrote that when he came up with big idea:

> No one ever said it would be too expensive or too time-consuming; people just pushed through the night to make things happen—again and again . . . endless caverns, crystalline constructions, and gleaming underground cities . . .[673]

The idea to make Doozers pogo is amazing, but not cheap. Making it happen took three hours for fourteen seconds of video. Henson was able to pay the *Fraggle Rock* writers, performers, and artists well because of the extra money from both CBC and HBO. They were able to construct lavish sets and beautiful creatures, and create unforgettable original music, because they had twice as many funders as the average show. And to get them, Henson had to make twice as many pitches.

For all the drawbacks that come with relentless pitching, I believe it is the single most important thing that can allow an artist to control his own financial destiny.

HOW TO
CULTIVATE YOUR PITCHIFICATION

So how can you become a pitchman? Find what it is that you can't shut up about. Henson had more success pitching projects that were *both* financially and artistically attractive. When you are selling good, marketable things like *Sesame Street*, you will find it an easier sell than when you are selling Wheels, Flutes, and Crowns, which are just marketable. It also helps that your "good" things have a potential payout, like *Sesame Street* toys or *Muppet Show* re-syndication.

But you may also find that, like Henson, you pitch more when you are trying to *avoid* something than when you are trying to get *toward* something. If so, think of pitching as your way out, and pitch as though your life depended on it. Your *artistic* life just might.

Above all, know that Henson was not thrilled to do promotion, either. Henson was a shy man with a quiet way of speaking. It was only in the last year of his life that he agreed to appear on camera regularly as himself as a recurring character in *The Jim Henson Hour*. Henson's preachification leads me to wonder—is the shyest, most reluctant self-promoter perhaps the *best* pitchman? If he finds something *worth* overcoming shyness to preach, perhaps no one can silence him.

As I write this, I am burning with the sting of a recent rejection from *Slate*. But it makes me smile to think that two years ago, *Slate* told me my essay "Weekend at Kermie's" wasn't for them, and instead of cutting it down to conform to their style, I made it even longer and made a list of thirty more editors. *The Awl* ran it, and when it went viral people tweeted things like, "This is the single best article I have read this year." When you make something really great on spec, it can be a risk, but ultimately it gives you the power to control your artistic destiny. If you can stomach failure, pitching allows you to say and do what *you* want, not just what the market wants.

How do you feel about pitching? How does it feel to be rejected? How does it feel to get the job? Does it get any easier with time? What do you do to pick yourself up, dust yourself off, and pitch again?

Because of the way Henson's negotiation with Disney turned sour—as we will explore in Lesson 10—I don't think it is possible to truly "get out" of the pitching game. It seems a part of the freelance artist lifestyle. In order to have your independence—your creative freedom—as an artist, you have to just keep pitching.

You can convince people of anything, as long as you try enough people, and as long as you really believe in it yourself. If you *believe* in your art, make a pitch for it today. Spend a day at the easel working on a pitch of some kind. Watch Jim Henson's impressive pitching for inspiration, and then go out and sell, sell, sell!

LESSON 9

NURTURE TALENT

AND GET OUT OF ITS WAY

To hear Henson's "employees" speak of him as their "fearless leader," it can sometimes seem over-the-top exultant. Longtime Muppets writer Jerry Juhl often spoke of "the joys that Jim gave us"[674] when recounting his time on *Fraggle Rock* and other projects. It's a bit hard to believe if you only hear about it—maybe they're all acting or brainwashed—but when you see Frank Oz tear up during a CNN interview at the loss of his friend and mentor, it dispels all cynicism.[675]

We intuitively know that Henson was a "good boss." But how should we define a "good boss," and better yet, how can we become one? Brian Henson has said of his father, "He taught me to identify a person's talent, nurture that talent, and encourage them to look to themselves for a solution."[676]

A good boss, like a good teacher, empowers his employees. This, though, is too easy to *say* and very hard to actually *do*. Maybe I could do it once or twice, but every day for thirty years? Most of us have egos that get in the way, worrying we will be thought of as too soft, slow, or indecisive. According to one article, Henson's wife,

Jane, "once said that Jim is so patient she sometimes wants to kick him."[677] Jim Henson had what was indeed a very *rare* management style—one of radical kindness, a compassion so strong it seems to most of us like a violent denial of one's own ego.

In our era of interconnected gadgets, we tend to exalt the self-made men of Silicon Valley, hardheaded—and antisocial—entrepreneurs like Steve Jobs, because they cut through the traditional business model and invented their own way of doing business. Yet biographers paint Jobs as egotistical to the point that it *hurt* others. According to David Price, "He made a habit of informing Atari engineers that they were moronic and their designs were lousy."[678] Price continues:

> While many at Apple admired Jobs's vision and perfectionism, he had an obnoxious side that antagonized employees up and down the ranks. Jef Raskin, originator of the Macintosh project, made an eleven-point list of the reasons Jobs was impossible to work with and later resigned from the company. (Item 3: "Does not give credit where due." Item 4: "Often reacts ad hominem." Item 10: "Often irresponsible and inconsiderate.")[679]

Steve Jobs's beautiful products have enticed many of us try to think more like Jobs in our own careers. WWSJD? What would Steve Jobs do? However, insulting arrogance is not *necessary* for a successful career in art or innovation.

Jim Henson's career also changed the world as we know it—and with *Sesame Street* shown round the world, probably more than we know. It's easy to spot Apple's influence in the physical world, but Henson's lessons are so imbedded in our psyches we don't even notice them. Generation X and Millennials can credit Henson with much of their idealism. And as we might expect from these generations of lovers and dreamers, Henson's management style was radically kind, radically gentle, and unlike Jobs, it bore a causal link to the kind of success an artist truly *wants*. In *Of Muppets and Men*, Henson says:

> The kind of comedy we do depends on being able to work in a certain atmosphere—it's something we work consciously to create. . . . If we didn't manage to maintain a friendly atmosphere, we'd be in deep trouble.[680]

It is easy for CEOs to *say* that they want to foster creativity, but it takes a radical approach to actually create that kind of environment. To foster collaboration, Steve Jobs designed the Pixar building to have only two bathrooms—both in the front lobby, *forcing* people to interact more and combine their ideas. Yet this is superficial and dictatorial, and it seems designed to ensure bladder discomfort. The real way to create innovation and collaboration is by setting an example—starting with oneself. Jerry Juhl has called Henson's spirit "infectious":

> One of the images that I think we all have of Jim that we've seen repeatedly is Jim standing in the studio with his hand in the air and a puppet and he's laughing uncontrollably. Everything has come to a complete stop, and that kind of infectious enthusiasm kind of spread through all casts and crews, and Jim balanced that with a desire to do the work as well as possible. So you were working at the top of your form, but you were also having as much fun as possible, and I think that was very infectious.[681]

Henson's leadership is noteworthy. Dave Goelz remarked recently, "We had a [*Fraggle Rock*] reunion last year, and many past employees came. Over and over we heard them say it was the best job they ever had."[682] Those employees have had over twenty years since Henson's death in which to experience the alternatives.

Martin Baker, one of Henson's producers said, "You can't replace someone like that—he was [a] true one off—you don't replace them."[683] As uncommon as Henson was as a leader, I hope this isn't true. I hope his management style can be replicated. Let us imagine for a minute that *anyone* can manage talent like Henson. What might that look like? First, let us distinguish Henson's approach from those who resemble him most.

ALTERNATIVES: WALT

Comparisons between Walt Disney and Henson are ubiquitous, and for good reason—it is almost uncanny how these two visionaries line up. Starting from the ground up, each created a successful business by making quality popular art that would last for generations. As artists, they had much in common.

Disney had a knack for seeing *character*—in animals and people. Animators Thomas and Johnston recalled:

> Walt . . . would get up at the story meetings, enter his trance, and suddenly transform himself uninhibitedly into . . . an old hunting dog. "Y'know this old guy would come snuffin' along like a vacuum cleaner, his muzzle spread all over the ground," Walt would say as he recalled a dog from his childhood in Marceline and turned himself into that dog. . . . He would imitate the expressions of the dog, and look from one side to the other, and raise first

> one brow and then the other as he tried to figure things out.[684]

It is eerily similarly to hear Henson speak of a family hound:

> He was so expressive. I would watch this dog for hours. Just in the area of the dog's eyes and eyebrows, you could read an enormous world of emotion going by.[685]

Both men owned their own companies yet were capable of getting into the mind of a goofy mutt. By studying the subtle expressions that give a character emotion and depth, each could transform this awareness into lifelike characters.

When it came to managing their companies, both recognized the importance of a "relaxed" environment for artists. Gabler compared the mood of Disney Studios in the 1930s to the "jocularity and informality" of a college campus:

> "[M]aybe an Ivy League campus," said one employee. . . . [O]ne new artist wrote friends, "If this is not a crazy house, then I don't know what is."[686]

And it seems that this excited *feeling* somehow made it into Disney's pictures themselves. Gossip columnist Hedda Hopper said of Disney's studio, "The whole atmosphere is conducive to the lightheartedness and gayety that you find in Disney's pictures."[687] There were often "sophomoric pranks" at the Hyperion studio, such as Ward Kimball coming to work dressed in a gorilla outfit. The humor and fraternity of the place calls to mind the cottage of the seven dwarfs on a scale of hundreds.

Similarly, pranks were common in Henson's workshops and studios, often perpetrated by Dave Goelz and Steve Whitmire. A mouse on a string terrorized Caroly Wilcox's puppet shop. Lew Grade's limo was mooned on the highway by a bus filled with Muppeteers and crew.[688]

Jerry Nelson paints the right image of "playfulness," describing a recording session for an underwater number:

> I wish there was footage of us trying to gargle and then sing. We all tried it, even Jim. We were all cracking up at each other. It was hilarious.[689]

Jerry Juhl described the world of the Muppets as one of "affectionate anarchy."[690]

And both Henson and Disney nurtured their talented artists. Disney drove his animators to night classes at the Chouinard Art Institute, and then hired the teacher, Donald Graham, to set up the "great Disney Art School," teaching figurative drawing, "the effect of gravity on mass, and how flesh and muscle move."[691]

Henson likewise nurtured homegrown talent, as he explained to Judy Harris:

> The whole process of learning our style and becoming good at it takes nearly a year, I would say, at least. . . . [W]henever we're in production, we try to have a couple of people working with us on a—not exactly apprenticed—but the new people learning. . . . [Y]ou just have to do it a lot until it gets natural and totally without thinking.[692]

And both have been called perfectionists or, to be more flattering, *adherents to quality*.

Gabler writes:

> Walt said to me, "Mickey wouldn't think this way," said storyman Leo Salkin.[693]

Henson said something similar to *SNL* writer Alan Zweibel:

> Jim Henson's reading the pages, and he gets to a line and he says, "Oh, Skred wouldn't say this."[694]

This kind of loyalty to the characters can seem crazy, but in many ways, being a visionary means protecting your vision. Mickey and Kermit would not be "characters" had Disney and Henson not *known* them—who they were and weren't.

Both men became workaholics to get the kind of quality they wanted. Behind each Muppet and Disney film lay hours of rehearsal, screen tests, and outtakes. As we know, Henson once spent 233 takes trying to get a drum to roll out a door to his liking, trying to match the practice try.[695] David Lazer said he had "a whim of steel."[696] Similarly, Disney was detail-oriented, observable in the way he fine-tuned every detail of *Snow White*: slightly lowering a dwarf's fanny or removing two of a hummingbird's six pick-ups.[697] And as we saw in Lesson 6, Disney's attention to quality could become the kind of micromanagement that most artists find damaging to their talent. Both men asked for great quality from their artists, yet, on closer inspection, Henson and Disney could not appear more different.

NOT WALT

Disney had a vision that was not just strong, but unilateral and absolute. Gabler writes that, "for all the talk of collaboration, no one at the studio doubted that the job was less to exhibit his own talent than to realize on-screen what Walt was visualizing in his head."[698] "He could be brutal,"[699] said one animator, in his criticism. We have seen this perfectionism in action: "God help you," a writer warned, if you took his idea in the wrong direction. Disney's eyebrow would shoot up and he would tell the writer he simply didn't "get it."[700] Disney's iconic raised eyebrow signifies his strong will—something we admire him for today—but you did not want to be on the wrong side of that eyebrow.

And, unlike Henson, "Walt thought nothing of firing someone who he felt had outlived his usefulness, calling it 'weeding out marginal people' or getting rid of 'deadwood.'"[701] From the earliest days, Ub Iwerks remembered Disney spending his lunch breaks not socializing, but practicing his signature. Some of the animators felt hurt when their names were left off the credits, and Disney's were so clearly stamped over the whole picture. But when someone suggested giving internal awards to boost morale, he said, "If there's going to be any awards made, I'm going to get them."[702]

This attitude was part of what led roughly 700 of Disney's animators to strike in 1941. One animator said, "He was a genius at using someone else's genius." As touched on earlier, one picket sign read, "1 Genius Against 1,200 Guinea Pigs" and another, "Walt Disney and the 700 Dwarfs."[703] By contrast, Henson's employees never went on strike, except in nationwide movements, such as when Juhl participated in a national writers' strike. England in the seventies was a time of many union strikes, and this occasionally affected *The Muppet Show*. Yet when, during the production of *The Muppet Show*, England's power company workers went on strike, they "put out a news release stating that they would not cut the power anywhere while *The Muppet Show* was being broadcast." According to Joseph Bailey, they wanted to keep the public on their side.[704]

Unlike Disney, Henson happily listened to others and incorporated their visions into his own. Christopher Finch writes that he was "generous in that he is always open to suggestion":[705]

> Henson is a good listener and if someone has an idea that is better than his own, he accepts it without hesitation. It is because of this that the others listen to him and accept direction without feeling resentment.[706]

Caroll Spinney adds:

> One of the wonderful aspects of Jim's genius was his openness to new ideas from the people around him. . . . Jim used several of my suggestions, like having a child sit with one of the puppets in an unscripted bit, talking about letters or numbers.[707]

Assistant Alex Rockwell remembered one thing of Henson above all:

> [H]is total generosity . . . a good idea could come from anywhere . . . even this guy who I think was the janitor in the building would come up to him almost every other day and have an idea, and Jim would sit and actually really listen to the idea and if he liked it he would actually comment on it and say, "Write it down."[708]

Of course, not everyone's vision *can* be incorporated into the Muppets. As we saw with Skred at *SNL*, sometimes Henson needed to protect his characters. Yet, unlike Disney, Henson seemed to reject suggestions with gentle tact. Harry Belafonte explained, "If my suggestion was good, he accepted it without question. If he rejected a suggestion, he would always explain why it wouldn't work."[709]

Brillstein wrote, "Jim was not the kind to act stubborn. . . . If I had a counterargument, he always listened and considered it fairly."[710] While Disney seemed to have no problem shutting another artist down, Brillstein said Henson was careful not to stunt another's creativity:

> When I made a suggestion, if Jim liked it, I knew right away. Otherwise, he'd give me one of two reactions. "Hmmmm" meant "not good, not bad." Silence meant he was thinking it through. . . . It was hard for him to say no to anybody.[711]

And unlike Disney, Henson tried to avoid firing his employees at all costs. Oz recalled one prop specialist prone to mistakes that Henson didn't have the heart to fire. If Henson had been as devoted to his vision as Walt Disney, he would not have tolerated this frustration, but since the feeling of the Muppets required a certain "friendly atmosphere," Henson put his *people* first, knowing it would help them make better art.

In contrast to Disney's egotism, Henson took the time to give his artists credit in all the ways he could. Duncan Kenworthy said that Frank Oz called Henson "the great appreciator" in that "he appreciated everything and it extended to not just the performances, but also to any expertise that anyone had."[712] In an early interview, he praised Oz as "the one person most responsible for the wild humor of the Muppets."[713] One would think Henson would have given himself that award.

Though Walt Disney was an unforgettable entrepreneur, Henson's care for others seemed to supersede his perfectionism, and in that he is decidedly different from Disney. It is possible to attribute Disney's egotism and unawareness of others to his tough homesteader upbringing, his Depression-era success, his harrowing job as an ambulance-driver in WWI, or his missing out on a collegial university experience. Henson attended college in the post-war boom of the fifties, allowing him a longer maturation process. Moreover, for Disney to make the world's first animated feature, his studio had to grow rapidly to over a thousand people, and this alone seems to require a tighter sense of control. Yet even if we set aside the exterior factors, Henson and Disney were simply two different men.

A student of mine, Caitlin Hatakeyama noticed an interesting difference in the way journalists described the two men's reasons for making art. To Disney, animation was "a way of . . . finding absolute control,"[714] whereas to Henson, puppetry was "a way of hiding."[715] Henson said it himself: "I've certainly always been a very shy person."[716] Though Henson's shyness and reluctance to hurt others might *sound* weak, especially in business, it is a powerful quality that may in fact be the best way to manage talented artists, since *self*-control allows a person to hold back, do no harm, and to listen more than he talks, to truly appreciate and nurture the talent of *others*.

ALTERNATIVES: LORNE

Since Disney's management style was more controlling than Henson's, perhaps a better comparison is to *Saturday Night Live* producer Lorne Michaels. On *SNL*, with Michaels's "not ready for prime time" cast, perfectionism was thrown out the window in favor of rawer *human* talent and collaboration. Surely, Michaels is another of the twentieth century's great visionaries and *herders* of artists. It seems he was just as driven as Disney or Henson. According to Lily Tomlin:

> Lorne just believed in what he was doing and nobody was going to get in his way. . . . His willpower outlasted everybody else's. He cared the most about this show. Everyone else cared more about something else.[717]

Michaels was a contemporary of Henson's and they shared much of the spirit of the 1970s. Michaels appreciated good work. In *Live from New York*, the wonderful oral history by Tom Shales and James Miller, Gwyneth Paltrow called Michaels "a fan of comedy and talent."[718] Unlike Disney, he gave his comedians the freedom to innovate, experiment, play—often overly hard, as with John Belushi or Chris Farley. Alec Baldwin noted, "He was very laissez-faire about the way he conduct[ed] the whole thing."[719] Though partying can seem "unprofessional," it is in fact the essence of collaboration, as *Sesame Street*—a much tamer group—cast member Sonia Manzano said:

> At the beginning, the cast was really close. I mean we would party together. We would go out all the time. And I'm convinced that makes great things happen.[720]

Like Henson, Michaels often worked all night. An informal "boss," Michaels had no problem smoking pot in the office with his staff.[721] Jerry Nelson said that Henson maybe smoked "a little grass,"[722] and one of his puppeteers, Richard Hunt, brought it to parties.[723] Lorne Michaels was so informal that Will Farrell didn't even know he'd been hired.[724] This sounds eerily similar to the stories of Henson hiring Caroll Spinney and Joseph Bailey, unbeknownst to them. Perhaps most similarly to Henson, Michaels was described by Steve Martin as patient.[725]

Chevy Chase said, "He can't fire anyone."[726] Even more Henson-like, after Dan Aykroyd put his fist though Michaels's office wall, Michaels didn't show anger, only disappointment, albeit through what Al Franken called a "heavy, heavy sarcasm."[727]

That the two men worked together on the first year of *SNL* is interesting. Henson said, "I really respect Lorne."[728] Michaels said, "I have enormous respect for Jim."[729] Yet the two parted ways in 1975, working two separate shows on two separate continents and with increasingly different management styles.

NOT LORNE

More than a few of Michaels's performers thought of him as a father figure, and this makes artistic sense, because if his comedians felt childlike, they could better play and convey a sense of fun to the audience. One of Henson's builders said he was a "father figure" for her.[730] Yet Michaels seems to be a very *specific* kind of father. Some described him as "manipulative"[731] or "infantilizing."[732]

"He didn't compliment us too much,"[733] said one cast member. Of praise, Tina Fey said, "He does not give it out so easily. And that just makes you want to get praise and approval from him more."[734] While Michaels appreciated comedy in the abstract, he seldom praised those he asked to do it. By contrast, Henson seemed to conduct his crew *through* appreciation, as Goelz said:

> He was aware of all the disciplines in the studio, and he would suggest an additional light in the shot, but do so in a very gentle unassertive way, and pretty soon the lighting guy would start to realize, hey this guy really knows what he—he appreciates what *I'm* doing too, and Jim did that with everybody, he was aware of all the jobs in the studio.[735]

If Michaels was the father who made you successful to *finally* earn his respect, Henson was the father who made you successful by treating you with that respect from the start and making you want to live up to it.

Brillstein said euphemistically of Michaels, "He is the most articulate guy in the world,"[736] meaning "talkative." David Cross recalled his first time meeting Michaels, he sat down in Michaels's office and was given an impromptu lecture on "alternative comedy" lasting a half hour.[737] This is very different from the image of Henson listening to a janitor. While Michaels loved to hear himself *talk*, Henson loved to *listen*. And while Michaels was stingy with praise, Henson was reluctant to ever give criticism. "He always used praise," said Kevin Clash. "He never had to tell us when it wasn't working. We knew it."[738]

Puppeteer Fran Brill recalled this as essential:

> The whole Muppet thing works best when people are free and open and feel like nobody will criticize you. And Jim was incredible like that. He'd expect you to do the best you can, but he also knew where you came from.[739]

Henson was indeed the "great appreciator," so much so that he never seemed to stigmatize failure the way the rest of us do. Dave Goelz called it his "generosity":

> A very common image that I'm sure is burned into all of us is Jim watching the playback on a monitor of some other people's characters, and just *laughing*. He on one hand was intent on refining every take, every subsequent take, but at the same time, he enjoyed every one for what was good about it, and we, I remember, most of us couldn't do that. We watched playbacks and thought, ughhh, blew that, blew that, gotta get that cue faster. He was just very delighted to be a part of it all, and [the] next take was better.[740]

Most of us think that we *need* negative feedback to know what to do better next time. But as Goelz said, Henson himself used *delight* in the positive aspects of his work to make the next one better. He didn't *need* shame, and he didn't give it to others. When he met Caroll Spinney for the first time, Spinney had just bombed on stage at a puppetry festival. Goelz recalled, "Jim said, "I really loved what you were *trying* to do." And he was absolutely sincere about it."[741]

Henson appreciated Spinney's performance on the level of concept, even if the execution was terrible. An artist has his own internal judge of quality, and it's not necessary, Henson knew, to point his mistakes out to him.

This radical abstention from criticism can be seen as *weak*. Duncan Kenworthy explained:

> He would never ever say, and this was actually to a fault, if he didn't like something, if he thought something hadn't

> been done well, he would never ever say that, and he'd say, "Hey, I wonder if we just should *try*. . ." and somehow he would turn the corner and it would be a positive. "Let's try it a different way." He would never say, "God, *that* doesn't work."[742]

Henson's inability to criticize can be described as a weakness, but maybe, as adults, we are too afraid to let ourselves be criticized as weak. We are tough on ourselves and tough on others. But perhaps a better way to improve is to stop criticizing ourselves and simply appreciate what is good about our work, so that the next take will be better. As an artist, it is essential to first treat one's own talent humanely. From there, it is easier to treat others this same way. Oz said Henson kept a "gentle rein on us lunatics."[743] Being *gentle* in business is certainly an uncommon approach, but one that may suit creative companies the best.

A COMPASSIONATE MANAGEMENT STYLE CENTER-OUT ORGANIZATION

Remember the four terrible bosses of *The Muppet Musicians of Bremen*? As Kermit said, "The villains [in the story] are all people. I hope none of you take that personally." One is miserly, one fearful, one lazy, and one angry, and they are all four of them thieves. By contrast, Kermit tells us, "The heroes of our story are all animals." The animals are natural musicians—artists.

These four were the worst bosses an artist could have. By contrast, Henson was the opposite of each one. He didn't get angry. Far from lazy, he worked harder than anyone in his company. He was not fearful, but legendarily fearless. Instead of miserly, Henson was generous, going over budget in order to give others the time and space to create. What made Henson's business *different* was that it didn't start out with a traditional organizational hierarchy—with an orderly chain of command of unbreakable ranks—and as it grew, Henson Associates remained informal, with inspiration coming from the center, rather than orders coming from above.

Bad bosses make their work harder for themselves, because the more greedy, fearful, angry, and lazy you are, the harder it becomes to compel others to do good work. If you are not productive as a boss, then it becomes necessary to *trick* your workers into productivity. On the other hand, by being fearless, hardworking, generous, and calm, Henson's attitude easily spread out in a contagious way to those around him.

Ironically, it is a cowardly person who is afraid of being seen as weak. In contrast, Henson's crew thought of him as both "gentle" and "fearless." In a quote we've seen before, Jerry Nelson expressed something important about the way Henson led:

> We called Jim Henson "fearless leader" and there was a reason for that. Because Jim would try all kinds of things, and he was not afraid to try something new, and if he could see it happening in his mind's eye and knew that it would work, he would *dog* it until it worked. . . . I think we always wanted to give Jim exactly what he was looking for.[744]

A leader who is fearless doesn't need to lead by criticizing or controlling—he can lead by example, inspiring others to try just as hard as he does to do his best. Jim Henson inspired people to do huge amounts of work, but he did so by giving of himself. Juhl said of him:

> Year after year we watched him push himself beyond what we could possibly imagine. You had to try to keep up with the guy—it only seemed fair.[745]

Essentially, Henson didn't need to lead by manipulating others. He simply set the tone with his behavior, and allowed it to radiate outward from the center. Henson discovered this almost *anarchic* style of management in his early days working with Jerry Juhl and Jane Henson. Recall that, as Jerry Juhl has said, "In the beginning, it was just Jim and Jane and me and the three of us did everything. We all did a lot of writing together at first."[746] An informal group like this, formed by peers and which makes its own rules, resembles a rock group or a street gang more than a company, that is, all but the most *garage-y* of start-ups.

Perhaps this is why Henson's business managers are quoted so often in a recent Henson biography criticizing Henson's organization method.[747] David Lazer didn't think he gave out enough "attaboys" or lavish praise. And when Henson called the office, he "was not preoccupied by office organization charts, so he would call and speak to whomever he wished," which caused confusion, according to Al Gottesman.[748] But expecting Henson Associates to look like a traditional business would be a mistake, since it was Henson's "collective" approach that made the business possible in the first place.

Rank didn't matter to Henson the way it would to a normal businessman. And for an artist interested in collaborating, it shouldn't. In another strange similarity between Henson and Disney, both men tried to express their gratitude to their employees with a bonus system—Disney after *Snow White*,[749] and Henson after he secured a lucrative deal with Disney.[750] In both cases, what was meant as a gesture of generosity was met with resentment, when employees inevitably compared their bonuses to one another and felt unfairly slighted. *Why did he get more than me? I deserve more than her.*

Henson's ranking of his employees is anathema to artistic collaboration. Top-down management works well for corporations, but for an artist-entrepreneur, a center-out approach makes the most sense. Henson was right to talk to whoever answered the phone. Lazar may have wanted Henson to give out more "attaboys" to his employees,[751] but the kind of appreciation Henson gave was not a manipulative managerial technique. It was genuine.

The center-out model is what we typically see in a rock group or gang, with a charismatic center orbited by others. It takes a certain amount of comfort with chaos to work like this. For that reason, like a clique, Henson Associates was very careful about whom they let in.

When Henson made *Fraggle Rock*, there was a very long audition process. Juhl recalled searching endlessly for the songwriters:

> I walked into this office for the first time, and the desk was just *heaped* with cassettes. It was like every songwriter in Canada who liked to work in children's media had sent a cassette and there were hundreds of them, so I wound up for several days, when I wasn't at a meeting or sleeping, I had one of these cassettes plugged in.[752]

But once a person was *in*, control was relaxed, so that the artist was free to create. The songwriters chosen, Phil Balsam and Dennis Lee, produced a total of three original songs per episode, and according to producer Larry Mirkin, none were ever rejected.[753] Balsam and Lee had already been working together before *Fraggle Rock*, as had the three mimes who performed the bodies of the Gorgs. And here lies an interesting distinction.

When Henson set up a special effects group called the Creature Shop, Duncan Kenworthy joined on. Kenworthy, who came from a business background, recalled the decision to hire a friend:

> Henson suggested John Stephenson. . . . I had thought about John, but he's a good friend of mine. It would have almost been nepotism to have offered him the job. Jim said, "We should all be so lucky as to go through life working only with friends."[754]

Even though many hires are nepotistic today, care is taken to make them appear meritocratic, because that is theoretically the best and fairest way to find talent. Yet if we shift the lens a bit and view things from inside the operation, this is how a troupe of artists *works*—like a good group of friends. To criticize a motorcycle gang or garage band of cronyism would be nonsensical, because it's not a government, corporation, or any kind of compulsory power structure. It's more like a utopia—a tiny society formed on its own foundation. No one would call the Beatles unfair because they didn't extend their search for drummers beyond their familiar Liverpool circle. Working with friends tends to increase the emotional bonds that keep employees dedicated to the project.

Henson didn't seem to see things through the typical business lens. He saw the human side of the equation and the benefits it would lend to art. And while it may seem that Henson's business model is not particularly "scalable" in business terms, this is only half true. Henson's organization could never have succeeded as a cast of thousands all working on one thing. And as we will see in the next lesson, problems arose when the company grew too large. But during those same years, Henson was remarkably successful in setting up small offshoot groups, with the spirit of his original start-up, on two different continents.

What makes Henson so special was not that he was able to create his unique business model once, with Jane and Jerry Juhl, but that he understood the process enough to *set up* these groups—which could function on their own in his absence—and help them grow.

SETTING UP STREET GANGS
THE CREATURE SHOP AND *FRAGGLE ROCK*

Two good examples of satellite Hensonian groups are the London Creature Shop and Toronto's *Fraggle Rock*. Both these 1980s projects came to be self-sustaining in that Henson didn't need to be in the studio—or even in the country—for it all to work. If we look at the similarities between these groups, we can derive a formula for scaling the start-up mentality that artists and innovators need to thrive: instead of growing *bigger*, Henson's groups grew more *numerous*.

In setting up both of these projects, Henson needed to give the crews two things—the *time* and *space* to co-create their worlds. Both time and space require money. For the Creature Shop, this originally meant that the artists would be paid from the budget of the films they were working on, yet that model had to change, because when a project inevitably ended, many of the best collaborators left for other jobs and couldn't be brought back. Writer Anthony Minghella recalled packing up after a job was over. Henson stopped him, saying it "was no good reason to leave . . . just because the project was over."[755] Matt Bacon wrote in his book *No Strings Attached: The Inside Story of Jim Henson's Creature Shop*:

> At the end of *Labyrinth*, rather than laying everyone off, Jim wanted to start a permanent workshop, where research and development could be continued. The idea was to increase the likelihood of getting involved in new projects by having a new facility. Henson said, "By keeping a group of people together, we are staying closer to what we've always done with the Muppets, where we had our own builders. That way you can make it better every time and build on your past work."[756]

Time and space to create. John Stephenson explained that was no small order:

> The Creature Shop was really a 24-hour place—it just never stopped and it still remains the atmosphere. [Henson would] be able to wake up in the middle of the night and ring me up for my opinion on new ideas.[757]

A twenty-four-hour place is expensive. Ultimately, to "keep a group of people together," Henson had to sacrifice part of his artistic vision, having the Creature Shop do work for commercials, even though he would have preferred not to, and making the "costumes" for *Teenage Mutant Ninja Turtles*, even though it glamorized realistic violence, something Henson had once called "criminal."[758] But neither of these reservations was more important than keeping the Creature Shop people *together*. Without pay, the Muppets in *Muppets Take Manhattan* tell Kermit, "We've had some job offers," and scatter around the country.

When *The Muppet Show* ended, Jerry Juhl recalled:

> We were gonna relax. We could pack and go home at last. And then Jim said, "No, before you go home, the day after the wrap party, I'm holding this big meeting at the hotel ballroom in London so we can talk about the *next* show."[759]

Henson's next idea was an international children's show that would become *Fraggle Rock.* In developing *Fraggle Rock*, Henson brought together a core group of people—Jerry Juhl, Jocelyn Stevenson, Michael Frith, and Duncan Kenworthy—and allowed them to create the world, starting with a book of lists, for instance, "What we know about the Fraggles." Juhl said:

> This was one of the joys that Jim gave us on this project, because we were coming off of a successful show and Jim was willing to let us take the time to really develop the show completely and carefully and slowly and think about it. And that led us to a whole series of meetings that took place on and off through the next year or so.[760]

They met first "in a very grand conference room in London's Hyde Park Hotel,"[761] according to Frith—twenty-five people sitting in the ballroom,[762] sketching and making notes on hotel stationery. While Henson was away working on *The Dark Crystal,* he let the Fraggle co-creators stay in his house near the Hampstead Heath in London. There were meetings in Long Island and other locations over the next year.[763] Henson put *his own money* into the development of this project, even before a network stepped in to fund it.

The money that would allow the *Fraggle Rock* group to *stay* together came from two networks, HBO and CBC. The Canadian network gave them studio time, a crew, and a little money, and

HBO gave them "the cash," in Kenworthy's words—an amount generous enough to allow the artists to do their best.[764] The *Fraggle Rock* set was not a twenty-four-hour place, but with one fourteen-second Doozer pogo scene taking three hours to film, there was sometimes overtime.[765] When Stevenson wrote a scene featuring a flooded Gorg basement, the whole crew stayed until six in the morning to make it work. When she proposed the idea, "everyone said, sure, we can do that."[766] They could do it, because there was enough money to buy them time and space.

Giving collaborators time and space is akin to giving them Gladwell's ten thousand hours, but Henson also gave them something more: ownership of their work. For *The Dark Crystal,* each design team in the Creature Shop oversaw their creature from start to finish, essentially giving engineers the creative authority of artists. Bacon explains it was "another unusual move in a business in which art is usually very different from engineering. The designers would make their own clay sculpture, mould-making, latex casting, final texturing, and painting, and even their own costume-printmaking," According to Henson, "It makes them feel more involved, more in control.'"[767] Director Gary Kurtz said they found it "much more satisfying."[768] Giving an artist not just credit but creative control over his work makes managerial sense. It also makes artistic sense.

When each character has been shepherded to the film by a single builder, the character's evolution starts to resemble the way real creatures evolve. Henson said that the creatures in *The Dark Crystal* are "the result of sort of many generations of growth."[769] Bacon notes: "Just like living creatures, *The Dark Crystal* Skeksis, Mystics, Garthim, and others evolved."[770] Giving each creator control of his character resulted in lifelike art.

Henson also allowed great freedom to the writers and designers to conceptualize *Fraggle Rock*. As head writer Jerry Juhl said, "Jim was willing to let us take the time to really develop the show completely and carefully and slowly and think about it."[771] Juhl then gave this same respect to his staff writers. Jocelyn Stevenson explained:

> As almost every writer has said, the unique thing about this show was when you wrote a script, at the end of the show it was still your script. Nobody had taken it away, rewritten it, and pounded it into something that you hadn't written. The words were your words. [Jerry Juhl] helped you shape it, but he never took it away and rewrote it, which is so often done.[772]

Similarly, each puppeteer performed the same character for all four years, and that produced both job satisfaction and a realism that was particularly lifelike.

At both the London Creature Shop and Toronto's *Fraggle Rock*, Henson set up workspaces that were "Muppetty" in nature—they did not function as business-as-usual, but instead employed his uncommon management style. Anthony Minghella described the Creature Shop as "a barely controlled chaos,"[773] and pictures show a staggering number of workspaces filled with self-directed projects. *Fraggle Rock* producer Larry Mirkin said of its work environment:

> What you would hope it would be like to do this show—because of what was on-screen—was really and truly what it was like to do this show. It was a lot of fun for all of us the entire time.[774]

RADICAL KINDNESS
NEVER MAD

We have seen that—unlike the bad boss in *The Muppet Musicians of Bremen*—Henson held himself back from being angry or critical of others, but even that is an understatement. *Sesame Street Unpaved* describes an event that might have made Henson upset, or at least flummoxed:

> A bullfrog did "what bullfrogs do, right on Jim," said Bob [McGrath of *Sesame Street*]. Bob didn't think that Jim would be able to keep his composure, but he did. They continued the scene as if nothing had ever happened and finished the bit.[775]

Alex Rockwell said Henson "would never lose his temper," and, for balance, followed that with a qualifier—"once, a very mild angry moment."[776] Rollie Krewson said:

> I remember *one* time during *The Muppet Show* when he got mad, and all he did was flip the pages of a book really quickly, and that was it. That's the only way that you knew that he was upset. He was always really calm about everything.[777]

When asked if he ever got angry, Henson said another show's director had exasperated him. "Doing guest spots can be very difficult," he said.[778] Using a word like "difficult" displays a radical self-reserve on Henson's part, a desire to give the world only the good parts of himself, only what is positive and generous. Henson *held back*, which is one of the hardest things for a boss to do.

A very funny 1973 *Sesame Street* skit illustrates why. Bert feels cold. He asks Ernie if there is a draft, and before Bert can say anything else, Ernie snaps into action.

> **Ernie:** Wouldn't want you feeling cold. I'll just get you something so that you won't feel cold any longer. Just a moment. Wait right there. [Ernie puts a shawl, hat, and coat on Bert.]
> **Bert:** The shawl is enough. [Ernie wraps a muffler around Bert's mouth so he can't talk.]
> **Ernie:** How do you feel now, Bert? I can't hear you, Bert! [Ernie pulls down the muffler]
> **Bert:** I feel hot, I feel broiling hot!
> **Ernie:** Oh, you do, well just a second, Bert, wait right there. I have just what you need! [Ernie brings an ice bag, opens a window, and turns on an electric fan.]
> **Ernie:** Okay, Bert? How's that, Bert? Feel better now, Bert?
> **Bert:** Leave me alone![779]

Bert is totally exasperated by Ernie's help. When we micromanage the creative work of others, we tend to do more harm than good. Bert is perfectly capable of regulating his own temperature. But a bad boss who doesn't listen is incapable of helping someone do good work. By disregarding Bert's own agency, Ernie winds up making Ptolemaic short-term fixes that will never get Bert back to the natural state he was in at the start of the sketch. A good boss would have left Bert alone.

It is likely the talk-show director who made Henson angry was one of these micromanagers who did not listen. From frustrating experiences like this, Henson could understand the director-performer relationship from both sides of the camera lens. With this knowledge, Henson *held back* a good deal in order to, at the very least, *do no harm*. Still, though Henson never seemed to get angry, human beings *do*. So where does that anger *go*?

Dave Goelz said, "Jim's characters . . . were all part of him, but none more so than Kermit, who occupied the exact same relationship to *The Muppet Show* characters as Jim did to his employees."[780] On *The Muppet Show*, we often see Kermit's temper snap out of exasperation—it is one of the funniest parts of every show, because every other scene seems to test his patience so. Henson once said Kermit was "more playful, less hesitant than I am," and that Kermit "can say things I hold back."[781] It seemed that Henson channeled his frustration into an outlet that ultimately *helped* his employees rather than stifling them—through successful comedy.

A few recent books have argued for the virtues of introversion,[782] but few of us picture introverts being *best* suited to managing a company. Clearly, there is a link between masterpiece puppeteering and shyness, because, as Morley Safer noted of the Muppeteers:

> All are extremely shy men, almost tongue-tied without the Muppets close at hand. They find it easier to speak through the pig or Gonzo or the others than through the faces God gave them.[783]

Richard Hunt told the *Washington Post*, "Puppeteers are not always comfortable in social situations. They like anonymity."[784]

For years, Frank Oz was afraid to speak on camera, even in character.[785] According to Oz, "I didn't do voices for four years, I was so scared. I had no confidence whatsoever."[786] Yet Henson patiently waited for him to get comfortable, which paid off. Ultimately, Oz would be his best performer. It also took some time for Dave Goelz to work up the confidence to transition from a builder to a puppeteer of lead characters, and he too would become one of the best. Henson said:

> You get a talented performer, like a Dave or a Frank, and then any character they do just starts to bloom and blossom because of all that they put into it.[787]

There is likely something about timidity that leads to masterpiece puppeteering—perhaps because overcoming such reservations takes a heroic leap of courage, and that coupled with critical taste can overcome anything. But shyness can also lead to effective leadership, because an introverted person is one with a massive amount of self-control.

It comes down to a simple rule of human nature: it is hard to root for someone who has hurt you with callousness. There is a great passage in Adam Grant's *Give and Take* about the differences in the level of success attained by "givers" and "takers" at work. Grant writes that while givers can often occupy the bottom rungs of companies, as we might expect, Grant says, they also occupy the very top:

> Givers, takers, and matchers all can—and do—achieve success. But there's something distinctive that happens when givers succeed: it spreads and cascades. When takers win, there's usually someone else who loses. Research shows that people tend to envy successful takers and look for ways to knock them down a notch. In contrast, when [givers] win, people are rooting for them and supporting them, rather than gunning for them. Givers succeed in a way that creates a ripple effect, enhancing the success of people around them.[788]

Instead of asking people to work harder, Henson showed them how. Instead of criticizing his employees, Henson criticized no one. Instead of taking credit, he gave it to others. And instead of controlling his employees, Jim Henson controlled himself—his temper. For most of us, anger is the hardest emotion to tame. So how did Henson do it?

He meditated:

> I spend a few minutes in meditation and prayer each morning. I find this really helps me to start the day with a good frame of reference. As part of my prayers, I thank whoever is helping me—I'm sure somebody or something is—I express gratitude for all my blessings and I try to forgive the people that I'm feeling negative toward. I try hard not to judge anyone, and I try to bless everyone who is a part of my life, particularly anyone with whom I am having any problems.[789]

With meditation setting the tone of each day, Henson's attitude seems less like self-*control* and more like self-*guiding*, or leading *himself* by example. He started out with an attitude of compassion and let that inspire the rest of his day.

Moreover, when Henson performed, the camera system that he set up became a kind of feedback loop that was inherently meditative, in that it showed Henson parts of himself as though they were someone else. He described the performance as close to an out-of-body feeling:

> Working the way we do, watching a monitor, you become rather separated from that personality. It's a nice thing in that you watch the screen and the screen becomes a living

> creature. I mean Kermit to me is alive on the screen there. And very often you have fun, you just play with it, you try things, you experiment a little bit.[790]

This separation or distance from one's emotions is almost Buddhist in the awareness it brings. The camera makes the separation between the reactive self and the perceiving self quite explicit. Henson was literally watching himself lose his temper as Kermit. This must've led to some wisdom in terms of his relationship to anger. Instead of getting mad that he was getting mad—as most of us do—and compounding the problem, Henson simply let that emotion come and go, appreciating it on the level of comedy. With meditation, more than *restricting* or *controlling* himself, Henson was able to *coach* or *guide* himself to grow better without stigmatizing his present failings.

By engineering the start of his day with meditation and working in a manner that promoted self-acceptance, Henson seems to have totally avoided outbursts of real, *damaging* anger. And as a result, people were "rooting" for him, rather than "gunning" for him, to use Grant's words. Perhaps it's because he was a "giver" boss that, to this day, Henson still has such a cult following.

Mel Brooks once said of the Muppets, "Their comedy and what they mean stand for one thing—the meek shall inherit the Earth."[791] Henson's success shows us that this is sometimes true.

LET PEOPLE SURPRISE YOU
GET OUT OF THE WAY

According to Jamie Courtier, a designer at Henson's Creature Shop, "There is no formula for design. You just do what you have to do to make it work."[792] So, for example, on *Fraggle Rock*, of all the various crystalline Doozer constructions appearing in four years of the show, there was never a note given to the prop builders on how to build one. Each one was designed according to the specifications of its builder.

Henson once explained the benefits of improv: "Frank can ad-lib scenes funnier than he would have thought about if you asked him beforehand."[793] Part of the effect of characters being performed by *two* people was to push more improvisation. Gorgs, for instance, were a symbiosis of a mime and a radio-puppeteered head remotely controlled by a second performer. Sprocket's upper and lower halves were performed by two puppeteers. The relationship between the two performers is symbiotic and unspoken. Karen Prell, who performed the right hand of Henson's Convincing John, explained:

> You'd just jump into it and explore and discover with him and, the same way, if you were just kinda open to the energy and went with it, you would surprise yourself.[794]

This is the ultimate goal of artists—to surprise oneself by one's own performance—because only by doing this can we surprise our audience. As a boss, when you *want* your employees to surprise you, it is counterintuitive to tell them exactly what to do. Henson, like Lorne Michaels and unlike Walt Disney, wanted to be surprised, and perhaps this is why both the Muppets and *SNL* have such an *aliveness* to them, even in reruns.

It takes a good deal of self-directedness to surprise your boss. "My experience with Jim," said Jocelyn Stevenson, "was that if you knew what you wanted to do, he would do everything to help you. What he didn't like were people that sort of said, I don't know what I want to do—I don't like what I'm doing but I don't know what I want to do. He sort of had no time for that."[795] Because Stevenson had her own vision, Henson supported her move from publishing to television. Even though she'd never written for TV, when she asked Henson, "Could I try writing for the show?" Henson said, "Yeah, great. And if it doesn't work out, you can go back to the books."[796] Henson was happy to be surprised by his writers. As a boss, he wanted *you* to explore *your* vision.

David Bowie said he was not micromanaged when he wrote the songs for Henson's *Labyrinth*: "I must say that Jim gave me a completely free hand with it."[797] Another composer, Paul Williams, said:

> Working with Jim Henson was probably the easiest collaboration of my life—he lacked the diva gene. He had a sweetness about him and I don't think he ever got emotionally pulled off course. But I've also never worked with anybody that spent less time over my shoulder. I mean, I've worked on projects that were very successful, where a lot of the time, this was going on. [Looks over shoulder and says, "Yeah, yeah."] It's hard to work when the phone's ringing every two hours.[798]

As Williams implied, micromanagement can drain artists of their creativity. Head of the puppet workshop, Caroly Wilcox said Henson "trusted us to invent. That's what's so much fun in puppets is creating, and to be given the chance to create was something Jim did for all of us."[799] Bacon writes that even though Henson had started development on the Roald Dahl project *The Witches*, when Nicolas Roeg came on to direct it, Henson "took a backseat, remaining as executive producer, and let Roeg's creative vision shape the film."[800] Someone with "the diva gene" would have a hard time taking "a backseat," and yet to do so creates the most surprising results.

One scene in *The Great Muppet Caper* was a complete surprise. Trying to get out of committing to Kermit's dangerous plan, the gang devolves into excuses. Kermit silences everyone with the word, "Quiet!" In the space created, we hear the puppet Janice: "So I said, 'Listen, mother, it's my life, and if I want to live on a beach and walk around naked . . .'[801]

The perfect non sequitur like this comes from giving artists enough rope—as they say—to hang themselves. Such surprises are often the most memorable moments in a film, because they make us feel alive with possibility. But in an anarchic group of artists like Henson's, if *everyone* follows his own vision, how do you get them all to go together?

SYNTHESIS
SYMPHONY OF CREATIVES

Henson's goal as a leader was, as Steve Whitmire said, "seeing to it that this person does what they need to do well."[802] But in addition to everyone doing their best, they also needed to know what exactly they were working *toward*. *Fraggle Rock* producer Larry Mirkin often said, "we were all working in service of the best idea."[803] Karen Prell noted this was different than many "ego-driven" productions.[804] But if Henson didn't criticize or control or even know what the "best" was supposed to look like, how did he elicit the "best" from his people?

As we saw in Lesson 6, Sculptor Wendy Midener designed the heads of the gelflings in *The Dark Crystal* by a process of trial and error, with Henson (and artist Brian Froud) appreciating the results:

> I started by sculpting tiny heads in Plasticine, and I work very quickly, so I would just keep sculpting them, turning

> them out. And Jim and Brian would come by and say, yes, well I like that, but change the eyes, change the mouth.[805]

I like *that*, Henson would say, but what if we *try*—and then he would ask for another take. Just as when he performed, he noticed what was good about the take and then tried it one more time, without criticism. This is a familiar trick for teachers—saying it's still not quite there yet. *You can do better than this*. Since this trial-and-error process is how many artists already work, as Midener did, it seems like the natural way to coax the best from people.

And while Henson outwardly spoke of his artist's *strengths*, he clearly had to manage their *weaknesses* silently, behind the scenes. Jane Henson said, "There's a lot of ad-libbing on set,"[806] but Jerry Nelson told a fan interviewer that it was *Brian* Henson who finally let him improvise. "With Jim and Frank," he said, "you had to stay exactly where the script was."[807] It might be surprising, but Henson did not let *everyone* follow their vision.

Frank Oz and Dave Goelz, on the other hand, were encouraged to improvise. Juhl said, "Some performers are stronger at the ad-libbing than the others, that's Frank's strong suit. It's very rare where we'll have to write anything for him, he goes in a lot and just does his thing."[808] Finch wrote, "Oz's humor is a sudden release of energy, a surge of comic inventiveness that is in direct proportion to his habitual seriousness."[809] Likewise, Gonzo's character was found when a chicken extra wasn't cooperating. He explains that he ad-libbed:

> "Nice legs though!"
>
> Jim cracked up. That weird attraction to chickens just made [Gonzo] so strange, and it was something Jim liked a lot. So Gonzo soon got a chicken girlfriend, Camilla.[810]

If you were good at improv, Henson would let you do it. But Nelson's strength was not his humor, it was his voice. Oz and Goelz, it could be said, didn't have Nelson's rhythm or pitch control.

In a documentary called *Down at Fraggle Rock*, Henson indeed makes sure to mention everyone's strengths:

> One of the great things about Jerry is his voice. He has a remarkable control, and his voice has sort of a cutting edge that records very well.
>
> Kathy succeeds in bringing a tenderness to Mokey that is very special.
>
> Karen has taken and enriched the personality of Red Fraggle with wonderful energy and fun.
>
> Dave is quite a funny fellow. He has a very offbeat sense of humor.
>
> Steve . . . has become one of our leading and very funniest performers.
>
> We're excited about some of the new challenges Richard has taken on, like directing.[811]

Henson appreciated everyone for what they did well. But in order to get everyone doing their best, each artist had to ultimately cede to *the best idea*, and Henson did not allow *every* idea to enter his creations. Rob Mills was the mime who performed Junior Gorg on *Fraggle Rock* and started learning to puppeteer. He recalled being thrilled when Henson, guest-directing, asked who was doing the red creature in the back. Mills proudly said, "I am," and Henson said, "Yeah, don't do that."[812] It seems that his inexperienced "upstaging" didn't help. It threw off the shot, because everyone else was swaying collectively. It was uncharacteristically abrupt, because of the difficulty of the group shot and Henson's increasingly limited time, but the spirit resembles his usual approach: *let's try another take.*

Henson understood that best way to talk about weaknesses is to turn them into strengths. In an abstract sense, all puppeteers create a strength out of their weaknesses. Richard Hunt suggested on *60 Minutes* that puppeteers are often shy because when they really let loose, they are thought to be crazy:

> People walk in here and they look at us and we show them around the shop, and they see all these puppets, and you go and put one on and do a different weird voice and they look at you like, that's magical, but the guy's *nuts*![813]

In casting puppeteers, Henson was looking for that rare person who came most alive through a puppet. Interestingly, two Muppet performers, Spinney[814] and Angus,[815] have cerebral palsy. Two puppeteers, Hunt and Clash, have identified themselves as homosexual. In the not-so-distant past, these differences from the norm might have been seen as something "wrong" with you, and they may have led to shyness or being discriminated against. But in Henson's repertory company of performers, difference could be a powerful advantage.

Ultimately, difference is a positive thing for a symphony of creatives. All of Disney's princesses would never be able to coexist in one film. On the other hand, groups of Muppets can sometimes get together, numbering in the hundreds with no two quite the same. The strength of using "odd" characters such as Fozzie or Janice is that they tend to all find a *space* in the symphony. While there is room for only four or so flutes, there can be instruments of all timbres because each one can fill in a gap another has left.

HAVE A BEER IN YOUR OFFICE FRIDGE

Business *structure*, corporate *ladder*: is anything in life really that simple? Certainly not at Henson Associates. Martin Baker was a producer for Henson. He recently reminisced:

> People say to me "what was it like working for Jim Henson" and I always correct them and say "you don't work for Jim Henson, you work with Jim Henson"—and it was that subtle difference which made him who he was. He was one of those people, unique in many ways, yes he was clearly the boss and you were the employee, but he never made you feel that way. I say working with Jim was a lot like going to work with your best friend every day.[816]

You don't work *for* Henson, you work *with* him. Are these just pretty elegiac words, or is there something practical and actionable we can take away from them?

It is commonly accepted that wolf packs are hierarchical, ruled by an alpha male. Yet in the scientific community this assumption was challenged in 1999 by L. David Mech, who noted this was only observed in packs that were artificially confined.[817] In natural self-chosen groups, the pack instead had the structure of a family, with the "leaders" being naturally the "parents." Acts of "dominance" in a family look more like protection, affection, grooming, feeding, or teaching. In cages, wolves fight for rank. Aggression is their weapon and hierarchy rules their days.

But most of the time, wolves behave this way because we make them. And so do human societies when they are effectually "trapped" in unnatural groups like ship sailors, prison inmates, or corporate desk-mates. It is entirely possible to have a management structure with no "top dog."

Jerry Juhl said:

> When it comes to characters, it's all a collaborative effort with writers and performers. We all have a family quality that picks itself up in the writing what with all the time we spend together.[818]

Mark Saltzman, a *Sesame Street* writer, said the Muppets had "a very fuzzy, Grateful Dead kind of sensibility."[819] *A Muppets Family Christmas* brought together many of Henson's performers to literally resemble a family. And while some of the younger performers certainly saw him as a "father figure,"[820] two of his best puppeteers—Spinney and Nelson—were a few years older than Henson. For many collaborators, Henson was more like a brother.

When working for Henson, your role seemed to matter more than your rank—contractors, business partners, producers, benefactors, and managers all seemed like part of the puzzle, interconnected, but no one *above* another. "Peoples," said Pete in *The Great Muppet Caper*, "is peoples." Utopias like these have failed for countries like the USSR or in twenty-four-hour situations like the California communes of the sixties, but it seemed to work for Henson Associates, where people weren't "trapped" but chose to be there because they liked the work. In a small start-up where workers could leave and go home, a hierarchy-less system worked. The Muppets' affectionate anarchy might just be the best management model an artist can have.

From early on in Henson's career, he managed to find himself almost entirely bossless. Of *Sam and Friends*, he said:

> I was convinced no one else at the station ever watched the show because there was never a complaint or any attempt at censorship of any kind.[821]

Producer Lew Grade gave Henson "a promise of creative independence"[822] on *The Muppet Show* and his first two movies."[823] Of *The Dark Crystal*, Henson said:

> There was no pressure from anyone but ourselves because we were the ones doing this from the beginning. Lew Grade, who financed the film, never put any pressure on us.[824]

Finch wrote, "Lord Grade's hands-off policy has been vital to the success of the enterprise."[825] Likewise, about *Fraggle Rock*, which had two funders in CBC and HBO. Mirkin said, "In the four years that we did the show, we never had a script note from either network."[826]

Having no boss was something that must've had a profoundly freeing psychological effect on Henson. He knew the value of it. With no boss over *him*, it likely seemed natural to step back and share the freedom he felt with others. I have no doubt that he *sought out* hands-off investors like Grade and HBO; it was no coincidence that he continued to find himself bossless. The first step toward being an uncommon boss is to find a way to have *no* boss.

In the *Fraggle Rock* episode "The Gorg Who Would Be King," the Fraggles teach Junior Gorg that it's possible to have no boss. Junior, being a prince, is steeped in the hierarchy of his father the king, so he has a hard time understanding how the Fraggles operate.

> **Junior:** Wow, you must be the boss around here.
> **Wembley:** Me? No, Fraggles don't have any bosses.
> **Junior:** You mean you don't have somebody like my daddy who tells you what to do?
> **Wembley:** No, we each lead ourselves, and we all lead each other.[827]

The Fraggles then sing a song explaining, "You can never ever ever . . . be the boss of someone else. You just gotta be the boss—of just *yourself*."[828]

This somewhat subversive song seems to say, *Lead by example.* When Henson—the boss—came to *Fraggle Rock* to direct or puppeteer, Terry Angus said the mood didn't turn serious:

> We were still just a bunch of clowns, basically, and Jim was the biggest clown of all. He kept the atmosphere so light that nobody knew the boss was there anyway. Very rarely were we conscious of, "Okay, the boss is here. Maybe we ought to be a bit better." He was just one of us.[829]

In a hierarchy where pecking order is important, there is much competition and aggression, but in Henson's business, much of that could be channeled into the work itself. "Upstaging" was a common practice that was *encouraged* on set, where one character would steal the show, even if he was not supposed to be the star. And it is likely much of Henson's own egotism was channeled into various haughty characters, such as the Mayor of Waterville, Link Hogthrob, the Vanguard of the Poohbahs, or the Ritual Master Skeksis. Henson delighted in this kind of role:

> I was doing the ritual master, who's sort of a high priest, very pompous, arrogant. And I enjoyed that. I think there's probably a part of me that's that way, and it so that sort of comes out while you're doing it.[830]

With his most pompous self coming *out* on screen, Henson was able to enjoy the thrill of power while his true self could afford to be a bit more humble.

Finch noted the odd function of Henson's office during the making of *The Muppet Show*:

> Here too is a small refrigerator stocked with soft drinks, beer and cider. Unrefrigerated bottles of soda water and cider are stored in crates. . . . [T]his is Jim Henson's office, but you will not often find him in it. . . . [H]owever, it is used by just about everybody else. . . . Jerry Juhl making amendations to a freshly typed script; an Italian interviewer watching tapes; Dave Goelz, during a break, fetching himself a tonic water from the refrigerator.[831]

If you can walk into your boss's office, open a refrigerator, and have a beer, that beer in a sense kills convention, and the conventional *idea* of a boss. Henson did this again when he told a reporter he hired a boss. If you can hire and fire your boss, are they really a boss at all? Henson's business seemed more like a family, where dominance is replaced with teaching, training the employees to become their own bosses.

A case in point is Bonnie Erickson, who notes:

> I joined Jim as a freelance costume designer for *The Frog Prince* in 1970. . . . Jim cleverly gave me a place to work

> at the brilliant and mischievous Donald Sahlin's worktable. . . . Don also became a mentor, sharing tricks and techniques. . . . At the same time I was learning about business from Jim. . . . [O]nce we completed that first year of *The Muppet Show* I felt I could leave. . . . [I]t was time for me to establish a business. . . . When I told Jim I was leaving he said, "Well, I know this is what you need to do. And we're not going to lose touch." Luckily, we never did. Jim became one of our first clients, hiring me for productions like *Fraggle Rock*, *Bunny Picnic*, *Christmas Toy* and to consult on licensed product for *Sesame Street* where I was a creative director for fourteen years.[832]

Henson didn't seem worried that his designer was leaving or would somehow compete with him. He *wanted* Erickson to be her own boss. Knowing what it was like for himself as an artist to own a company seems to have made him want that same freedom for her.

Maybe superficially, the "hierarchy" shifted when Erickson started her own company. She went from employee to contractor. Henson went from boss to client. Yet these titles don't seem to matter as much as the more essential relationship—between collaborators. As two artists working together, the *status* of it all would only get in the way.

HOW TO
BECOME A RADICAL ENABLER

The first step to becoming a good boss is to throw off all bosses, if not literally—by starting a business—then emotionally, as much as you can, by thinking of yourself as the only boss of *yourself*. What can you do to encourage more independence in yourself and others?

Henson was lucky that the WTOP channel *didn't* check in on him at *Sam and Friends*. But in later scenarios, he negotiated for total creative control. Whenever it is possible to get control of your project, fight for it. Start by acting as though you already have it. As the saying goes, it is better to ask for forgiveness than permission.

When you *are* the boss, you control everything. Yet many bosses still don't *feel* in control, and in their insecurity they exert excessive control over others. If you are the boss, trust yourself. Banish fear from your thoughts through meditation, and use meditative activities that help you to understand what Henson said:

> You're not the victim, but instead you're the one who's doing it. . . . [Y]ou are the person who ha[s] control of your life.[833]

When you have watched your emotions on television as much as Henson had, you surely have a greater awareness of them and how they affect others. Don't stigmatize your faults or failures—the ways you negatively affect others. Instead, look at what you're doing *well*, and then try again. By carefully observing your emotions and trying to do better, you can more fully *create* the world you want.

Your leadership needs to start with you. Like the participants in the show *Undercover Boss*, Henson knew exactly how difficult his employees had it, because even while he ran the company, he also performed at the bottom rung—the puppeteer. In the filming of *The Muppets Take Manhattan*, he was at the mercy of director Frank Oz, who could be demanding. Even if you don't have experience doing what your workers do, you need to find a way to learn about it. By asking your employees to teach you what they do, you not only empower them, but you can better conduct them like Henson, the "great appreciator."

Try not to rank your collaborators, even it comes from generosity. Henson was mistaken to dole out bonuses of different amounts in 1990,[834] but years earlier, he had a much better idea. According to entertainment blogger and Disney expert Jim Hill, under Henson, "the Muppeteers received royalties from all merchandise sold relating to their characters."[835] Giving an artist a share of the profits for the characters they create is the best way to be generous, because it doesn't create a static ranking. With profit sharing, the reward you give can grow infinitely over time. It is surprising that Disney did not think it necessary to continue giving Muppet performers this kind of Henson-like generosity.

It would be naïve to think Jim Henson was a *perfect* boss. Brian Jay Jones's biography chronicles many of the problems that Henson Associates faced in the late 1980s when Henson hired management consultants to "look at the structure of the organization" and identify "holes in the chain of command."[836] When Henson was spread too thin in what I call his "producerman" years, it seemed like the best way out was to become a small company again—by selling his merchandising department to Disney. While I don't think "organization" experts would have helped Henson, I do agree that Henson's unique center-out model works best when it is kept to a manageable size. In the next lesson, we will take a closer look at what an artist can learn from these troubled years.

Henson Associates' chaotic structure may have exacerbated his problems in the late 1980s, but at the same time, it was this same anarchic style that made the company possible in the first place, and that anarchy allowed the company to entertain over a hundred nations in 1981. As a boss, Henson was best suited to lead smaller groups, where innovation and creativity thrive. For most artists, this is exactly where we want to be anyway, not at the helm of a corporate behemoth. Henson may not have been the perfect boss, but for many artists struggling today, his methods seem pretty attractive and pretty rare.

While it is possible to find bosses like this today, it might be better still to *be* a boss like this. It is hard to change a calcified business model. It is hard enough to change another person. The easiest person to change is yourself, and that is easiest to do when you are your own boss. Jim Henson's spirit was decidedly entrepreneurial. The inner calm that he brought to his leadership stemmed from a fundamental *satisfaction* with the amount of control he had over his life.

If we are the ones in control of our lives, it becomes only natural to be other-directed, since our own plans, once achieved, start to bore us. Being surprised by the talents of others is the antidote to boredom. The way to encourage others to surprise you is to work with them—not above or below them, but with them—and to try to have *fun* doing it. And most importantly, exercise your appreciation of others.

Point out what someone has done really *well.* Let that be the next thing you do. If there's no one around you right now, then be a *good boss* and heap some well-earned praise on your best employee—yourself. What are you doing really well? Let that feeling of accomplishment inspire you.

LESSON 10

YOUR COMPANY IS YOURS ALONE

YOU'RE STUCK WITH WHAT YOU'VE MADE

The real key to making money as an artist is copyright—owning it, investing in it, and licensing it—as noted in a 1999 *Kidscreen* article:

> Looking back, Brian Henson believes the first milestone for the Henson brand was his father's decision at age 20 to retain ownership and control of his characters. "I think that is really the root of why he was so successful," says Henson. "He really had a gut instinct for business."[837]

It should be obvious by now how copyright made Henson rich—to put it crudely, Fisher-Price and other toy manufacturers paid Henson a good deal to license his characters; in addition, videos, record albums, and books made up another infinite profit stream, since these things can be made once and duplicated cheaply. All of this relies on copyright—owned by Henson and licensed to others.

But copyright isn't just important "for business," it's also important for art. Owning one's work firstly means being able to protect it from being changed or exploited by others. And secondly, it allows the artist to recycle one's previous works in an organic cycle of growth. When an artist can freely build on his previous successes and failures, he can keep doing what works and use what doesn't for scrap parts.

"Jim never wasted an idea,"[838] according to the Henson archivist Karen Falk, who ought to know best, because she has catalogued all of those ideas since the eighties. "Monster Eats Machine" became the Munchos Monster, who became Cookie Monster. Plans for a Broadway show became *Muppet Show* skits and then fed into *The Muppets Take Manhattan*. As we saw, Henson's reaction to failure was not to feel shame, but simply to appreciate what was good about it and to try to make the next take better. You should never waste an idea, even if it's terrible. There's likely something in there that *could* work.

A fertile creative mind can turn failure into the next success, but to do so, it needs to own everything it does. If the Munchos Monster had not been Henson's intellectual property, then there would never have been a Cookie Monster. Many artists today allow others to own copyrights for their work. Henson worked for only those companies—Frito-Lay, in the Munchos Monster scenario—that would allow him to own the copyright. We have seen that Brillstein would counsel him to take jobs for the money, but he'd pass:

> "Not this one," he'd say, "because they want to *own* the character." Jim's rule was simple: Don't sell anything.[839]

You should always fight to *own your own work.* Copyright allows artists to build upon what they've done. Not only does your art grow organically, but as an artist-entrepreneur, so does your career—it grows like a tree. A tree grows out of the ground, and it can build only on what came before. Once a trunk or a limb is made, you are stuck with it. You can grow in a new direction, but you can't start over on new roots. You're stuck in place. Since your career thus far is what *you* have to work with, it is imperative you have the rights to build off it.

STAY PRIVATE
THINK TWICE ABOUT GOING PUBLIC

Henson never wanted to talk about money with reporters. *Time* wrote, "He is secretive as a nesting hen when asked to talk figures."[840] the *Saturday Evening Post* wrote, "But exactly how many millions [the Henson empire is worth] the company refuses to disclose as detrimental to the Muppets' overall image."[841] We can understand why—with reporters, it's easy for your message to go *off* message. On the second season of *The Muppet Show,* Kermit is visited by a reporter from "The Daily Scandal," who tries to tease out gossipy features no matter what Kermit does:

> "Listen, I'm sorry, but we don't allow any reporters backstage during the show."
>
> "What a headline! *Muppets ban press. Reporter thrown out by frog.*"
>
> "Wait. On the other hand, can I offer you a cup of coffee?"
>
> "What a headline. *Frog bribes reporter. Muppets desperate for publicity.*"

"Uh, this isn't gonna be easy."

"Say, is it true you're dropping a lot of stuff from the show this year?"

"No, no, not particularly."

"Oh. *Muppets reliant on same old tired junk.*"

"Wait, on the other hand, we have a lot of brand new innovative stuff!"

"Oh, *Muppets changing format. Desperate to sustain show.*"

"I never knew the press could be so depressing."[842]

But the reason Henson could avoid talking money when he wanted to talk art was that, legally, he was not required to disclose any of that information—his company wasn't public. From the very beginning, Jim Henson's company has been a private, family-owned company. Henson never sold shares, and there is very good reason for that.

A fellow artist-entrepreneur, Walt Disney, was vocally *against* issuing public stock. During the golden age of *Snow White*, Disney bragged, "We don't have to make profits for any stockholders. New York investors can't tell us what kind of picture they want us to make or hold back."[843]

Yet Disney did eventually cave due to pressure from Roy, and in 1940, Disney issued stock to the public.[844] Another entertainment mogul, George Lucas, said he turned down the chairmanship of Disney in the eighties. "I don't want to run a public company," Lucas said.[845] For artists, a public company means having many bosses, and less artistic freedom.

Pixar had a public offering in 1995, scheduled by primary investor Steve Jobs to reap the benefits of *Toy Story*'s success. But ultimately this model was unsustainable, and they decided *not* to remain an independent public company, but instead to operate as a wing of Disney, to trade market volatility for Disney's protection. Writer Karen Paik explained why being a publicly traded company was so risky:

> Once Pixar went public, it had been protected by its track record of perfection at the box office, which . . . earned it the latitude from its shareholders to make decisions as it saw fit. But in the expensive and often fickle movie business, it's dangerous to be in a place where you have to rely on perfection to keep your head above water.[846]

As Paik speculates, "a spell of bad luck" could leave Pixar at the mercy of its shareholders, that is, told what to do *artistically* by the business side. As long as Pixar artists maintained a perfect track record, shareholders would leave them alone, but how long could they stay perfect? Part of their reason for merging with Disney was to avoid the fickleness of public investors. Of course, even before going public, Pixar had to answer to Steve Jobs, and Disney had to answer to Bank of America, but clearly, answering to a faceless mob—by turns impulsively bullish and bearish—seemed more worrisome to these artists than answering to a single, human lender with whom they had already established a relationship and could reason.

While Henson was alive, the shares of his company were owned by only two people, Jim and Jane Henson. Though he would have to seek funding at times from producer Lew Grade and networks for expensive projects, for the most part, his enterprise was funded by its own products—commercial work and merchandise. To never have to deal with stockholders' desires—which can often be shortsighted, greedy, or fearful—was certainly a blessing for Henson. It allowed him to control the destiny of his own company, answering only to his own artistic standards of excellence. Building a reputation takes patience, investing even when the profits take a dip. While stockholders tend to make a fuss about this year's merchandising sales, Larry Mirkin said of Henson, "He took a longer view about it."[847]

OWN EVERYTHING YOU DO
PAY UP TO BUY YOURSELF BACK

Owning your work has clear financial benefits, but it can be incredibly costly. One instance in which the risk paid off was in the case of Henson's early commercials. In 1957, Henson made an ad for Wilkins Coffee that became the "number one, most popular commercial"[848] in the Washington area. Because these ads played only in local markets, Henson was able to repackage them and sell them to other coffee companies in other regions. Henson explained that many paychecks grew out of the ads for Wilkins Coffee:

> They got a lot of talk, and so then the advertising agency started syndicating them and they would sell them to a coffee company in Boston, another coffee company in New York. . . . [S]o for a while there—I bought my contract from that agency and then I was producing them—the same things around the country. And so we had up to about a dozen or so clients going at the same time. At the point, I was making a lot of money.[849]

It's funny to think someone could make more money on *local* TV, but it was actually a blessing to have a small market with these commercials. Falk explains: "Jim could make the same ads for the new client easily by just changing the name in the script and the packaging during the shoot."[850] This became even more lucrative when he bought his contract from the middle-man ad agency. Henson made a lot of money this way, firstly by owning the copyright, rather than letting the coffee company keep it, and secondly by buying his contract back from the ad agency. It paid off. However, the cost of buying himself back would be even greater in the case of *The Dark Crystal*.

Henson said in 1982 of the film, "Of all projects that I've ever worked on, it's the one I'm most proud of."[851] The film had a high budget from Grade, whose "hands-off policy [had] been vital to the success of the enterprise,"[852] but just before the film was scheduled to release, Henson's angel funder was forced to sell his company to Robert Holmes à Court, a British businessman with a very different idea about the relationship between art and profits. Writer David Odell recalls Henson's worry that the new producers, fearful that they had spent too much, would "try to cut their losses by skimping on publicity and promotion."[853]

Brillstein recalls:

> He called me and announced he wanted to buy back the movie.
>
> "You're out of your mind," I said. "What are you going to do with it?"
>
> "I'll control its destiny," he said. "I love it."
>
> "But Sir Robert will want fifteen million."
>
> "I don't care."
>
> "Tell you what. I'll come to your office right now with a Gucci bag filled with fifteen million in cash. Take a look at it. Say good-bye to it."
>
> "Bernie," he said patiently. "Remember ten years ago

> in your kitchen you said I'd be free to do what I want? Artistic freedom? I'm calling it in."[854]

Odell continues:

> Holmes à Court said "Sold!" and Jim was the proud owner of *The Dark Crystal.* Jim had broken the one rule they warn you about in Hollywood: Never put your own money in your movie.[855]

The film was only a moderate success. Brillstein said, "It was costly in the short term, but eventually we made back all but a million. Jim didn't mind. He just wanted to own his own stuff. End of subject."[856] If Brillstein is correct, then the movie made them $14 million by 1999, and for all their hard work, Henson Associates *lost* a million. However, Henson saw beyond the world as it was—a place of fuzzy TVs and VHS cassettes. In the early eighties, he said of high-resolution cable television, "Certainly, that will come." Continuing, he said, "Hopefully . . . we're gonna have some wide-screen images at home, it'll be wonderful, and when we do that, and then I'm gonna release *Dark Crystal* to television."[857]

Sure enough, the new millennium saw the popularization of DVDs—lossless, crisp-imaged Digital Video Disks—and affordable wide-screen televisions. According to Odell in 2012, *The Dark Crystal* had "become a classic and a terrific seller on DVD, largely to people in their thirties who fell in love with it when they were kids."[858] Sony even asked The Henson Company, as it was later known, if they could produce a fantasy film in the same vein hoping to attract a similar cult following, resulting in Neil Gaiman's 2005 film *MirrorMask.*[859] In the long view, Henson's decision to buy back the film paid off. And yet, in the short term, it was thought a foolish choice by many, and at the very least, it was a *risky* choice.

While most of us can't write a check for $15 million, we quite often have the ability to negotiate for the ownership of our work to, as Henson said, "control its destiny." Yet a phrase like this is almost too mythic to be understood. In practical terms, what does it mean to control a work's destiny? It's not just who gets the profits, or how the film will be marketed and released.

Pixar presents a good example of a company that could not control the destiny of their movie, because their distributor and funder, The Walt Disney Company, owned the rights to 1995's *Toy Story* along with its characters.[860] This, along with other contractual headaches, put Pixar in a terrible situation—one in which they had to choose between going independent (and losing *Toy Story*) or joining Disney (which at that time was run by management they distrusted). John Lasseter explained:

> Steve Jobs stayed at the negotiating table with Disney about two to three years longer because of me. Because I wanted our characters. These characters are like our children, and it just killed me to think of the people who forced *Cinderella II* into existence making sequels to our films, running our characters into the ground.[861]

Because of the deal they'd made with Disney, Pixar couldn't control the destiny of *Toy Story*—Disney could churn out low-quality, direct-to-video products for the hungry stay-at-home market with little care for narrative continuity or cinematic magnificence. Disney had already attempted to make a direct-to-video sequel to *Toy Story*, but because they were artists, Pixar went to great effort to make *Toy Story 2* and *3* themselves, without skimping on quality. One can imagine that if Henson had *not* bought back *The Dark Crystal*, we might have seen any number of gelfling spin-offs made to conform to whatever the top-grossing video of the day demanded: crime-fighting ninja gelflings, babytalk sing-a-long gelflings, or preteen pop-starlet gelflings.

When Henson bought his contract from the Chicago ad agency, he was clearly buying himself back, because what he purchased was his right to control his future work. When he bought *The Dark Crystal*, the work had already been made, yet it was such a personal film for Henson that it likely *felt* like a part of himself. When John Lasseter says that Buzz and Woody are "like our children," this should not be a surprise to artists. Like children, artworks can be separated from the artist, and yet a parent can never truly "let go." And in business—when we arrange our fiscal contracts—it makes sense to set up a scenario that conforms to this feeling. As an artist, you very likely will return to the characters again, if not as a sequel, then in some way, shape, or form. It will be a part of you that you will have a real problem with *someone else* owning.

Yet, with all we know about Henson—owning everything he did—how could he ever decide, as he did in 1990, to enter into negotiations with Michael Eisner to sell his characters to Disney?

THE DISNEY SALE
HIS MOTIVES AND THEIRS

Disney in 1990 was acquiring *many* properties. In *The Disney Touch,* Ron Grover explains why the 1980s was such a time of change—and growth—for Disney. After Walt's death, the company was failing, and in 1984, Roy E. Disney—Walt's nephew—staged a shareholder coup and got rid of the old management led by Walt's son-in-law Ron Miller and in his place installed a new, experienced corporate leadership: CEO Michael Eisner (the former vice president of ABC), Chairman Jeffrey Katzenberg (the former president of production at Paramount), and President Frank Wells (the former president of Warner Brothers). According to one Disney-produced documentary, it was a time of "optimistic growth and aggressive investment"[862] into new sectors, with the company acquiring sports teams, cruise ships, TV networks, record labels, other studios, and publishing companies.[863] But Disney was strategic; as often as not, it decided *not* to buy a company, as was the case with SeaWorld. Grover, drawing from extensive interviews with Eisner and Disney insiders, explains:

> Disney's decision to reject the Harcourt deal had boiled down to one fundamental question: Were the SeaWorld properties so unique that Disney could not create something similar or better, and at a lower price?[864]

Because Disney could undercut SeaWorld with its own aquatic park, it didn't bother buying it. On the other hand, they agreed to buy Henson's Company. Grover explains why:

> In many ways, the Muppet deal was a classic Disney acquisition. The Muppets were irreplaceable assets, characters that had been created by Henson's genius and elevated to their current popularity through years of nurturing. They were not the kinds of assets that could be created by forming a new division of Disney or giving an assignment to existing creative personnel.[865]

Henson's art was not something Disney could make copies of cheaply. So Eisner arranged to buy the Muppet feature films and television series, and the trademarks and copyrights associated with them.[866] Going forward, any profits made by exploiting Kermit would go to Disney, and Eisner was counting on Kermit being "what industry executives call 'evergreen,'"[867] defined in the *New York Times* as:

> Properties that can be introduced to a new generation of children every few years. Such characters can be recycled not just on films and television, but on books, lunch boxes, T-shirts and other products.[868]

Eisner was on the lookout for "evergreens," which he seemed to be collecting. According to the *Wall Street Journal*:

> Disney needs new characters because there's always a risk with Disney of overexposing the characters they do have, says one analyst, adding that the Roger Rabbit characters aren't enough to supply fresh characters.[869]

Another likely motivation of Disney's—though hidden—was that Henson was Disney's competition. Buying him would silence his ability to take profits away from Disney. Though this motive was not announced by Disney, it was clearly a factor, because they *did* try to limit Henson's other characters. According to *Forbes*:

> [The *Sesame Street* Muppets] are controlled by Children's Television Workshop—[but] Disney wanted to limit their use, presumably to enhance the value of the Muppets it was buying.[870]

And it was also reported in the *Washington Post* that *Sesame Street* characters would no longer be able to use the name "Muppets" if the deal closed.[871] If Disney was to corner the market in family entertainment—which it had done in the 2000s, acquiring Marvel Comics, Pixar Studios, and Lucasfilm—it had to have the Muppets in its collection. But why would *Henson* want to sell? The reason would have to be pretty compelling to make a man who cared so much for creative control to give up his copyrights.

Grover writes that Disney agreed to pay Henson "nearly $150 million in Disney stock for the rights to Kermit, Miss Piggy, and the rest of the Muppet characters. . . . Henson himself had agreed to a 10-year contract to work—exclusively—with Disney on TV shows and films."[872] The number is large, although Disney stock is not the same as money, it's more like power—over Disney. Yet for Henson, the motive was more about the ten years than the $150 million.

To Henson, Disney must've looked like the ideal angel funder, willing to write a check for his expensive projects. Joan Ganz Cooney explained in *Street Gang*, "Disney was promising to back any movie project Jim wanted to do. That was huge."[873] The promise to fund *any* project was paramount to the barrier-breaking Henson, who was eager to experiment with 3-D movies and theme-park rides, which were too costly to produce on his own. And in Eisner's overtures, he clearly saw echoes of Lew Grade's hands-off policy. Over lunch with Cooney in 1989, Henson said, "I want the kind of creative freedom that I'll have there [at Disney] without the burden of fund-raising."[874] Clearly, business had taken its toll on Henson. At age fifty, he was still having to pitch his ideas to networks and often being disappointed, as when NBC cancelled *The Jim Henson Hour* after only five episodes. Cooney continues:

> Jim was fine with turning over the classic Muppets to Disney because he was tired of running the company, tired of having to raise money for every project.[875]

He told his agent, Bernie Brillstein, the same thing:

> His overhead was enormous, and it was tough on him. Even though he had expert assistance from guys like David Lazer, Jim needed to get out from under the organizational albatross that drained his creative energy. You can have the top people in the world, but the buck stops at the boss. People would go to Jim directly about everything and he hardly had the time. He was an artist first and foremost, and he needed to concentrate on his work and come up with magnificent ideas like he always had. With Disney's money and machinery, Jim could be fully creative.[876]

In his mind, the Disney deal would allow Henson to make more art and have to do less business. Because in fact, he didn't sell his *entire* company to Disney, just the branch that made the money—"the licensing and publishing businesses of Henson Associates,"[877] according to *The Los Angeles Times*. Michael Davis writes:

> The deal did not include Henson's production company and the core creative talent who worked in the United States and in the London offices of the Henson Creature Shop.[878]

Henson was keeping his creative team, his production company, and his Creature Shop, and jettisoning the licensing and publishing—the business—departments. According to the *Washington Post*:

> With the sale still on the boards, Henson cut his staff of about 120 in half to trim away business operations that

> were not part of the production entity. Most of those laid off were not members of the creative staff and were absorbed by Disney to minister to the properties after they are acquired.[879]

Henson was keeping his artists and tech people, and landing them a lucrative distribution deal with an entertainment legend. It seemed like a deal made in heaven. What Disney wanted most was the licensing business, and that was what Henson wanted *least*. They were willing to give him what he wanted *most*, a ten-year contract with an angel funder to make great art.

So, to make the deal, Henson bought out his wife's thirty-five shares in the company in July 1987 by agreeing to pay her any proceeds made from them in the merger.[880] He also gave Brillstein "a check for $7 million" to compensate for their agreement coming to an end.[881] At this point, Henson was the sole owner and stakeholder in his business. He was in the perfect position for an artist.

Yet Henson was about to give up an artist's greatest asset—copyright—because he was weary of business and believed he could start over.

OUR POOR BOY
THE SOLDIER AND THE HEARTLESS GIANT

Jim Henson chose to direct two episodes of his extravagant 1988 folktale series *The Storyteller*: "The Heartless Giant" and "The Soldier and Death." The *New York Times* wrote that the stories were made of "scary, beguiling, contradictory ideas."[882] Henson said of these fairy tales, "the stories have a lot of substance—they work for the present day."[883]

Indeed, the episodes Henson directed seem to have a strange resonance with this period in his life. Falk summarizes their themes:

> "The Soldier and Death," based on a Russian story about a soldier who cheats death and "The Heartless Giant," the story about a Giant and a prince grappling with friendship and betrayal."[884]

Like "The Shoemaker and the Elves," "The Soldier and Death" is an allegory about the life of an artist. By becoming an artist—singing and dancing—the wandering soldier cheats death and lives forever. On his way home from the war, the soldier meets a beggar and learns to whistle a "ruby whistle" along with the beggar's fiddle, and though they are both terrible musicians, he enjoys himself so much he gives the man one of his last three biscuits. A few beggars later, the soldier can not only fiddle but dance too, play cards, and call animals into a magic sack that compels them to obey. With his pack of magic cards, he beats the devils at their card game and becomes a king. One of them gives him the ability to see death—a puppet the *New York Times* called "at once a hooded fetus and ethereal crone."[885] On his deathbed, the soldier cleverly calls death into his sack. He becomes immortal.

It is a dark tale, but remember that Henson himself earned a kind of immortality through his art. He was a self-taught artist who collaborated with others like himself, just as the soldier danced and played with the beggar. "The one couldn't fiddle, the other couldn't whistle. And quite happy they both were."[886] Henson's generosity toward his collaborators, like the soldier's biscuit, earned him friendship and loyalty, and the pack of cards can be seen as the ability to negotiate in business—something artists notoriously lack. With the magic cards, the soldier could *beat* the devils. The sack represents copyright—the ability to turn what naturally flies free—ideas—into property. The soldier called birds, beasts, devils, and death into the sack. Henson called in movie scripts, VHS tapes, Big Bird, and Piggy.

Yet the soldier's story does not end happily. The people in his kingdom *want* to die because the world has become meaningless without death. So, eventually, the soldier sets death free, but he himself is doomed to wander the earth forever:

> He was condemned to watch while others aged and died, but death would not come for him. No, the soldier, old chip and dried beef, lived on and on and on . . .[887]

Anthony Minghella's beautiful script stops short of calling the soldier a poor soul, but the storyteller's dog judges the tale rightly when he says, "So sad."[888]

"The Soldier and Death" tells the tale of a man who becomes immortal—by using art, business, and copyright. In the late 1980s, Jim Henson also seemed weary of his responsibilities—"playing cards" with networks and keeping his licensing business going with characters that never grew old.

In the producerman phase of Henson's career, he and Jane split up. While many of his collaborators were marrying one another—Brian Froud and Wendy Midener, Michael Frith and Kathryn Mullen—Henson legally separated from Jane in July 1987.[889] He lived in a luxury Central Park bachelor-pad apartment at the Sherry-Netherland hotel, which he spent much time in 1983 and 1984 renovating. He drove a BMW in New York and a Mercedes convertible in Hollywood.[890] He filmed *A Muppet Family Christmas* in 1987, ironically coming together with all his employees precisely when his own family was no longer all together.

As a producer, he excelled at bringing groups together, but he was only marginally a *part* of them. He guest-starred on *Fraggle Rock* and guest-directed two episodes of *The Storyteller*. Perhaps it is a romantic notion to compare Henson to Citizen Kane in the Big Table Years—where the wealthier one gets, the more *distance* one finds between himself and his fellow man. Yet it is hard not to see the "poor old boy" overtones of "The Soldier and Death" in Henson's endless wanderings. Falk writes, "May 1988 was a typically hectic month for Jim," with trips to New York, London, Scotland, Plymouth, Stockholm, Detroit, New York again, and Yugoslavia.[891]

His assistant at the time was Alex Rockwell, who noted that in the late eighties, "even Jim had not been able to make a successful Muppet movie for some time."[892] This was disappointing. Frank Oz once said, "Jim didn't think of it in hit terms."[893] And yet, when the movies didn't do well, he was forced to care, because it meant it would be harder to get his next project made. While he may not have wanted to think about hits versus flops, he had to. He noted hits and non-hits in his *Red Book*:

> 5/20/1980—Empire Strikes Back opens in London—YODA big hit.
> 3/19/1982—First preview Dark Crystal in Washington, DC—not great.
> 7/12/1982—Preview Dark Crystal in Detroit—a bit better.
> 12/16/1987—Muppet Family Christmas airs. Great Reviews—great rating. I go over for UK Party.[894]

In his own words, he sounds wearied of business:

> Eliminating the dealmaking, administrative aspect of what I did was attractive. I was spending a lot more time on business than production.[895]

But like the soldier, Henson didn't really *get* to stop. And the lesson I take from this is that you *can't* really sell your company and keep control of your art. Henson thought he was getting *artistic freedom*, like he did when he licensed *Sesame Street* products, or like when Lew Grade funded the Muppet Show, and even *more* than that even, because Disney was better at toys than he was and better at marketing than Lew Grade, and with Disney, he would have just *one* funder to worry about—one that he trusted, and one with enough money to make the magical projects he had in mind.

However, in hindsight, Henson seems to have misjudged the Disney Company—at least Disney under Eisner, Wells, and Katzenberg. Cooney said that "Henson went into the initial discussions thinking 'Eisner would be a male Joan Cooney.'"[896] But despite Henson's long relationship with Eisner dating back to the mid-sixties,[897] Disney's lawyers were overly aggressive. According to *Newsweek*:

> Henson staffers say they felt uncomfortable working with the hard-driving Disney people. A few months after the deal was announced, according to Henson employees, Jim Henson and about 25 staffers were flown to Florida for a get-acquainted meeting. Jeffrey Katzenberg, chairman of Walt Disney Studios, asked Henson how things were going. Henson said he was happy except that he found Disney's negotiators "offensive." He reportedly went on to say, "All I really want out of this is a fair deal." Katzenberg

> supposedly responded: "Fair deal! Get out of the '60s, pal. You're in Hollywood now."[898]

This betrayal at the hands of a friend calls to mind the story of "The Heartless Giant." The tale begins with the warning:

> On the whole, there is absolutely no reason to be afraid of giants. Giants are gentle, perfectly harmless, very affectionate. Unless of course, the giant has no heart in his body.[899]

The *heartless* giant, we learn, is unpleasant because he's hidden his heart, which "gave him too much trouble—all those giant feelings. In its place was a wasp's nest, ready to swarm."[900] The good prince Leo doesn't believe this warning and befriends the giant, even sets him free. Finally Leo goes to find the giant. When he discovers that the giant has turned Leo's brothers to stone, he still doesn't try to slay the heartless giant. Innocent Leo thinks he can *reform* the giant—by putting his heart back.

The tale would be predictive of the next year of Henson's life, 1989. At the time, the Disney Company was a giant entertainment conglomerate, and one whose heart—Walt Disney—was no longer around. On the whole, there is nothing wrong with a large corporation, as long as it has a "heart." Walt had been the heart—*he* who makes *art.* He was the creator who started the corporation in the first place, for human reasons. But Walt Disney died in 1966, and his son-in-law was replaced by seasoned entertainment executives. In the 1980s, the giant was being driven not by a heart but by a swarm of wasps—acquisitive capitalists who were not themselves artists.

Like Leo's brothers turned to stone, many of the best children's characters were eventually turned into toys by Disney. By acquiring the copyright to Winnie the Pooh and Pinocchio, they were frozen in time, and they became the property of the giant. Still, even seeing what the giant had done to his brothers, Leo believed he could save both his brothers *and* the giant.

Henson always liked Disney, and he liked Michael Eisner. The *Los Angeles Daily News* reported:

> Eisner was an old friend. While a junior programming executive at ABC in the mid-1960s, Eisner worked with Henson to develop a television series pilot. In the late 1960s, Eisner again tried to develop a Muppet television show with Henson. Neither project ever made it on the air, but a mutual professional respect was established.
>
> "I wouldn't have made this deal with anyone else," [Henson] said.[901]

Henson, by joining Disney, could have filled the lacuna where Walt Disney once sat. With the heart of the Disney corporation replaced, there would be nothing wrong with the giant. He would be "perfectly harmless, very affectionate."

In "The Heartless Giant," Leo lives with the giant, becoming his servant. He cleans the house, looking for the giant's heart, but the giant tricks him, not wanting to reveal its location. Just as the giant tried to trick Leo by telling him his heart was under the stair when it wasn't, Disney would not give Henson a simple "fair deal." Run by what was effectively a triad of Roys, rather than a partnership between a Roy and a Walt, it was interested in profit above all. This triad had been installed for one purpose—to save Disney by turning the company around, *financially*. What they really wanted from Henson was not what he had hoped for. Those ten years started to feel like a lifetime of servitude. Cooney explained Henson's misgivings:

> What really caused him immense grief, and I think contributed to his lack of physical resistance was the contract provision dealing with his personal services. Jim would have been exclusively theirs for the rest of his life. He would be permitted to work on *Sesame Street* for two weeks a year, but that was it. Jim wanted to sign only a five-year deal for his personal services, not fifteen, and Disney said no. In fairness, Disney was about to pay him $150 million, and for what? But Jim was feeling like a caged bird, physically and personally trapped. He just wanted to fly away. You want to say that's what killed him.[902]

Medically, it makes no sense to say that Henson's rare strep infection was a result of his problems with the Disney deal. Yet Henson was clearly under stress because of the way the deal was turning out. Of the nine episodes of *The Storyteller*, only two have tragic endings, and those are the two Henson chose to direct. In the end of "The Heartless Giant," Leo tells his grandchildren that he did give the giant his heart back, and he did reform. "Because you see," said the storyteller, "despite all that took place, a little boy once met a giant, and they became friends." But Leo told the story he wished had been true. In reality, the giant died, because Leo could not stop his brothers' revengeful hearts.

Let's go back in time for a moment and imagine the Disney story *did* go differently. Brillstein's memoir offers us a window into what could have been:

> In the early '80s, knowing Disney was vulnerable, Jim wanted to make a run at taking over the company, which was still under its old management team of Ron Miller and Roy Disney. It was just idle talk that never went anywhere, and then Michael Eisner, Frank Wells, and Jeff Katzenberg took over.[903]

It's almost possible to imagine a world where Jim Henson ran the Disney Company, a gentle giant. Had he gotten to the company before the greed-is-good eighties had taken their course, the Disney Company would have a very different culture today.

But it would have meant Henson would be running a much bigger company, and that seemed to be something he was quite resistant to do.

BECOMING DISNEY
SMALL COMPANY, BIG COMPANY

For an artist-entrepreneur, it makes a lot of sense to keep your business small. The bigger you get, the more time you have to spend on business and the more businesspeople you need to hire. As noted earlier, in 2012, the Disney Company employed 156,000 people.[904] To put this in context, consider The Henson Company's 300 and Pixar's 850.[905] One of the reasons Pixar did not want to be independent was that it would have had to expand. Ed Catmull explained, "All of a sudden there would be another two to three hundred businesspeople in the company, and that would be a risk to the culture.[906]

Henson also preferred to keep the business small. In the article "Jim Henson Content with His Kingdom," he is quoted as saying:

> I've never particularly wanted to have a large organization. The trick is to try to stay small enough to be creative but still be able to do all the projects we want to do—and not get so big where you spend all your time just managing people and trying to keep everybody working together.[907]

At that time, 1987, the company employed "more than 100 people in three cities."[908] Disney, when he was making his first movie was already well over 1,000. A 1973 article said the Disney Company had 20,000 employees.[909]

Still, when Henson made his first movie in 1979, the *New York Times* wrote, "the externals of his business are beginning to take on a Disneylike aspect."[910] Henson disagreed:

> "I'm slightly uncomfortable with all the people who want to say things like that about me," Henson responded to the comparison, "'cause I like Disney but I don't ever particularly want to do what he did. He built this great, huge empire. I'm not particularly inclined to do that. You get that large a thing going and I'm not sure that the quality of the work can be maintained." He smiled sheepishly. "It seems that I'm bigger now than I thought I would be."[911]

If a company's profits depend on quality—as an artist-entrepreneur's do—then a small company is ideal for maintaining quality control.

The animated *Muppet Babies* series is a good case in point. Henson's company was growing bigger in the eighties, and as the *New York Times* said in "Mr. Muppet's Empire Is Thriving," he was on five networks at once—NBC, ABC, CBS, HBO, and PBS.[912]

Muppet Babies was very loosely based on the original characters and was directed at children under seven years old. The animation was outsourced overseas and new voice actors and songwriters were brought in to reinterpret the characters. Brillstein explained that it was his idea, a business idea:

> I convinced him to okay the animated series *Muppet Babies*. . . . Not everyone on [Henson's] informal council—Frank Oz, Jerry Juhl, Diana Bergenfield, David Lazer, Jim's wife, Jane, and I—wanted to. But The Henson Company had nothing on the air. I believed *Muppet Babies* would give Jim a presence and merchandising income while he pursued other interests. I was right.[913]

In effect, Henson's business manager, Brillstein, was advising him to spread himself thin—to produce more shows than he could effectively quality control—to become a bigger company than an artist can sustain.

The results were good by the standards of Saturday morning cartoons, but not by the high standards of the rest of the Muppet productions. *Muppet Babies* won Daytime Emmys consistently for its first four years, and yet it was too cutesy for parents to enjoy. It pandered. Jeffrey Scott's scripts are like the candy-cigarette version of Muppets. They encourage imagination—Henson's message—but the animation is in the dated, comic-book style of the eighties, the same as *G.I. Joe* or *Transformers.* It has the disposable feeling of a Happy Meal.

As executive producer, Henson *tried* to oversee the quality of the show. He set the mission and tone of the show with his notes. He made suggestions for possible storylines. He met with the animation companies before making a selection. His partner, Marvel Studios, kept Henson abreast of the casting progress, and he flew to LA to approve and fine-tune the ultimate lineup.[914] Of course,

Henson decided to do the series "for the right reasons," because he wanted to reach out to children where they were—watching cartoons on Saturday—with a different kind of message, one about the co-existence of different perspectives and being open-minded. Yet *Muppet Babies* does not have the stamp of timeless quality of Henson's other works. While many parents today buy vintage *Sesame Street* and *Fraggle Rock* DVDs to show their kids, age hasn't been kind to the *Muppet Babies* cartoon.

Henson didn't want his company to grow any bigger, to sacrifice any more quality. Selling his assets to Disney would allow him to downsize. Steve Whitmire explained:

> [Jim Henson] said, ". . . What I'd like to do is reduce the size of our company and get back to being just a small production company and just do our work." I think he was tired of the big corporate aspect of everything. . . . Having the company grow into this big corporate thing. He just wanted to cut back and get back to just creating stuff. I think the idea was Disney would look after the publishing and licensing and the legal side of the business, and he would be able to just do work and direct and perform and that sort of thing. So that was his goal.[915]

And yet, as much as Henson did not want to be a big company, he did want to be Disneylike in one aspect—creating his own theme-park attractions. Archivist Karen Falk describes Henson's ambitious concepts:

> A food ride where the cars shaped like carrots and beets would travel into a mouth, get chewed in some fashion,

> enter the bloodstream and end up in a cell. There was the Five Senses Ride that went into the nose, eyes, ears and mouth, perhaps connecting with the food ride, allowing riders to send messages to the brain. Another ride might highlight different regions of the country and include an aural component where the visitor could hear regional accents. Jim thought about people traveling through time, seeing life on earth develop before them, or using his *Muppet Show* characters as guides on a trip through theater history, providing Nerf tomatoes to throw in the Shakespearean section.[916]

Henson essentially wanted the job of an imaginer—the ability to dream big. His joining with Disney would allow him to test the limits of possibility with the "interactive, cinematic *Jim Henson's Muppet*Vision 3D*" attraction, which now runs at both Disney World and Disneyland.[917]

And according to one Disney expert, Henson might have left an even bigger impact on Disneyland. Plans were drawn up for a publicity stunt where Mickey, Donald, and the gang were to go on vacation for a year, leaving the park in the hands of Kermit's weirdos. Jim Hill wrote:

> Once Mickey had turned over the keys to this theme park over to Kermit in January of 1991 (in what was sure to have been a well-attended photo-op), the Muppets were to have . . . well, Muppetized the place. This was to have involved ripping up the much-photographed Mickey-shaped planter in front of the Main Street U.S.A. train station and then temporarily replacing it with a Kermit-shaped one. Not to mention throwing a crudely-painted

> canvas sign over the Disneyland entrance marquee so that this theme park would then be identified as Muppetland. But the pièce de résistance of Lindquist's Muppets-take-over-Disneyland publicity stunt—the part of Jack's promotional sketch that was almost certain to garner worldwide press coverage—involved several hundred gallons of Kermit-the-Frog green paint. You see, what Jack wanted to do (just for the year of 1991, mind you) was paint all 147 feet of the Matterhorn green.[918]

While Henson wanted a small company, he also wanted Disney's one-of-a-kind playground and the funding that made it possible. In this light, the Disney deal seemed like a perfect arrangement. On the other hand, mergers can be tricky.

MERGER PROBLEMS
CULTURE CLASH—WHAT WENT WRONG

In *The Muppets at Disneyland*, a 1990 TV special, Kermit meets Mickey, and it doesn't go smoothly. Kermit's gang runs loose in the park without tickets. A security guard played by Charles Grodin says, "I'll pay anything to capture the Muppets." Confinement is a theme. Rowlf is netted by a dog catcher right after he says, "I don't know what to do with all this incredible freedom." Fozzie is forced to panhandle: "A little money for some funny." Money is another theme, since the Muppets haven't paid admission. "Kermit usually handles all that stuff for us," they say. Scooter explains that a new character was brought in to be "cute" so the rest of the cast didn't have to. Rizzo irreverently reminds the Disneyland guards that rodents *are* allowed in the park with a wisecrack: "Oh yeah, does your boss *Mickey* know that?"

This is not unlike the real difficulties of the merger. According to Cooney, "Everyone [at Henson Associates] said it's been awful. It was clear that they've been having a severe culture clash."[919] One Henson writer, Mark Saltzman, said, "I was surprised about [the] Disney [merger] because Disney is a corporate entity and Jim and the Muppets have a very fuzzy, Grateful Dead kind of sensibility."[920] The *Washington Post* said, "[T]he inner circle has always operated in an informal manner that contrasts sharply with Disney's closely structured style. . . . In Hollywood, the Disney name is synonymous with rigid, aggressive corporate control. The Henson atelier is informal and respect for the artist is the first rule."[921]

In *Newsweek*, Larry Reibstein wrote:

> Disney has a reputation for vigorously defending copyrights on its own characters. Lawyers point to its suit two years ago against the Academy of Motion Picture Arts and Sciences for using *Snow White* in the opening number of the Oscars show. Said one copyright lawyer, "Disney writes the book on being tough. They'll sue anybody and anything."[922]

The *Washington Post* cited "one of Henson's representatives" as saying, "You'd have to call Michael Eisner and say, 'This is where it's gone with your overzealous robots. . . . If it continues this way, the deal won't close."[923]

One point of conflict between Henson and Eisner was *Sesame Street*. Since the licensing rights had become the source of independence for the nonprofit Children's Television Workshop, Henson felt he owed it to Cooney, CTW's chairman, to keep it separate. Eisner, on the other hand, wanted to buy Big Bird and wouldn't take no for an answer. According to Cooney, after Henson had expressed his annoyance, Eisner invited her and Henson to a "peace lunch" during which he was "his most charming self," and then he pressed the issue, which "stopped Jim cold":

> Jim turned to Michael and said, "You did it again!"
> Michael said, "I did what?"
> Jim said, "You mentioned *Sesame Street*."
> Michael said, "Jim, I'm so sorry, I didn't mean to."
> But the damage was done at that moment, . . . and it remained a real issue with Jim deep down.[924]

Sesame Street licensing revenues were more than a cash cow for Henson and Cooney; they ensured creative freedom. If Disney owned Big Bird, his cuteness level and educational message would be subject to Disney's shareholders.

Disney also made the typical business demand that products be made faster and cheaper to maximize profits. The *Washington Post* reported:

> A source close to the Henson studio says Disney offended Muppeteers by suggesting that they could quickly train personnel to operate the Muppet characters. "I don't think they understood that it took Jim years to get a single puppeteer up to speed," says Cooney.[925]

Former Henson employee Jim Hill remembered this was a "major sticking point" in the negotiations:

> The story around the Henson studio back then was that Disney wanted a stable of several puppeteers per character. This would enable them to churn out product whenever

> and however they deemed necessary. The Muppeteers, however, believed these characters were individual to themselves and that multiple puppeteers would disintegrate the characters' personalities. There couldn't be more than one Kermit or more than one Miss Piggy. This small-town approach to entertainment didn't fit in with Disney's big plans for the Muppet characters.
> . . . The other angle to this roadblock was an amazing piece of information I learned from my co-workers. I was told, and I don't know if this is still the case, that the Muppeteers [under Henson] received royalties from all merchandise sold relating to their characters.[926]

Disney wanted to take away both the Muppet performers' creative ownership of their characters and their financial ownership of toy royalties; this is clearly not an "artist-first" business philosophy. One editorialist in the *St. Petersburg Times* pointed out that when a "Disney stock analyst" for Merrill Lynch described the merger, he managed to use the word "exploit" only twice. The editorial pointed out that Eisner earned $40.2 million that year. Nothing leads us to believe Henson or Cooney took anywhere near that kind of salary. The corporate ladder breeds a very different kind of approach to taking care of one's creative "assets."

Peggy Charren, president of Action for Children's Television, explained another difference, this time philosophical: "None of the Disney characters worry about the way the world works like the Muppets do."[927] The editorial goes on to imagine that Donald Duck never pondered why his skin was the color it was, as Kermit has. It is unlikely that a merger like this can end happily without a good deal of struggle.

Pixar's negotiations with Michael Eisner's Disney were similarly troubled. When Pixar was negotiating with Eisner, Steve Jobs broke off talks altogether with Disney until Eisner was replaced. Ironically, the same man who put Eisner in power, Roy E. Disney, staged a coup again in 2004. He wrote a letter to Eisner blaming him for many of the company's mistakes:

> You have had a very successful first 10-plus years at the company . . . but since Frank [Wells's] untimely death in 1994, the Company has lost its focus, its creative energy, and its heritage. . . . The perception by all of our stakeholders—consumers, investors, employees, distributors and suppliers—[is] that the company is rapacious, soul-less, and always looking for the "quick buck" rather than long-term value which is leading to a loss of public trust.[928]

Walt's nephew Roy E. wanted the old Disney back. Though new leadership had indeed "saved" the company financially, it had bankrupted its spirit. Roy then told Jobs, "When the wicked witch is dead, we'll be together again,"[929] and indeed, when Roy succeeded in making Bob Iger the new CEO, Pixar joined Disney.

Time will tell how the Pixar-Disney merger fares, but their past has certainly been a bumpy road simply because they were two different companies with two different cultures. We saw the trouble Woody, Buzz Lightyear, and the rest of Andy's toys had trying to fit into a big daycare business like Sunnyside in *Toy Story 3*. Written after tense negotiations between Pixar and Disney, the film was about culture clash, but it ends happily when the charming but despotic Lotso has been ousted and a "groovy" Ken doll is put in charge. Perhaps Pixar will succeed because they knew what they were getting into with their merger. Lasseter had even been fired from Disney in the early eighties after his experiments with digital animation. Just before the merger, Pixar's Chief Technical Officer Ed Catmull told his employees, "Our number-one priority [is] protecting the culture that we'[ve] built and the way our people work together. A real creative community is a rare thing."[930]

WE WILL LIVE FOREVER
ON THE IMMORTALITY OF KERMIT

Unexpectedly to fans and family alike, Jim Henson died on May 16, 1990, at the age of fifty-three of a particularly aggressive strep infection. Too ill to work for the first time in his life, Henson died at New York Hospital surrounded by his wife Jane and children. According to Steve Whitmire, many collaborators also congregated in a waiting room:

> Frank [Oz], [manager] David Lazer, [designer] Michael Frith, [puppeteer] Kathy Mullen, [puppeteer] Jerry Nelson, [daughters] Lisa, Cheryl, Heather, and Jane. . . . The doctor took Frank aside, then he came over and he kind of broke up a little, but he said, "well, at" whatever time it was, which I don't remember, "Jim passed away." And that's all he said.[931]

Besides the shattering personal loss, Henson Associates was left rudderless. The company's logo was Kermit the Frog, and it seemed as though they needed Kermit in order to keep the company going.

Brian Henson recalled, "It took a while for us to decide what we were going to do with Kermit, as a family—just the family involved in that decision of how Kermit would continue and how we would do it."[932] At the urging of Disney, they filmed a special called *The Muppets Celebrate Jim Henson* in which death is acknowledged, but Kermit returns in the last scene, played by Steve Whitmire. According to *The Disney Touch*:

> With Henson's sudden death, the deal which had not yet been signed fell into uncertainty. Now, Disney executives began trying to put together a memorial for Henson in the form of a TV special. Long-time Henson collaborator Frank Oz agreed to direct the Disney special, which would use the Muppet characters in short film pieces. CBS was interested, as was NBC. Eisner, who had been out of town at the time of Henson's death, called to New York to discuss the project with Henson's widow. A day into the planning, she decided against doing the show.[933]

There was resistance to the special, in part because, at the same time, a real memorial was being held in New York on a short five-day notice at the Cathedral of Saint John the Divine, according to Henson's instructions.[934] At the service, no one wore black, a big Dixieland band played "When the Saints Go Marching In," and friends and puppets sang many of Henson's favorite songs. Big Bird sang a lilting "Bein' Green," and as Davis describes, "Just before Big Bird trudged off, he looked skyward and said, 'Thank you, Kermit.'"[935] Big Bird—and many others—assumed that *Kermit* had died.

Author Michael Davis laments an irreplaceable loss:

> It's very hard for me to watch Ernie and Bert's "Have Yourself a Merry Little Christmas" duet in Christmas Eve on *Sesame Street.* It makes me so sad, I just couldn't watch

> it this year. Because what it always brings me back to is that it can't happen again.[936]

But the business model of copyright demands that it happen again. And, today, Ernie and Bert sing together—without Henson or Oz. It's very peculiar, since the characters seem so close to the personalities of these men. Willard Scott went so far as to say, "Jim was not simply the voice of Kermit. Kermit was the soul of Jim."[937] Cheryl Henson said,

> Kermit is so much my father's character. . . . Kermit was the first character that my father really allowed to be himself. . . . I think Steve does a wonderful job of Kermit, but it's not quite the same. Kermit, to me, will always be my father's Kermit.[938]

Puppeteer Terry Angus said of the new Kermit:

> It doesn't have the same authority that Jim's Kermit had, but hey, Steve is not Jim, and I am not Jim. We can impersonate Jim, but we can't really be him.[939]

Keeping the Muppets group together means keeping Kermit alive, and yet, prior to Henson's death, no fully developed Muppet character had ever been transferred to a new puppeteer like this.

Muppets writer Jerry Juhl said:

> We would never want a performer to be doing a copycat imitation, it's a true acting job in that sense. Since our comedy is character-based, they can't be static. They need to be able to grow. . . . I'm a strong believer in having the

> main characters evolve and keeping them fresh and finding new places to put them. Otherwise, they would just be corporate icons.[940]

Yet Kermit has rather become a corporate icon, for financial reasons. The 1998 "Mickey Mouse Protection Act," as it is called, extended copyright protection to a full seventy years beyond the creator's death. Trademark law, by contrast, is valid indefinitely—as long as Mickey represents Disney, or Kermit represents the Muppets Holding Company—that is, as long as a company uses a character as a logo. Essentially, forever.

Did Henson really want Kermit to live forever?

The Dark Crystal contains much of Henson's philosophy. The movie's writer, Dave Odell, called it "spiritual" and called Henson a "spiritual searcher" who "developed his own ideas that seemed to combine a little bit of . . . various philosophies."[941] In the film, the race of "cruel" Skeksis live in the castle, guarding their power source—the crystal—and chant, "We will live forever!" On the other hand, the natural wizards, the gentle Mystics, die in peace. Skeksis fight death and die in agony. It is not a reach to interpret the message of this film as saying that it is better to accept death as a part of life than to "cheat death" as the Skeksis do.

According to the *Washington Post*:

> Henson had two objectives when he decided to sell to Disney. He put the Muppets in a sort of Valhalla, where the Disney experts could package and promote them for all time. The deal also allowed Henson to get away from the bureaucracy so he could focus on and fund new productions.[942]

Ostensibly, it would appear that putting Kermit in Valhalla seems to be a motive for Henson. And though the Disney-Henson merger devolved into "invective-filled"[943] lawsuits in 1990, Henson's heirs did eventually decide to sell the Muppet copyrights to Disney in 2004 and used the money from the sale to keep their current projects going. When asked how they feel about it, the usual answer is: "It's what my father wanted."[944]

However, I think it is more fair to say this is what he wanted in 1990 in a specific context, along with many other things. More than feeling a powerful need to keep Kermit alive, Henson seems to have felt a weary responsibility to do so. My guess is that he didn't know if it was really *possible*. More importantly, *as an artist*, Henson would rather have done more interesting things like big fantasy movies and 3-D, rather than keeping a corporate icon in suspended animation. Henson had spoken to Whitmire about replacing him as Kermit, but not necessarily after his death. Brian Henson said, "I think he was starting to feel like, 'I love the Muppets, but I have more in me.'"[945] We could imagine Whitmire as Kermit might free up a still-living Henson to do other things.

It's possible that his main reason for the Disney deal was to have the "creative freedom" to *not have* to keep Kermit alive—to get someone else, someone who valued that—to take that burden off his back.

Michael Davis wrote:

> Henson had successfully propelled Kermit into an orbit few characters ever reach. Keeping him there for generations hence would be a business worry Henson would no longer have to shoulder if he sold to Disney. Plus, he could still be around for the fun part: providing Kermit's voice, movements, and expressions as a paid performer.[946]

Unfortunately, Henson didn't get to be around for the fun part. And just as Kermit's future was uncertain, so was the future of Henson Associates. Henson hadn't groomed a protégé who could take over *both* the business *and* the creative aspects of the company. Indeed, such a person would be hard to find. Eventually, Henson's daughter Lisa—a former president at Columbia Pictures—became the CEO, and Brian—a puppeteer/director/producer—became chairman. The company continues to innovate and contribute to children's entertainment, without the Muppets. Like the Disney Company in the years after Walt's death, the company has had trouble finding its financial footing. But while they haven't hit upon the same success as Jim Henson, they continue to create new projects like *Bear in the Big Blue House*, *Sid the Science Kid*, the off-Broadway hit *Stuffed and Unstrung*, and the creatures in *Where the Wild Things Are*. One gets the sense that it is in this small company, still family-run, that Kermit's energy was meant to live on—perhaps not in the same copyrightable shape, but in the same spirit of collective creativity.

HOW TO RETAIN OWNERSHIP

Henson's role as an artist-entrepreneur gave him great freedom—artistic freedom—that rested on his copyrights and the shares of stock he owned in his own company. His rule had been simple: "Own everything." And it feels symbolic that the year we lost Jim Henson was the year he broke this rule. Reading about culture clashes, merger problems, and lawsuits can make an artist weary of business, but let us go back to that moment when Jim Henson owned all the shares to his company and all the copyrights. That is how we would all like to be as artist-entrepreneurs.

It's tempting to cash out. Many tech start-ups *start* just so that someone big will buy them out. Yet, for an artist, it is harder to truly cash *out*, because the things you've made are not mere impersonal gadgets or algorithms; they are extensions of your personality. They are more like our children. Protect your art. Hold onto it. Control its destiny.

Jim Henson chose to sell the Muppets because he was ready to move on to other things, yet even when you *think* you can leave your project in someone else's hands, the giant who wants to buy them may demand more than you're willing to give. Like Disney wanting the *Sesame Street* characters in addition to the Muppets, it is often not enough to sell *part* of your work—a savvy corporation will want it *all*, effectively turning you into its servant.

Henson was hopeful to see the goodness in everyone, and most of his stories end with the villain being reformed, but that's not the case in "Happy Girl Meets a Monster." In this early *Ed Sullivan* sketch, the girl, an optimist, can't convince the monster, a pessimist, to see things positively, no matter how hard she tries. He eats her flowers, shoots her singing bird. With a sneaky look in her eye, the girl says:

> You're so perfectly awful that it's beautiful. I'm sure that you've tried all your life to be perfectly awful. Working and working year after year just to be as bad as possible. And now all your toil and self-sacrifice has made you a success. You set yourself a goal and you have succeeded. Perfection is a beautiful goal to strive for. You should be congratulated. Yes, you're so awful it is truly awful. You're a perfect example of beautiful awfulness.[947]

As she flatters him, the monster starts to shrink. When he is small enough, she *flattens* him with a fly swatter, then says to the camera: "You have to talk your troubles down to a size where you can handle them."[948]

You can't change everyone, the skit implies. Though Henson most often practiced the philosophy "invite the outside in," he could only do that if he had a *house* to invite them into. If the outside owns your house, well then, something is off. Although it may not have seemed like it, in 1989, Henson was in a position of *power* in the negotiation with Disney—his giant *had* a heart. When the merger seemed to be destructive, he could very well have walked away from the deal.

Be aware that if your business becomes too big, quality will be hard to maintain. But do not be tempted by the words of even bigger giants who tell you that you can go back to being small by shaking hands with them. Like a very tall tree, you must continue to try to stand on your own weight. You cannot go back in time—the only ways to shrink are to prune back or to fall. You might try cutting back—layoffs. A better strategy is prevention—to keep your company manageable *from the start.*

It is baffling that Henson groomed a protégé for Kermit but didn't train someone to run his company. Yet Disney before him had the same trouble—how do you replace the irreplaceable? Both companies were family run in the years after their creators' deaths, and both reached the brink of failure. In order to right themselves, the Disney Company went corporate, and The Henson Company sold its most successful characters. This does not lead an artist to be very optimistic about the health of his company without him, but perhaps that is as it should be.

When watching Henson's films and shows, one notices a very *healthy* relationship with death—Mr. Hooper's death on *Sesame*

Street and Mudwell's death on *Fraggle Rock* seem intended to teach children that death is a part of life. In the end of *The Dark Crystal*, both races cruel and wise are "made whole" and *leave* the universe, telling Jen and Kira to take care of each other, not abuse the crystal's power, and "make their world in its light." I think that must be what Henson would want the artists who come after him to do.

CONCLUSION

MAKE YOUR WORLD IN ITS LIGHT

What Jim Henson did with his life was amazing. He seemed to approach his career with the idea that he could *do* anything, so what was *worth* doing?

Sesame Street, *The Muppet Show*, and *Fraggle Rock* have inspired children from 1969 to the present—all over the world. Those works of art inspire us to be kind, lighthearted, accepting, and creative. Henson's work has had a deceptively powerful effect on a generation of creatives. *Sesame Street* tells us that it's okay to stay innocent, and as a result, Generation Henson values art and collaboration in some cases more than it values financial security. *Time* wrote that Henson "helped sustain the qualities of fancifulness, warmth and consideration that have been threatened by our coarse, cynical age."[949] As Mel Brooks has wisely said, the Muppets stand for one thing: "The meek shall inherit the earth."[950] I think he was right. There are kinder people walking the earth today *because* of Henson. In many ways, the meek have *already* inherited it.

The message to children in *Labyrinth* was to grow up and yet stay innocent at the same time. In the last episode of *Fraggle Rock*, we are told, "You cannot leave the magic." This is the way Henson lived his life. Though he was the head of a large company, he had a sense of wonder about life that celebrated its surprises, its people, and their humor. I have heard young people declare in their most mature voices, "Professor, sometimes you just *have* to be cutthroat." I don't think Henson believed that rubbish.

To my mind, Henson had just about the best attitude toward money that an artist can have. I would be inspired if people living today—if *you*—could somehow hit upon Henson's powerful and uncommon entrepreneurship, and prove it is possible to re-create the kind of magic he left us.

I've drawn some surprisingly serious analyses from Henson's "children's" shows. But I'm not alone: as we've seen, Dave Odell Henson called a "spiritual searcher,"[951] who "developed his own ideas that seemed to combine a little bit of theosophy, Hinduism, Taoism, and various new age philosophies,"[952] and surely these philosophical insights appear in the film.

Odell recalled that many of the themes were "accidental":

> I pointed out to Jim once the similarity in the endings of *The Dark Crystal* and *The Muppet Movie*. The roof falls away and the puppets are bathed in a blast of light from heaven, which seems to solve all their problems. I asked him if it was a personal symbol of something, like the Christian paraclete or the beginning of Genesis: "Let there be light." He said he had never connected the two scenes in his mind, but he found strange echoes of things were always turning up in his work.[953]

Art helps us uncover what we believe through self-exploration, and often we uncover ideas we didn't know we had. At the same time,

Henson's themes were often planned explicitly. In his 1978 developmental notes for *The Dark Crystal*, Henson described the two sides, what could perhaps be called good and evil, if Henson believed in this duality, which he didn't. Evil just wasn't a part of Henson's worldview; to him, people were just different. Here, he sums up the Skeksis and the Oours, who would later become the Mystics:

SKEK-SIS	OO-URS
in charge military	brotherly love
science–technology	lover of beauty
operations–business	spiritual
treasurers–	generosity
food–glutton	lover of animals
rituals–intellectual	wisdom
pleasure/sensual	self denying
power	guilty
self-centered–selfish–ego	giving–sharing
vanity	un-self–looks mess
cruel–blood thirsty	healer–herbs–plants
devious–scheming	loving–open
lazy–indolent	hard working–diligent[954]

This conflict—between business and spirituality—should look familiar; it went all the way back to 1968's "Business, Business," which uses many of the very same words. And there are clear parallels between it and Henson's own biographical statement, "Maintaining a balance between art and business has always been a part of what I do."[955] The parallels I've drawn between *The Gift* and Henson are also not unfounded. *Fraggle Rock* writer David Young said he gave *The Gift* to Jerry Juhl and Jocelyn Stevenson, and that "they all had that kind of energy" at *Fraggle Rock*.[956]

Henson may have been more of a visual artist than a writer, but he most definitely had a message. Odell recalls that Henson wanted him to understand his philosophy before he wrote *The Dark Crystal*. He gave Odell a copy of another philosophical book called *Seth Speaks*, and it later showed up in the movie:

> [Henson] had a lot of copies of this book and gave them away to people. (He also gave a copy to Brian Froud.) I was flattered that Jim wanted me to understand his spiritual insights before we collaborated. . . . One of Jim's favorite lines that I wrote in *The Dark Crystal* script was when Aughra asks Jen where his master is, and Jen says he's dead. Aughra looks around suspiciously and mutters, "He could be anywhere then." I couldn't have written that if I hadn't read the Seth book.[957]

The *Seth Speaks* book contained many interesting ideas about the nature of creativity, such as that it is possible to create "multidimensional" art using one's life the way a painter uses pigment and canvas. Your life is your art. After Henson gave Jocelyn Stevenson a copy of *Seth Speaks*, she wrote the *Fraggle Rock* episode "Believe it or Not," which deals with the idea that we create our own reality, something Henson himself professed:

> I believe that we form our own lives, that we create our own reality, and that everything works out for the best. I know that I drive some people crazy with what seems to be ridiculous optimism, but it has always worked for me.[958]

It is possible Henson got this idea from *Seth Speaks*, but it is more likely he found resonance in the book with his own philosophy. According to *Seth Speaks*, nothing is due to luck:

> The great artists, for example, did not emerge out of a particular time simply because they were born into it, or [because] those conditions were favorable. . . . Periods of renaissance—spiritual, artistic, or psychic—occur because the intense inner focus of those involved in the drama are directed toward those ends.[959]

Essentially, this "intense inner focus" of artists can create a new reality. Henson truly believed this and lived his life accordingly. He felt what we might call "self-actualized," saying:

> Most people, and particularly kids, don't realize that they are in control of their lives and they're the ones that are going to make the decisions and they're the ones that are going to make it either way. Usually adolescence is a time when kids feel that the world is doing it to them. . . . Somewhere in there, you have to learn that you're not the victim, but instead you're the one who's doing it. . . . All of a sudden you realize that you are the person who had control of your life.[960]

If *The Dark Crystal* can be read as a parable of our modern "culture wars," now is the time for the Mystics to return to the castle. In the film, the land was dying because the beings themselves were fragmented into gross caricatures. Instead of a race of whole beings, the Skeksis became all-greedy and the Mystics became all-artist. Each being was starving a part of itself. To become whole, the artist needs to join with his opposite—the businessman.

Maybe the roof won't fall away to reveal an all-encompassing light, but maybe our own lives will become better, stronger, more creative. Perhaps our lives will serve as multidimensional art for others yet to come.

Can ten lessons comprise a foolproof system to make money from your art? *Fraggle Rock* mocks the very notion of rules ensuring success. In "Gobo's School for Explorers," Gobo learns the hard way that you can't just blindly follow the rules and ignore your own intuition. No true explorer would let a set of rules tell him what to do. He'd have to see for himself.

If you disagree with anything in these lessons, trust your intuition. What do *you* see in Henson's life? I have shown you what I've seen, not so that you will trust it without testing it, but instead to show you an example of how you might think about Henson in a new way—not just as a familiar memory from childhood, but as someone whose career was remarkable and perhaps similar to your own. You don't need ten lessons to see that connection—you need the *spirit* of the lessons.

More than that, what we *really* need is a hero. Henson is perhaps the only entrepreneur I would trust as a mentor, because of the way he lived his life. Through delving into his decisions, their outcomes, and his motives, I've learned more about business than I thought possible. Though it's too soon to tell if I'll make *millions*, I'm getting incrementally closer. If you're reading this, I have at least succeeded in publishing my first book. By picturing Henson and the way he lived his life, I can envision myself successful. It seems to be working.

More than anything, I'm incredibly grateful that I've had the chance to work on this project for the last few years—doing something I love that feels important to me—and that with the income from teaching and a book advance, I could afford to do so. While I had a lot of support, it is a dream that came from me, and I knew that it was my responsibility to make it happen. No one was going to write it for me. And it reminds me of something Jim Henson said: "The feeling of accomplishment is more real and satisfying than finishing a good meal or looking at one's accumulated wealth."[961] When you make your heart the boss of your life, you can accomplish things that no one can take away from you. They can take away the money, but for artists, it's never really about the money.

Whether you are a painter, a writer, or inventor—if you feel *emboldened* by what Henson has done, then know that you have it in you to do it, too. Before you read this book, you were already quite Henson-like, because you learned his values through the art. As you continue in your career, I hope you will find your mind returning to these ideas. Henson's approach to money has been helpful to me, and I hope it can be helpful to you.

I hope you will talk about these ideas with other artists. Find others like yourself who are interested in *both* art and money and discuss your heroes, your careers, your dreams. What have you tried? What has worked for you? What did you learn from Henson, and what have you learned from others? If you want, write to me. You can contact me on my website ElizabethHydeStevens.com. I'm always happy to explore these concepts.

Consider one more thing. At the age of twenty-eight, Jim Henson did something very smart. He started a career journal that would later become *Jim's Red Book*. It was a pocket-sized book with a cloth cover, and he wrote in playful script:

The life and
times of
THE MUPPETS
As documented by
Jim Henson
and begun this 7th
day of June, in the
year of our Lord 1965

Henson wrote short one-line descriptions all of the important things that had occurred in his career so far—in a section called "Ancient History." And he continued to add events until 1988. A journal like this is meditative, because it allows you to see your career more objectively, more playfully. By turning it into a narrative, it allows you to treat your own life as a kind of art. Add to this career—let it grow.

Art and money are very often in conflict, and yet, while Jim Henson was clearly aware of this conflict, his career proves that they *can* be combined in a meaningful way that adds *value* to the world. You can do something like this, too. How do I know it's possible? Because someone did it already—Jim Henson.

There are millions of people out there who'll tell you it can't be done. They are the naysayers, the been-there-done-thats, the people in the audience who know the ending already. Believe in the never-before. The miracle. The surprise. Because no one knows the future.

Even the smartest scientist and the most jaded historian will tell you he has no idea what tomorrow will bring.

Jim Henson believed that we create our own reality. Do you?

ENDNOTES

1. Sullivan, "Muppets Magic."
2. Hyde, *Gift: Creativity and the Artist*, 26.
3. Ibid., 359.
4. Ibid., 360.
5. Ibid., 369.
6. Brillstein, *Where Did I Go Right?*, 109–10.
7. Freeman, "Muppets on His Hands," 52.
8. Finch, *Jim Henson: The Works*.
9. Henson, *Youth '68*.
10. Clines, "Mr. Muppet's Empire."
11. Grover, *Disney Touch*, 216.
12. Odell, *Dark Crystal: Creation Myths*, afterword.
13. Davis, *Street Gang*, 5.
14. Brillstein, *Where Did I Go Right?*, 111.
15. Davis, *Street Gang*, 50.
16. CNN, "Remembering Jim Henson."
17. Hyde, *Gift: Creativity and the Artist*, 358–9.
18. Ibid.
19. Larry Mirkin, e-mail to E. H. Stevens, June 20, 2013.
20. Freedman, "It's a Muppet Invasion."
21. Harris, "Muppet Master."
22. Borgenicht, *"Sesame Street" Unpaved*, 171.
23. Falk, *Jim Henson's Red Book*, Jan. 13, 1966.

24. Hyde, *Gift: Creativity and the Artist*, 360.
25. Harris, "Muppet Master."
26. Ibid.
27. Davis, *Street Gang*, 150–51.
28. Ibid., 203.
29. Ibid., 205.
30. Brillstein, *Where Did I Go Right?*, 109–10.
31. Ibid.
32. Ibid.
33. Ibid.
34. Ibid.
35. Davis, *Street Gang*, 203.
36. Ibid., 150–51.
37. Ibid., 5.
38. Ibid.
39. Rockwell, "Frances: Interview."
40. Skow, "Those Marvelous Muppets."
41. Brillstein, *Where Did I Go Right?*, 111.
42. Odell, *Dark Crystal: Creation Myths*, afterword.
43. Davis, *Street Gang*, 204.
44. Falk, *Jim Henson's Red Book*, Nov. 9, 1971.
45. Ibid.
46. Ibid.
47. *St. Petersburg Times*, "Acquisitions, Mergers and Muppets."
48. Falk, *Jim Henson's Red Book*, Mar. 8, 1977.
49. Finch, *Jim Henson: The Works*, 153.
50. Falk, *Jim Henson's Red Book*, Mar. 8, 1977.
51. Ibid.
52. Whitmire, "My Week with Steve."
53. Falk, *Jim Henson's Red Book*, Sept. 20–24, 1971.
54. Nelson, "Chat with Jerry Nelson."

55. Spinney, *Wisdom of Big Bird*, 132.
56. Finch, *Of Muppets and Men*, 60.
57. Henson, *Fraggle Rock—First Season*, bonus material.
58. Falk, *Jim Henson's Red Book*, Nov. 9, 1971.
59. Hyde, *Gift: Creativity and the Artist*, 358–9.
60. Larry Mirkin, e-mail to E. H. Stevens, June 20, 2013.
61. Falk, *Jim Henson's Red Book*, Sept. 20–24, 1971.
62. Harris, "Muppet Master."
63. CNN, "Remembering Jim Henson."
64. Falk, *Jim Henson's Red Book*, Oct. 14, 1970.
65. Paik, *To Infinity and Beyond!*, 291.
66. Finch, *Jim Henson: The Works*, 153.
67. Falk, *Jim Henson's Red Book*, Dec. 1975.
68. Falk, *Jim Henson's Red Book*, Apr. 21, 1986.
69. Brillstein, *Where Did I Go Right?*, 109–10.
70. Oz, "Interview with Frank Oz."
71. Falk, *Jim Henson's Red Book*, July 31, 1954.
72. Falk, *Jim Henson's Red Book*, June 1954.
73. Harris, "Muppet Master."
74. Ibid.
75. Falk, *Jim Henson's Red Book*, July 31, 1954.
76. Harris, "Muppet Master."
77. Ibid.
78. Ibid.
79. Falk, *Jim Henson's Red Book*, July 31, 1954.
80. Davis, *Street Gang*, 82.
81. Falk, *Jim Henson's Red Book*, July 31, 1954.
82. Jerry Seinfeld, interview by Larry Wilde.
83. Falk, *Jim Henson's Red Book*, July 31, 1954.
84. Falk, *Jim Henson's Red Book*, May 6, 1959.
85. Smith, "Jim Henson Dies at 53."

86. CNN, "Remembering Jim Henson."
87. Falk, *Jim Henson's Red Book*, Dec. 15, 1961.
88. Bacon, *No Strings Attached*, 51.
89. Gabler, *Walt Disney*, 162.
90. Hyde, *Gift: Creativity and the Artist*, 66.
91. Ibid., 63–4.
92. Ibid., 64.
93. Henson, *It's Not Easy Being Green.*
94. Hyde, *Gift: Creativity and the Artist*, 64.
95. Ibid.
96. Ibid., 67.
97. Freeman, "Muppets on His Hands," 51.
98. Henson, *It's Not Easy Being Green*, 58.
99. Hyde, *Gift: Creativity and the Artist*, 63.
100. Henson, *Fraggle Rock—First Season*, bonus material.
101. Goelz, "Gonzo Puppeteerism."
102. Davis, *Street Gang*, 300.
103. CNN, "Remembering Jim Henson."
104. Falk, *Jim Henson's Red Book*, May 5, 1985.
105. Spinney, *Wisdom of Big Bird*, 132.
106. Ibid.
107. Worron, "Frank Oz Talks about Miss Piggy."
108. Bailey, *Memoirs of a Muppet Writer*, 221.
109. Ibid., 16.
110. Falk, *Jim Henson's Red Book*, Nov. 24, 1965.
111. Falk, *Jim Henson's Red Book*, Sept. 23–24, 1976.
112. Falk, *Jim Henson's Red Book*, Sept. 21, 1986.
113. Henson, *It's Not Easy Being Green*, 57.
114. Emmens, "Muppet Mania," 31.
115. CNN, "Remembering Jim Henson."
116. Henson, *It's Not Easy Being Green*, 49.

117. Davis, *Street Gang,* 306–7.
118. Ibid., 307.
119. Nuwer, "Muppets on the Move," 70.
120. Gabler, *Walt Disney*, 162.
121. CNN, "Remembering Jim Henson."
122. Henson, *Best of The Muppet Show*, "Dudley Moore."
123. Falk, *Jim Henson's Red Book*, Dec. 25, 1979; May 5, 1980.
124. Falk, *Jim Henson's Red Book*, May 4–10, 1971.
125. Henson, *It's Not Easy Being Green*, 49.
126. Gabler, *Walt Disney*, 325.
127. CNN, "Remembering Jim Henson."
128. Falk, *Jim Henson's Red Book*, Sept. 23, 1980.
129. Falk, *Jim Henson's Red Book*, Sept. 4, 1980.
130. Harris, "Muppet Master."
131. Falk, *Jim Henson's Red Book*, June 1958.
132. Freeman, "Muppets on His Hands," 52.
133. CNN, "Remembering Jim Henson."
134. Henson, *It's Not Easy Being Green*, 68.
135. Spinney, *Wisdom of Big Bird*, 153.
136. Henson, *Fraggle Rock—First Season*, "The Thirty-Minute Work Week."
137. Gladwell, *Outliers*, 50.
138. Ibid., 49.
139. Ibid.
140. Ibid., 50.
141. Ibid., 39.
142. Ibid., 47.
143. Ibid., 55.
144. Ibid., 42.
145. Gladwell, "Q and A with Malcolm."
146. Ibid.

147. Henson, "Muppet Musicians of Bremen."
148. Falk, *Jim Henson's Red Book*, Dec. 15, 1961.
149. Mischer, "Muppets Celebrate Jim Henson."
150. Henson, *It's Not Easy Being Green*, 9.
151. CNN, "Remembering Jim Henson."
152. Henson, *It's Not Easy Being Green*, 112.
153. Falk, *Jim Henson's Red Book*, May 28, 1959.
154. Gabler, *Walt Disney*, 51.
155. Spinney, *Wisdom of Big Bird*, 150.
156. Finch, *Of Muppets and Men*, 21.
157. Henson, *Fraggle Rock—Second Season*, "Mokey and the Minstrels."
158. Henson, *Fraggle Rock—Second Season*, bonus material.
159. "Puppeteers of America Festival," YouTube video, posted by "enterthedome."
160. Henson, *It's Not Easy Being Green*, 73.
161. Falk, *Jim Henson's Red Book*.
162. Falk, *Jim Henson's Red Book*, May 28, 1959.
163. Falk, *Jim Henson's Red Book*, Feb. 1955.
164. Davis, *Street Gang*, 83 and 259.
165. Falk, *Jim Henson's Red Book*, June 1958.
166. Harris, "Muppet Master."
167. Culhane, "Muppets in Movieland."
168. Falk, *Jim Henson's Red Book*, Aug. 1961.
169. Ibid.
170. Falk, *Jim Henson's Red Book*, Dec. 17, 1985.
171. Freeman, "Muppets on His Hands," 126.
172. McLellan, "Jerry Juhl, 67."
173. Juhl, "Written in Foam."
174. Oz, "Magic Behind the Muppets."
175. Freeman, "Muppets on His Hands," 52.

176. Bacon, *No Strings Attached*, 19.
177. Ibid., introduction.
178. Henson, *Fraggle Rock—First Season*, bonus material.
179. Harris, "Muppet Master."
180. Angus, "Reflections in Fleece."
181. Harris, "Muppet Master."
182. Falk, *Jim Henson's Red Book*, Sept. 1970.
183. Falk, *Jim Henson's Red Book*, June 1–3, 1970.
184. Falk, *Jim Henson's Red Book*, Sept. 1970.
185. Angus, "Reflections in Fleece."
186. Henson, *Fraggle Rock—First Season*, bonus material.
187. Ibid.
188. Ibid.
189. Ibid.
190. Ibid.
191. Finch, *Of Muppets and Men*, 65.
192. Whitmire, "My Week with Steve."
193. Ibid.
194. Ibid.
195. Bacon, *No Strings Attached*, 15.
196. Harris, "Muppet Master."
197. Reibstein, "Kermit vs. Mickey Mouse."
198. Goelz, "Gonzo Puppeteerism."
199. Rockwell, "Frances: Interview."
200. Spinney, *Wisdom of Big Bird*, 24–25.
201. Angus, "Reflections in Fleece."
202. Bailey, *Memoirs of a Muppet Writer*, 13.
203. Ibid., 14.
204. Ibid., 16.
205. Ibid., 35.
206. Ibid., 115.

207. Falk, *Jim Henson's Red Book*, Dec. 1975.
208. Spinney, *Wisdom of Big Bird*, 31.
209. Davis, *Street Gang*, 304.
210. Spinney, *Wisdom of Big Bird*, 150.
211. Zuckerman, "Actor Who Created Big Bird."
212. CNN, "Remembering Jim Henson."
213. Bailey, *Memoirs of a Muppet Writer*, 123.
214. Ibid., 19.
215. Goelz, "Gonzo Puppeteerism."
216. Falk, *Jim Henson's Red Book*, Dec. 15, 1979.
217. Bailey, *Memoirs of a Muppet Writer*, 275.
218. Associated Press, "Talk Show Host for Boss."
219. Shemin, *Behind the Scenes*.
220. Henson, *Fraggle Rock—First Season*, bonus material.
221. Prell, "Interview with Muppeteer."
222. Whitmire, "My Week with Steve."
223. Nelson, "Chat with Jerry Nelson."
224. Angus, "Reflections in Fleece."
225. Zuckerman, "Actor Who Created Big Bird."
226. Nelson, "Chat with Jerry Nelson."
227. Davis, *Street Gang*, 312.
228. Falk, *Jim Henson's Red Book*, Nov. 1, 1981.
229. *Muppet Wiki*, "Michael K. Frith."
230. Davis, *Street Gang*, 77.
231. Falk, *Jim Henson's Red Book*, May 29, 1979.
232. Culhane, "Muppets in Movieland."
233. Spinney, *Wisdom of Big Bird*, 133.
234. Ibid., 58.
235. Ibid., 135–6.
236. Davis, "Michael Davis Interview."
237. Brillstein, *Where Did I Go Right?*, 54.

238. Harris, "Muppet Master."
239. Freeman, "Muppets on His Hands," 52.
240. Harris, "Muppet Master."
241. Hyde, *Gift: Creativity and the Artist*, 361.
242. Falk, *Jim Henson's Red Book*, Oct. 9, 1966.
243. Bacon, *No Strings Attached*, 92.
244. Henson, *Fraggle Rock—Second Season*, bonus material.
245. Ibid.
246. Falk, *Jim Henson's Red Book*, Jan. 10, 1968.
247. CNN, "Remembering Jim Henson."
248. Falk, *Jim Henson's Red Book*, Apr. 1968.
249. Falk, *Jim Henson's Red Book*, May 10–12, 1966.
250. Falk, *Jim Henson's Red Book*, Nov. 1957.
251. Henson, *Sam and Friends*, "C'est Ci Bon."
252. Henson, *Sam and Friends*, "Promo 1961."
253. Henson, *Sam and Friends*, "Kermit Plays the Banjo."
254. Falk, *Jim Henson's Red Book*, Nov. 1957.
255. Falk, *Jim Henson's Red Book*, Dec. 13–15, 1966.
256. Falk, *Jim Henson's Red Book*, Aug. 23–27, 1965.
257. Falk, *Jim Henson's Red Book*, Sept. 27, 1965.
258. Falk, *Jim Henson's Red Book*, Dec. 4, 1967.
259. Falk, *Jim Henson's Red Book*, Jan. 21, 1966.
260. Falk, *Jim Henson's Red Book*, Mar. 6, 1967.
261. Falk, *Jim Henson's Red Book* Apr. 3, 1965.
262. Falk, *Jim Henson's Red Book*, Oct. 1967.
263. Falk, *Jim Henson's Red Book*, Jan. 25, 1964.
264. Ibid.
265. Falk, *Jim Henson's Red Book*, Oct. 1967.
266. Falk, *Jim Henson's Red Book*, June 3, 1968.
267. Falk, *Jim Henson's Red Book*, Oct. 1963.
268. Falk, *Jim Henson's Red Book*, Jan. 10, 1968.

269. Falk, *Jim Henson's Red Book*, Mar. 11, 1969.
270. Falk, *Jim Henson's Red Book*, Feb. 27, 1969.
271. Henson, "Flapsole Sneakers."
272. Ibid., (caption).
273. Graeber, "And a Frog Shall Lead Them."
274. Falk, *Jim Henson's Red Book*, June 25–26, 1969.
275. Ibid.
276. Ibid.
277. Henson, *Wilson's Meats Meeting Films*, "Film #2."
278. Henson, *Wilson's Meats Meeting Films*, "Film #1."
279. Seligmann, "Jim Henson: 1936–1990."
280. Henson, *Wilkins Coffee Commercials*.
281. Henson, *Ideal Toys Commercial*.
282. Gladwell, *Tipping Point*.
283. Falk, *Jim Henson's Red Book*, Jan. 25, 1964.
284. Falk, *Jim Henson's Red Book*, Dec. 4, 1967.
285. Falk, *Jim Henson's Red Book*, Jan. 25, 1964.
286. Falk, *Jim Henson's Red Book*, Aug. 23–27, 1965.
287. Harris, "Muppet Master."
288. Henson, *Wilson's Meats Meeting Films*, "Film #1."
289. Bailey, *Memoirs of a Muppet Writer*, 27.
290. Henson, *Wilson's Meats Meeting Films*, "Film #2."
291. Falk, *Jim Henson's Red Book*, June 1958.
292. Finch, *Jim Henson: The Works*.
293. Museum of the Moving Image, "Jim Henson's Fantastic World."
294. Finch, *Jim Henson: The Works*.
295. Falk, *Jim Henson's Red Book*, Sept. 1, 1964.
296. Museum of the Moving Image, "Jim Henson's Fantastic World."
297. *Muppet Wiki*, "Wilkins Coffee."

298. Davis, *Street Gang*, 150.
299. Brillstein, *Where Did I Go Right?*, 109.
300. *Sesame Workshop*, "Our Mission."
301. Davis, *Street Gang*, 65.
302. Ibid., 121–2.
303. Falk, *Jim Henson's Red Book*, Mar. 11, 1969.
304. Ibid.
305. Davis, *Street Gang*, 73.
306. Ibid.
307. Gould, "'Hey, Cinderella.'"
308. Davis, *Street Gang*, 212.
309. Falk, *Jim Henson's Red Book*, Oct. 30, 1975.
310. Falk, *Jim Henson's Red Book*, May 30–31, 1981.
311. Falk, *Jim Henson's Red Book*, Oct. 30, 1975.
312. Falk, *Jim Henson's Red Book*, Feb. 11, 1977.
313. Ibid.
314. Falk, *Jim Henson's Red Book*, Mar. 15, 1988.
315. *Kermiclown's Muppets Videos Trade Page.*
316. Henson, "Forests."
317. Rockwell, "Frances: Interview."
318. CNN, "Remembering Jim Henson."
319. Hyde, *Gift: Creativity and the Artist*, 359.
320. Harris, "Muppet Master."
321. Henson, *Sell, Sell, Sell.*
322. Henson, *Youth '68.*
323. Rockwell, "Frances: Interview."
324. Donald, "Julianna Donald Interview."
325. Hyde, *Gift: Creativity and the Artist*, 358.
326. Davis, *Street Gang*, 258.
327. Henson, *Muppet Show Pitch Reel.*
328. Culhane, "Muppets in Movieland."

329. Davis, *Street Gang*, 150.
330. Henson, *It's Not Easy Being Green*, 112.
331. Henson, *Fraggle Rock—First Season*, bonus material.
332. *Muppet Wiki*, "Richard Nixon."
333. Bailey, *Memoirs of a Muppet Writer*, 90.
334. Falk, *Jim Henson's Red Book*, Nov. 21, 1977.
335. Falk, *Jim Henson's Red Book*, Nov. 21, 1978.
336. Falk, *Jim Henson's Red Book*, Dec. 1, 1986.
337. Falk, *Jim Henson's Red Book*, Mar. 30, 1976.
338. Bell, *American Puppet Modernism*, 2.
339. Ibid., 50.
340. Culhane, "Muppets in Movieland."
341. Leal, "Muppets and Money," 213–14.
342. CNN, "Remembering Jim Henson."
343. Brillstein, *Where Did I Go Right?*, 109–10.
344. Henson, *Fraggle Rock—First Season*, bonus material.
345. McLellan, "Jerry Juhl, 67."
346. Ibid.
347. Falk, *Jim Henson's Red Book*, June 16, 1971.
348. Freeman, "Muppets on His Hands."
349. Falk, *Jim Henson's Red Book*, Aug. 13, 1974.
350. Ibid.
351. Falk, *Jim Henson's Red Book*, Aug 30, 1975.
352. Rockwell, "Frances: Interview."
353. Skow, "Those Marvelous Muppets."
354. Nuwer, "Muppets on the Move," 70.
355. Ibid.
356. Bailey, *Memoirs of a Muppet Writer*, 54.
357. Borgenicht, *"Sesame Street" Unpaved*, 14.
358. Henson, *Fraggle Rock—First Season*, bonus material.
359. Ibid.

360. Ibid.
361. Ibid.
362. Davis, *Street Gang*, 165.
363. Falk, *Jim Henson's Red Book*, May 10–12, 1966.
364. Bell, *American Puppet Modernism*, 2.
365. Freeman, "Muppets on His Hands."
366. Falk, *Jim Henson's Red Book*, Jan. 13, 1966.
367. Ibid.
368. McLellan, "Jerry Juhl, 67; His Scriptwriting Breathed Life into the Muppets."
369. Hyde, *Gift: Creativity and the Artist*, 27.
370. Bacon, *No Strings Attached*, 15.
371. Henson, *Fraggle Rock—Third Season*, bonus material.
372. Sullivan, *Muppets Magic.*
373. Ibid.
374. Ibid.
375. Henson, *Muppet Movie.*
376. Henson, *It's Not Easy Being Green*, 49.
377. Culhane, "Muppets in Movieland," 4.
378. Mitgang, "Muppets Turn 30."
379. Falk, *Jim Henson's Red Book*, Apr. 21, 1968.
380. Falk, *Jim Henson's Red Book*, Feb. 26, 1968.
381. Ibid.
382. Emmens, "Muppet Mania."
383. Ibid.
384. Odell, *Dark Crystal: Creation Myths*, afterword.
385. Mitgang, "Muppets Turn 30."
386. Bacon, *No Strings Attached*, 71.
387. Davis, *Street Gang*, 281.
388. Spinney, *Wisdom of Big Bird*, 136.
389. Falk, *Jim Henson's Red Book*, May 16, 1980.

390. Davis, *Street Gang*, 301.
391. Ibid., 244.
392. Spinney, *Wisdom of Big Bird*, 110.
393. Ibid., 136.
394. Freedman, "It's a Muppet Invasion."
395. Henson, *Muppets Take Manhattan.*
396. Harris, "Muppet Master."
397. Nuwer, "Muppets on the Move"; Freeman, "Muppets on His Hands."
398. Harris, "Muppet Master."
399. Ibid.
400. Bunce, *Christian Science Monitor*, "Mr. Muppet."
401. Mischer, "Muppets Celebrate Jim Henson."
402. Christensen, "How Will You Measure?"
403. Hyde, *Gift: Creativity and the Artist*, 28.
404. CNN, "Remembering Jim Henson."
405. Gabler, *Walt Disney*, 246.
406. Ibid., 174.
407. Henson, *World of Dark Crystal.*
408. Gabler, *Walt Disney*, 354.
409. Ibid., 246–7.
410. Whitmire, "My Week with Steve."
411. Henson, *Fraggle Rock—First Season*, bonus material.
412. Henson, *World of "Dark Crystal."*
413. Shemin, *Behind the Scenes.*
414. Ibid.
415. Falk, *Jim Henson's Red Book*, Sept. 4, 1980.
416. Henson, *Muppets Take Manhattan.*
417. CNN, "Remembering Jim Henson."
418. Nelson, "Chat with Jerry Nelson."
419. Falk, *Jim Henson's Red Book*, July 1983.

420. Larry Mirkin, E. H. Stevens, June 21, 2013.
421. Finch, *Of Muppets and Men*, 21.
422. Henson, *Best of The Muppet Show* "Edgar Bergen."
423. Skow, "Those Marvelous Muppets."
424. Ibid.
425. Henson, *Fraggle Rock—Second Season*, "Mokey and the Minstrels."
426. Finch, *Of Muppets and Men*, 137.
427. Gabler, *Walt Disney*, 285.
428. Safer, *60 Minutes*, "Backstage on 'The Muppet Show'."
429. Gabler, *Walt Disney*, 272.
430. Ibid.
431. Paik, *To Infinity and Beyond!*, 63.
432. Ibid.
433. Finch, *Of Muppets and Men*, 21.
434. Brillstein, *Where Did I Go Right?*, 111.
435. Davis, *Street Gang*, 5.
436. Hyde, *Gift: Creativity and the Artist*, 362.
437. Nelson, "Chat with Jerry Nelson."
438. Brillstein, *Where Did I Go Right?*, 101.
439. Davis, *Street Gang*, 150.
440. CNN, "Remembering Jim Henson."
441. Falk, *Jim Henson's Red Book*, Oct. 21–24, 1970.
442. Davis, *Street Gang*, 118.
443. Culhane, "Muppets in Movieland."
444. Ibid.
445. Freberg, "Stan Freberg Talks."
446. Hyde, *Gift: Creativity and the Artist*, 56.
447. Bailey, *Memoirs of a Muppet Writer*, 69.
448. Nelson, "Interview with Legendary Muppeteer."
449. Freeman, "Muppets on His Hands," 53.

450. Ibid.
451. Harris, "Muppet Master."
452. Freeman, "Muppets on His Hands," 52.
453. Culhane, "Muppets in Movieland."
454. Freeman, "Muppets on His Hands," 53.
455. Clines, "Mr. Muppet's Empire."
456. Freeman, "Muppets on His Hands," 53.
457. *The Kuklapolitan Website*, "Frequently Asked Questions."
458. Falk, *Jim Henson's Red Book*, Mar. 22, 1969.
459. Henson, "Future of Video & Cable."
460. Henson, "Jim Henson on *Labyrinth*."
461. Nelson, "Chat with Jerry Nelson."
462. Falk, *Jim Henson's Red Book*, June 1, 1960.
463. Ibid.
464. Henson, "Jim Henson on *Labyrinth*."
465. Henson, *It's Not Easy Being Green*, 54.
466. Emmens, "Muppet Mania."
467. Gabler, *Walt Disney*, 245.
468. "Puppeteers of America Festival," YouTube video, posted by "enterthedome."
469. Paik, *To Infinity and Beyond!*, 289.
470. Price, *Pixar Touch*, 235.
471. Catmull, "How Pixar Fosters Creativity."
472. Falk, *Jim Henson's Red Book*, June 5–8, 1988.
473. Henson, "Future of Video & Cable."
474. Falk, *Jim Henson's Red Book*, Sept. 10–12, 1970.
475. Bacon, *No Strings Attached*, 133.
476. Fal, *Jim Henson's Red Book*, Sept. 10–12, 1970.
477. Whitmire, "My Week with Steve."
478. Ibid.
479. Catmull, "How Pixar Fosters Creativity," 68.

480. Ibid., 70.
481. Finch, *Of Muppets and Men*, 69.
482. Ibid., 55.
483. Gabler, *Walt Disney*, 367.
484. Finch, *Of Muppets and Men*, 55–6.
485. Prell, "Interview with Muppeteer."
486. Ibid.
487. Bacon, *No Strings Attached*, 19.
488. Prell, "Interview with Muppeteer."
489. Clines, "Mr. Muppet's Empire."
490. Harris, "Muppet Master."
491. Ibid.
492. Falk, *Jim Henson's Red Book*, July 27–28, 1985.
493. Finch, *Of Muppets and Men*, 115.
494. Henson, *It's Not Easy Being Green*, 54.
495. Falk, *Jim Henson's Red Book*, Feb. 1955.
496. Falk, *Jim Henson's Red Book*, Mar. 7, 1955.
497. Harris, "Muppet Master."
498. Falk, *Jim Henson's Red Book*, May 14–17, 1984.
499. Gabler, *Walt Disney*, 55–6.
500. Paik, *To Infinity and Beyond!*, 46–7.
501. Hoover's, Inc., 2011 and 2012.
502. Gabler, *Walt Disney*, 351.
503. Finch, *Jim Henson: The Works*, 163.
504. Culhane, "Muppets in Movieland."
505. Masters, "Disney's Muppet Miasma."
506. Reibstein, "Kermit vs. Mickey Mouse."
507. Culhane, "Muppets in Movieland."
508. Iwerks, *Pixar Story*.
509. Gabler, *Walt Disney*, 47.
510. *Muppet Wiki*, "Larry Jameson."

511. Henson, *Fraggle Rock—Second Season*, "Doozer Contest."
512. Catmull, "How Pixar Fosters Creativity," 71.
513. Ibid., 68.
514. Gabler, *Walt Disney*, 84.
515. Ibid., 329.
516. Falk, *Jim Henson's Red Book*, June 1960.
517. Archive of American Television, *Archive Interviews on Jim Henson*.
518. Brillstein, *Where Did I Go Right?*, 54.
519. Ibid.
520. Ibid., 329.
521. *Muppet Wiki*, "Jim Henson Company."
522. Falk, *Jim Henson's Red Book*, Sept. 1, 1964.
523. Ibid.
524. Brillstein, *Where Did I Go Right?*, 109.
525. Ibid., 110.
526. Davis, "Michael Davis Interview."
527. Gabler, *Walt Disney*, 83.
528. Ibid., 57.
529. Ibid., 329.
530. Ibid., 161.
531. Brillstein, *Where Did I Go Right?*, 330.
532. Ibid., 329–30.
533. Gabler, *Walt Disney*, 350.
534. Ibid., 284.
535. Bunce, *Christian Science Monitor*, "Mr. Muppet."
536. Hyde, *Gift: Creativity and the Artist*, 359.
537. Ibid.
538. Davis, *Street Gang*, 149.
539. Ibid., 150–51.
540. Ibid., 151.

541. Ibid., 92.
542. Brillstein, *Where Did I Go Right?*, 330.
543. Davis, *Street Gang*, 142.
544. Archive of American Television, *Archive Interviews on Jim Henson.*
545. Davis, *Street Gang*, 92.
546. Ibid.
547. Brillstein, *Where Did I Go Right?*, 110.
548. Ibid.
549. Price, *Pixar Touch*, 61.
550. Reibstein, "Kermit vs. Mickey Mouse."
551. Masters, "Disney's Muppet Miasma."
552. Reibstein, "Kermit vs. Mickey Mouse."
553. Brown, "Muppets Deal."
554. Price, *Pixar Touch*, 164–65.
555. Ibid.
556. Bailey, *Memoirs of a Muppet Writer*, 35.
557. Price, *Pixar Touch*, 232.
558. Paik, *To Infinity and Beyond!*, 285.
559. Whitmire, "My Week with Steve."
560. Freeman, "Muppets on His Hands."
561. Falk, *Jim Henson's Red Book*, Nov. 25, 1971.
562. Bailey, *Memoirs of a Muppet Writer*, 139.
563. Ibid., 16–17.
564. Ibid., 115.
565. Falk, *Jim Henson's Red Book*, Mar. 1, 1972.
566. Ibid.
567. Emmens, "Muppet Mania."
568. Brillstein, *Where Did I Go Right?*, 101.
569. Falk, *Jim Henson's Red Book*, May 16, 1980.
570. Finch, *Of Muppets and Men*, 24.

571. Falk, *Jim Henson's Red Book*, Nov. 11, 1981.
572. Bailey, *Memoirs of a Muppet Writer*, 143.
573. Brillstein, *Where Did I Go Right?*, 150–51.
574. Davis, *Street Gang*, 312.
575. Falk, *Jim Henson's Red Book*, Nov. 1, 1981.
576. Finch, *Of Muppets and Men*, 20–21.
577. Ibid.
578. Culhane, "Muppets in Movieland."
579. Finch, *Of Muppets and Men*, 65.
580. Brillstein, *Where Did I Go Right?*, 147.
581. Ibid., 148.
582. Ibid., 149.
583. Jones, *Jim Henson: The Biography*, 315.
584. Henson, "Future of Video & Cable."
585. Brillstein, *Where Did I Go Right?*, 111.
586. Henson, *Muppet Movie.*
587. Falk, *Jim Henson's Red Book*, Dec. 20, 1983.
588. Brillstein, *Where Did I Go Right?*, 147–48.
589. Henson, *Muppet Movie.*
590. Gabler, *Walt Disney*, 63.
591. Leal, "Muppets and Money," 213.
592. Falk, *Jim Henson's Red Book*, Dec. 22, 1968.
593. Brillstein, *Where Did I Go Right?*, 146.
594. Finch, *Of Muppets and Men*, 21.
595. Henson, *Fraggle Rock—First Season*, bonus material.
596. Brillstein, *Where Did I Go Right?*, 338.
597. Henson, *Sell, Sell, Sell.*
598. Juhl, "Written in Foam."
599. Ibid.
600. Ibid.
601. Hyde, *Gift: Creativity and the Artist*, 72.

602. Falk, *Jim Henson's Red Book*, July 31, 1954.
603. Falk, *Jim Henson's Red Book*, Sept. 1, 1964.
604. Ibid.
605. Falk, *Jim Henson's Red Book*, Dec. 1964.
606. Henson, *Tales of the Tinkerdee.*
607. Falk, *Jim Henson's Red Book*, Dec. 1964.
608. Falk, *Jim Henson's Red Book*, Feb. 15, 1966.
609. Ibid.
610. Falk, *Jim Henson's Red Book*, Apr. 18, 1966.
611. Falk, *Jim Henson's Red Book*, Feb. 21, 1966.
612. Brillstein, *Where Did I Go Right?*, 101.
613. Davis, *Street Gang*, 164–65.
614. Ibid., 189.
615. Falk, *Jim Henson's Red Book*, Mar. 22, 1969.
616. *Kermiclown's Muppets Videos Trade Page.*
617. Falk, *Jim Henson's Red Book*, Dec. 20, 1970.
618. Finch, *Of Muppets and Men*, 21.
619. Falk, *Jim Henson's Red Book*, Apr. 6, 1973.
620. Falk, *Jim Henson's Red Book*, Aug. 13, 1974.
621. Falk, *Jim Henson's Red Book*, Aug. 30, 1975.
622. Henson, Muppet Show Pitch Reel.
623. Falk, *Jim Henson's Red Book*, Aug. 30, 1975.
624. Brillstein, *Where Did I Go Right?*, 147–48.
625. Falk, *Jim Henson's Red Book*, Aug. 30, 1975.
626. Falk, *Jim Henson's Red Book*, Jan. 1978.
627. Falk, *Jim Henson's Red Book*, Dec. 21, 1979.
628. Goelz, "Gonzo Puppeteerism."
629. Brillstein, *Where Did I Go Right?*, 149.
630. Falk, *Jim Henson's Red Book*, July 27, 1974.
631. Emmens, "Muppet Mania," 31.
632. CNN, "Remembering Jim Henson."

633. Ibid.
634. Rockwell, "Frances: Interview."
635. Harris, "Muppet Master."
636. Falk, *Jim Henson's Red Book*, Sept. 13, 1983.
637. Henson, *Fraggle Rock—First Season*, bonus material.
638. Ibid.
639. Nelson, "Interview with Legendary Muppeteer."
640. Falk, *Jim Henson's Red Book*, July 21, 1988.
641. Falk, *Jim Henson's Red Book*, Jan. 26, 1988.
642. Henson, *Fraggle Rock—First Season*, bonus material.
643. Brillstein, *Where Did I Go Right?*, 327–28.
644. Ibid.
645. Ibid.
646. Falk, *Jim Henson's Red Book*, Aug. 8, 1988.
647. Finch, *Jim Henson: The Works*, 44.
648. Falk, *Jim Henson's Red Book*, Oct. 9, 1966.
649. Ibid.
650. Ibid.
651. Falk, *Jim Henson's Red Book*, May 9, 1974.
652. Falk, *Jim Henson's Red Book*, Oct. 31, 1983.
653. Freeman, "Muppets on His Hands," 53.
654. Ibid.
655. Falk, *Jim Henson's Red Book*, Mar. 7, 1973.
656. Ibid.
657. Ibid.
658. Falk, *Jim Henson's Red Book*, June 19, 1981.
659. Falk, *Jim Henson's Red Book*, Mar. 27, 1975.
660. Falk, *Jim Henson's Red Book*, June 5, 1979.
661. Falk, *Jim Henson's Red Book*, Sept. 30, 1982.
662. Ibid.
663. Falk, *Jim Henson's Red Book*, June 19, 1981.

664. Brillstein, *Where Did I Go Right?*, 331.
665. Shemin, *Behind the Scenes.*
666. Henson, *Sell, Sell, Sell.*
667. Falk, *Jim Henson's Red Book*, Oct. 1966.
668. Ibid.
669. Brillstein, *Where Did I Go Right?*, 148.
670. Henson, *Fraggle Rock—First Season*, bonus material.
671. Nelson, "Chat with Jerry Nelson."
672. Larry Mirkin, phone call with author, Feb. 15, 2013.
673. Henson, *Fraggle Rock—Third Season*, bonus material.
674. Henson, *Fraggle Rock—First Season*, bonus material.
675. CNN, "Remembering Jim Henson."
676. Henson, *It's Not Easy Being Green*, 84.
677. Emmens, "Muppet Mania," 28.
678. Price, *Pixar Touch*, 79.
679. Ibid., 65.
680. Finch, *Of Muppets and Men*, 22.
681. Henson, *Fraggle Rock—First Season*, bonus material.
682. Falk, *Jim Henson's Red Book*, Feb. 2, 1973.
683. Baker, "Interview: Martin Baker."
684. Gabler, *Walt Disney*, 209.
685. Engstrom, "Davis and Henson Changed Entertainment."
686. Gabler, *Walt Disney*, 238–9.
687. Ibid., 24.
688. Bailey, *Memoirs of a Muppet Writer*, 131.
689. Nelson, "Interview with Legendary Muppeteer."
690. Davis, *Street Gang*, 150.
691. Gabler, *Walt Disney*, 174–5.
692. Harris, "Muppet Master."
693. Gabler, *Walt Disney*, 209.
694. Shales and Miller, *Live from New York*, 80.

695. Shemin, *Behind the Scenes*.
696. Larry Mirkin, phone call with author, Feb. 15, 2013.
697. Gabler, *Walt Disney*, 246.
698. Ibid.
699. Ibid., 208.
700. Ibid., 354.
701. Ibid., 353.
702. Ibid., 354–5.
703. Ibid., 367.
704. Bailey, *Memoirs of a Muppet Writer*, 129.
705. Finch, *Of Muppets and Men*, 34.
706. Ibid., 65.
707. Spinney, *Wisdom of Big Bird*, 132.
708. Rockwell, "Frances: Interview."
709. Finch, *Of Muppets and Men*, 112.
710. Brillstein, *Where Did I Go Right?*, 110.
711. Ibid., 331.
712. Henson, *Fraggle Rock—First Season*, bonus material.
713. Freeman, "Muppets on His Hands," 126.
714. Gabler, *Walt Disney*, 55.
715. Davis, *Street Gang*, 4.
716. Museum of the Moving Image, "Jim Henson's Fantastic World."
717. Shales and Miller, *Live from New York*, 565.
718. Ibid., 568.
719. Ibid., 566.
720. Borgenicht, *"Sesame Street" Unpaved*, 118.
721. Shales and Miller, *Live from New York*, 568.
722. Jones, *Jim Henson: The Biography*, 226.
723. Stein, "Tribute to Richard Hunt."
724. Shales and Miller, *Live from New York*, 581.

725. Ibid., 583.
726. Ibid., 589.
727. Ibid., 593.
728. Harris, "Muppet Master."
729. CNN, "Remembering Jim Henson."
730. Shemin, *Behind the Scenes.*
731. Shales and Miller, *Live from New York*, 594.
732. Ibid., 562.
733. Ibid., 558.
734. Ibid., 559.
735. Henson, *Fraggle Rock—First Season*, bonus material.
736. Shales and Miller, *Live from New York*, 564.
737. Cross, interview by Marc Maron.
738. Henson, *It's Not Easy Being Green*, 93.
739. Davis, *Street Gang*, 251.
740. Henson, *Fraggle Rock—First Season*, bonus material.
741. Ibid.
742. Ibid.
743. Mischer, "Muppets Celebrate Jim Henson."
744. Shemin, *Behind the Scenes.*
745. Henson, *It's Not Easy Being Green*, 57.
746. Juhl, "Written in Foam."
747. Jones, *Jim Henson: The Biography*, 294–5, 377, 421–2.
748. Ibid., 294–5.
749. Gabler, *Walt Disney*, 355.
750. Jones, *Jim Henson*, 447.
751. Ibid., 377.
752. Henson, *Fraggle Rock—First Season*, bonus material.
753. Ibid.
754. Bacon, *No Strings Attached*, 19.
755. Ibid., introduction.

756. Ibid., 19.
757. Ibid., 51.
758. Mitgang, "Muppets Turn 30."
759. Henson, *Fraggle Rock—First Season*, bonus material.
760. Ibid.
761. Henson, *Fraggle Rock—Third Season*, DVD liner notes.
762. Henson, *Fraggle Rock—First Season*, bonus material.
763. Ibid.
764. Ibid.
765. Larry Mirkin, phone call with author, Feb. 15, 2013.
766. Henson, *Fraggle Rock—Third Season*, bonus material.
767. Bacon, *No Strings Attached*, 24.
768. Henson, *World of "Dark Crystal."*
769. Ibid.
770. Bacon, *No Strings Attached*, 23.
771. Henson, *Fraggle Rock—First Season*, bonus material.
772. Henson, *Fraggle Rock—Second Season*, bonus material.
773. Bacon, *No Strings Attached*, introduction.
774. Henson, *Fraggle Rock—First Season*, bonus material.
775. Borgenicht, "*Sesame Street" Unpaved*, 95.
776. Rockwell, "Frances: Interview."
777. Shemin, *Behind the Scenes.*
778. Finch, *Of Muppets and Men*, 64.
779. Sesame Street "529."
780. Henson, *It's Not Easy Being Green*, 96.
781. Seligmann and Leonard, "Jim Henson: 1936–1990."
782. See, e.g., *The Introvert Advantage* (2002) by Marti Olsen Laney; *The Introvert's Way* (2012) by Sophia Dembling; *Quiet: The Power of Introverts* (2013) by Susan Cain; and *Introvert Power* (2013) by Laurie Helgoe.
783. Safer, *60 Minutes,* "Backstage on 'The Muppet Show'."

784. Rosenfeld, "Big Hand for Puppet Connection."
785. Shemin, *Behind the Scenes.*
786. "Puppeteers of America Festival," YouTube video, posted by "enterthedome."
787. Harris, "Muppet Master."
788. Grant, *Give and Take.*
789. Henson, *It's Not Easy Being Green*, 49.
790. Henson, "*The Muppets Take Manhattan* Interviews."
791. Freeman, "Muppets on His Hands," 126.
792. Bacon, *No Strings Attached*, 41.
793. Henson, "*Muppets Take Manhattan* Interviews."
794. Henson, *Fraggle Rock—First Season*, bonus material.
795. Swanson, "Show #39."
796. Ibid.
797. Falk, *Jim Henson's Red Book*, Feb. 15, 1985.
798. Shemin, *Behind the Scenes.*
799. Ibid.
800. Bacon, *No Strings Attached*, 64.
801. Henson, *Great Muppet Caper.*
802. Whitmire, "My Week with Steve."
803. Henson, *Fraggle Rock—First Season*, bonus material.
804. Ibid.
805. Henson, *World of Dark Crystal.*
806. Finch, *Of Muppets and Men*, 88.
807. Nelson, "Chat with Jerry Nelson."
808. Juhl, "Written in Foam."
809. Finch, *Of Muppets and Men*, 74.
810. Nelson, "Chat with Jerry Nelson."
811. Henson, *Down at Fraggle Rock.*
812. Henson, *Fraggle Rock—Final Season*, bonus material.
813. Safer, *60 Minutes*, "Backstage on 'The Muppet Show'."

814. Davis, *Street Gang*, 95.
815. Angus, "Reflections in Fleece."
816. Baker, "Interview: Martin Baker."
817. Mech, "Dominance in Wolf Packs."
818. Juhl, "Written in Foam."
819. Masters, "Disney's Muppet Miasma."
820. Shemin, *Behind the Scenes.*
821. Smith, "Creator of Muppets Dies."
822. Finch, *Of Muppets and Men*, 21.
823. Ibid., 65.
824. Henson, "Future of Video & Cable."
825. Ibid.
826. Henson, *Fraggle Rock—First Season*, bonus material.
827. Henson, *Fraggle Rock—Final Season*, "Gorg Who Would Be King."
828. Ibid.
829. Angus, "Reflections in Fleece."
830. Henson, *World of "Dark Crystal."*
831. Finch, *Of Muppets and Men*, 60.
832. Falk, *Jim Henson's Red Book*, Oct. 1976.
833. Henson, *It's Not Easy Being Green*, 118.
834. Jones, *Jim Henson: The Biography*, 447.
835. Hill, "When the Muppeteers Were Fretting."
836. Jones, *Jim Henson: The Biography*, 421.
837. Fry, "Milestones."
838. Graeber, "And a Frog Shall Lead Them."
839. Brillstein, *Where Did I Go Right?*, 109.
840. Skow, "Those Marvelous Muppets."
841. Nuwer, "Muppets on the Move," 66.
842. Henson, *Best of The Muppet Show*, "George Burns."
843. Gabler, *Walt Disney*, 330.

844. Ibid., 331.
845. Lucas, "Billionaire Down on Capitalism."
846. Paik, *To Infinity and Beyond!*, 291–92.
847. Larry Mirkin, phone call with author, Feb. 15, 2013.
848. Harris, "Muppet Master."
849. Ibid.
850. Falk, *Jim Henson's Red Book*, Mar. 13–14, 1969.
851. Henson, *World of "Dark Crystal."*
852. Finch, *Of Muppets and Men*, 65.
853. Odell, *Dark Crystal: Creation Myths*, afterword.
854. Brillstein, *Where Did I Go Right?*, 111.
855. Odell, *Dark Crystal: Creation Myths*, afterword.
856. Brillstein, *Where Did I Go Right?*, 111.
857. Henson, "Future of Video & Cable."
858. Odell, *Dark Crystal: Creation Myths*, afterword.
859. *Muppet Wiki*, "MirrorMask."
860. Paik, *To Infinity and Beyond!*, 284.
861. Ibid., 285.
862. Disney, *Snow White.*
863. Ibid.
864. Grover, *Disney Touch*, 218.
865. Ibid., 217.
866. Ibid.
867. Reibstein, "Kermit vs. Mickey Mouse."
868. Stevenson, "Muppets Join Disney Menagerie."
869. Turner, "Look Out, Kermit."
870. Gubernick, "Did Mickey Shaft Kermit?"
871. Masters, "Disney's Muppet Miasma."
872. Grover, *Disney Touch*, 217.
873. Davis, *Street Gang*, 312.
874. Ibid., 311.

875. Ibid., 312.
876. Brillstein, *Where Did I Go Right?*, 328.
877. Adler, "Estate-Tax Burden Cancels Deal."
878. Davis, *Street Gang*, 312.
879. Masters, "Disney's Muppet Miasma."
880. Gottesman v. United States of America. 05 Civ. 8212.
881. Brillstein, *Where Did I Go Right?*, 329.
882. Clines, "Mr. Muppet's Empire."
883. Falk, *Jim Henson's Red Book*, Apr. 25–30, 1988.
884. Ibid.
885. Clines, "Mr. Muppet's Empire."
886. Henson, *Storyteller*.
887. Ibid.
888. Ibid.
889. Gottesman v. United States of America. 05 Civ. 8212.
890. Falk, *Jim Henson's Red Book*, May 1973.
891. Falk, *Jim Henson's Red Book*, May 17–18, 1988.
892. Rockwell, "Frances: Interview."
893. CNN, "Remembering Jim Henson."
894. Falk, *Jim Henson's Red Book*.
895. Brown, "Muppets Deal."
896. Davis, *Street Gang*, 313.
897. Brown, "Muppets Deal."
898. Reibstein, "Kermit vs. Mickey Mouse."
899. Henson, *Storyteller*.
900. Ibid.
901. Brown, "Muppets Deal."
902. Davis, *Street Gang*, 313.
903. Brillstein, *Where Did I Go Right?*, 327.
904. Hoover's, Inc., 2012.
905. Ibid.

906. Paik, *To Infinity and Beyond!*, 291.
907. Guttman, "Jim Henson Content."
908. Ibid.
909. *Time,* "Disney after Walt."
910. Culhane, "Muppets in Movieland."
911. Ibid.
912. Clines, "Mr. Muppet's Empire."
913. Brillstein, *Where Did I Go Right?*, 331.
914. Falk, *Jim Henson's Red Book.*
915. Whitmire, "My Week with Steve."
916. Falk, *Jim Henson's Red Book*, Feb. 25, 1988.
917. Ibid.
918. Hill, "Muppetty Takeover of Disneyland."
919. Masters, "Disney's Muppet Miasma."
920. Ibid.
921. Ibid.
922. Reibstein, "Kermit vs. Mickey Mouse."
923. Masters, "Disney's Muppet Miasma."
924. Davis, *Street Gang*, 314.
925. Masters, "Disney's Muppet Miasma."
926. Hill, "When the Muppeteers Were Fretting."
927. *St. Petersburg Times*, "Acquisitions, Mergers and Muppets."
928. Price, *Pixar Touch*, 233–34.
929. Ibid., 234.
930. Paik, *To Infinity and Beyond!*, 290.
931. Whitmire, "My Week with Steve."
932. CNN, "Remembering Jim Henson."
933. Grover, *Disney Touch*, 217.
934. CNN, "Remembering Jim Henson."
935. Davis, *Street Gang*, 10.
936. Davis, "Michael Davis Interview."

937. Engstrom, "Davis and Henson Changed Entertainment."
938. CNN, "Remembering Jim Henson."
939. Angus, "Reflections in Fleece."
940. Juhl, "Written in Foam."
941. Odell, *Dark Crystal: Creation Myths*, afterword.
942. Masters, "Disney's Muppet Miasma."
943. Reibstein, "Kermit vs. Mickey Mouse."
944. Museum of the Moving Image, "Friends and Family."
945. CNN, "Remembering Jim Henson."
946. Davis, *Street Gang*, 312.
947. Sullivan, *Muppets Magic.*
948. Ibid.
949. Brillstein, *Where Did I Go Right?*, 150.
950. Freeman, "Muppets on His Hands," 126.
951. Odell, *Dark Crystal: Creation Myths*, afterword.
952. Ibid.
953. Ibid.
954. Falk, *Jim Henson's Red Book*, Feb. 6, 1978.
955. Freedman, "It's a Muppet Invasion."
956. David Young, phone call with author, Jan. 24, 2013.
957. Odell, *Dark Crystal: Creation Myths*, afterword.
958. Henson, *It's Not Easy Being Green*, 9.
959. Roberts, *Seth Speaks*, 57.
960. Henson, *It's Not Easy Being Green*, 118.
961. Henson, *It's Not Easy Being Green*, 58.

ACKNOWLEDGMENTS

Publishing this book has been the biggest thrill of my life. I owe the world to everyone who has helped me. I had a great publishing team—Jason Allen Ashlock and Adam Chromy from Movable Type Management, editors Julia Cheiffetz and Carly Hoffmann, and copyeditor Jodie Young. I was met with generosity by the artists and thinkers in this book—David Young, Larry Mirkin, Christopher Cerf, Jocelyn Stevenson, Karen Prell, Lewis Hyde, Karen Falk, and Adam Grant. Though I never met them, Henson's collaborators have inspired me deeply—Frank Oz, Jerry Juhl, Jane Henson, Jerry Nelson, Richard Hunt, Dave Goelz, Steve Whitmire, Kathryn Mullen, Michael Frith, Louise Gold, Jon Stone, Joe Raposo, Jeff Moss, Paul Williams, Kenneth Ascher, Philip Balsam, Dennis Lee, Joan Ganz Cooney, and all the writers, illustrators, puppet builders, engineers, businesspeople, and artists who gave us these works of art. I owe much to the careful research of others, including biographers Christopher Finch, Neal Gabler, Michael Davis, Judy Harris, and countless Muppets fans who have kept this information alive for the rest of us. Thank you to the creators and contributors to Muppet Wiki, Tough Pigs, Muppet Central, Muppet Mindset, and the MuppetCast, including Andrew Leal, Kenneth Plume, Joe Hennes, Phillip Chapman, D.W. McKim, Ryan Dosier, and Grant Baciocco for their wonderful interviews.

Brilliant editors have so kindly helped me to publish articles on this subject—Carrie Frye, Choire Sicha, Alex Balk, Benjamin Samuel, Doree Shafrir, C. Max Magee, Mark Armstrong, Isaac Fitzgerald, and Alex Ludlum. Thank you to all who helped me get here: Lauren Goldrich, Jess Grose, Mike Welch, Ron and Nancy Standring, Mike and Janet Robinson, Anna Oliver, Andrew Innes, JoAnn Castano, Allison Caso, Maria Hamel, Jessica Silk, Phil Chaffee, Brandon Freeman, Karl Ljungquist, The Kilgore Trout Home for Wayward Writers (CJ Hauser, Lauren Belski, David Greenwood, Wythe Marschall, Erin Harte, Stephen Aubrey, Rosemary Midsary, Helen Rubinstein, and Christine Rath), Jeremy Meyers, Megan Elizabeth Morris, Carlin Trammel, Jilly Gagnon, Nora Fussner, Karen Russell, Teddy Wayne, George Saunders, Stephen Elliott, Maria Bustillos, my amazing writing teachers at the Brooklyn College MFA Program (Michael Cunningham, Francisco Goldman, Meera Nair, Jenny Offill, Joshua Henkin, Ellen Tremper, and Elaine Brooks), Liza Hebert and the Modern Culture and Media Department at Brown University, Alex Steele and Gotham Writers' Workshop, Chris Walsh, Anna Dalby and the Writing Program at Boston University, all my students in WR100 and WR150 at BU, Caitlin Hatakeyama and Ethan Higgins, the North Andover Public Schools and their excellent teachers (Judith Hillner, Ann Ericson, Thomas Rooney, Gerald Sanford, Tom McGowan, Paul and Mary Julie Gregoire, and especially Millie Matasso), to public broadcasting, to public libraries and coffee shops where I have worked (Outpost, Bloc 11, Diesel Café, and the Brooklyn, North Andover, Natick, Somerville, and Cambridge Public Libraries), Greg Skorupka, Linda Phoummalayvane Standring, Jarrod Standring, Jay Standring, Corinna Hoey Standring, Judy and Stuart Cleland, Ben and Joanne Hyde, Kathy Stevens, Beth Stevens, Judy Wehrer, Jeffy Dunmire, and Cornelia Harris, all my cousins, my incredible

Gram, Caroline Rockwell Stevens, the amazing artists Christopher Cooley, Emi Brady, and Karl Stevens, the talented photographer Natalia Boltukhova, and my dear friend Helen Rubinstein.

Most importantly, I could not have finished this book without my accountability partner and bestie, Cristina Kennedy; my loving and encouraging partner, Tim Standring; my sister, Kate Innes, who loves me so much it's silly; my brother, Nat Stevens, who always makes me smile; and my dad, Horace Nathaniel Stevens, who is the wisest man I know.

Thank you to my mother, Joanne Hyde Stevens, for all her love, and to Jim Henson for his art. Your memories keep me strong, and I am forever grateful.

ABOUT THE AUTHOR

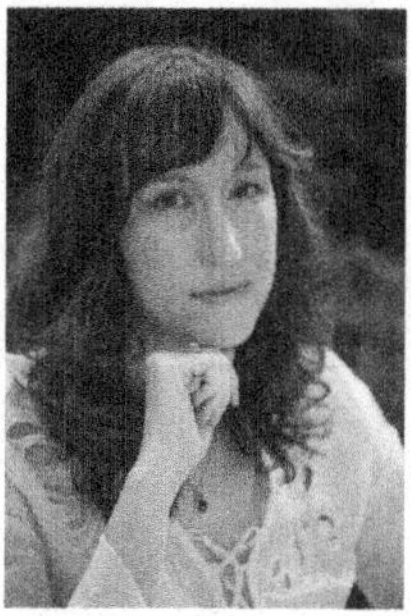

Elizabeth Hyde Stevens created the Muppets, Mickey, and Money research course at Boston University. Her analysis of Jim Henson's career has appeared online at *The Awl*, *The Millions*, *Electric Literature*, and *Rolling Stone*. In 2011, her essay "Weekend at Kermie's" was viewed over 160,000 times. Called "a long, brilliant thinkpiece" on Twitter, it was praised by Internet curators Brain Pickings, *Mother Jones*, Longreads, Longform, *Wired*, IMDB, IFC, *Reader's Digest*, and Kurt Loder. Stevens attended public school in North Andover, Massachusetts, and went on to study art semiotics at Brown University and creative writing at the Brooklyn College MFA program. She is a member of the Brooklyn writers' collective The Kilgore Trout Home for Wayward Writers and teaches fiction at Gotham Writers' Workshop. Her writing has earned the Himan Brown Award and the Somerville Arts Council Fellowship for Literature. Everything she knows about business she learned from watching *Sesame Street*.

BIBLIOGRAPHY

Adler, Leslie. "Estate-Tax Burden Cancels Muppets Deal with Disney." *Los Angeles Times*, Dec. 18, 1990. http://articles.latimes.com/1990-12-18/business/fi-6919_1_estate-tax.

Advertising Age. "Corporate Creatures Prove that They're Muppet Fans, Too." Oct. 19, 1987.

Angus, Terry. "Reflections in Fleece: An Interview with Muppeteer Terry Angus." By Kenneth Plume. *Muppet Central Articles*, Sept. 18, 1998. http://www.muppetcentral.com/articles/interviews/angus1.shtml.

Archive of American Television. *Archive Interviews on Jim Henson and the Muppets.* Archive of American Television, accessed May 13, 2013. http://www.youtube.com/watch?v=dz3OENAP4RM.

Associated Press. "Company News: Disney Counterclaim in Suit over Muppets." *New York Times*, Apr. 25, 1991. http://www.nytimes.com/1991/04/25/business/company-news-disney-counterclaim-in-suit-over-muppets.html?scp=4&sq=company news disney henson&st=cse.

———. "Survey Says Many Would Like Talk Show Host for Boss." Associated Press, accessed Apr. 21, 1980. LexisNexis Academic.

Bacon, Matt. *No Strings Attached: The Inside Story of Jim Henson's Creature Shop*. New York: Macmillan, 1997.

Bailey, Joseph A. *Memoirs of a Muppet Writer: You Mean Somebody Actually Writes That Stuff?* New York: Walnut Press, 2011.

Baker, Martin A. "Interview: Martin Baker." By Andrew Latimer. *TV Bomb*, May 2011. http://www.tvbomb.co.uk/?p=8461.

Bell, John. *American Puppet Modernism.* New York: Palgrave Macmillan, 2008.

Borgenicht, David. "*Sesame Street*" *Unpaved.* New York: Hyperion Books, 1998.

Brillstein, Bernie. *Where Did I Go Right?: You're No One in Hollywood Unless Someone Wants You Dead.* Boston: Little, Brown, 1999.

Brown, Corrie. "Muppets Deal Began in April." *Palm Beach Post*, Aug. 31, 1989.

Bunce, Alan. *Christian Science Monitor.* "Mr. Muppet." May 23, 1990.

Catmull, Ed. "How Pixar Fosters Collective Creativity." *Harvard Business Review* (Sept. 2008): 65–72.

Christensen, Clayton. *How Will You Measure Your Life?* Filmed talk for TEDxBOSTON. Posted July 17, 2012. http://www.youtube.com/watch?v=tvos4nORf_Y.

Cirillo, Joan J. "Kermit Sets $10 Million UNICEF Goal; Miss Piggy Already Gave." Associated Press, Aug. 24, 1980. LexisNexis Academic.

Clines, Frances X. "Mr. Muppet's Empire Is Thriving." *New York Times*, Oct. 25, 1987. http://www.nytimes.com/1987/10/25/arts/television-mr-muppet-s-empire-is-thriving.html?pagewanted=all&src=pm.

CNN. "Remembering Jim Henson." Apr. 27, 1999. Accessed May 23, 2012. LexisNexis Academic.

Cross, David. *WTF Podcast.* Interview by Marc Maron. Apr. 8, 2012.

Culhane, John. "The Muppets in Movieland." *New York Times*, June 10, 1979.

Davis, Michael. "Michael Davis Interview." *Tough Pigs Interviews.* By Joe Hennes. Jan. 25, 2009.

———. *Street Gang: The Complete History of "Sesame Street."* New York: Viking, 2008.

Disney, Walt. *Snow White and the Seven Dwarfs.* Walt Disney Video, 2001. DVD.

Donald, Julianna. "Julianna Donald Interview." *Muppet Mindset Interviews.* By "The British Correspondent." June 10, 2010. http://themuppetmindset.blogspot.com/2010/06/juliana-donald-interview.html.

Drapkin, Jennifer. "Q&A." *Smithsonian* 37.4 (2006): 37.

Dun & Bradstreet. *D & B WorldBase* (database). Accessed May 22, 2012. LexisNexis.

Emmens, Carol A. "Jim Henson and the People behind the Muppet Mania." *School Library Journal* 31.1 (1984): 27.

Engstrom, John. "Davis and Henson Changed the World of Entertainment; Mastermind of *Sesame Street* and Muppets Was a Gentle Soul." *Seattle Post-Intelligencer*, May 17, 1990.

Falk, Karen. *Jim Henson's Red Book.* The Jim Henson Company, Sept. 2010. http://www.henson.com/jimsredbook/.

Finch, Christopher. *Jim Henson: The Works.* New York: Random House, 1993.

———. *Of Muppets and Men: The Making of "The Muppet Show."* New York: Knopf, 1981.

Freberg, Stan. "Stan Freberg Talks about Jim Henson." Interview by Grant Baciocco. *The GrantCast, episode 001*, aired Sept. 24, 2011. http://www.mrgrant.com/2011/09/gc-episode-001/.

Freedman, Adele. "It's a Muppet Invasion." *Globe and Mail* (Toronto, Canada), Dec. 25, 1982.

Freeman, Don. "Muppets on His Hands." *Saturday Evening Post* 251.8 (1979): 50–126.

Fry, Andy. "Milestones." *Kidscreen* (website), posted Dec. 1, 1999. http://kidscreen.com/1999/12/01/27471-19991201/.

Gabler, Neal. *Walt Disney: The Triumph of the American Imagination*. New York: Vintage, 2006.

Gladwell, Malcolm. *Outliers: The Story of Success*. New York: Little, Brown, 2008.

———. *The Tipping Point: How Little Things Can Make a Big Difference*. New York: Little, Brown, 2000.

———. "Q and A with Malcolm." *Gladwell.com*, accessed June 30, 2012. http://gladwell.com/outliers/outliers-q-and-a-with-malcolm/.

Goelz, Dave. "Gonzo Puppeteerism: An Interview with Muppeteer Dave Goelz." By Kenneth Plume. *Muppet Central Articles*, Jan. 28, 2000. http://www.muppetcentral.com/articles/interviews/goelz1.shtml.

Gottesman v. United States of America. 05 Civ. 8212. U.S. Dist. 2007. Accessed May 24, 2012. LexisNexis Academic.

Gould, Jack. "'Hey, Cinderella' Given as A.B.C. Classic." *New York Times*, Apr. 11, 1970.

Graeber, Laurel. "And a Frog Shall Lead Them: Henson's Legacy." *New York Times*, Aug. 18, 2011. http://www.nytimes.com/2011/08/19/arts/design/jim-hensons-fantastic-world-at-museum-of-the-moving-image.html?_r=1&adxnnl=1&adxnnlx=1337799839-FTUilpbBHuquXQv0BnwkDw.

Grant, Adam. *Give and Take*. New York: Viking, 2013.

Grover, Ron. *The Disney Touch: How a Daring Management Team Revived an Entertainment Empire*. Burr Ridge, IL: Irwin, 1991.

Gubernick, L. "Did Mickey Shaft Kermit?" *Forbes* 147.9 (1991): 44.

Guttman, Monika. "Jim Henson Content with His Kingdom." *St. Petersburg Times* (Florida), Dec. 15, 1987.

Harmetz, Aljean. "*Star Wars* and Muppet Wizards Team Up in *Labyrinth*." *New York Times*, Sept. 15, 1985. http://www.nytimes.com/1985/09/15/arts/star-wars-and-muppet-wizards-team-up-in-labyrinth.html?pagewanted=all.

Harris, Judy. "Muppet Master." *Cinefantastique* 13:4 (Apr./May 1984), accessed on Judy Harris's personal website, May 22, 2012. http://users.bestweb.net/~foosie/henson.htm.

Hayes, Constance L. "Company News: Disney and Henson in Muppet Settlement." *New York Times*, May 1, 1991. http://www.nytimes.com/1991/05/01/business/company-news-disney-and-henson-in-muppet-settlement.html.

Henson, Jim. *Best of The Muppet Show*. Time Life Video, 2001. DVD.

———. *Down at Fraggle Rock*. Henson Associates and HBO, 1987.

———. *Flapsole Sneakers*. Short film [1968?]. Accessed July 19, 2013. http://www.youtube.com/watch?v=fHHHTST1hgE.

———. "Forests." National Wildlife Federation, 1988. Film. http://www.youtube.com/watch?v=IXA0P6Hn96M.

———. *Fraggle Rock—Complete Final Season*. Written by Jerry Juhl and Jocelyn Stevenson. Lionsgate/HIT Entertainment, 2009. DVD.

———. *Fraggle Rock—Complete First Season*. Written by Jerry Juhl and Jocelyn Stevenson. Lionsgate/HIT Entertainment, 2008. DVD.

———. *Fraggle Rock—Complete Second Season*. Written by Jerry Juhl and Jocelyn Stevenson. Lionsgate/HIT Entertainment, 2006. DVD.

———. *Fraggle Rock—Complete Third Season*. Written by Jerry Juhl and Jocelyn Stevenson. Lionsgate/HIT Entertainment, 2007. DVD.

———. *The Great Muppet Caper*. Henson Associates and ITC Films, 1981. DVD.

———. *Ideal Toys Commercial*. 1966. Short film. Accessed July 19, 2013. http://www.youtube.com/watch?v=iHGPxfpyFzA.

———. *Inside the Labyrinth*. Directed by Desmond Saunders. Sony Pictures Home Entertainment, 1987. DVD.

———. *It's Not Easy Being Green and Other Things to Consider*. New York: Hyperion, 2005.

———. "Jim Henson on *Labyrinth*." Interview by John C. Tibbets. University of Kansas, Kansas City, 1986. Accessed May 13, 2013, http://www.youtube.com/watch?v=EpS7O-vBgIo.

———. "Jim Henson: The Future of Video & Cable." Interview by John A. Gallagher. 1982. Originally archived by *TVDays.com* in "The Directors Series." Accessed May 13, 2013. http://www.youtube.com/watch?v=UoSutaKx0Ag.

———. *The Muppet Movie*. Henson Associates and ITC Films, 1979. Feature film.

———. "Muppet Musicians of Bremen." *Tales from Muppetland*. 1972. Television special.

———. *Muppet Show Pitch Reel*. 1975. Short film. Accessed July 19, 2013. http://www.youtube.com/watch?v=9KorhvVQRUM.

———. "*Muppets Take Manhattan* Interviews." *Muppets Take Manhattan*, DVD. Columbia Tristar Pictures and Jim Henson Home Entertainment, 2001.

———. *Sam and Friends*. Washington, DC: WRC-TV/NBC. 1955–1961. Television series. Accessed Jul 18, 2013. http://www.youtube.com/watch?v=W9R5dov0VIw, etc.

———. *Sell, Sell, Sell*. Muppet Meeting Films, 1975. Accessed July 19, 2013. http://www.youtube.com/watch?v=k8BKR2GkVBw.

———. *The Storyteller*. Written by Anthony Minghella. Jim Henson Home Entertainment, 2003. DVD.

———. *Tales of the Tinkerdee.* Directed by Carl Degan. Unaired television pilot. 1962.

———. *Wilkins Coffee Commercials.* 1957–1961. Short films. Accessed July 19, 2013. http://www.youtube.com/watch?v=ZxLyuw5bdyk.

———. *Wilson's Meats Meeting Films.* 1965. Short films. Accessed July 19, 2013. http://www.youtube.com/watch?v=w282YjrFIGE.

———. *The World of "The Dark Crystal."* Sony Pictures Home Entertainment, 1983. DVD.

———. *Youth '68: Everything's Changing . . . or Maybe It Isn't.* Directed by Jon Stone. *NBC Experiment in Television.* NBC: Apr. 19, 1968. Television documentary. Accessed Aug. 25, 2011. Paley Center for the Media, New York.

Hill, Jim. "The Muppetty Takeover of Disneyland that Almost Happened." *Huffington Post*, Dec. 19, 2011. http://www.huffingtonpost.com/jim-hill/disney-muppets-henson_b_1141087.html.

———. "When the Muppeteers Were Fretting about the Mouse." *Jim Hill Media* (blog), Sept. 22, 2005. http://jimhillmedia.com/guest_writers1/b/chris_barry/archive/2005/09/23/1725.aspx.

Hoover's, Inc. "Pixar Animation Studios, Inc.," "The Disney Company," and "The Jim Henson Company, Inc." company records. Accessed May 22, 2012. LexisNexis Academic.

Hyde, Lewis. *The Gift: Creativity and the Artist in the Modern World.* New York: Vintage, 2007.

Iwerks, Leslie. *The Pixar Story.* Disney/Pixar, 2007. Netflix.

Jones, Brian Jay. *Jim Henson: The Biography.* New York: Ballantine Books, 2013.

Juhl, Jerry. "Written in Foam: An Interview with Muppet Writer Jerry Juhl." By D.W. McKim and Phillip Chapman. *Muppet*

Central Articles, July 24, 1998. http://www.muppetcentral.com/articles/interviews/juhl1.shtml.

Kermiclown's Muppets Video Trade Page. Accessed July 19, 2013. http://kermiclownvideos.com/.

Kuklapolitan Website, The. "Frequently Asked Questions." Accessed Jul. 19, 2013. http://kukla.tv/faq.html.

Leal, Andrew. "Muppets and Money." In *Kermit Culture: Critical Perspectives on Jim Henson's Muppets*, edited by Jennifer C. Garlen and Anissa M Graham. Jefferson, NC: McFarland, 2009.

Lipinski, Jed. "It's Not Easy Making Green." *Fast Company* 160 (2011): 68. Accessed Mar. 30, 2012. Business Source Complete.

Lucas, George. "George Lucas: Billionaire Down on Capitalism." Interview by Charlie Rose. *CBSnews.com*. Jan. 20, 2012. http://www.cbsnews.com/8301-505271_162-57362574/george-lucas-billionaire-down-on-capitalism/#ixzz1k0lQ0OhS.

Marr, Merissa. "Why Miss Piggy Wore Prada: Disney Relaunches Muppets." *Wall Street Journal*, May 19, 2005.

Masters, Kim. "Disney's Muppet Miasma." *Washington Post*, June 30, 1990.

McLellan, Dennis. "Jerry Juhl, 67; His Scriptwriting Breathed Life into the Muppets." *Los Angeles Times*, Oct. 6, 2005. http://articles.latimes.com/2005/oct/06/local/me-juhl6.

McShane, Larry. "Muppet Creator Jim Henson Dead at 53." Associated Press, May 16, 1990. Accessed May 23, 2012. LexisNexis Academic.

Mech, L. David. "Alpha Status, Dominance, and Division of Labor in Wolf Packs." *Canadian Journal of Zoology* 77 (1999): 1196–1203. http://www.npwrc.usgs.gov/resource/mammals/alstat/index.htm.

Miller, S. "Empire of the Imagination." *Variety*, Dec. 11, 1995.

Mirkin, Larry. "The *Fraggle Rock* Complete Collection." *The Jim Henson Company Podcast*, Sept. 17, 2008.

Mischer, Don. "The Muppets Celebrate Jim Henson." Written by Jerry Juhl. Television special. Nov. 21, 1990.

Mitgang, Lee. "Kermit and the Muppets Turn 30." Associated Press, Jan. 4, 1986. Accessed May 23, 2012. LexisNexis Academic.

Muppet Wiki. http://muppet.wikia.com/wiki/Muppet_Wiki.

Museum of the Moving Image. "Jim Henson: Friends and Family." Panel discussion, New York, Sept. 18, 2011.

———. "Jim Henson's Fantastic World." Exhibit/documentary. Museum of the Moving Image. New York, Aug. 18, 2011.

Nelson, Jerry. "A Chat with Jerry Nelson." By Joe Hennes. *Tough Pigs Interviews*, Dec. 8, 2009. http://www.toughpigs.com/a-chat-with-jerry-nelson-part-1/.

———. "Interview with Legendary Muppeteer Jerry Nelson." By Ryan Dosier. *Muppet Mindset Interviews*, Nov. 12, 2010. http://themuppetmindset.blogspot.com/2010/11/interview-with-legendary-muppeteer.html.

———. "Still Counting: An Interview with Muppeteer Jerry Nelson." By Kenneth Plume. *Muppet Central Articles*, Mar. 1, 1999. http://www.muppetcentral.com/articles/interviews/nelson1.shtml.

Nuwer, Hank. "Muppets on the Move." *Saturday Evening Post* 252.9 (1980): 66–71.

Odell, David. Afterword to *The Dark Crystal: Creation Myths. Volume 2*, by Josh Dysart, Brian Froud, Alex Sheikman, and Lizzy John. Los Angeles: Archaia Entertainment, 2013.

Oz, Frank. "Interview with Frank Oz." By Kenneth Plume. *IGN.com*, Feb. 10, 2000. http://www.ign.com/articles/2000/02/10/interview-with-frank-oz-part-1-of-4.

———. "Magic Behind the Muppets." *Times* (London), Nov. 24, 2012.

Paik, Karen. *To Infinity and Beyond!: The Story of Pixar Animation Studios.* San Francisco: Chronicle Books, 2007.

Prell, Karen. "Animateer Karen Prell: An Interview with Muppeteer, Animator and Writer." By Kenneth Plume and Phillip Chapman. *Muppet Central Articles*, Sept. 11, 1998. http://www.muppetcentral.com/articles/interviews/prell.shtml.

Price, David. *The Pixar Touch.* New York: Vintage, 2009.

"Puppeteers of America Festival, 1989, at MIT—Frank Oz and Jim Henson." YouTube video. Posted by "enterthedome." Accessed May 13, 2013. http://www.youtube.com/watch?v=_PYzMluU3uQ.

Reibstein, L., and J. Taliaferro. "Kermit vs. Mickey Mouse." *Newsweek* 117.17 (1991): 42.

Roberts, Jane. *Seth Speaks: The Eternal Validity of the Soul.* Englewood Cliffs, NJ: Prentice-Hall, 1972.

Rockwell, Alex. "Frances: Interview with Alex Rockwell." By Grant Baciocco. *The Jim Henson Company Podcast*, Aug. 20, 2008. http://www.henson.com/podcast.php?content=41.

Rosenfeld, Megan. "A Big Hand for the Puppet Connection; At the Smithsonian: Kermit Moves In." *Washington Post*, June 9, 1980.

Safer, Morley. "Backstage on 'The Muppet Show'." *60 Minutes.* CBS, Mar.17, 1979. http://www.dailymotion.com/video/x3e5f7_the-muppet-show-making-of_creation#.UbjkhOfqnKi.

Seligmann, J., and E. Leonard. "Jim Henson: 1936–1990." *Newsweek* 115.22 (1990): 79.

Sesame Workshop. "Our Mission." *Sesame Workshop.* July 19, 2013. http://www.sesameworkshop.org/about-us/our-mission/.

Shales, Tom. *Washington Post.* "Ta-Dahhh! It's Jim Henson Creator of Kermit the Frog and King of the Muppets: The Creator of Kermit the Frog and the King of the Muppets." Jan. 29, 1977.

Shales, Tom, and James Andrew Miller. *Live From New York: An Uncensored History of "Saturday Night Live."* Boston: Little, Brown, 2003.

Shemin, Craig. *Behind the Scenes in Frogtown Hollow*. Wacky Hijinx Films, 2005. DVD.

Skow, John. "Those Marvelous Muppets: How Kermit, Miss Piggy & Co. Captivate 235 Million People a Week." *Time* 112.26 (1978): 70.

Smith, J. Y. "Jim Henson, Creator of Muppets, Dies at 53." *Washington Post*, May 17, 1990.

Spinney, Caroll. *The Wisdom of Big Bird (And the Dark Genius of Oscar the Grouch): Lessons from a Life in Feathers.* New York: Villard, 2003.

St. Petersburg Times (Florida). "Editorial: Acquisitions, Mergers and Muppets." Aug. 30, 1989.

Stein, Jessica Max. "Tribute to Richard Hunt." Lecture at Longstockings Bookstore, New York, Aug. 16, 2011.

———. *The Rainbow Connection: Richard Hunt, Gay Muppeteer.* Brooklyn: Long Walk, 2010.

Stevenson, Richard W. "Company News: In Thaw, Henson and Disney Strike Deal on Home Videos." *New York Times*, Dec. 19, 1991. http://www.nytimes.com/1991/12/19/business/company-news-in-thaw-henson-and-disney-strike-deal-on-home-videos.html.

———. "Muppets Join Disney Menagerie." *New York Times*, Aug. 29, 1989.

Sullivan, Ed. *Muppets Magic from "The Ed Sullivan Show"!* SOFA Entertainment, 2003. DVD.

Swanson, Steve. "Show #39." *MuppetCast*, Jan. 6, 2008. http://muppetcast.com/WordPress/archives/56.

Time. "Disney after Walt Is a Family Affair." *Time* 102.5 (1973): 68.

Turner, Richard. "Look Out, Kermit: Disney's Next Meal May Be Muppets—Buying Henson Associates Might Let Mickey Mouse Avoid 'Overexposing'." *Wall Street Journal*, Aug. 1, 1989.

Wagner, Erica. "My Family and Other Muppets." *Times* (London), Dec. 2, 2012.

Whitmire, Steve. "My Week with Steve." Interview by Joe Hennes. *Tough Pigs Interviews*, Oct. 13, 2008. http://www.toughpigs.com/my-week-with-steve-day-1/.

———. "Ratting Out: An Interview with Muppeteer Steve Whitmire." By Kenneth Plume. *Muppet Central Articles*, July 19, 1999. http://www.muppetcentral.com/articles/interviews/whitmire1.shtml.

Worron, Trish. "TV Talk: Frank Oz Talks about Miss Piggy." Associated Press, Sept. 17, 1982. Accessed May 23, 2012. LexisNexis Academic.

Zuckerman, Esther. "The Actor Who Created Big Bird Makes About $314,000 a Year." *Atlantic Wire*, Oct. 9, 2012. http://www.theatlanticwire.com/entertainment/2012/10/actor-who-created-big-bird-makes-about-314000-year/57774/.

Kindle Serials

This book was originally released in Episodes as a Kindle Serial. Kindle Serials launched in 2012 as a new way to experience serialized books. Kindle Serials allow readers to enjoy the story as the author creates it, purchasing once and receiving all existing Episodes immediately, followed by future Episodes as they are published. To find out more about Kindle Serials and to see the current selection of Serials titles, visit www.amazon.com/kindleserials.

Made in the USA
Monee, IL
04 September 2026

60923198R00277